# The Field of Cultural Production

# The Field of Cultural Production

## Essays on Art and Literature

Pierre Bourdieu

*Edited and Introduced by*
*Randal Johnson*

Polity Press

This edition © Polity Press 1993

Copyright © Preface and Editor's Introduction: Randal Johnson
Copyright © Chapters 1 and 3: Elsevier Science Publishers B.V. 1983
Copyright © Chapter 2: Sage Publications Ltd, 1986
Copyright © Chapters 4, 5 and 6: Pierre Bourdieu. English translation © Claud
    DuVerlie, 1986
Copyright © Chapter 7: The University of Chicago, 1988. All rights reserved
Copyright © Chapters 8 and 10: Blackwell Publishers, 1968, 1989
Copyright © Chapter 9: Pierre Bourdieu, 1987. English translation © Polity Press,
    1993

First published 1993 by Polity Press
in association with Blackwell Publishers

Editorial office:
Polity Press
65 Bridge Street
Cambridge CB2 1UR

Marketing and production:
Blackwell Publishers
108 Cowley Road
Oxford OX4 1JF, UK

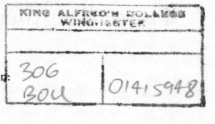

ISBN 0 7456 09864
ISBN 0 7456 09872 (pbk)

A CIP catalogue record for this book is available from the British Library.

Typeset in 10½ on 12 pt Sabon
by TecSet Ltd, Wallington, Surrey
Printed in Great Britain by T. J. Press (Padstow) Ltd, Padstow, Cornwall

This book is printed on acid-free paper.

# Contents

## Part III The Pure Gaze: Essays on Art

# Preface

This volume brings together Pierre Bourdieu's major essays on art, literature and culture, published between 1968 and 1987. It includes articles appearing in English for the first time, others which have been previously published in books and journals but are not always readily accessible, and a series of three lectures presented as the Christian Gauss Seminars in Criticism at Princeton University in 1986, here published for the first time in any language. Complete bibliographical information for each essay is given below.

Chapter 1, 'The Field of Cultural Production, or: The Economic World Reversed' was originally published in *Poetics* (Amsterdam), 12/4–5 (1983), pp. 311–56, translated by Richard Nice (Amsterdam: Elsevier Science Publishers).

Chapter 2, 'The Production of Belief: Contribution to an Economy of Symbolic Goods' was originally published as 'La production de la croyance: contribution à une économie des biens symboliques' in *Actes de la recherche en sciences sociales*, 13 (February 1977), pp. 3–43. The abbreviated translation, by Richard Nice, previously appeared in *Media, Culture and Society*, 2/3 (July 1980), pp. 261–93, and in Richard Collins et al. (eds), *Media, Culture and Society: A Critical Reader* (London: Sage, 1986), pp. 131–63. Reprinted with kind permission of Sage Publications Ltd.

Chapter 3, 'The Market of Symbolic Goods' was originally published as 'Le marché des biens symboliques' in *L'année sociologique*, 22 (1971), pp. 49–126. The abbreviated translation, by R. Swyer, first appeared in *Poetics* (Amsterdam), 14/1–2 (April 1985), pp. 13–44.

Chapter 4, 'Is the Structure of *Sentimental Education* an Instance of Social Self-analysis?', Chapter 5, 'Field of Power, Literary Field and Habitus', and Chapter 6, 'Principles for a Sociology of Cultural Works', were presented as the Christian Gauss Seminars in Criticism at Princeton University in 1986. They were translated by Claud DuVerlie.

Chapter 7, 'Flaubert's Point of View', translated by Priscilla Parkhurst Ferguson, was originally published in *Critical Inquiry*, 14/3 (Spring 1988), pp. 539–62. It also appears in Philippe Desan, Priscilla Parkhurst Ferguson and Wendy Griswold (eds), *Literature and Social Practice* (Chicago: University of Chicago Press, 1988). The version included here has been slightly abbreviated.

Chapter 8, 'Outline of a Sociological Theory of Art Perception', was originally published as 'Éléments d'une théorie sociologique de la perception artistique', *Revue internationale des sciences sociales*, special issue on 'Les arts dans la société', 20/4 (1968), pp. 5–14. The English translation first appeared in *International Social Science Journal*, 20 (Winter 1968), pp. 589–612.

Chapter 9, 'Manet and the Institutionalization of Anomie', was originally published as 'L'institutionnalisation de l'anomie', *Les Cahiers du Musée national d'art moderne*, 19–20 (June 1987), pp. 6–19. It was translated by Juliette Parnell.

Chapter 10, 'The Historical Genesis of a Pure Aesthetic', translated by Charles Newman, was originally published in *The Journal of Aesthetics and Art Criticism*, 46, special issue (1987), pp. 201–10. It also appears in R. Shusterman (ed.), *Analytic Aesthetics* (Oxford, New York: Blackwell, 1989).

R. J.
Gainesville, Florida

# Editor's Introduction
## Pierre Bourdieu on Art, Literature and Culture

Since the early 1970s Pierre Bourdieu has become a major theoretical voice in the critical study of cultural practices.[1] Bourdieu's analytical method represents a fruitful alternative to many of the immanent modes of analysis – ranging from New Criticism and various brands of formalism to structuralism and deconstruction – which have dominated literary studies during this period. His work converges with and in many ways anticipates the renewed interest in the socio-historical ground of cultural production exemplified in different ways by 'New Historicism', depth hermeneutics, studies of the institutional framework of literature and literary criticism and, in a broad sense, cultural studies. It addresses, directly or indirectly, such issues as aesthetic value and canonicity, subjectification and structuration, the relationship between cultural practices and broader social processes, the social position and role of intellectuals and artists and the relationship between high culture and popular culture, all of which have become increasingly prevalent in cultural debate since the 1970s. Perhaps most importantly, Bourdieu dissects the relationship between systems of thought, social institutions and different forms of material and symbolic power, revealing certain affinities with thinkers such as Michel Foucault, of whom he was a friend and colleague at the Collège de France.

Bourdieu's wide-ranging work cuts across established academic disciplines and provides a powerful and highly productive model for social analysis in diverse fields of activity. In the elaboration of his theory of practice he has written on linguistic exchange, the political uses of language, museum attendance, the social uses of photography, marriage rites and ritual exchange among the Kabyle and the social origins and trajectories of French university students, academics and intellectuals, to mention only a few of the many areas he has addressed in over twenty books and hundreds of articles.[2]

Throughout its many facets, Bourdieu's work combines rigorous empirical analysis with a highly elaborate theoretical frame. One of its central concerns is the role of culture in the reproduction of social structures, or the way in which unequal power relations, unrecognized as such and thus accepted as legitimate, are embedded in the systems of classification used to describe and discuss everyday life – as well as cultural practices – and in the ways of perceiving reality that are taken for granted by members of society.[3]

Bourdieu argues, especially in *Distinction*, that systems of domination find expression in virtually all areas of cultural practice and symbolic exchange, including such things as preferences in dress, sports, food, music, literature, art and so on, or, in a more general sense, in *taste*.[4] As he remarks, 'taste classifies, and it classifies the classifier. Social subjects, classified by their classifications, distinguish themselves by the distinctions they make, between the beautiful and the ugly, the distinguished and the vulgar, in which their position in the objective classifications is expressed or betrayed.' Although they do not create or cause class divisions and inequalities, 'art and cultural consumption are predisposed, consciously and deliberately or not, to fulfil a social function of legitimating social differences' and thus contribute to the process of social reproduction.[5] Like Foucault, Bourdieu sees power as diffuse and often concealed in broadly accepted, and often unquestioned, ways of seeing and describing the world; but unlike Foucault, in Bourdieu's formulation this diffuse or symbolic power is closely intertwined with – but not reducible to – economic and political power, and thus serves a legitimating function.

Bourdieu's work on the cultural field constitutes a forceful argument against both Kantian notions of the universality of the aesthetic and ideologies of artistic and cultural autonomy from external determinants. He provides an analytical model which reintroduces, through the concept of *habitus*, a notion of the agent – which structuralism had excluded from social analysis – without falling into the idealism of Romantic conceptions of the artist as creator (or *subject*) which still informs much literary and art criticism today. At the same time, with the concept of *field*, he grounds the agent's action in objective social relations, without succumbing to the mechanistic determinism of many forms of sociological and 'Marxian' analysis. The essays included in this volume contribute, in a very fertile and often provocative manner, to transcending false dichotomies between internal and external readings, texts and institutions, literary and sociological analysis, popular and high culture. Bourdieu convincingly argues against essentialist concepts of art and the (still) dominant charismatic vision of the artist, both of which tend to efface the objective position of art and cultural practice in the field of social relations. His theory of practice thus calls into question many of the underlying presuppositions and *doxa* which have long guided the study of literature and art.

In this brief introduction, I will attempt to summarize the major features of Bourdieu's mode of analysis as they relate to the study of art and literature. Since his work on the cultural field is inseparable from his broader concerns, even such a limited purpose requires a certain contextualization within the general thrust of his work as a whole. At the same time, I have no intention of providing a thorough overview or a critical analysis of Bourdieu's work, or of situating it, except in a broad sense, within the multiple theoretical positions in the social sciences and philosophy with which his work implicitly or explicitly engages. In the first part of the introduction I will outline some of the basic tenets of Bourdieu's theory of practice. In the second, I will turn towards his application of that theory to the literary/artistic field (henceforth referred to simply as the cultural field). Then, in the third, I will focus on his theory of art perception and aesthetics.

I

Bourdieu first turned his attention to the field of cultural production in a series of seminars held at the École Normale Supérieure, and later at the École Pratique des Hautes Études, starting in the 1960s.[6] Much of his work prior to that time had been, in his own words, that of a 'blissful structuralist' engaged in ethnographic studies of Algerian peasant communities.[7] Through those studies he had come to see the limitations of structuralism and had begun formulating his own theory and methodology as a means of overcoming a series of dichotomies (individual vs society, freedom vs necessity, and so forth) which had, in his view, impeded the development of a scientific approach to human practice. He subsumed these dichotomies under the central epistemological dichotomy between 'subjectivism' and 'objectivism' or, as he sometimes puts it, between social phenomenology and social physics.[8]

Subjectivism represents a form of knowledge about the social world based on the primary experience and perceptions of individuals and includes such intellectual currents as phenomenology, rational action theory and certain forms of interpretive sociology, anthropology and linguistic analysis (what Volosinov calls 'individualistic subjectivism').[9]

In the literary field this would include all idealistic and essentialist theories based on the charismatic ideology of the writer as 'creator'. Objectivism, on the other hand, attempts to explain the social world by bracketing individual experience and subjectivity and focusing instead on the objective conditions which structure practice independent of human consciousness. It is found in many social theories, including Saussurean semiology, structural anthropology and Althusserian Marxism.[10]

Both subjectivism and objectivism fail to account for what Bourdieu refers to as the 'objectivity of the subjective'.[11] Subjectivism fails to grasp the social ground that shapes consciousness, while objectivism does just the opposite, failing to recognize that social reality is to some extent shaped by the conceptions and representations that individuals make of the social world. In his critique of objectivism Bourdieu writes, in the conclusion to *Distinction*, that 'the representation which individuals and groups inevitably project through their practices and properties is an integral part of social reality. A class is defined as much by its *being-perceived* and by its *being*, by its consumption – which need not be conspicuous to be symbolic – as much as by its position in the relations of production.'[12] Yet his reservations about objectivism (which Bourdieu finds more acceptable than subjectivism in that it is a necessary first step in any social analysis) in no way imply acceptance of theories which posit some sort of creative free will with the ability to constitute meaning, or that the constituted significations of actions and works should be reduced to the conscious intentions of their authors.[13] In Bourdieu's theory, symbolic aspects of social life are inseparably intertwined with the material conditions of existence, without one being reducible to the other.

In an attempt to transcend this false dichotomy, Bourdieu sought to develop a concept of agent free from the voluntarism and idealism of subjectivist accounts and a concept of social space free from the deterministic and mechanistic causality inherent in many objectivist approaches.[14] Bourdieu's *genetic sociology* or *genetic structuralism* – which should under no circumstances be identified or confused with Lucien Goldmann's methodology – thus combines an analysis of objective social structures with an analysis of the genesis, within particular individuals, of the socially constituted mental structures which generate practice.[15]

It was within this framework that Bourdieu developed the concepts of *habitus* and *field*. The notion of habitus was conceived as an alternative to the solutions offered by subjectivism (consciousness, subject, etc.) and a reaction against structuralism's 'odd philosophy of action' which reduced the agent to a mere 'bearer' (*Träger*: for the Althusserians) or 'unconscious' expression (for Lévi-Strauss) of structure. Bourdieu first introduced into his theory the notion of habitus – a concept borrowed from Scholastic philosophy but also used, in a different but not totally unrelated sense, by thinkers such as Hegel, Husserl and Mauss – on the occasion of the French edition of Erwin Panofsky's *Architecture gothique et pensée scolastique*.[16] On one level Bourdieu compares the notion to Chomsky's generative grammar, in that it attempts to account for the creative, active and inventive capacities of human agents, but without – and here he distances himself from Chomsky – attributing it to a universal mind. In sum, habitus represented a 'theoretical intention . . . to get out from under the philosophy of consciousness without doing away with the agent, in its truth of a practical operator of object constructions'.[17]

Bourdieu formally defines habitus as the system of 'durable, transposable dispositions, structured structures predisposed to function as structuring structures, that is, as principles which generate and organize practices and representations that can be objectively adapted to their outcomes without presupposing a conscious aiming at ends or an express mastery of the operations necessary in order to attain them. Objectively "regulated" and "regular" without being in any way the product of obedience to rules, they can be collectively orchestrated without being the product of the organizing action of a conductor.'[18]

The habitus is sometimes described as a 'feel for the game', a 'practical sense' (*sens pratique*) that inclines agents to act and react in specific situations in a manner that is not always calculated and that is not simply a question of conscious obedience to rules. Rather, it is a set of dispositions which generates practices and perceptions. The habitus is the result of a long process of inculcation, beginning in early childhood, which becomes a 'second sense' or a second nature. According to Bourdieu's definition, the dispositions represented by the habitus are 'durable' in that they last throughout an agent's lifetime. They are 'transposable' in that they may generate practices in multiple and diverse fields of activity, and they are 'structured structures' in that they inevitably incorporate the objective social conditions of their inculcation. This accounts for the similarity in the habitus of agents from the same social class and authorizes speaking of a class habitus (in *Distinction*, for example, Bourdieu shows statistically how the working-class habitus generates analogous preferences across a broad range of cultural practices). Finally, the dispositions of the habitus are 'structuring structures' through their ability to generate practices adjusted to specific situations.

The habitus does not negate the possibility of strategic calculation on the part of agents, but it functions in a quite different manner. In

Bourdieu's words, 'This system of dispositions – a present past that tends to perpetuate itself into the future by reactivation in similarly structured practices, an internal law through which the law of external necessities, irreducible to immediate constraints, is constantly exerted – is the principle of the continuity and regularity which objectivism sees in social practices without being able to account for it; and also of the regulated transformations that cannot be explained either by the extrinsic, instantaneous determinisms of mechanistic sociologism or by the purely internal but equally instantaneous determination of spontaneist subjectivism.'[19]

Agents do not act in a vacuum, but rather in concrete social situations governed by a set of objective social relations. To account for these situations or contexts, without, again, falling into the determinism of objectivist analysis, Bourdieu developed the concept of field (*champ*). According to Bourdieu's theoretical model, any social formation is structured by way of a hierarchically organized series of fields (the economic field, the educational field, the political field, the cultural field, etc.), each defined as a structured space with its own laws of functioning and its own relations of force independent of those of politics and the economy, except, obviously, in the cases of the economic and political fields. Each field is relatively autonomous but structurally homologous with the others. Its structure, at any given moment, is determined by the relations between the positions agents occupy in the field. A field is a dynamic concept in that a change in agents' positions necessarily entails a change in the field's structure.

The formulation of the notion of field also represented an attempt to apply what Bourdieu, borrowing from Cassirer, calls a *relational* mode of thought to cultural production. This requires a break with the ordinary or substantialist perception of the social world in order to see each element in terms of its relationships with all other elements in a system from which it derives its meaning and function. Bourdieu's initial elaboration of the concept of intellectual field (in the 1966 article 'Intellectual Field and Creative Project') was still excessively dependent on a substantialist perspective.[20] The recognition of the importance of objective relationships between positions, as opposed to interactions among agents, came through a critical reading of Max Weber's sociology of religion.[21]

In any given field, agents occupying the diverse available positions (or in some cases creating new positions) engage in competition for control of the interests or resources which are specific to the field in question. In the economic field, for example, agents compete for economic capital by way of various investment strategies using accumulated economic capital. But the interests and resources at stake in fields are not always material, and competition among agents – which Bourdieu sees as one universal invariant property of fields – is not always based on conscious calculation. In the cultural (e.g. literary) field, competition often concerns the authority inherent in recognition, consecration and prestige. This is especially so in what Bourdieu calls the sub-field of restricted production, that is, production not aimed at a large-scale market. Authority based on consecration or prestige is purely symbolic and may or may not imply possession of increased economic capital. Bourdieu thus developed, as an integral part of his theory of practice, the concept of *symbolic power* based on diverse forms of capital which are not reducible to economic capital. Academic capital, for example, derives from formal education and can be measured by degrees or diplomas held. Linguistic capital concerns an agent's linguistic competence measured in relation to a specific linguistic market where often unrecognized power relations are at stake.[22]

Two forms of capital are particularly important in the field of cultural production. *Symbolic capital* refers to degree of accumulated prestige, celebrity, consecration or honour and is founded on a dialectic of knowledge (*connaissance*) and recognition (*reconnaissance*).[23] *Cultural capital* concerns forms of cultural knowledge, competences or dispositions. In *Distinction*, the work in which he elaborates the concept most fully, Bourdieu defines cultural capital as a form of knowledge, an internalized code or a cognitive acquisition which equips the social agent with empathy towards, appreciation for or competence in deciphering cultural relations and cultural artefacts. He suggests that 'a work of art has meaning and interest only for someone who possesses the cultural competence, that is, the code, into which it is encoded'. The possession of this code, or cultural capital, is accumulated through a long process of acquisition or inculcation which includes the pedagogical action of the family or group members (family education), educated members of the social formation (diffuse education) and social institutions (institutionalized education).[24]

Like economic capital, the other forms of capital are unequally distributed among social classes and class fractions. Although the different forms of capital may be mutually convertible under certain circumstances (for example, the proper kind and amount of academic capital may be converted into economic capital through advantageous placement in the job market), they are not reducible to each other. Possession of economic capital does not *necessarily* imply possession of cultural or symbolic capital, and vice versa. Bourdieu, in fact, analyses the field of cultural production as an 'economic world reversed' based on a 'winner loses' logic, since economic success (in literary terms, for example, writing a best seller) may well signal a barrier to specific consecration and symbolic power.

It is important to recognize, however, that Bourdieu's use of economic terminology does not imply any sort of economism or economic reductionism. In fact, he sees the economic field *per se* as simply one field among others, without granting it primacy in the general theory of fields. To enter a field (the philosophical field, the scientific field, etc.), to play the game, one must possess the habitus which predisposes one to enter that field, that game, and not another. One must also possess at least the minimum amount of knowledge, or skill, or 'talent' to be accepted as a legitimate player. Entering the game, furthermore, means attempting to use that knowledge, or skill, or 'talent' in the most advantageous way possible. It means, in short, 'investing' one's (academic, cultural, symbolic) capital in such a way as to derive maximum benefit or 'profit' from participation. Under normal circumstances, no one enters a game to lose. By the same token, no one enters the literary field – no one writes a novel, for example – to receive bad reviews.

In each and every field, certain interests are at stake even if they are not recognized as such; a certain 'investment' is made, even if it is not recognized as an investment. These interests and investments can be analysed in terms of an economic logic without in any way reducing them to economics, for the structural *homology* between fields does not imply structural *identity*. The idea that there are different kinds of capital which are invested in different fields of activity in accordance with the specific interests of the field in question (and of the agents involved) allows Bourdieu to develop what he calls a 'general science of the economy of practices', within which one can analyse 'all practices, including those purporting to be disinterested or gratuitous, and hence non-economic, as economic practices directed toward the maximising of material or symbolic profit'.[25] It is up to the analyst to establish through research what the specific interests of the field are and what strategies of accumulation (which may or may not be based on conscious calculation) are employed by the agents involved.

Bourdieu elaborated and refined the concepts of habitus and field in the process of analysing the field of cultural production which is inseparable from his broader theory of practice. He rejects the idea, implicit in many prevailing forms of immanent analysis (and perhaps taken to its extreme in Baudrillard's sign fetishism), that symbolic forms and systems of exchange can somehow be set apart from other modes of practice. He posits instead a correspondence between social and symbolic structures based on the systematic unity of social life and the existence of structural and functional homologies among all fields of social activity. The transfer of concepts from one field to another, Bourdieu suggests, possesses 'an eminent heuristic virtue, the one that the epistemological tradition recognizes in analogy' and makes it possible for him to attain a greater level of generalization of his theoretical principles.[26]

## II

Bourdieu's theory of the cultural field might be characterized as a radical contextualization. It takes into consideration not only works themselves, seen relationally within the space of available possibilities and within the historical development of such possibilities, but also producers of works in terms of their strategies and trajectories, based on their individual and class habitus, as well as their objective position within the field. It also entails an analysis of the structure of the field itself, which includes the positions occupied by producers (e.g. writers, artists) as well as those occupied by all the instances of consecration and legitimation which make cultural products what they are (the public, publishers, critics, galleries, academies and so forth). Finally, it involves an analysis of the position of the field within the broader field of power. In short, Bourdieu's theory of the field of cultural production and his extremely demanding analytical method encompass the set of social conditions of the production, circulation and consumption of symbolic goods.[27]

   The very complexity of Bourdieu's model ensures that it does not fall into the reductionism of either purely internal readings or modes of external analysis of cultural texts. The full explanation of artistic works is to be found neither in the text itself, nor in some sort of determinant social structure. Rather, it is found in the history and structure of the field itself, with its multiple components, and in the relationship between that field and the field of power. As Bourdieu has put it, 'The theory of the field [leads] to both a rejection of the direct relating of individual biography to the work of literature (or the relating of the "social class" of origin to the work) and also to a rejection of internal analysis of an individual work or even of intertextual analysis. This is because *what we have to do is all these things at the same time.*'[28]

   For Bourdieu, the specific economy of the cultural field is based on a particular form of *belief* concerning what constitutes a cultural (e.g. literary, artistic) work and its aesthetic or social value. In its most traditional and canonical form – institutionalized in many universities around the world – this belief involves the autonomy of the work from external determinants and an essentialist notion of the absolute value of the work *per se*. But as Bourdieu notes, both the autonomy of the artistic field and theories of pure art are fairly recent phenomena, dating, in the form we know them today, from only the nineteenth century.[29] By the same token, aesthetic value, itself socially constituted, is radically contingent on a very complex and constantly changing set of circumstances involving multiple social and institutional factors.[30] Literature, art and their respective producers do not exist independently of a complex institutional framework which authorizes, enables, empowers and legitimizes them. This framework must be incorporated into any analysis that pretends to provide a thorough understanding of cultural goods and practices.

The notion of field provides a means of going beyond internal analysis (whether formalist or hermeneutic) and external explication, both of which Bourdieu sees as inadequate and reductive. Bourdieu identifies two central theoretical traditions in internal analysis. The first derives from the neo-Kantian philosophy of symbolic forms and from traditions which seek universal, ahistorical structures as the basis of the literary or poetic construction of the world.[31] The second, which Bourdieu sees as the more powerful tradition since it lends a degree of scientificity to the analytical endeavour, is that of structuralism.

Bourdieu's objection to strictly internal analysis – ranging, in literary criticism, from different brands of formalism to Anglo-American New Criticism, French *explication de textes*, and structuralist and deconstructuralist readings of isolated texts – is quite simply that it looks for the final explanation of texts either within the texts themselves (the object of analysis, in other words, is its own explanation) or within some sort of ahistorical 'essence' rather than in the complex network of social relations that makes the very existence of the texts possible. Bourdieu directs this critique at *all* modes of internal analysis, whether conducted on a broad scale, such as Foucault's 'field of strategic possibilities', which seeks the explanatory principle of discourse in the field of discourse itself, or in more narrow concerns with 'textuality', such as in the work of the Russian Formalists.[32]

Bourdieu may well agree with Jakobson's statement that the true subject of literary science is 'that which makes a given work a literary work', but he would certainly disagree that 'that which makes a given work a literary work' is, as Jakobson would have it, 'literariness', especially when seen in terms of form alone.[33] Tynjanov's concept of the 'literary system' comes closer to Bourdieu's formulation in that it recognizes in every period the coexistence of opposing literary schools, either consecrated or striving for consecration. The literary system is not harmonious, but rather is driven by conflict in which one aesthetic construction negates opposing constructions. Formal properties are thus understood relationally, that is, in opposition to other formal properties.[34] Yet for Bourdieu the concept of literary system is ultimately inadequate, for it fails to recognize that formal properties, both past and present, are themselves socially and historically constituted, and it remains imprisoned by immanent modes of analysis.

By isolating texts from the social conditions of their production, circulation and consumption, formalist analysis eliminates from consideration the social agent as producer (e.g. the writer), ignores the objective social relations in which literary practice occurs and avoids the questions of precisely what constitutes a work of art at a given historical moment and of the 'value' of the work, which constantly changes in accordance with structural changes in the field. Internal explication, furthermore, ignores the fact that 'what makes a given work a literary work' is a complex social and institutional framework which authorizes and sustains literature and literary practice.

Bourdieu suggests that 'it can only be an unjustifiable abstraction (which could fairly be called reductive) to seek the source of the understanding of cultural productions in these productions themselves, taken in isolation and divorced from the conditions of their production and utilization, as would be the wish of *discourse analysis*, which, situated on the border between sociology and linguistics, has nowadays relapsed into indefensible forms of internal analysis. Scientific analysis must work to relate to each other two sets of relations, the space of works or discourses taken as differential stances, and the space of the positions held by those who produce them.'[35] To be fully understood, literary works must be reinserted in the system of social relations which sustains them. This does not imply a rejection of aesthetic or formal properties, but rather an analysis based on their position in relation to the universe of possibilities of which they are a part. In this universe of belief one must consider, in other words, 'not only the material production but also the symbolic production of the work, i.e. the production of the value of the work or, which amounts to the same thing, of belief in the value of the work' ('The Field of Cultural Production', chapter 1 in this volume). This includes recognition of the functions of artistic mediators (publishers, critics, agents, *marchands*, academies and so forth) as producers of the meaning and value of the work. Rather than an instance of individual creativity (in accordance with a Romantic conception) or 'literariness' (as the formalists would have it), each work thus becomes an expression of the field as a whole. Within this framework, internal analysis alone is indeed untenable and reductive.

Bourdieu's opposition to external modes of analysis, especially other sociological approaches, derives from the mechanistic determinism which characterizes many of them. He takes issue with analysts who attempt, through quantitative or qualitative methods, to relate works directly to the social origin of their authors, or who seek an explanation in the groups which have commissioned works or for whom works are intended.[36] Along these same lines, he rejects Lucien Goldmann's theory of a 'transindividual subject' and the idea that the structure of a specific work 'reflects' or expresses the world view of the social group or class that produced it.[37]

The first problem with most statistical methods of analysis is that they rarely question the 'sample' employed, using, more often than not, a classification of authors borrowed from standard literary histories, memoirs, and biographies. In other words, the sample tends to include only consecrated writers, frequently omitting those writers, now considered minor, who may have occupied an important position in the field at the time of their literary activity, even if only in a negative sense – (that is, occupying a position in opposition to those writers now consecrated). A thorough statistical analysis would have to include the totality of the literary field: both great and minor writers, both those who are now consecrated and those who have been relegated to oblivion by literary historiographers in accordance with specific yet normally unspecified symbolic interests. Even then, statistical analysis alone would at best result in only a superficial and partial identification of certain empirically verifiable regularities such as social origin or formal education, without being able to understand truly the fundamental characteristics of writers or even how 'the writer' is defined at a certain historical moment. This definition – Who can legitimately be called a writer? What is legitimate literary practice? – is one of the key stakes of symbolic struggle in the literary field, and failure to understand it often results in the blind acceptance of the dominant definition of literary legitimacy.[38]

The second and perhaps more serious problem with statistical analysis – as with other forms of analysis which attempt to establish a direct link between the social origins of writers and the significance of their work – derives from what Bourdieu calls the literary field's weak degree of institutionalization. The literary field – like all other fields, but especially those whose stakes are largely symbolic – is relatively autonomous from the demands of politics and economics. There are no ultimate, legally constituted arbiters of literary quality or value, which is unstable and constantly changing over time. Strategies and trajectories of writers tend to be individual – which does not mean that they are totally subjective or the product of conscious calculation – and highly differentiated, even among agents of a similar social background. The literary field does not follow the laws that apply in other fields which may be more amenable to sociological analysis based on traditional categories. It is a field where effort is not necessarily rewarded with success, where the value accorded to specific positions or honours (for example, membership of the Academy in France) may vary greatly according to the agent in question, where supply attempts to create demand rather than vice versa, where seniority has little bearing on career paths, and where writers with many different social and geographical backgrounds coexist, often having little in common other than their mutual interest in literature.[39] There can thus be no direct, mechanistic correlation between the writer's objective position in society and the type of writing he or she will produce.

Bourdieu also takes issue with 'reflection theories', which suppose homologies between the structure of works and the social structure, or between works and the world view of social interests of a specific class. To suggest, in the manner of Lukács and Goldmann, that the writer is somehow an unconscious spokesman for a group is, for Bourdieu, simply to invert the Romantic myth of the poet *vates*. Reducing the writer to a sort of 'medium', this approach assumes a perfect correlation between the group and the mode of expression without questioning how one defines the group whose world view is supposedly expressed through the work's structure. It takes for granted that one fully understands the world view of the group in question and that that world view is somehow homogeneous. Bourdieu suggests that 'one ought to examine the presuppositions, all extremely naïve, of these imputations of spiritual inheritance, which can always be reduced to the supposition that a group can act *directly*, as final cause (function), on the production of the work' ('Principles for a Sociology of Cultural Works', chapter 6 in this volume).

By conceiving of literary works as expressions not of the author but rather of the social class of which he or she is a member, by seeing the author as merely one who lends coherence to the 'mental structure' of his or her class, and by positing works as collective products of social groups, such approaches also ignore the objective conditions of the production, circulation and consumption of symbolic goods. They thus fall prey to the objectivism which Bourdieu finds unacceptable in much structuralist analysis. Artistic works, in Bourdieu's view, are produced by agents existing in objective sets of social relations which are not limited to those of 'class' and which fulfil specific functions for those agents which must be brought into the analysis.

Reflection theories, no matter how elaborate or 'euphemized', neglect the relative autonomy of the literary field. This problem is addressed by, for example, Mikhail Bakhtin, who suggests that literature is part of, and cannot be understood outside of, the 'total context' of a given period's culture. Social and economic factors clearly affect literature, but only through their effect on culture as a whole; their impact on literature *per se* occurs only through the mediation of the entire culture.[40] To counter what he calls the 'short circuit effect' of approaches that posit a direct connection between art and social structure, Bourdieu developed the theory of the field as a social universe with its own laws of functioning. External determinants can have an effect only through transformations in the structure of the field itself. In other words, the field's structure *refracts*, much like a prism, external determinants in terms of its own logic, and it is only through such refraction that external factors can have an effect on the field. The degree of autonomy of a particular field is measured precisely by its ability to refract external demands into its own logic.[41]

Finally, Bourdieu criticizes the failure of external analysis to consider works of art as possessing a specific language. This, as we have seen, does not mean that he accepts the formalist contention that literary language alone, or 'literariness', can provide an adequate explanation of literature or literary practice, even when seen, as by Tynjanov, as the result of the historical, yet still internal, dialect of a literary system. The analysis of literary form or language is an essential part of literary study, but has full meaning only when viewed relationally – or, broadly speaking, intertextually – and when reinserted into the objective field of social relations of which it is part and from which it derives. In Bourdieu's view, one cannot ignore 'the balance of forces between social agents [e.g., writers, critics, etc.] who have entirely real interests in the different possibilities available to them as stakes and who deploy every sort of strategy to make one set or the other prevail' ('The Field of Cultural Production', chapter 1 below). Only a method which retains a notion of intertextuality, seen as a system of differential stances, and reintroduces a notion of agent (i.e. producer), acting (consciously or unconsciously) within a specific set of social relations, can transcend the seemingly irreconcilable differences between internal and external readings of artistic works. This is precisely the method that Bourdieu has developed with his notions of field and habitus.

To summarize very briefly, Bourdieu's method attempts to incorporate three levels of social reality: (1) the position of the literary or artistic field within what he calls the *field of power* (i.e. the set of dominant power relations in society or, in other words, the ruling classes); (2) the structure of the literary field (i.e. the structure of the objective positions occupied by agents competing for legitimacy in the field as well as the objective characteristics of the agents themselves); and (3) the genesis of the producers' habitus (i.e. the structured and structuring dispositions which generate practices).

The cultural (literary, artistic, etc.) field exists in a subordinate or dominated position within the field of power, whose principle of legitimacy is based on possession of economic or political capital. It is situated *within* the field of power because of its possession of a high degree of symbolic forms of capital (e.g. academic capital, cultural capital), but in a dominated position because of its relatively low degree of economic capital (when compared with the dominant fractions of the dominant classes). It is for this reason that Bourdieu refers to intellectuals as pertaining to the dominated fraction of the dominant class. Although fully within the field of power (except when the cultural practices in question comprise what is often referred to as 'folklore'), the cultural field possesses a relative autonomy with respect to its economic and political determinations.

The field of cultural production is structured, in the broadest sense, by an opposition between two sub-fields: the field of restricted production and the field of large-scale production. The field of restricted production concerns what we normally think of as 'high' art, for example 'classical' music, the plastic arts, so-called 'serious' literature. In this sub-field, the stakes of competition between agents are largely symbolic, involving prestige, consecration and artistic celebrity. This, as Bourdieu often writes, is production for producers. Economic profit is normally disavowed (at least by the artists themselves), and the hierarchy of authority is based on different forms of symbolic profit, e.g. a profit of disinterestedness, or the profit one has on seeing oneself (or being seen) as one who is not searching for profit. It is in this sense that the cultural field is a universe of belief. The symbolic power of this sub-field's products is sustained by a vast social apparatus encompassing museums, galleries, libraries, the educational system, literary and art histories, centres for the performing arts and so forth.

The degree of autonomy of a specific realm of activity is defined by its ability to reject external determinants and obey only the specific logic of the field, governed by specific forms of symbolic capital. In Bourdieu's words, again in 'The Field of Cultural Production', 'in the most perfectly autonomous sector of the field of cultural production, where the only audience aimed at is other producers (e.g. Symbolist poetry), the economy of practices is based, as in a generalized game of "loser wins", on a systematic inversion of the fundamental principles of all ordinary economies, that of business (it excludes the pursuit of profit and does not guarantee any sort of correspondence between investments and monetary gains), that of power (it condemns honours and temporal greatness), and even that of institutionalized cultural authority (the absence of any academic training or consecration may be considered a virtue)'. The very logic of the restricted field of production makes it conducive to formal experimentation and innovation (diverse avant-garde movements are situated at this extreme of the field).

The field of large-scale production involves what we sometimes refer to as 'mass' or 'popular' culture: privately owned television, most cinematic productions, radio, mass-produced literature (the Harlequin or Mills & Boon romance, for example). Sustained by a large and complex culture industry, its dominant principle of hierarchization involves economic capital or 'the bottom line'. Its very nature and its dependence on the broadest possible audience make it less susceptible to formal experimentation, although, as Bourdieu notes in 'The Market of Symbolic Goods' (chapter 3 in this volume), it frequently borrows from the restricted field of production in attempts to renew itself.

The cultural field constitutes, as Bourdieu indicates in the subtitle to the lead essay in this volume, an 'economic world reversed', in that the autonomous pole, based on symbolic capital and thus subject only to internal demands, is marked positively, and the opposite pole, based on subordination to the demands of economic capital, is marked negatively. Between these poles is a range of cultural practices which combine the two principles of legitimacy to various degrees. Bourdieu thus refers to two principles of hierarchization which constitute the stakes of struggle in the field: the heteronomous principle, based on external factors, and the autonomous principle, based on specific interests. This fundamental opposition, however, is cut through with multiple additional opposi-tions, (for example between genres or between different approaches to the same genre). While today these principles are found in the opposi-tion between 'mass' and 'elite' culture, they may vary according to the specific country in question and the specific historical moment of analysis. In his discussion of the literary field in nineteenth-century France, for example, Bourdieu analyses these opposing principles through the opposition between bourgeois art (notably the theatre), social art, and art for art's sake. Social art occupies a thoroughly ambiguous position in relation to the other two in that it appeals to external functions (like bourgeois art) while at the same time rejecting (like art for art's sake) the dominant principle of hierarchy in the field of power.

The cultural field is, furthermore, structured by the distribution of available positions (e.g. consecrated artist vs striving artist, novel vs poetry, art for art's sake vs social art) and by the objective characteristics of the agents occupying them. The dynamic of the field is based on the struggles between these positions, a struggle often expressed in the conflict between the orthodoxy of established traditions and the heret-ical challenge of new modes of cultural practice, manifested as *prises de position* or position-takings. Bourdieu sometimes refers to position-takings as the 'space of creative works', but they may refer to both internal (e.g. stylistic) and external (e.g. political) positionings. The space of position-takings can only be defined as a system of differential stances in relation to other possible position-takings, past and present. This is where a notion of intertextuality comes into the analysis. Unlike intertextuality as conceived by Bakhtin or Kristeva, however, which tends to relate texts only to other texts, for Bourdieu texts must be analysed both in relation to other texts and in relation to the structure of the field and to the specific agents involved.

Bourdieu posits a homology between the space of position-takings and the space of positions in the field, so that conflicts between different position-takings in fact constitute particular manifestations of the structure of the latter. In *Homo Academicus* he offers the Barthes–Picard polemic, a 'quarrel of the Ancients and the Moderns', as an example of such conflict, which he sees as a 'rationalized retranslation' of the opposition between the posts each critic held, between the social sciences and literary studies or, in institutional terms, between the École des Hautes Études and the Sorbonne, respectively.[42] The polemic, in other words, is not simply between two individuals, but rather is inscribed in the broader conflict between orthodoxy and heresy which constitutes the central dialectic of change in the cultural field. The same principle applies to the process of 'banalization' and 'debanalization' described by the Russian Formalists and to what Weber describes as a process of 'routinization' and 'deroutinization' in the religious field. As Bourdieu puts it in 'Principles for a Sociology of Cultural Works', 'the process that carries works along is the product of the struggle among agents who, as a function of their position in the field, of their specific capital, have a stake in conservation, that is routine and routinization, or in subversion, i.e. a return to sources, to an original purity, to heretical criticism, and so forth'.

The relationship between positions and position-takings is mediated by the dispositions of the individual agents, their feel for the game. Agents' strategies are a function of the convergence of position and position-taking mediated by habitus. In his discussion of Flaubert's *Sentimental Education* (see chapter 4 in this volume), Bourdieu shows how the characters' habitus shapes their inclination to play the game to win or lose, to augment, preserve or squander their inherited capital. Strategies also account for agents' trajectories in the field.

*Strategy* and *trajectory* are two key concepts in Bourdieu's theory of the field. *Strategy* may be understood as a specific orientation of practice. As a product of the habitus, strategy is not based on conscious calculation but rather results from unconscious dispositions towards practice. It depends both on the position the agent occupies in the field and on what Bourdieu calls the state of the 'legitimate problematic' – the issues or questions over which confrontation takes place, which constitute the stakes of struggle in the field and which orient the search for solutions. *Trajectory*, as defined in 'Principles for a Sociology of Cultural Works', 'describes the series of positions successively occupied by the same writer in the successive states of the literary field, being understood that it is only in the structure of a field that the meaning of these successive positions can be defined'. The trajectory is one way in which the relationship between the agent and the field is objectified. It differs from traditional biography in that it does not search, as does Sartre in his study of Flaubert, for some sort of 'original project' that determines and unifies all subsequent developments in a writer's life. It concerns, rather, the objective positions successively occupied in the field. Symbolic forms (e.g. novels or other forms of artistic works) constitute another way in which the relationship between the agent and the field is objectified and, as we have seen, can only be understood relationally.

Bourdieu's model necessarily involves different levels of analysis which account for different aspects of cultural practice, ranging from the relationship between the cultural field and the broader field of power to the strategies, trajectories and works of individual agents. All levels of analysis, each composed of multiple components, must be taken into consideration to gain a full understanding of cultural works. Although represented here only schematically, the significance of Bourdieu's model for contemporary criticism, especially those tendencies concerned with the relations between literature/art and its socio-historical ground, should be clear.

Bourdieu's model might, for example, provide theoretical and methodological rigour to a formulation such as that of Edward Said's 'affiliations', defined as an 'implicit network of peculiarly cultural associations between forms, statements, and other aesthetic elaborations, on the one hand, and, on the other, institutions, agencies, classes, and amorphous social forces'. According to Said, such affiliations anchor writers and their texts in a complex system of cultural relationships which include the 'status of the author, historical moment, conditions of publication, diffusion and reception, values drawn upon, values and ideas assumed, a framework of consensually held tacit assumptions, presumed background, and so on'.[43] Although at first glance similar to Bourdieu's model, Said's formulation is largely intuitive and ultimately vague, and it never really inquires into the socially and historically constituted institutional framework which in fact sustains literary practice. Nor does it ever inquire into the objective position that criticism itself – and therefore the critic – occupies in the field of social relations.[44]

Bourdieu's work coincides in a number of ways with the 'New Historicism', identified primarily with Stephen Greenblatt and the journal *Representations*. Like Bourdieu, the New Historicism has attempted to develop a methodology that would avoid the reductionism both of internal, formalist and of external, more frankly sociological or Marxian paradigms of criticism. It has sought to refigure the literary field, especially that of the English Renaissance, by resituating works 'not only in relationship to other genres and modes of discourse but also in relationship to contemporaneous social institutions and non-discursive practices'.[45] It posits, again like Bourdieu, that formal and historical concerns are inseparable, that human consciousness and thought are socially constituted, and that possibilities of action are socially and historically situated and defined.[46] But Bourdieu would almost certainly take issue with New Historicism's 'post-structuralist textualization of history', which ultimately downplays the importance of an extra-textual social and historical ground and the mediating role of the field of cultural production.[47]

During the 1980s the question of the formation and perpetuation of canons has come increasingly to the fore in Anglo-American literary and cultural criticism. Discussions of the canon inevitably impinge on broader questions of aesthetic, literary and cultural value as well as on the constitution, preservation and reproduction of authority and symbolic power in the field. The literary canon has explicitly become both the site and the stake of contention as different groups have argued for its rearrangement along lines more favourable to their divergent interests and agendas.[48] Bourdieu's model suggests that such struggles in fact constitute the dynamic of change in the cultural field, for what is always at stake – in struggles between the Ancients and the Moderns, between consecrated artists and the avant-garde, between competing visions of the canon or competing methodologies – is the legitimate definition of literature and literary practice.

The legitimacy and authority of a specific critical interpretation derive at least in part from the legitimacy and authority of those who propagate it, or, to put it another way, from their objective position as authorized *lectores* (as opposed to *auctores*) in the literary field. A canonical vision of a literary school, movement or writer represents a structure of authority in the field; we would be naïve to assume that it is innocent or disinterested. As Bourdieu writes in 'The Field of Cultural Production', 'Every critical affirmation contains, on the one hand, a recognition of the value of the work which occasions it . . . and on the other hand an affirmation of its own legitimacy. All critics declare not only their judgement of the work but also their claim to the right to talk about it and judge it. In short, they take part in a struggle for the monopoly of legitimate discourse about the work of art, and consequently in the production of the value of the work of art.' There is, as Bourdieu has said, an interest in disinterestedness.

At stake in the literary field, and more specifically in the field of criticism is, among other things, the authority to determine the legitimate definition of the literary work and, by extension, the authority to define those works which guarantee the configurations of the literary canon. Such a definition is both positive, through selection of certain literary values, and negative, through its exclusion of others. The establishment of a canon in the guise of a universally valued cultural inheritance or patrimony constitutes an act of 'symbolic violence', as Bourdieu defines the term, in that it gains legitimacy by misrecognizing the underlying power relations which serve, in part, to guarantee the continued reproduction of the legitimacy of those who produce or defend the canon.

One of the major tenets of Bourdieu's theory and method – and one which goes back to his ethnographic studies in Algeria and to his break with structuralism – concerns the need to objectify and analyse the relationship between the analyser and his or her object of analysis. Failure to do so frequently results in the analyser assuming a privileged position (always self-attributed) and effacing relations of power that may be inherent in the relationship. It is for this reason that Bourdieu takes issue, for example, with Derrida's 'deconstruction' of Kant's *Critique of Judgement*, since it only goes halfway, failing to question its own position in the philosophical field. It thus remains, in Bourdieu's words, 'subject to the censorships of the pure reading'.[49] In this respect Bourdieu's work (for instance, *Homo Academicus*) represents an exemplary self-referentiality, constantly questioning and verifying its own presuppositions.

## III

Bourdieu's theory of the field of cultural production covers, as indicated above, both the material and the symbolic production of cultural works, which entails taking into account the multiple mediators which contribute to the works' meaning and sustain the universe of belief which is the cultural field. If cultural works are produced in objective historical situations and institutional frameworks by agents using different strategies and following different trajectories in the field, the reception of such works, regardless of the level of that reception, also takes place in specific historically constituted situations. Works have significance for certain groups and individuals based on their own objective position, cultural needs and capacities for analysis or symbolic appropriation. A discussion of the reception of cultural works thus implies a consideration of the values and systems of classification brought to bear on them at different moments. As already noted, such systems constitute the stakes of symbolic struggle in the cultural field and embody frequently unrecognized relations of power. Much of Bourdieu's work on art, literature and culture – in particular *Distinction* – has been concerned precisely with the ways in which culture contributes to domination and to the process of social reproduction.

The three essays in the final section of this volume all deal with the art world. Taken together, they represent an encapsulation of the overriding concerns of Bourdieu's model: the reconstruction of an artistic field at a given moment, its relationship to the field of power, the heretical challenge of a specific artist, the transformation of the hierarchy of legitimacy as a result of that challenge, and the long-term implications of that transformation in terms of the aesthetic appropriation of artistic works. The essays' central focus is, ultimately, the development of the pure gaze – focusing on form rather than function – which characterizes cultivated appreciation of art works up to the present.

The pure gaze came into being with the emergence of an autonomous artistic field capable of formulating and imposing its own values and its own principles of legitimacy while at the same time rejecting external sanctions and demands. This entails, obviously, the emergence of a group of producers motivated by pure artistic intention. Bourdieu suggests that, at least in France, such an autonomous field came into being only in the 1860s with the breakdown of the academic system, which imposed a set of official pictorial and aesthetic values institutionally reinforced by the École des Beaux-Arts, the Salon and other competitions. In the final analysis, academic values were sanctioned and guaranteed by the state, which encompassed the specific institutions in question.

The breakdown of the academic system occurred in particular through Manet's revolutionary refusal to abide by institutional impositions and his rejection of academic norms. He especially repudiated its injunction, based on a learned tradition steeped in classical culture, that a painting have a narrative content, that it 'say' something, and that it deal only with 'high' or 'noble' themes considered appropriate to legitimate painting. Hence the scandal caused, for example, by (among other works) his *The Absinthe Drinker*. In pictorial terms, Manet's heretical challenge rejected the academy's aesthetic of the 'finish', which sought to eliminate all traces of the artist's work and to impose conventional forms of composition and colour schemes. With Manet, and the Impressionists after him, narrative and drama lose their privileged position, and painting, in its most legitimate form, ceases to refer to anything but itself. Form, in other words, replaces function. The breakdown of the academic system led to the emergence of new groups of artists who no longer recognized a single source of legitimation and who increasingly rejected aesthetic values other than those based on the specific interests of the field. The system's monolithic authority was replaced, as Bourdieu describes it in 'Manet and the Institutionalization of Anomie' (chapter 9 in this volume), by 'the plurality of competing cults of multiple uncertain gods'.

The pure gaze is thus inseparable from the existence of an autonomous artistic field. It is also inseparable – when one shifts to the level of ontogenesis – from very specific conditions of acquisition, a fact born out by empirical research. Bourdieu's initial study of the artistic field was made in the mid-1960s when a research team he directed undertook a survey of art museum attendance in Western Europe. The results of the survey were published in 1966 under the title *L'Amour de l'art*.[50] Without going into the details of his survey and analysis, suffice it to say that Bourdieu found, perhaps not surprisingly, that regular museum attendance increases with increasing levels of education, to the point where, although theoretically open to all, art museums become 'almost the exclusive domain of cultivated classes'.[51] They thus have all the outward appearances of legitimacy, since the only ones excluded are those who exclude themselves. Simply verifying the correlation between educational level – or level of cultural aspiration – and museum attendance through statistical analysis is, however, insufficient for understanding why certain classes exclude themselves from what might be seen as a potentially edifying experience.

Access to works of art cannot be defined solely in terms of physical accessibility, since works of art exist only for those who have the means of understanding them. Comprehension involves a decoding operation, and the ability to decode works of art as they are meant to be decoded (that is, according to the values established in the artistic field) is not a universally shared natural talent, since it involves much more than the direct and immediate apprehension of the work. Artistic competence is a form of knowledge which permits the beholder to situate the work of art in relation to the universe of artistic possibilities of which it is part. As Bourdieu writes in 'Outline of a Sociological Theory of Art Perception' (chapter 8 in this volume), 'The perception of the work of art in a truly aesthetic manner, that is, as a signifier which signifies nothing other than itself, does not consist of considering it "without connecting it with anything other than itself, either emotionally or intellectually" . . , but rather of noting its *distinctive stylistic features* by relating it to the ensemble of the works forming the class to which it belongs, and to these works only'. Artistic competence, defined in this manner, is the result of a long process of inculcation which begins (or not) in the family, often in conformity with its level of economic, academic and cultural capital, and is reinforced by the educational system. It also involves prolonged exposure to works of art. The understanding of a work of art thus depends fully on the possession of the code into which it has been encoded, and this is neither a natural nor a universally distributed capability. Competence in this process of appropriation, which Bourdieu sometimes refers to as an 'aesthetic disposition', is a form of cultural capital, which, like other forms of capital, tends to follow unequal patterns of accumulation.

The role of the educational system – at least in France – is particularly important in this respect, not because it offers systematic programmes in art appreciation (in fact, it tends to be oriented towards a *literary* culture), but rather because it tends to cultivate a certain familiarity with legitimate culture and to inculcate a certain attitude towards works of art. In other words, even dealing as it does in the main with literary works, the educational system tends to create a transferable cultural disposition to appreciate academically sanctioned works of art and an equally transferable aptitude for artistic classification. These dispositions gradually become attached to certain academic and social status groups. The transferability of the aesthetic disposition allows knowledge and taste to be arranged into 'constellations', closely associated with educational level, 'such that a typical structure of preferences and knowledge in matters of painting is very likely to be linked to a similar structure of knowledge and tastes in classical music or even in jazz or cinema'.[52]

In an ideal situation in which education serves a true democratic function and is available to all on a truly equal basis, its impact should be to provide all students with the same or at least a similar aesthetic disposition. But Bourdieu's work in the sociology of education has shown, to the contrary, that schooling serves to reinforce, rather than diminish, social differences. The culture it transmits is largely that of the dominant classes, and it tends to perceive and classify as 'natural' talent, and thus 'natural' superiority, levels of knowledge among students which are in fact largely the result of an informal learning process taking place within the family. The educational system transforms social hierarchies into academic hierarchies and, by extension, into hierarchies of 'merit'. As Bourdieu writes, 'It is sufficient to give free play to the laws of cultural transmission for cultural capital to be added to cultural capital and for the structure of the distribution of cultural capital between social classes to be thereby reproduced.'[53]

Cultural competence and the aesthetic disposition participate in the perpetuation of social differences to the extent that they are taken to be natural talents available to all on an equal basis and thus not recognized as the result of a specific process of cultural transmission and training which is in fact not available to all. Bourdieu refers in 'Outline of a Sociological Theory of Art Perception' to the paradox of the process by which the realization of culture becomes *natural*, to the extent that it is only achieved 'by negating itself as such, that is, as artificial and artificially acquired, so as to become second nature, a habitus, . . . so completely freed from the constraints of culture and so little marked by the long, patient training of which it is the product that any reminder of the conditions and the social conditioning which have rendered it possible seems to be at once obvious and scandalous'. Cultural capital thus participates in the process of domination by legitimizing certain practices as 'naturally' superior to others and by making these practices seem superior even to those who do not participate, who are thus led, through a negative process of inculcation, to see their own practices as inferior and to exclude themselves from legitimate practices.

The implication of Bourdieu's theory is that any form of analysis which overlooks the social ground of aesthetic taste tends to establish as universal aesthetic and cultural practices which are in fact products of privilege. It is in this sense that Bourdieu discusses at great length, especially in *Distinction*, the homology of lifestyles – drawing connections, for example, between taste in art and taste in food – and the differences between taste of distinction and taste for necessity. Taste of distinction, of which artistic competence and the aesthetic disposition are part, implies freedom from economic necessity, the ability to keep necessity at arm's length, and permits the distant and detached relationship to works of art required by a pure aesthetic. The submission to necessity by those less endowed with cultural and economic capital corresponds, on the other hand, to a more functional and pragmatic aesthetic based on the schemes of perception of everyday life and the frequent rejection of the gratuitousness associated, for example, with formal experimentation.

Through a very elaborate empirical analysis of class tastes and lifestyles, Bourdieu offers a radical critique – outlined most explicitly in the 'Postscript' to *Distinction*, titled 'Towards a "Vulgar" Critique of "Pure" Critiques' – of Kantian aesthetics. Bourdieu argues that the aesthetics of 'pure' taste are based on a refusal of 'impure' taste, or taste reduced to the pleasure of the senses, as well as on a refusal of the facile.

This refusal, however, is not universally accessible. Rather, the opposition between 'pure' and 'impure' or 'barbarous' taste is grounded, like the difference between the tastes of distinction and the taste for necessity, in the opposition between the cultivated and the uncultivated or between the dominant and the dominated. In Kant's words, ' "Taste that requires an added element of charm and emotion for its delight, not to speak of adopting this as the measure of its approval, has not yet emerged from barbarism" '.[54]

A pure aesthetic expresses, in rationalized form, the ethos of a cultured elite or, in other words, of the dominated fraction of the dominant class. As such, it is a misrecognized social relationship: 'The denial of lower, coarse, vulgar, venal, servile – in a word, natural – enjoyment, which constitutes the sacred sphere of culture, implies an affirmation of the superiority of those who can be satisfied with the sublimated, refined, disinterested, gratuitous, distinguished pleasures forever closed to the profane. That is why art and cultural consumption are predisposed, consciously and deliberately or not, to fulfil a social function of legitimating social differences.'[55]

Bourdieu's work in the sociology of culture attempts to reinsert issues such as the meaning and value of works into the multiple and complex set of historically constituted social relations which authorize and sustain them. He presents a powerful model which calls into question many of the presuppositions guiding widely received notions of the social role and function of culture and opens new horizons for the study of cultural works and practice.

# Part I

---

*The Field of Cultural
Production*

# 1

# The Field of Cultural Production, or: The Economic World Reversed

O Poésie, ô ma mère mourante
Comme tes fils t'aimaient d'un grand amour
Dans ce Paris, en l'an mil huit cent trente:
Pour eux les docks, l'Autrichien, la rente
Les mots de bourse étaient du pur hébreu.

Théodore de Banville, Ballade de ses regrets
pour l'an 1830

## PRELIMINARIES

Few areas more clearly demonstrate the heuristic efficacy of *relational* thinking than that of art and literature. Constructing an object such as the literary field[1] requires and enables us to make a radical break with the substantialist mode of thought (as Ernst Cassirer calls it) which tends to foreground the individual, or the visible interactions between individuals, at the expense of the structural relations – invisible, or visible only through their effects – between social positions that are both occupied and manipulated by social agents which may be isolated individuals, groups or institutions.[2] There are in fact very few other areas in which the glorification of 'great individuals', unique creators irreducible to any condition or conditioning, is more common or uncontroversial – as one can see, for example, in the fact that most analysts uncritically accept the division of the corpus that is imposed on them by the names of authors ('the work of Racine') or the titles of works (*Phèdre* or *Bérénice*).

To take as one's subject of study the literary or artistic field of a given period and society (the field of Florentine painting in the quattrocento or the field of French literature in the Second Empire) is to set the history of art and literature a task which it never completely performs, because it fails to take it on explicitly, even when it does break out of the routine of monographs which, however interminable, are necessarily inadequate (since the essential explanation of each work lies outside each of them, in the objective relations which constitute this field). The task is that of constructing the space of positions and the space of the position-takings [*prises de position*] in which they are expressed. The science of the literary field is a form of *analysis situs* which establishes that each position – e.g. the one which corresponds to a genre such as the novel or, within this, to a sub-category such as the 'society novel' [*roman mondain*] or the 'popular' novel – is subjectively defined by the system of distinctive properties by which it can be situated relative to other positions; that every position, even the dominant one, depends for its very existence, and for the determinations it imposes on its occupants, on the other positions constituting the field; and that the structure of the field, i.e. of the space of positions, is nothing other than the structure of the distribution of the capital of specific properties which governs success in the field and the winning of the external or specific profits (such as literary prestige) which are at stake in the field.

The *space of literary or artistic position-takings*, i.e. the structured set of the manifestations of the social agents involved in the field – literary or artistic works, of course, but also political acts or pronouncements, manifestos or polemics, etc. – is inseparable from the *space of literary or artistic positions* defined by possession of a determinate quantity of specific capital (recognition) and, at the same time, by occupation of a determinate position in the structure of the distribution of this specific capital. The literary or artistic field is a *field of forces*, but it is also a *field of struggles* tending to transform or conserve this field of forces. The network of objective relations between positions subtends and orients the strategies which the occupants of the different positions implement in their struggles to defend or improve their positions (i.e. their position-takings), strategies which depend for their force and form on the position each agent occupies in the power relations [*rapports de force*].

Every position-taking is defined in relation to the *space of possibles* which is objectively realized as a *problematic* in the form of the actual or potential position-takings corresponding to the different positions; and it receives its distinctive *value* from its negative relationship with the coexistent position-takings to which it is objectively related and which determine it by delimiting it. It follows from this, for example, that a position-taking changes, even when the position remains identical, whenever there is change in the universe of options that are simultaneously offered for producers and consumers to choose from. The meaning of a work (artistic, literary, philosophical, etc.) changes automatically with each change in the field within which it is situated for the spectator or reader.

This effect is most immediate in the case of so-called classic works, which change constantly as the universe of coexistent works changes. This is seen clearly when the simple *repetition* of a work from the past in a radically transformed field of compossibles produces an entirely automatic *effect of parody* (in the theatre, for example, this effect requires the performers to signal a slight distance from a text impossible to defend as it stands; it can also arise in the presentation of a work corresponding to one extremity of the field before an audience corresponding structurally to the other extremity – e.g. when an avant-garde play is performed to a bourgeois audience, or the contrary, as more often happens). It is significant that breaks with the most orthodox works of the past, i.e. with the belief they impose on the newcomers, often take the form of *parody* (intentional, this time), which presupposes and confirms *emancipation*. In this case, the newcomers 'get beyond' ['*dépassent*'] the dominant mode of thought and expression not by explicitly denouncing it but by repeating and reproducing it in a sociologically non-congruent context, which has the effect of rendering it incongruous or even absurd, simply by making it perceptible as the arbitrary convention it is. This form of heretical break is particularly favoured by ex-believers, who use pastiche or parody as the indispensable means of objectifying, and thereby appropriating, the form of thought and expression by which they were formerly possessed.

This explains why writers' efforts to control the reception of their own works are always partially doomed to failure (one thinks of Marx's 'I am not a Marxist'); if only because the very effect of their work may transform the conditions of its reception and because they would not have had to write many things they did write and write them as they did – e.g. resorting to rhetorical strategies intended to 'twist the stick in the other direction' – if they had been granted from the outset what they are granted retrospectively.

One of the major difficulties of the social history of philosophy, art or literature is that it has to reconstruct these spaces of original possibles which, because they were part of the self-evident givens of the situation, remained unremarked and are therefore unlikely to be mentioned in contemporary accounts, chronicles or memoirs. It is difficult to conceive of the vast amount of information which is linked to membership of a field and which all contemporaries immediately invest in their reading of works: information about institutions – e.g. academies, journals, magazines, galleries, publishers, etc. – and about persons, their relationships, liaisons and quarrels, information about the ideas and problems which are 'in the air' and circulate orally in gossip and rumour. (Some intellectual occupations presuppose a particular mastery of this information.) Ignorance of everything which goes to make up the 'mood of the age' produces a derealization of works: stripped of everything which attached them to the most concrete debates of their time (I am thinking in particular of the connotations of words), they are impoverished and transformed in the direction of intellectualism or an empty humanism. This is particularly true in the history of ideas, and especially of philosophy. Here the ordinary effects of derealization and intellectualization are intensified by the representation of philosophical activity as a summit conference between 'great philosophers'; in fact, what circulates between contemporary philosophers, or those of different epochs, are not only canonical texts, but a whole philosophical doxa carried along by intellectual rumour – labels of schools, truncated quotations, functioning as slogans in celebration or polemics – by academic routine and perhaps above all by school manuals (an unmentionable reference), which perhaps do more than anything else to constitute the 'common sense' of an intellectual generation. Reading, and *a fortiori* the reading of books, is only one means among others, even among professional readers, of acquiring the knowledge that is mobilized in reading.

It goes without saying that, in both cases, change in the space of literary or artistic possibles is the result of change in the power relation which constitutes the space of positions. When a new literary or artistic group makes its presence felt in the field of literary or artistic production, the whole problem is transformed, since its coming into being, i.e. into difference, modifies and displaces the universe of possible options; the previously dominant productions may, for example, be pushed into the status either of outmoded [*déclassé*] or of classic works.

This theory differs fundamentally from all 'systemic' analyses of works of art based on transposition of the phonological model, since it refuses to consider the field of position-takings in itself and for itself, i.e. independently of the field of positions which it manifests. This is understandable when it is seen that it applies relational thinking not only to symbolic systems, whether language (like Saussure) or myth (like Lévi-Strauss), or any set of symbolic objects, e.g. clothing, literary works, etc. (like all so-called 'structuralist' analyses), but also to the *social relations* of which these symbolic systems are a more or less transformed expression. Pursuing a logic that is entirely characteristic of symbolic structuralism, but realizing that no cultural product exists by itself, i.e. outside the relations of interdependence which link it to other products, Michel Foucault gives the name 'field of strategic possibilities' to the regulated system of differences and dispersions within which each individual work defines itself.[3] But — and in this respect he is very close to semiologists such as Trier and the use they have made of the idea of the 'semantic field' — he refuses to look outside the 'field of discourse' for the principle which would cast light on each of the discourses within it: 'If the Physiocrats' analysis belongs to the same discourses as that of the Utilitarians, this is not because they lived in the same period, not because they confronted one another within the same society, not because their interests interlocked within the same economy, but because their two options sprang from one and the same distribution of the points of choice, one and the same strategic field.'[4] In short, Foucault shifts on to the plane of possible position-takings the strategies which are generated and implemented on the sociological plane of positions; he thus refuses to relate works in any way to their social conditions of production, i.e. to positions occupied within the field of cultural production. More precisely, he explicitly rejects as a 'doxological illusion' the endeavour to find in the 'field of polemics' and in 'divergences of interests and mental habits' between individuals the principle of what occurs in the 'field of strategic possibilities', which he sees as determined solely by the 'strategic possibilities of the conceptual games'.[5] Although there is no question of denying the specific determination exercised by the possibilities inscribed in a given state of the space of position-takings — since one of the functions of the notion of the relatively autonomous field with its own history is precisely to account for this — it is not possible, even in the case of the scientific field and the most advanced sciences, to make the cultural order [*épistème*] a sort of autonomous, transcendent sphere, capable of developing in accordance with its own laws.

The same criticism applies to the Russian formalists, even in the interpretation put forward by Itamar Even-Zohar in his theory of the 'literary polysystem', which seems closer to the reality of the texts, if not to the logic of things, than the interpretation which structuralist readings (especially by Todorov) have imposed in France.[6] Refusing to consider anything other than the system of works, i.e. the 'network of relationships between texts', or 'intertextuality', and the — very abstractly defined — relationships between this network and the other systems functioning in the 'system-of-systems' which constitutes the society (we are close to Talcott Parsons), these theoreticians of cultural semiology or culturology are forced to seek in the literary system itself the principle of its dynamics. When they make the process of 'banalization' and 'debanalization' the fundamental law of poetic change and, more generally, of all cultural change, arguing that a 'deautomatization' must necessarily result from the 'automatization' induced by repetitive use of the literary means of expression, they forget that the dialectic of orthodoxy which, in Weber's terms, favours a process of 'routinization', and of heresy, which 'deroutinizes', does not take place in the ethereal realm of ideas, and in the confrontation between 'canonized' and 'non-canonized' texts. More concretely, they forget that the existence, form and direction of change depend not only on the 'state of the system', i.e. the 'repertoire' of possibilities which it offers, but also on the balance of forces between social agents who have entirely real interests in the different possibilities available to them as stakes and who deploy every sort of strategy to make one set or the other prevail. When we speak of a *field* of position-takings, we are insisting that what can be constituted as a *system* for the sake of analysis is not the product of a coherence-seeking intention or an objective consensus (even if it presupposes unconscious agreement on common principles) but the product and prize of a permanent conflict; or, to put it another way, that the generative, unifying principle of this 'system' is the struggle, with all the contradictions it engenders (so that participation in the struggle – which may be indicated objectively by, for example, the attacks that are suffered – can be used as the criterion establishing that a work belongs to the field of position-takings and its author to the field of positions).[7]

In defining the literary and artistic field as, inseparably, a field of positions and a field of position-takings we also escape from the usual dilemma of internal ('tautegorical') reading of the work (taken in isolation or within the system of works to which it belongs) and external (or 'allegorical') analysis, i.e. analysis of the social conditions of production of the producers and consumers which is based on the – generally tacit – hypothesis of the spontaneous correspondence or deliberate matching of production to demand or commissions. And by the same token we escape from the correlative dilemma of the charismatic image of artistic activity as pure, disinterested creation by an isolated artist, and the reductionist vision which claims to explain the act of production and its product in terms of their conscious or unconscious external functions, by referring them, for example, to the interests of the dominant class or, more subtly, to the ethical or aesthetic values of one or another of its fractions, from which the patrons or audiences are drawn.

Here one might usefully point to the contribution of Becker who, to his credit, constructs artistic production as a collective action, breaking with the naïve vision of the individual creator. For Becker, 'works of art can be understood by viewing them as the result of the co-ordinated activities of all the people whose co-operation is necessary in order that the work should occur as it does'.[8] Consequently the inquiry must extend to all those who contribute to this result, i.e. 'the people who conceive the idea of the work (e.g. composers or playwrights); people who execute it (musicians or actors); people who provide the necessary equipment and material (e.g. musical instrument makers); and people who make up the audience for the work (playgoers, critics, and so on)'.[9] Without elaborating all the differences between this vision of the 'art world' and the theory of the literary and artistic field, suffice it to point out that the artistic field is not reducible to a *population*, i.e. a sum of individual agents, linked by simple relations of *interaction* – although the agents and the *volume* of the *population* of producers must obviously be taken into account (e.g. an increase in the number of agents engaged in the field has specific effects).

But when we have to re-emphasize that the principle of position-takings lies in the structure and functioning of the field of positions, this is not done so as to return to any form of economism. There is a specific economy of the literary and artistic field, based on a particular form of belief. And the major difficulty lies in the need to make a radical break with this belief and with the deceptive certainties of the language of celebration, without thereby forgetting that they are part of the very reality we are seeking to understand, and that, as such, they must have a place in the model intended to explain it. Like the science of religion, the science of art and literature is threatened by two opposite errors, which, being complementary, are particularly likely to occur since, in reacting diametrically against one of them, one necessarily falls into the other. The work of art is an object which exists as such only by virtue of the (collective) belief which knows and acknowledges it as a work of art. Consequently, in order to escape from the usual choice between celebratory effusions and the reductive analysis which, failing to take account of the fact of belief in the work of art and of the social conditions which produce that belief, destroys the work of art as such, a rigorous science of art must, *pace* both the unbelievers and iconoclasts and also the believers, assert the possibility and necessity of understanding the work in its reality as a fetish; it has to take into account everything which helps to constitute the work as such, not least the discourses of direct or disguised celebration which are among the social conditions of production of the work of art *qua* object of belief.

The production of discourse (critical, historical, etc.) about the work of art is one of the conditions of production of the work. Every critical affirmation contains, on the one hand, a recognition of the value of the work which occasions it, which is thus designated as a worthy object of legitimate discourse (a recognition sometimes extorted by the logic of the field, as when, for example, the polemic of the dominant confers participant status on the challengers), and on the other hand an affirmation of its own legitimacy. All critics declare not only their judgement of the work but also their claim to the right to talk about it and judge it. In short, they take part in a struggle for the monopoly of legitimate discourse about the work of art, and consequently in the production of the value of the work of art. (And one's only hope of producing scientific knowledge – rather than weapons to advance a particular class of specific interests – is to make explicit to oneself one's position in the sub-field of the producers of discourse about art and the contribution of this field to the very existence of the object of study.)

The science of the social representation of art and of the appropriate relation to works of art (in particular, through the social history of the process of autonomization of the intellectual and artistic field) is one of the prerequisites for the constitution of a rigorous science of art, because belief in the value of the work, which is one of the major obstacles to the constitution of a science of artistic production, is part of the full reality of the work of art. There is in fact every reason to suppose that the constitution of the aesthetic gaze as a 'pure' gaze, capable of considering the work of art in and for itself, i.e. as a 'finality without an end', is linked to the *institution* of the work of art as an object of contemplation, with the creation of private and then public galleries and museums, and the parallel development of a corps of professionals appointed to conserve the work of art, both materially and symbolically. Similarly, the representation of artistic production as a 'creation' devoid of any determination or any social function, though asserted from a very early date, achieves its fullest expression in the theories of 'art for art's sake'; and, correlatively, in the representation of the legitimate relation to the work of art as an act of 're-action' claiming to replicate the original creation and to focus solely on the work in and for itself, without any reference to anything outside it.

> The actual state of the science of works of art cannot be understood unless it is borne in mind that, whereas external analyses are always liable to appear crudely reductive, an internal reading, which establishes the charismatic, creator-to-creator relationship with the work that is demanded by the social norms of reception, is guaranteed social approval and reward. One of the effects of this charismatic conception of the relation to the work of art can be seen in the cult of the virtuoso which appeared in the late nineteenth century and which leads audiences to expect works to be performed and conducted from memory – which has the effect of limiting the repertoire and excluding avant-garde works, which are liable to be played only once.[10]

The educational system plays a decisive role in the generalized imposition of the legitimate mode of consumption. One reason for this is that the ideology of 're-creation' and 'creative reading' supplies teachers – *lectores* assigned to commentary on the canonical texts – with a legitimate substitute for the ambition to act as *auctores*. This is seen most clearly in the case of philosophy, where the emergence of a body of professional teachers was accompanied by the development of a would-be autonomous science of the history of philosophy, and the propensity to read works in and for themselves (philosophy teachers thus tend to identify philosophy with the history of philosophy, i.e. with a pure *commentary* on past works, which are thus invested with a role exactly opposite to that of suppliers of problems and instruments of thought which they would fulfil for original thinking).

Given that works of art exist as symbolic objects only if they are known and recognized, that is, socially instituted as works of art and received by spectators capable of knowing and recognizing them as such, the sociology of art and literature has to take as its object not only the material production but also the symbolic production of the work, i.e. the production of the value of the work or, which amounts to the same thing, of belief in the value of the work. It therefore has to consider as contributing to production not only the direct producers of the work in its materiality (artist, writer, etc.) but also the producers of the meaning and value of the work – critics, publishers, gallery directors and the whole set of agents whose combined efforts produce consumers capable of knowing and recognizing the work of art as such, in particular teachers (but also families, etc.). So it has to take into account not only, as the social history of art usually does, the social conditions of the production of artists, art critics, dealers, patrons, etc., as revealed by indices such as social origin, education or qualifications, but also the social conditions of the production of a set of objects socially constituted as works of *art*, i.e. the conditions of production of the field of social agents (e.g. museums, galleries, academies, etc.) which help to define and produce the value of works of art. In short, it is a question of understanding works of art as a *manifestation* of the field as a whole, in which all the powers of the field, and all the determinisms inherent in its structure and functioning, are concentrated. (See Figure 1.)

THE FIELD OF CULTURAL PRODUCTION AND THE FIELD OF POWER

In figure 1, the literary and artistic field (3) is contained within the field of power (2), while possessing a relative autonomy with respect to it, especially as regards its economic and political principles of hierarchiza-

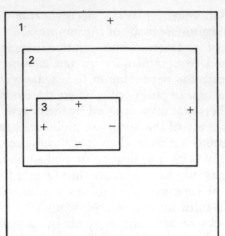

Figure 1

tion. It occupies a *dominated position* (at the negative pole) in this field, which is itself situated at the dominant pole of the field of class relations (1). It is thus the site of a double hierarchy: the *heteronomous* principle of hierarchization, which would reign unchallenged if, losing all autonomy, the literary and artistic field were to disappear as such (so that writers and artists became subject to the ordinary laws prevailing in the field of power, and more generally in the economic field), is *success*, as measured by indices such as book sales, number of theatrical performances, etc. or honours, appointments, etc. The *autonomous* principle of hierarchization, which would reign unchallenged if the field of production were to achieve total autonomy with respect to the laws of the market, is *degree specific consecration* (literary or artistic prestige), i.e. the degree of recognition accorded by those who recognize no other criterion of legitimacy than recognition by those whom they recognize. In other words, the specificity of the literary and artistic field is defined by the fact that the more autonomous it is, i.e. the more completely it fulfils its own logic as a field, the more it tends to suspend or reverse the dominant principle of hierarchization; but also that, whatever its degree of independence, it continues to be affected by the laws of the field which encompasses it, those of economic and political profit. The more autonomous the field becomes, the more favourable the symbolic power balance is to the most autonomous producers and the more clear-cut is the division between the field of restricted production, in which the producers produce for other producers, and the field of large-scale production [*la grande production*], which is *symbolically* excluded and discredited (this symbolically dominant definition is the one that the historians of art and literature *unconsciously* adopt when they exclude from their object of study writers and artists who produced for the market and have often fallen into oblivion). Because it is a good measure of the degree of autonomy, and therefore of presumed adherence to the disinterested values which constitute the specific law of the field, the degree of public success is no doubt the main differentiating factor. But lack of success is not in itself a sign and guarantee of election, and *poètes maudits*, like 'successful playwrights', must take account of a secondary differentiating factor whereby some *poètes maudits* may also be 'failed writers' (even if exclusive reference to the first criterion can help them to avoid realizing it), while some box-office successes may be recognized, at least in some sectors of the field, as genuine art.

Thus, at least in the most perfectly autonomous sector of the field of cultural production, where the only audience aimed at is other producers (as with Symbolist poetry), the economy of practices is based, as in a generalized game of 'loser wins', on a systematic inversion of the fundamental principles of all ordinary economies: that of business (it excludes the pursuit of profit and does not guarantee any sort of correspondence between investments and monetary gains), that of power (it condemns honours and temporal greatness), and even that of institutionalized cultural authority (the absence of any academic training or consecration may be considered a virtue).

One would have to analyse in these terms the relations between writers or artists and publishers or gallery directors. The latter are equivocal figures, through whom the logic of the economy is brought to the heart of the sub-field of production-for-fellow-producers; they need to possess, simultaneously, economic dispositions which, in some sectors of the field, are totally alien to the producers and also properties close to those of the producers whose work they valorize and exploit. The logic of the structural homologies between the field of publishers or gallery directors and the field of the corresponding artists or writers does indeed mean that the former present properties close to those of the latter, and this favours the relationship of trust and belief which is the basis of an exploitation presupposing a high degree of misrecognition on each side. These 'merchants in the temple' make their living by tricking the artist or writer into taking the consequences of his or her statutory professions of disinterestedness.

This explains the inability of all forms of economism, which seek to grasp this anti-economy in economic terms, to understand this upside-down economic world. The literary and artistic world is so ordered that those who enter it have an interest in disinterestedness. And indeed, like prophecy, especially the prophecy of misfortune, which, according to Weber, demonstrates its authenticity by the fact that it brings in no income, a heretical break with the prevailing artistic traditions proves its claim to authenticity by its disinterestedness.[11] As we shall see, this does not mean that there is not an economic logic to this charismatic economy based on the social miracle of an act devoid of any determination other than the specifically aesthetic intention. There are economic conditions for the indifference to economy which induces a pursuit of the riskiest positions in the intellectual and artistic avant-garde, and also for the capacity to remain there over a long period without any economic compensation.

## The Struggle for the Dominant Principle of Hierarchization

The literary or artistic field is at all times the site of a struggle between the two principles of hierarchization: the heteronomous principle, favourable to those who dominate the field economically and politically (e.g. 'bourgeois art') and the autonomous principle (e.g. 'art for art's sake'), which those of its advocates who are least endowed with specific capital tend to identify with degree of independence from the economy, seeing temporal failure as a sign of election and success as a sign of compromise.[12] The state of the power relations in this struggle depends on the overall degree of autonomy possessed by the field, that is, the extent to which it manages to impose its own norms and sanctions on the whole set of producers, including those who are closest to the dominant pole of the field of power and therefore most responsive to external demands (i.e. the most heteronomous); this degree of autonomy varies considerably from one period and one national tradition to another, and affects the whole structure of the field. Everything seems to indicate that it depends on the value which the specific capital of writers and artists represents for the dominant fractions, on the one hand in the struggle to conserve the established order and, perhaps especially, in the struggle between the fractions aspiring to domination within the field of power (bourgeoisie and aristocracy, old bourgeoisie and new bourgeoisie, etc.), and on the other hand in the production and reproduction of economic capital (with the aid of experts and cadres).[13] All the evidence suggests that, at a given level of overall autonomy, intellectuals are, other things being equal, proportionately more responsive to the seduction of the powers that be, the less well endowed they are with specific capital.[14]

The struggle in the field of cultural production over the imposition of the legitimate mode of cultural production is inseparable from the struggle within the dominant class (with the opposition between 'artists' and 'bourgeois') to impose the dominant principle of domination (that is to say – ultimately – the definition of human accomplishment). In this struggle, the artists and writers who are richest in specific capital and most concerned for their autonomy are considerably weakened by the fact that some of their competitors identify their interests with the dominant principles of hierarchization and seek to impose them even within the field, with the support of the temporal powers. The most heteronomous cultural producers (i.e. those with least symbolic capital) can offer the least reistance to external demands, of whatever sort. To defend their own position, they have to produce weapons, which the dominant agents (within the field of power) can immediately turn against the cultural producers most attached to their autonomy. In endeavouring to discredit every attempt to impose an autonomous principle of hierarchization, and thus serving their own interests, they serve the interests of the dominant fractions of the dominant class, who obviously have an interest in there being only one hierarchy. In the struggle to impose the legitimate definition of art and literature, the most autonomous producers naturally tend to exclude 'bourgeois' writers and artists, whom they see as 'enemy agents'. This means, incidentally, that sampling problems cannot be resolved by one of those arbitrary decisions of positivist ignorance which are dignified by the term 'operational definition': these amount to blindly arbitrating on debates which are inscribed in reality itself, such as the question as to whether such and such a group ('bourgeois' theatre, the 'popular' novel, etc.) or such and such an individual claiming the title of writer or artist (or philosopher, or intellectual, etc.) belongs to the population of writers or artists or, more precisely, as to who is legitimately entitled to designate legitimate writers or artists.

The preliminary reflections on the definitions of the object and the boundaries of the population, which studies of writers, artists and, especially, intellectuals, often indulge in so as to give themselves an air of scientificity, ignore the fact, which is more than scientifically attested, that the definition of the writer (or artist, etc.) is an issue at stake in struggles in every literary (or artistic, etc.) field.[15] In other words, the field of cultural production is the site of struggles in which what is at stake is the power to impose the dominant definition of the writer and therefore to delimit the population of those entitled to take part in the struggle to define the writer. The established definition of the writer may be radically transformed by an enlargement of the set of people who have a legitimate voice in literary matters. It follows from this that every survey aimed at establishing the hierarchy of writers predetermines the hierarchy by determining the population deemed worthy of helping to establish it. In short, the fundamental stake in literary struggles is the monopoly of literary legitimacy, i.e., *inter alia*, the monopoly of the power to say with authority who are authorized to call themselves writers; or, to put it another way, it is the monopoly of the power to consecrate producers or products (we are dealing with a world of belief and the consecrated writer is the one who has the power to consecrate and to win assent when he or she consecrates an author or a work – with a preface, a favourable review, a prize, etc.).

While it is true that every literary field is the site of a struggle over the definition of the writer (a universal proposition), the fact remains that scientific analysts, if they are not to make the mistake of universalizing the particular case, need to know that they will only ever encounter historical definitions of the writer, corresponding to a particular state of the struggle to impose the legitimate definition of the writer. There is no other criterion of membership of a field than the objective fact of producing effects within it. One of the difficulties of orthodox defence against heretical transformation of the field by a redefinition of the tacit or explicit terms of entry is the fact that polemics imply a form of recognition; adversaries whom one would prefer to destroy by ignoring them cannot be combated without consecrating them. The *'Théâtre libre'* effectively entered the sub-field of drama once it came under attack from the accredited advocates of bourgeois theatre, who thus helped to produce the recognition they sought to prevent. The *'nouveaux philosophes'* came into existence as active elements in the philosophical field – and no longer just that of journalism – as soon as consecrated philosophers felt called upon to take issue with them.

The *boundary* of the field is a stake of struggles, and the social scientist's task is not to draw a dividing line between the agents involved in it by imposing a so-called operational definition, which is most likely to be imposed on him by his own prejudices or presuppositions, but to describe a *state* (long-lasting or temporary) of these struggles and therefore of the frontier delimiting the territory held by the competing agents. One could thus examine the characteristics of this boundary, which may or may not be institutionalized, that is to say, protected by conditions of entry that are tacitly and practically required (such as a certain cultural capital) or explicitly codified and legally guaranteed (e.g. all the forms of entrance examination aimed at ensuring a *numerus clausus*). It would be found that one of the most significant properties of the field of cultural production, explaining its extreme dispersion and the conflicts between rival principles of legitimacy, is the extreme permeability of its frontiers and, consequently, the extreme diversity of the 'posts' it offers, which defy any unilinear hierarchization. It is clear from comparison that the field of cultural production demands neither as much inherited economic capital as the economic field nor as much educational capital as the university sub-field or even sectors of the field of power such as the top civil service – or even the field of the 'liberal professions'.[16] However, precisely because it represents one of the *indeterminate sites* in the social structure, which offer ill-defined posts, waiting to be made rather than ready made, and therefore extremely elastic and undemanding, and career paths which are themselves full of uncertainty and extremely dispersed (unlike bureaucratic careers, such as those offered by the university system), it attracts agents who differ greatly in their properties and dispositions but the most favoured of whom are sufficiently secure to be able to disdain a university career and to take on the risks of an occupation which is not a 'job' (since it is almost always combined with a private income or a 'bread-and-butter' occupation).

> The 'profession' of writer or artist is one of the least professionalized there is, despite all the efforts of 'writers' associations', 'Pen Clubs', etc. This is shown clearly by (*inter alia*) the problems which arise in classifying these agents, who are able to exercise what they regard as their main occupation only on condition that they have a secondary occupation which provides their main income (problems very similar to those encountered in classifying students).

The most disputed frontier of all is the one which separates the field of cultural production and the field of power. It may be more or less clearly marked in different periods, positions occupied in each field may be more or less totally incompatible, moves from one universe to the other more or less frequent and the overall distance between the corresponding populations more or less great (e.g. in terms of social origin, educational background, etc.).

## The Effect of the Homologies

The field of cultural production produces its most important effects through the play of the *homologies* between the fundamental opposition which gives the field its structure and the oppositions structuring the field of power and the field of class relations.[17] These homologies may give rise to ideological effects which are produced automatically whenever oppositions at different levels are superimposed or merged. They are also the basis of partial alliances: the struggles within the field of power are never entirely independent of the struggle between the dominated classes and the dominant class, and the logic of the homologies between the two spaces means that the struggles going on within the inner field are always overdetermined and always tend to aim at two birds with one stone. The cultural producers, who occupy the economically dominated and symbolically dominant position within the field of cultural production, tend to feel solidarity with the occupants of the economically and culturally dominated positions within the field of class relations. Such alliances, based on homologies of position combined with profound differences in condition, are not exempt from misunderstandings and even bad faith. The structural affinity between the literary avant-garde and the political vanguard is the basis of rapprochements, between intellectual anarchism and the Symbolist movement for example, in which convergences are flaunted (e.g. Mallarmé referring to a book as an *'attentat'* – an act of terrorist violence) but distances prudently maintained. The fact remains that the cultural producers are able to use the power conferred on them, especially in periods of crisis, by their capacity to put forward a critical definition of the social world, to mobilize the potential strength of the dominated classes and subvert the order prevailing in the field of power.

The effects of homology are not all and always automatically granted. Thus whereas the dominant fractions, in their relationship with the dominated fractions, are on the side of nature, common sense, practice, instinct, the upright and the male, and also order, reason, etc., they can no longer bring certain aspects of this representation into play in their relationship with the dominated classes, to whom they are opposed as culture to nature, reason to instinct. They need to draw on what they are offered by the dominated fractions, in order to justify their class domination, to themselves as well. The cult of art and the artist (rather than of the intellectual) is one of the necessary components of the bourgeois 'art of living', to which it brings a *'supplément d'âme'*, its spiritualistic point of honour.

Even in the case of the seemingly most heteronomous forms of cultural production, such as journalism, adjustment to demand is not the product of a conscious arrangement between producers and consumers. It results from the correspondence between the space of the producers, and therefore of the products offered, and the space of the consumers, which is brought about, on the basis of the homology between the two spaces, only through the competition between the producers and through the strategies imposed by the correspondence between the space of possible position-takings and the space of positions. In other words, by obeying the logic of the objective competition between mutually exclusive positions within the field, the various categories of producers tend to supply products adjusted to the expectations of the various positions in the field of power, but without any conscious striving for such adjustment.

If the various positions in the field of cultural production can be so easily characterized in terms of the audience which corresponds to them, this is because the encounter between a work and its audience (which may be an absence of immediate audience) is, strictly speaking, a *coincidence* which is not explained either by conscious, even cynical adjustment (though there are exceptions) or by the constraints of commission and demand. Rather, it results from the homology between positions occupied in the space of production, with the correlative position-takings, and positions in the space of consumption; that is, in this case, in the field of power, with the opposition between the dominant and the dominated fractions, or in the field of class relations, with the opposition between the dominant and the dominated classes. In the case of the relation between the field of cultural production and the field of power, we are dealing with an almost perfect homology between two chiastic structures. Just as, in the dominant class, economic capital increases as one moves from the dominated to the dominant fractions, whereas cultural capital varies in the opposite way, so too in the field of cultural production economic profits increase as one moves from the 'autonomous' pole to the 'heteronomous' pole, whereas specific profits increase in the opposite direction. Similarly, the secondary opposition which divides the most heteronomous sector into 'bourgeois art' and 'industrial' art clearly corresponds to the opposition between the dominant and the dominated classes.[18]

## THE STRUCTURE OF THE FIELD

Heteronomy arises from *demand*, which may take the form of personal *commission* (formulated by a 'patron' in Haskell's sense of a protector or client) or of the sanction of an autonomous *market*, which may be *anticipated* or *ignored*. Within this logic, the *relationship to the audience* and, more exactly, economic or political interest in the sense of interest in success and in the related economic or political profit, constitute one of the bases for evaluating the producers and their products. Thus, strict application of the autonomous principle of hierarchization means that producers and products will be distinguished according to their degree of success with the audience, which, it tends to be assumed, is evidence of their interest in the economic and political profits secured by success.

The duality of the principles of hierarchization means that there are few fields (other than the field of power itself) in which the antagonism between the occupants of the polar positions is more total (within the limits of the interests linked to membership of the field of power). Perfectly illustrating the distinction between relations of interaction and the structural relations which constitute a field, the polar individuals may never meet, may even ignore each other systematically, to the extent of refusing each other membership of the same class, and yet their practice remains determined by the negative relation which unites them. It could be said that the agents involved in the literary or artistic field may, in extreme cases, have nothing in common except the fact of taking part in a struggle to impose the legitimate definition of literary or artistic production.[19]

The hierarchy by degree of real or supposed dependence on audience, success or the economy itself overlaps with another one, which reflects the degree of specific consecration of the audience, i.e. its 'cultural' quality and its supposed distance from the centre of the specific values. Thus, within the sub-field of production-for-producers, which recognizes only the specific principle of legitimacy, those who are assured of the recognition of a certain fraction of the other producers, a presumed index of posthumous recognition, are opposed to those who, again from the standpoint of the specific criteria, are relegated to an inferior position and who, in accordance with the model of heresy, contest the legitimation principle dominant within the autonomous sub-field, either in the name of a new legitimation principle or in the name of a return to an old one. Likewise, at the other pole of the field, that of the market and of economic profit, authors who manage to secure 'high-society' successes and bourgeois consecration are opposed to those who are condemned to so-called 'popular' success – the authors of rural novels, music-hall artists, *chansonniers*, etc.

## The Duality of Literary Hierarchies and Genres

In the second half of the nineteenth century, the period in which the literary field attained its maximum autonomy, these two hierarchies seem to correspond, in the first place, to the specifically cultural hierarchy of the genres – poetry, the novel and drama – and secondarily to the hierarchy of ways of using them which, as is seen clearly in the case of the theatre and especially the novel, varies with the position of the audiences reached in the specifically cultural hierarchy.

> The literary field is itself defined by its position in the hierarchy of the arts, which varies from one period and one country to another. Here one can only allude to the effect of the hierarchy of the arts and in particular to the dominance which poetry, an intellectual art, exerted until the sixteenth century over painting, a manual art,[20] so that, for example, the hierarchy of pictorial genres tended to depend on their distance – as regards the subject and the more or less erudite manner of treating it – from the most elaborate model of poetic discourse. It is well known that throughout the nineteenth century, and perhaps until Duchamp, the stereotype which relegated the painter to a purely manual genre ('stupid as a painter') persisted, despite the increasing exchange of symbolic services (partly, no doubt, because the painters were generally less rich in cultural capital than the writers; we know, for example, that Monet, the son of a Le Havre grocer, and Renoir, the son of a Limoges tailor, were much intimidated in the meetings at the Café Guerbois on account of their lack of education). In the case of the field of painting, autonomy had to be won from the literary field too, with the emergence of specific criticism and above all the will to break free from the writers and their discourse by producing an intrinsically polysemic work beyond all discourse, and a discourse about the work which declares the essential inadequacy of all discourse. The history of the relations between Odilon Redon and the writers – especially Huysmans – shows in an exemplary way how the painters had to fight for autonomy from the *littérateur* who enhances the illustrator by advancing himself, and to assert the irreducibility of the pictorial work (which the professional critic is more ready to recognize).[21] The same logic can be used to analyse the relations between the composers and the poets: the concern to use without being used, to possess without being possessed, led some composers (Debussy, for example) to choose to set mediocre texts which would not eclipse them.

From the economic point of view, the hierarchy is simple and relatively stable, despite cyclical fluctuations related to the fact, for example, that the more economically profitable the various genres, the more strongly and directly they are affected by recession.[22] At the top of the hierarchy is drama, which, as all observers note, secures big profits – provided by an essentially bourgeois, Parisian, and therefore relatively restricted, audience – for a very few producers (because of the small number of theatres). At the bottom is poetry, which, with a few, very rare exceptions (such as a few successes in verse drama), secures virtually zero profit for a small number of producers. Between the two is the novel, which can secure big profits (in the case of some naturalist novels), and sometimes very big profits (some 'popular' novels), for a relatively large number of producers, from an audience which may extend far beyond the audience made up of the writers themselves, as in the case of poetry, and beyond the bourgeois audience, as in the case of theatre, into the *petite bourgeoisie* or even, especially through municipal libraries, into the 'labour aristocracy'.

From the point of view of the symbolic hierarchies, things are less simple since, as can be seen from Figure 2, the hierarchies according to distance from profits are intersected by hierarchies internal to each of the genres (i.e. according to the degree to which the authors and works conform to the specific demands of the genre), which correspond to the social hierarchy of the audiences. This is seen particularly clearly in the case of the novel, where the hierarchy of specialities corresponds to the hierarchy of the audiences reached and also, fairly strictly, to the hierarchy of the social universes represented.

The complex structure of this space can be explained by means of a simple model taking into account, on the one hand, the properties of the different arts and the different genres considered as economic enterprises (price of the product, size of the audience and length of the economic cycle) and, on the other hand, the negative relationship which, as the field increasingly imposes its own logic, is established between symbolic profit and economic profit, whereby *discredit* increases as the audience grows and its specific competence declines, together with the value of the recognition implied in the act of consumption. The different kinds of cultural enterprise vary, from an economic standpoint, in terms of the unit price of the product (a painting, a play, a concert, a book, etc.) and the cumulative number of purchasers; but they also vary according to the length of the production cycle, particularly as regards the speed with which profits are obtained (and, secondarily, the length of time during which they are secured). It can be seen that, although the opposition between the short cycle of products which sell rapidly and the long cycle of products which sell belatedly or slowly is found in each of the arts, they differ radically in terms of the mode of profit acquisition and therefore, because of the connection that is made between the size of the audience and its *social quality*, in terms of the objective and subjective relationship between the producer and the market.

There is every difference between painters who, even when they set themselves in the avant-garde, can expect to sell to a *small number of connoisseurs* (nowadays including museums) works whose value derives

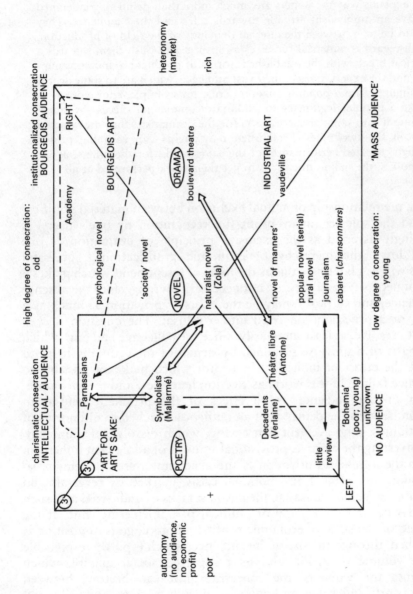

Figure 2 *French literary field in the second half of the 19th century; + = positive pole, implying a dominant position, − = negative pole, implying a dominated position*

partly from the fact that they are produced in limited numbers, and the writer who has to sell to an audience that is as wide as possible but one which, as it grows, is no doubt less and less composed of connoisseurs. This explains why the writers are, much more than painters, condemned to have an ambivalent attitude towards sales and their audience. They tend to be torn between the internal demands of the field of production, which regard commercial successes as suspect and push them towards a heretical break with the established norms of production and consumption, and the expectations of their vast audience, which are to some degree transfigured into a populist mission (Zola, for example, endeavoured to invoke a popular legitimacy to sublimate commercial success by transforming it into popular success). As for the dramatists, they are situated between the two poles. Established playwrights can earn big profits through repeated performances of the same work; for the others, as for composers, the main difficulty is to get their work performed at all.

Thus, the relationship of mutual exclusion between material gratification and the sole legitimate profit (i.e recognition by one's peers) is increasingly asserted as the exclusive principle of evaluation as one moves down the hierarchy of economic gratifications. Successful authors will not fail to see this as the logic of resentment, which makes a virtue of necessity; and they are not necessarily wrong, since the absence of audience, and of profit, may be the effect of privation as much as a refusal, or a privation converted into a refusal. The question is even harder to resolve, at least summarily, since the collective bad faith which is the basis of a universe sustained by denial of the economy helps to support the effort of individual bad faith which makes it possible to experience failure in this world as election hereafter, and the incomprehension of the audience as an effect of the prophetic refusal to compromise with the demands of an audience attached to old norms of production. It is no accident that ageing, which dissolves the ambiguities, converting the elective, provisional refusals of adolescent bohemian life into the unrelieved privation of the aged, embittered bohemian, so often takes the form of an emotional crisis, marked by reversals and abjurations which often lead to the meanest tasks of 'industrial art', such as vaudeville or cabaret, and of political pamphleteering. But, at the other end of the scale of economic profits, a homologous opposition is established, through the size of the audience, which is partly responsible for the volume of profit, and its recognized social quality, which determines the value of the consecration it can bestow, between bourgeois art, which has an honoured place in society, and industrial art, which is doubly suspect, being both mercantile and 'popular'.

Thus we find three competing principles of legitimacy. First, there is the specific principle of legitimacy, i.e., the recognition granted by the set of producers who produce for other producers, their competitors, i.e. by the autonomous self-sufficient world of 'art for art's sake', meaning art for artists. Secondly, there is the principle of legitimacy corresponding to 'bourgeois' taste and to the consecration bestowed by the dominant fractions of the dominant class and by private tribunals, such as *salons*, or public, state-guaranteed ones, such as academies, which sanction the inseparably ethical and aesthetic (and therefore political) taste of the dominant. Finally, there is the principle of legitimacy which its advocates call 'popular', i.e. the consecration bestowed by the choice of ordinary consumers, the 'mass audience'. It can be seen that poetry, by virtue of its restricted audience (often only a few hundred readers), the consequent low profits, which make it the disinterested activity *par excellence*, and also its prestige, linked to the historical tradition initiated by the Romantics, is destined to charismatic legitimation which is given to only a few individuals, sometimes only one per generation and, by the same token, to a continuous struggle for the monopoly of poetic legitimacy and a succession of successful or abortive revolutions: Parnassians against Romantics, Symbolists against Parnassians, neo-classicists against the early Symbolists, neo-Symbolists against neo-classicists.

> Although the break between poetry and the mass readership has been virtually total since the late nineteenth century (it is one of the sectors in which there are still many books published at the author's expense), poetry continues to represent the ideal model of literature for the least cultured consumers. As is confirmed by analysis of a dictionary of writers (such as the *Annuaire national des lettres*), members of the working and lower middle classes who write have too elevated an idea of literature to write realist novels; and their production does indeed consist essentially of poetry – very conventional in its form – and history.

The theatre, which directly experiences the immediate sanction of the bourgeois public, with its values and conformisms, can earn the institutionalized consecration of academies and official honours, as well as money. The novel, occupying a central position in both dimensions of the literary space, is the most dispersed genre in terms of its forms of consecration. It was broadly perceived as typical of the new mercantile literature, linked to the newspaper and journalism by serialization and the impact they gave to it, and above all because, unlike the theatre, it reached a 'popular' audience; with Zola and Naturalism it achieved a wide audience which, although socially inferior, provided profits equivalent to those of the theatre, without renouncing the specific demands of the art and without making any of the concessions typical of 'industrial' literature; and, with the 'society' novel [*roman mondain*], it was even able to win bourgeois consecrations previously reserved for the theatre.

## Genesis of a Structure

In this legitimacy conflict, the different positions in the literary field obviously govern the position-takings, which are the aesthetic retranslation of everything which separates the field of restricted production – above all poetry which, from the 1860s on, exists virtually in a closed circuit – from the field of large-scale production, with drama and, after 1875, the Naturalist novel. In fact, although it is justified inasmuch as it grasps transhistorical invariants, the representation of the field which one is obliged to give for the purpose of analysis remains artificial to the extent that it synchronizes writers and literary groups who are contemporary only in the abstract logic of an all-purpose chronology which ignores the *structural time-scales* specific to each field. Thus bourgeois drama, whose variation-time is that of common sense and bourgeois morality and which, while being strongly 'dated', does not grow old (but without becoming classic) because there is nothing to 'outmode' it and push it into the past, lives in the long time-scale of evergreen dramas (*Madame Sans-Gêne* or *La Dame aux Camélias*) or the ageless comedies of conjugal life. Poetry, by contrast, lives in the hectic rhythm of the aesthetic revolutions which divide the continuum of ages into extremely brief literary *generations*. The novel, which really enters the game with the break introduced by the Naturalist novel, followed by the 'psychological novel', lies between these two extremes.

> The fact that social age is largely independent of biological age is particularly apparent in the literary field, where generations may be less than ten years apart. This is true of Zola, born in 1840, and his recognized disciples of the *Soirées de Médan*, almost all of whom went on to found new groups: Alexis, born 1847; Huysmans, 1848; Mirbeau, 1848; Maupassant, 1850; Céard, 1851; and Hennique, 1851. The same is true of Mallarmé and his early disciples. Another example: Paul Bourget, one of the main advocates of the 'psychological novel', was only twelve years younger than Zola.

One of the most significant effects of the transformations undergone by the different genres is the transformation of their transformation-time. The model of permanent revolution which was valid for poetry tends to extend to the novel and even the theatre (with the arrival, in the

1890s, of *mise en scène*), so that these two genres are also structured by the fundamental opposition between the sub-field of large-scale production and the endlessly changing sub-field of restricted production. It follows that the opposition between the genres tends to decline as there develops within each of them an 'autonomous' sub-field, springing from the opposition between a field of restricted production and a field of large-scale production. The structure of the field of cultural production is based on two fundamental and quite different oppositions: first, the opposition between the sub-field of restricted production and the sub-field of large-scale production, i.e. between two economies, two time-scales, two audiences, which endlessly produces and reproduces the negative existence of the sub-field of restricted production and its basic opposition to the bourgeois economic order; and secondly, the opposition, within the sub-field of restricted production, between the consecrated avant-garde and the avant-garde, the established figures and the newcomers, i.e. between *artistic generations*, often only a few years apart, between the 'young' and the 'old', the 'neo' and the 'paleo', the 'new' and the 'outmoded', etc.; in short, between cultural orthodoxy and heresy.

The dualistic structure of the field of cultural production, which in the French case is expressed in the form of the opposition right bank, left bank (most clearly in the theatre), has thus been progressively constituted through a series of transformations of the field, particularly of the hierarchy of genres, which has led to the constitution of a highly autonomous sub-field of restricted production, continuously supported, in its claim to a specific autonomy, by its opposition to the sub-field of large-scale production, and characterized by a specific form of opposition, struggle and history.

Without endeavouring to describe here this complex set of partly independent processes, it is possible, with the aid of the work of Christophe Charle and Rémy Ponton,[23] to outline the evolution of the genres which widens the gap between the two sub-fields and leads to the increasing autonomization of the sub-field of restricted production. Whereas under the July Monarchy poetry and drama were at the top of the cultural hierarchy (and consequently attracted the majority of producers), with drama top in the economic hierarchy, under the Second Empire the novel joined drama at the top of the economic hierarchy, with Zola's enormous print runs (his novels had sold 2,628,000 copies by 1905) and substantial profits, without being symbolically discredited (so that it succeeded in attracting a large proportion of the newcomers). It did so because, thanks to its commercial successes, it no longer depended on the newspapers and serialization and because it won these successes without renouncing its literary pretensions. Over the same period, poetry, which continued to attract a large proportion of the newcomers, was progressively deprived of any audience other than the producers themselves. The crisis of the 1880s affected the Naturalist novelists severely, especially those of the second generation, as well as a proportion of the writers who, having started out as poets, converted into the novel genre, with the psychological novel, a cultural and especially a social capital much greater than that of their Naturalist rivals. This, as we have seen, had the effect of bringing into the novel the division into competing schools which already existed in poetry. Drama served as a refuge for unlucky novelists and poets, who came up against the protective barriers characteristic of the genre, the discreet devices for exclusion which, like a club, the closed network of critics and consecrated authors deploys to frustrate pretentious *parvenus*. Despite short-term setbacks, the endeavours of the Naturalists (in particular, Zola's effort to overthrow the hierarchy of the genres by transferring into drama the symbolic capital he had won among a new, non-theatregoing audience) and of the Symbolists mark the beginning, with Antoine's *Théâtre libre* and Paul Fort's and Lugné-Poe's *Théâtre de l'Oeuvre*, of the schism which henceforward made drama a bipolar field.[24] No doubt because it is the genre most directly constrained by the demand of an (at least initially) mainly bourgeois clientele, drama was the last literary form to develop an autonomous avant-garde which, for the same reasons, always remained fragile and threatened.

This process of transformation thus led to the establishment of an autonomous sub-field which is opposed to the heteronomous sub-field as an anti-economic economy based on the refusal of commerce and 'the commercial' and, more precisely, on the renunciation of short-term economic profits (linked to the short cycle of the field of large-scale production) and on recognition solely of *symbolic, long-term profits* (but which are ultimately reconvertible into economic profits). And, like Charle, we may see Zola's *J'accuse* as the culmination of this collective process of autonomization (and emancipation) – a prophetic break with the established order which asserts, in defiance of every *raison d'état*, the irreducibility of the values of truth and justice and, by the same token, the absolute independence of the guardians of these values, the intellectuals, explicitly defined as such in opposition to the constraints and seductions of economic and political life.

The parallelism between the economic expansion of the 1860s and the expansion of literary production does not imply a relationship of direct determination. Economic and social changes affect the literary field indirectly, through the growth in the cultivated audience, i.e. the potential readership, which is itself linked to increased schooling, at secondary and also at primary level. The existence of an expanding market, which allows the development of the press and the novel, also allows the number of producers to grow. The relative opening up of the field of cultural production due to the increased number of positions offering basic resources to producers without a private income had the effect of increasing the relative autonomy of the field and therefore its capacity to reinterpret external demands in terms of its own logic (denunciation of 'industrial literature' obscures the fact that, while the field is a source of constraints, it is also liberating, inasmuch as it enables new categories of producers to subsist without constraints other than those of the market). The Naturalist revolution, which marked a step towards autonomization, can thus be seen as the encounter between the new dispositions which were brought into the field by Zola and his friends, thanks to a modification of the tacit entry conditions (this is how the morphological changes have to be understood) and which found the conditions for their fulfilment in a transformation of the objective chances. Nor can the reversal which occurred in the 1880s be understood as a direct effect of external economic or political changes. In fact, the crisis of Naturalism is correlative with the crisis of the literary market, or more precisely, with the disappearance of the conditions which had previously favoured the access of new social categories to production and consumption. And the political atmosphere (the proliferation of *Bourses du travail*, the rise of the trades unions and the socialist movement, Anzin, Fourmies, etc.), which was not unconnected with the spiritualist revival in the bourgeoisie (and the many conversions among writers), was bound to strengthen the reaction against a literary group which scandalized by its productions, its manners and its position-takings (and, through the group, against the cultural pretensions of the rising fractions of the petite bourgeoisie and bourgeoisie) and encourage a return to forms of art which, like the psychological novel, maximize denial of the social world.

## Structure and Change

Changes which affect the structure of the field as a whole, such as major re-orderings of the hierarchy of genres, presuppose a concordance between internal changes, directly determined by modification of the chances of access to the literary field, and external changes which supply the new producers (the Romantics, the Naturalists, the Symbolists and the whole *fin-de-siècle* literary and artistic movement) and their new products with socially homologous consumers. This is not true to the same extent of changes which affect only the field of restricted production. These endless changes, which arise from the very structure of the field, i.e. the synchronic oppositions between the antagonistic positions (dominant/dominated, consecrated/novice, old/young, etc.), are largely independent of the external changes which may seem to determine them because they accompany them chronologically. This is true even when such internal changes owe their subsequent consecration mainly to a 'miraculous' encounter between (largely) independent causal series. This argument would have to be demonstrated, for example, in cases such as that of Mallarmé (or Debussy, or Fauré), in which the two opposing theses – the absolute independence of pure art, led solely by the autonomous logic of its own development, and the thesis of direct dependence on the historical situation – can both find arguments. Indeed, the *coincidence* between the properties of the social experience which privileged consumers may have had in a certain historical conjuncture and the properties of the work, in which are expressed the necessities inscribed in a *position* progressively instituted and containing a whole past and potential history, and in a *disposition*, itself progressively constituted through a whole social trajectory, is a sort of trap laid for those who, seeking to escape from internal reading of the work or the internal history of artistic life, condemn themselves to the *short circuit* of directly interrelating the period and the work. In such cases, both the period and the work are reduced to a few schematic properties, selected for the purposes of the argument, as in the Lukácsian or Goldmannian mythology of the writer as the unconscious spokesman of a group, which is simply an inversion of the Romantic myth of the poet *vates*.

Understanding a work of art, from Goldmann's standpoint, is a matter of understanding the social group from which and for which the artist composes his work, and which, at once patron and addressee, efficient cause and final cause, creates with and, as it were, through him.[25] But what is this group? The group the artist comes from – which may not coincide with the group from which his or her clients are drawn – or the group which is the main or favoured addressee – but *is* there always one? – of the production? There is no reason to suppose that the addressee, when there is one (the commissioner of the work, its dedicatee, etc.) is really the final, still less the efficient, cause of the work. At most he or she may be the occasional cause of an effort whose principle lies in the whole structure and history of the field of production and, beyond this, in the whole structure and history of the social field in question. To make the artist the unconscious spokesperson of a social group to which the work of art reveals what it unknowingly thinks or feels is to condemn oneself to assertions which would not be out of place in the wildest metaphysics, but which will have a familiar ring for readers of political theology: 'Between such art and such a social situation, can there be only a fortuitous encounter? Fauré, of course, did not intend it, but his *Madrigal* manifestly created a diversion in the year in which trade unionism won acceptance, in which 42,000 workers flung themselves into a 46-day strike at Anzin. He proposes individual love as if as a remedy for class warfare. In the end, it could be said that the *grande bourgeosie* turns to its composers and their dream-factories to provide the fantasies it politically and socially needs.'[26] To understand a piece by Fauré or Debussy or a poem by Mallarmé, without reducing it to its function of compensatory escapism, denial of social reality, flight into lost paradises, means first of all determining all that is inscribed in the position, i.e. in poetry as it defines itself around the 1880s, after a continuous process of purification, sublimation, begun in the 1830s with Théophile Gautier and the Preface to *Mademoiselle de Maupin*, taken further by Baudelaire and the Parnassians, and carried to its most evanescent extreme with Mallarmé and *le vertige du néant*; it also means determining all that this position owes to the negative relationship which opposes it to the Naturalist novel and associates it with everything that reacts against Naturalism, scientism and positivism – the psychological novel, which is obviously in the front line of the battle, but also figures such as Fouillée, Lachelier and Boutroux, who combat positivism in philosophy, or Melchoir de Voguë, who reveals the Russian novel and its mysticism, or all those who convert to Catholicism, etc. Finally, it would mean determining everything in Mallarmé's personal and family trajectory which predisposed him to occupy and fulfil a social position progressively shaped by its successive occupants, and in particular, the relationship, examined by Rémy Ponton,[27] between a downward social trajectory which condemns him to the 'hideous toil of a pedagogue' and pessimism, or hermetic, i.e. anti-pedagogic, use, of language, another way of breaking free of a social reality he refuses. One would then have to explain the 'coincidence' between the product of this set of specific factors and the diffuse expectations of a declining aristocracy and a threatened bourgeoisie, in particular their nostalgia for ancient grandeur, which is also expressed in the cult of the eighteenth century and the flight into mysticism and irrationalism.

Without ever being a direct reflection of them, the internal struggles depend for their outcome on the correspondence they may have with the external struggles between the classes (or between the fractions of the dominant class) and on the reinforcement which one group or another may derive from them, through homology and the consequent synchronisms. When the newcomers are not disposed to enter the cycle of simple reproduction, based on recognition of the 'old' by the 'young' – homage, celebration, etc. – and recognition of the 'young' by the 'old' – prefaces, co-optation, consecration, etc. – but bring with them dispositions and position-takings which clash with the prevailing norms of production and the expectations of the field, they cannot succeed without the help of external changes. These may be political breaks, such as revolutionary crises, which change the power relations within the field (the 1848 revolution strengthened the dominated pole, causing writers to shift, very temporarily no doubt, to the left, i.e. towards 'social art'), or deep-seated changes in the audience of consumers who, because of their affinity with the new producers, ensure the success of their products.

> In fact, one never observes either total submission – and erudite reproduction presupposes a form of regulated innovation, even an obligatory, limited, break with predecessors – or an absolute break – and a break with the immediately preceding generation (fathers) is often supported by a return to the traditions of the next generation back (grandfathers), whose influence may have persisted in a shadowy way. For example, though there is no need to emphasize how much the Parnassians maintain of the Romantic tradition, it is less obvious that they tapped a current of Hellenism which had lived on despite the Romantic break with imitations of Antiquity. Events such as the publication in 1819 of the works of Chénier, impregnated with Hellenism, the discovery of the Venus de Milo in 1820, the Greek War of Independence and the death of Byron, turn attention to Grecian Antiquity; Greek myths are revitalized by the prose poems of Ballanche (*Antigone*, 1814; *Orphée*, 1827), and at the height of the Romantic period, there are the works of Paul-Louis Courier and Maurice de Guérin.

In the field of restricted production, each change at any one point in the space of positions objectively defined by their difference, their *écart*, induces a generalized change – which means that one should not look for a specific *site* of change. It is true that the initiative of change falls almost by definition on the newcomers, i.e. the youngest, who are also those least endowed with specific capital: in a universe in which to exist is to differ, i.e. to occupy a distinct, distinctive position, they must assert their difference, get it known and recognized, get themselves known and recognized ('make a name for themselves'), by endeavouring to impose new modes of thought and expression, out of key with the prevailing modes of thought and with the doxa, and therefore bound to disconcert the orthodox by their 'obscurity' and 'pointlessness'. The fact remains that every new position, in asserting itself as such, determines a displacement of the whole structure and that, by the logic of action and reaction, it leads to all sorts of changes in the position-takings of the occupants of the other positions.

> As well as the countless labels too obviously intended to *produce* the differences they claim to express, one could point to 'manifestos', which often have no other content than the aim of distinguishing themselves

from what already exists, even if they do not all go so far as the founders of the *Revue de métaphysique et de morale* and explicitly declare the aim of 'doing something different'.[28] As for the transformations induced by the effect of the structure, a characteristic example can be found in the changes which the Naturalist novelists made in their style and themes – Maupassant with *Une vie* and Zola with *Le rêve* – in response to the success of the psychological novel,[29] and one may even suspect that the effect of the field explains some aspects of the sociology of Durkheim (classified by Bouglé among the representatives of the 'spiritualist initiative', alongside Bergson and Laberthonnière), in which Bouglé sees 'an effort to underpin and justify spiritualist tendencies in a new way'.[30]

Because position-takings arise quasi-mechanically – that is, almost independently of the agents' consciousness and wills – from the relationship between positions, they take relatively invariant forms, and being determined relationally, negatively, they may remain virtually empty, amounting to little more than a *parti pris* of refusal, difference, rupture. Structurally 'young' writers, i.e. those less advanced in the process of consecration (who may be biologically almost as old as the 'old' writers they seek to oust),[31] will refuse everything their 'elders' (in terms of legitimacy) are and do, and in particular all the indices of *social ageing*, starting with the signs of consecration, internal (academies, etc.) or external (success), whereas the 'old' writers will regard the social non-existence (in terms of success and consecration) and also the 'obscurity' of their young rivals as evidence of the voluntaristic, forced character of some endeavours to overtake them (as Zola puts it, 'a gigantic, empty pretension').

The 'young' have an interest in describing every advance in the internal hierarchy of the sub-field of restricted production as an advance in the hierarchy of the field of cultural production as a whole, and therefore contest the independence of the internal hierarchy (cf. the contesting of the 'mandarins'). They may point to the fact that while 'bourgeois' consecration (academy places, prizes, etc.) is primarily awarded to writers who produce for the mass market, it also goes to the most acceptable members of the consecrated avant-garde (and the *Académie Française* has always made room, to a varying extent at different periods, for producers from the field of restricted production). It is also clear that the opposition, within the 'autonomous' field, between professional writers, whose activity obliges them to lead an organized, regular, quasi-bourgeois life, and the 'bohemian' world of 'proletaroid intellectuals' who live on the odd jobs of journalism, publishing or teaching, may give rise to a political division, as was seen at the time of the Paris Commune.[32]

The history of the field arises from the struggle between the established figures and the young challengers. The ageing of authors, schools and works is far from being the product of a mechanical, chronological, slide into the past; it results from the struggle between those who have made their mark (*fait date* – 'made an epoch') and who are fighting to persist, and those who cannot make their own mark without pushing into the past those who have an interest in stopping the clock, eternalizing the present stage of things.[33] 'Making one's mark', initiating a new epoch, means winning recognition, in both senses, of one's difference from other producers, especially the most consecrated of them; it means, by the same token, creating a new position, ahead of the positions already occupied, in the vanguard. (Hence the importance, in this struggle for survival, of all distinctive marks, such as the names of schools or groups – words which make things, distinctive signs which produce existence.) The agents engaged in the struggle are both contemporaries – precisely by virtue of the struggle which synchronizes them – and separated by time and in respect of time: avant-garde writers have contemporaries who recognize them and whom they recognize – apart from other avant-garde writers – only in the future; consecrated writers recognize their contemporaries only in the past. The emergence of a group capable of 'making an epoch' by imposing a new, advanced position is accompanied by a displacement of the structure of temporally hierarchized positions opposed within a given field; each of them moves a step down the temporal hierarchy which is at the same time a social hierarchy; the avant-garde is separated by a generation from the consecrated avant-garde which is itself separated by another generation from the avant-garde that was already consecrated when it made its own entry into the field.[34] Each author, school or work which 'makes its mark' displaces the whole series of earlier authors, schools or works. As Shklovsky points out,[35] each period excludes certain hackneyed subjects: Tolstoy forbids mention of the 'romantic Caucasus' or moonlight, while Chekhov, in one of his juvenilia, lists the newly unacceptable commonplaces. Because the whole series of pertinent changes is present, practically, in the latest (just as the six figures already dialled on a telephone are present in the seventh), a work or an aesthetic movement is irreducible to any other situated elsewhere in the series; and *returns* to past styles (frequent in painting) are never 'the same thing', since they are separated from what they return to by negative reference to something which was itself the negation of it (or the negation of the negation, etc.).[36]

That is why, in an artistic field which has reached an advanced stage of this history, there is no place for *naïfs*; more precisely, the history is immanent to the functioning of the field, and to meet the objective demands it implies, as a producer but also as a consumer, one has to possess the whole history of the field.[37]

> Here it would be appropriate to point to the ideal-typical opposition between Rousseau and Duchamp. Rousseau, the painter as object, who does something other than what he thinks he is doing, does not know what he does, because he knows nothing of the field he stumbles into, of which he is the *plaything* (it is significant that his painter and poet 'friends' stage parodic consecration scenes for him); he is made by the field, a 'creator' who has to be 'created' as a legitimate producer, with the character of 'Douanier Rousseau', in order to legitimate his product.[38] By contrast, Duchamp, born into a family of painters, the younger brother of painters, has all the tricks of the artist's trade at his fingertips, i.e. an art of painting which (subsequently) implies not only the art of producing a work but the art of self-presentation; like the chess-player he is, he shows himself capable of thinking several moves ahead, producing art objects in which the production of the producer as artist is the precondition for the production of these objects as works of art; he admires Brisset as 'the Douanier Rousseau of philology' and invents the 'ready-made', a 'manu-factured object promoted to the dignity of an *objet d'art* by the symbolic authority of the artist' (quite unlike Rousseau, who makes 'assisted ready-mades' but shamefacedly conceals his sources, e.g. for *Le lion mangeant les explorateurs*); even when he uses mythical or sexual symbols, he refers to an esoteric, alchemical, mythological or psychoana-lytic culture; and he always situates himself at the second degree, even when he disabuses his exegetes of the sophisticated interpretations they have given of his works.

## POSITIONS AND DISPOSITIONS

### *The Meeting of Two Histories*

To understand the practices of writers and artists, and not least their products, entails understanding that they are the result of the meeting of two histories: the history of the positions they occupy and the history of their dispositions. Although position helps to shape dispositions, the latter, in so far as they are the product of independent conditions, have an existence and efficacy of their own and can help to shape positions. In no field is the confrontation between positions and dispositions more continuous or uncertain than in the literary and artistic field. Offering positions that are relatively uninstitutionalized, never legally guaran-teed, therefore open to symbolic challenge, and non-hereditary (al-though there are specific forms of transmission), it is the arena *par excellence* of struggles over job definition. In fact, however great the effect of position – and we have seen many examples of it – it never operates mechanically, and the relationship between positions and *position-takings* is mediated by the dispositions of the agents.

> Likewise, morphological changes never produce their effects *mechanically*. For example, the influx, in the 1850s, of a large number of writers living with precarious means on the lower edges of the field is retranslated into a redefinition of the post, i.e. of the image of the writer, his sartorial symbolism, his political attitudes, his preferred haunts (café rather than *salon*), etc. More generally, a *numerus clausus* has the effect of protecting a definition of the function, and an increase in the number of legitimate performers of the function – whether architects, doctors or teachers – is sufficient to change the function more or less radically, through the objective devaluation which automatically ensues, the struggle by the guardians of the post to preserve the rarity which previously defined it, and the endeavours of the new occupants to adapt the position to their dispositions.

The 'post' of poet as it presents itself to the young aspirant in the 1880s is the crystallized product of the whole previous history. It is a position in the hierarchy of literary crafts, which, by a sort of effect of *caste*, gives its occupants, subjectively at least, the assurance of an essential superiority over all other writers; the lowest of the poets (Symbolist, at this time) sees himself as superior to the highest of the (Naturalist) novelists.[39] It is a set of 'exemplary figures' – Hugo, Gautier, etc. – who have composed the character and assigned roles, such as, for intellectuals (after Zola), that of the intellectual as the champion of great causes. It is a cluster of representations – that of the 'pure' artist, for example, indifferent to success and to the verdicts of the market – and mechanisms which, through their sanctions, support them and give them real efficacy. In short, one would need to work out the full social history of the *long, collective labour* which leads to the progressive invention of the crafts of writing, and in particular to *awareness* of the *fundamental law* of the field, i.e. the theory of art for art's sake, which is to the field of cultural production what the axiom 'business is business' (and 'in business there's no room for feelings') is to the economic field.[40] Nor, of course, must one forget the role of the mechanism which, here as elsewhere, leads people to make a virtue of necessity, in the constitution of the field of cultural production as a space radically independent of the economy and of politics and, as such, amenable to a sort of pure theory. The work of real emancipation, of which the 'post' of artist or poet is the culmination, can be performed and pursued only if the post encounters the appropriate dispositions, such as disinterestedness and daring, and the (external) conditions of these virtues, such as a private income. In this sense, the collective invention which results in the post of writer or artist has to be endlessly repeated, even if the objectification of past discoveries and the recognition ever more widely accorded to an activity of cultural production that is an end in itself, and the will to emancipation that it implies, tend constantly to reduce the cost of this permanent reinvention. The more the autonomizing process advances, the more possible it becomes to occupy the position of producer without having the properties – or not all of them, or not to the same degree – that had to be possessed to produce the position; the more, in other words, the newcomers who head for the most 'autonomous' positions can dispense with the more or less heroic sacrifices and breaks of the past.

The position of 'pure' writer or artist, like that of intellectual, is an institution of freedom, constructed against the 'bourgeoise' (in the artists' sense) and against institutions – in particular against the state bureaucracies, academies, salons, etc. – by a series of breaks, partly cumulative, but sometimes followed by regressions, which have often been made possible by diverting the resources of the market – and therefore the 'bourgeoisie' – and even the stage bureaucracies.[41] Owing to its objectively contradictory intention, it exists only at the lowest degree of institutionalization, in the form of words ('avant-garde', for example) or models (the avant-garde writer and his or her exemplary deeds) which constitute a tradition of freedom and criticism, and also, but above all, in the form of a field of competition, equipped with its own institutions (the paradigm of which might be the *Salon des refusés* or the little avant-garde review) and articulated by mechanisms of competition capable of providing incentives and gratification for emancipatory endeavours. For example, the acts of prophetic denunciation of which *J'accuse* is the paradigm have become, since Zola, and perhaps especially since Sartre, so intrinsic to the personage of the intellectual that anyone who aspires to a position (especially a dominant one) in the intellectual field has to perform such exemplary acts.[42] This explains why it is that the producers most freed from external constraints – Mallarmé, Proust, Joyce or Virginia Woolf – are also those who have taken most advantage of a historical heritage accumulated through collective labour against external constraints.

Having established, in spite of the illusion of the constancy of the thing designated, which is encouraged by the constancy of the words artist, writer, bohemian, academy, etc., what each of the positions is at each moment, one still has to understand how those who occupy them have been formed and, more precisely, the shaping of the dispositions which help to lead them to these positions and to define their way of operating within them and staying in them. The field, as a field of possible forces, presents itself to each agent as a *space of possibles* which is defined in the relationship between the structure of average chances of access to the different positions (measured by the 'difficulty' of attaining them and, more precisely, by the relationship between the number of positions and the number of competitors) and the dispositions of each agent, the subjective basis of the perception and appreciation of the objective chances. In other words, the objective probabilities (of economic or symbolic profit, for example) inscribed in the field at a given moment only become operative and active through 'vocations', 'aspirations' and 'expectations', i.e. in so far as they are perceived and appreciated through the schemes of perception and appreciation which constitute a habitus. These schemes, which reproduce in their own logic the fundamental divisions of the field of positions – 'pure art'/ 'commercial art', 'bohemian'/'bourgeois', 'left bank'/'right bank', etc. – are one of the mediations through which dispositions are adjusted to positions. Writers and artists, particularly newcomers, do not react to an 'objective reality' functioning as a sort of stimulus valid for every possible subject, but to a 'problem-raising situation', as Popper puts it; they help to create its intellectual and affective 'physiognomy' (horror, seduction, etc.) and therefore even the symbolic force it exerts on them. A position as it appears to the (more or less adequate) 'sense of investment' which each agent applies to it presents itself either as a sort of necessary locus which beckons those who are made for it ('vocation') or, by contrast, as an impossible destination, an unacceptable destiny or one that is acceptable only as temporary refuge or a secondary, accessory position. This sense of social direction which orients agents, according to their modesty or daring, their disinterestedness or thirst for profit, towards the risky, long-term investments of journalism, serials or the theatre, is the basis of the astonishingly close correspondence that is found between positions and dispositions, between the social characteristics of 'posts' and the social characteristics of the agents who fill them. The correspondence is such that in all cases of coincidence and concordance in which the position is in a sense materialized in the dispositions of its occupants, it would be equally wrong to impute everything solely to position or solely to dispositions.

The mechanistic model that is, more or less consciously, put into operation when social origin, or any other variable, is made the principle of a linear series of determinations – e.g. father's occupation, more or less crudely defined, determining position, e.g. occupational position, which in turn determines opinions – totally ignores the effects of the field, in particular those which result from the way in which the influx of newcomers is quantitatively and qualitatively regulated.[43] Thus the absence of statistical relation between the agents' social origin and their *position-takings* may result from an unobserved transformation of the field and of the relationship between social origin and *position-taking*, such that, for two successive generations, the same dispositions will lead to different *position-takings*, or even opposing ones (which will tend to cancel each other out).

There is nothing mechanical about the relationship between the field and the habitus. The space of available positions does indeed help to determine the properties expected and even demanded of possible candidates, and therefore the categories of agents they can attract and above all *retain*; but the perception of the space of possible positions and trajectories and the appreciation of the value each of them derives from its location in the space depend on these dispositions. It follows as a point of method that one cannot give a full account of the relationship obtaining at a given moment between the space of positions and the space of dispositions, and, therefore, of the set of *social trajectories* (or constructed biographies),[44] unless one establishes the configuration, at the moment, and at the various critical turning-points in each career, of the space of available possibilities (in particular, the economic and symbolic hierarchy of the genres, schools, styles, manners, subjects, etc.), the social value attached to each of them, and also the meaning and value they received for the different agents or classes of agents in terms of the socially constituted categories of perception and appreciation they applied to them.

It would be quite unjust and futile to reject this demand for complete reconstitution on the ground (which is undeniable) that it is difficult to perform in practice and in some cases impossible (for example, a special study would be required in order to determine, for each relevant period, the *critical points* in the trajectories corresponding to each field, which are often unquestioningly assumed to be situated where they are today). Scientific progress may consist, in some cases, in identifying all the presuppositions and begged questions implicitly mobilized by the seemingly most impeccable research, and in proposing programmes for fundamental research which would really raise all the questions which ordinary research treats as resolved, simply because it has failed to raise them. In fact, if we are sufficiently attentive, we find numerous testimonies to this perception of the space of possibilities. We see it for example in the image of the great predecessors, who provide the terms for self-definition, such as the complementary figures of Taine and Renan, for one generation of novelists and intellectuals, or the opposing personalities of Mallarmé and Verlaine for a whole generation of poets; more simply, we see it in the exalted vision of the writer's or artist's craft which may shape the aspirations of a whole generation: 'The new literary generation grew up thoroughly impregnated with the spirit of 1830. The verses of Hugo and Musset, the plays of Alexandre Dumas and Alfred de Vigny circulated in the schools despite the hostility of the University; an infinite number of Mediaeval novels, lyrical confessions and despairing verses were composed under cover of classroom desks.'[45] One could quote whole pages in which Cassagne evokes the adolescent enthusiasms of Maxime Ducamp and Renan, Flaubert and Baudelaire or Fromentin. But one can also quote this very significant passage from *Manette Salomon*, in which Goncourt and Goncourt show that what attracts and fascinates in the occupation of artist is not so much the art itself as the artist's lifestyle, the artist's life (the same logic nowadays governs the diffusion of the model of the intellectual): 'At heart, Anatole was called by art much less than he was attracted by the artist's life. He dreamt of the studio. He aspired to it with a schoolboy's imaginings and the appetites of his nature. He saw in it those horizons of Bohemia which enchant from a distance: the novel of Poverty, the shedding of bonds and rules, a life of freedom, indiscipline and disorder, every day filled with accident, adventure and the unexpected, an escape from the tidy, orderly household, from the family and its tedious Sundays, the jeering of the bourgeois, the voluptuous mystery of the female model, work that entails no effort, the right to wear fancy dress all year, a sort of unending carnival; such were the images and temptations which arose for him from the austere pursuit of art.'[46]

Thus, writers and artists endowed with different, even opposing dispositions can coexist, for a time at least, in the same positions. The structural constraints inscribed in the field set limits to the free play of dispositions; but there are different ways of playing within these limits. Thus, whereas the occupants of the dominant positions, especially in economic terms, such as bourgeois theatre, are strongly homogeneous, the avant-garde positions, which are defined mainly negatively, by their opposition to the dominant positions, bring together for a certain time writers and artists from very different origins, whose interests will sooner or later diverge.[47] These dominated groups, whose unity is essentially oppositional, tend to fly apart when they achieve recognition, the symbolic profits of which often go to a small number, or even to only one of them, and when the external cohesive forces weaken. As is shown by the progressive separation between the Symbolists and the Decadents (analysed below), or the break-up of the Impressionist group, the factor of division does in this case lie in dispositions, the basis of aesthetic and political position-takings whose divergencies are felt the more strongly when associated with unequal degrees of consecration.[48]

Starting out from the same, barely marked, position in the field, and defined by the same opposition to Naturalism and the Parnasse group – from which Verlaine and Mallarmé, their leaders, were each excluded – the Decadents and the Symbolists diverged as they attained full social identity.[49] The latter, drawn from more comfortable social backgrounds (i.e. the middle or upper bourgeoisie or the aristocracy) and endowed with substantial educational capital, are opposed to the former, who are often the sons of craftsmen and virtually devoid of educational capital, as the *salon* (Mallarmé's 'Tuesdays') to the café, the right bank to the left bank and bohemia, audacity to prudence,[50] and, in aesthetic terms, as 'clarity' and 'simplicity' based on 'common sense' and 'naïveté' to a hermeticism based on an explicit theory which rejects all the old forms; politically, the Symbolists are indifferent and pessimistic, the Decadents committed and progressive.[51] It is clear that the field-effect which results from the opposition between the two schools, and which is intensified by the process of institutionalization that is needed to constitute a fully-fledged literary group, i.e. an instrument for accumulating and concentrating symbolic capital (with the adoption of a name, the drawing-up of manifestos and programmes and the setting-up of aggregation rites, such as regular meetings), tends to consecrate and underscore the critical differences. Verlaine, skilfully making a virtue of necessity, celebrated naïveté (just as Champfleury countered 'art for art's sake' with 'sincerity in art') whereas Mallarmé, who sets himself up as the theorist of 'the enigma in poetry', found himself pushed ever further into hermeticism by Verlaine's striving for sincerity and simplicity.[52] And as if to provide a crucial proof of the effect of dispositions, it was the richest Decadents who joined the Symbolists (Albert Aurier) or drew closer to them (Ernest Raynaud), whereas those Symbolists who were closest to the Decadents in terms of social origin, René Ghil and Ajalbert, were excluded from the Symbolist group, the former because of his faith in progress and the latter, who ended up as a realist novelist, because his works were not considered sufficiently obscure.

## The Habitus and the Possibles

The propensity to move towards the economically most risky positions, and above all the capacity to persist in them (a condition for all avant-garde undertakings which precede the demands of the market), even when they secure no short-term economic profit, seem to depend to a large extent on possession of substantial economic and social capital.

This is, first, because economic capital provides the conditions for freedom from economic necessity, a private income [*la rente*] being one of the best substitutes for sales [*la vente*], as Théophile Gautier said to Feydeau: 'Flaubert was smarter than us . . . He had the wit to come into the world with money, something that is indispensable for anyone who wants to get anywhere in art.'[53]

> Those who do manage to stay in the risky positions long enough to receive the symbolic profit they can bring are indeed mainly drawn from the most privileged categories, who have also had the advantage of not having to devote time and energy to secondary, 'bread-and-butter' activities. Thus, as Ponton shows,[54] some of the Parnassians, all from the petite bourgeoisie, either had to abandon poetry at some stage and turn to better-paid literary activities, such as the 'novel of manners', or, from the outset, devoted part of their time to complementary activities such as plays or novels (e.g. François Coppée, Catulle Mendès, Jean Aicard), whereas the wealthier Parnassians could concentrate almost exclusively on their art (and when they did change to another genre, it was only after a long poetic career). We also find that the least well-off writers resign themselves more readily to 'industrial literature', in which writing becomes a job like any other.

It is also because economic capital provides the guarantees [*assurances*] which can be the basis of self-assurance, audacity and indifference to profit – dispositions which, together with the flair associated with possession of a large social capital and the corresponding familiarity with the field, i.e. the art of sensing the new hierarchies and the new structures of the chances of profit, point towards the outposts, the most exposed positions of the avant-garde, and towards the riskiest investments, which are also, however, very often the most profitable symbolically, and in the long run, at least for the earliest investors.

The sense of investment seems to be one of the dispositions most closely linked to social and geographical origin, and, consequently, through the associated social capital, one of the mediations through which the effects of the opposition between Parisian and provincial origin make themselves felt in the logic of the field.[55] Thus we find that as a rule those richest in economic, cultural and social capital are the first to move into the new positions (and this seems to be true in all fields: economic, scientific, etc.). This is the case with the writers around Paul Bourget, who abandoned Symbolist poetry for a new form of novel which broke with Naturalism and was better adjusted to the expectations of the cultivated audience. By contrast, a faulty sense of investment, linked to social distance (among writers from the working class or the petite bourgeoisie) or geographical distance (among provincials and foreigners) inclines beginners to aim for the dominant positions at a time when, precisely because of their attractiveness (due, for example, to the economic profits they secure, in the case of the Naturalist novel, or the symbolic profits they promise, in the case of Symbolist poetry) and the intensified competition for them, the profits are tending to decline. It may also make them persist in declining or threatened positions when the best-informed agents are abandoning them. Or again, it may lead them to be drawn by the attraction of the dominant sites towards positions incompatible with the dispositions they bring to them, and to discover their 'natural place' only when it is too late, i.e. after wasting much time, through the effect of the forces of the field and in the mode of relegation. An ideal-typical example of this is Léon Cladel (1835–92), the son of a Montauban saddler, who came to Paris in 1857, joined the Parnasse movement and, after seven years of fairly impoverished bohemian existence, returned to his native Quercy and devoted himself to the regionalist novel.[56] The whole oeuvre of this eternally displaced writer is marked by the antinomy between his dispositions, linked to his starting-point, to which he eventually returned, and the positions he aimed at and temporarily occupied: 'His ambition was to glorify his native Quercy, a Latin soil trodden by rustic Hercules, in a sort of ancient, barbarous *"geste"*. In distilling the arrogant poses of village champions from furious peasant scuffles, Cladel aspired to be numbered among the modest rivals of Hugo and Leconte de Lisle. Thus were born *Ompdrailles* and *La Fête votive de Bartholomé-Porte-Glaive*, bizarre epics, pastiching the *Iliad* and the *Odyssey* in inflated or Rabelaisian language.'[57] Tension and incoherence, oscillating between parody and utter seriousness, are manifest in this project of describing the peasants of Quercy in the style of Leconte de Lisle: 'Being instinctively led' he writes in the preface to his novel *Celui-de-la-croix-aux-boeufs* (1878), 'towards the study of plebeian types and milieux, it was almost inevitable that there would sooner or later be a conflict between the coarse and the refined.'[58] Always out of step, Cladel was a peasant among the Parnassians (who, objectively and subjectively, placed him with the 'populace', like his friend Courbet),[59] and a petit-bourgeois among the peasants of his native region. Not surprisingly, the very form and content of the rustic novel to which he resigned himself, in which rehabilitation gives way to self-indulgent depiction of peasant savagery, express the contradictions of a position entirely defined by the trajectory which led to it: 'A beggar's son, a beggar dreamer, he had an innate love of village life and country people. If, from the outset, without any shilly-shallying, he had sought to render them with that holy roughness of touch which distinguishes the early manner of the master painters, perhaps he would have made a place for himself among the most sparkling young writers of his generation.'[60]

But these forced returns to the 'people' are only particular cases of a more general model. And all the evidence suggests that the confrontation, within the artistic and literary field, with bourgeois, Parisian artists and writers, which impels them towards the 'people', induces writers and artists of working-class or petit-bourgeois origin to accept themselves for what they are and, like Courbet, to mark themselves positively with what is stigmatized – their provincial accent, dialect, 'proletarian' style, etc. – but the more strongly, the less successful their initial attempts at *assimilation* have been. Thus, Champfleury, a writer from very modest provincial petit-bourgeois origins, after having for some time been 'torn between two tendencies, a realism *à la* Monnier and German-style poetry, Romantic and sentimental',[61] found himself impelled towards militant realism by the failure of his first endeavours and perhaps especially by consciousness of his difference, provoked by contact or objective competition with the Parisian writers, which sent him towards 'the people', i.e. to realism in his manner and to objects excluded from the legitimate art of the day. And this negative return to the people is no less ambiguous, and suspect, than the regionalist writers' retreat to the peasantry. Hostility to the libertarian audacities and arbitrary populism of the bourgeois intellectuals can be the basis of an anti-intellectual populism, more or less conservative, in which 'the people' are once again merely a projection in fantasy of relations internal to the intellectual field. A typical example of this field-effect can be seen in the trajectory of the same Champfleury, who, after having been the leader of the young realist writers of 1850 and the 'theorist' of the realist movement in literature and painting, was increasingly eclipsed by Flaubert and then by the Goncourts and Zola. He became a state official at the Sèvres porcelain factory and set himself up as the historian of popular imagery and literature, and, after a series of shifts and turns, the official theorist (awarded the Légion d'Honneur in 1867) of a conservatism based on exaltation of popular wisdom – in particular, of the resignation to hierarchies that is expressed in popular arts and traditions.[62]

Thus, it is within each state of the field that – as a function of the structure of the possibles which are manifested through the different positions and the properties of the occupants (particularly with respect to social origin and the corresponding dispositions), and also as a function of the positions actually and potentially occupied within the field (experienced as success or failure) – the dispositions associated with a certain social origin are specified by being enacted in structurally marked practices; and the same dispositions lead to opposite aesthetic or political positions, depending on the state of the field in relation to which they have to express themselves. One only has to consider the example of realism in literature or painting to see the futility of the attempts of some contemporary critics to relate the characteristics of this art directly to the characteristics of the social group – the peasantry – from which its inventors or advocates (Champfleury or Courbet) originate. It is only within a determinate state of an artistic field, and in the relationship with other artistic positions and their occupants, themselves socially characterized, that the dispositions of the realist painters and artists, which might have been expressed elsewhere in other forms of art, were fulfilled in a form of art which, within that structure, appeared as a form of aesthetic and political revolt against 'bourgeois' art and artists (or the spiritualist criticism which supported them) and, through them, against the 'bourgeois'.

To make this argument fully convincing, one would have to show how habitus, as systems of dispositions, are effectively realized only in relation to a determinate structure of positions socially marked by the social properties of their occupants, through which they manifest themselves. Thus, nothing would be more naïve than to endeavour to understand the differences between the *Théâtre de l'Oeuvre* and the *Théâtre libre* solely in terms of the differences of habitus between their respective founders, Lugné-Poe, the son of a Parisian bourgeois, and Antoine, a provincial petit-bourgeois.[63] Yet it seems quite impossible to understand them solely on the basis of the structural positions of the two institutions which, initially at least, seem to reproduce the opposition between the founders' dispositions. This is only to be expected, since the former are the realization of the latter in a certain state of the field, marked by the opposition between Symbolism, which is more bourgeois – not least in the characteristics of its advocates – and Naturalism, which is more petit-bourgeois. Antoine, who, like the Naturalists, and with their theoretical support, defined himself against bourgeois theatre, proposed a systematic transformation of *mise en scène*, a *specific* theatrical revolution based on a coherent thesis. Emphasizing milieu over characters, the determining context over the determined text, he made the stage 'a coherent, complete universe over which the director is sole master'.[64] By contrast, Lugné-Poe's 'scrappy but fertile' directing, which defined itself in relation to bourgeois theatre, but also in relation to Antoine's innovations, led to performances described as 'a mixture of refined invention and sloppiness'; inspired by a project that was 'sometimes demagogic, sometimes elitist', they brought together an audience in which anarchists rubbed shoulders with mystics.[65] In short, without exploring any further an opposition which appears everywhere, between the writers, newspapers or critics who support one or the other, between the authors performed and the content of the works, with, on one side, the 'slice of life', which in some ways resembles vaudeville, and, on the other, intellectual refinements inspired by the idea, enunciated by Mallarmé, of the multi-levelled work, it can be seen that the opposition between class dispositions receives its particular content in a particular space. There is every reason to think that, as this case suggests, the weight of dispositions – and the explanatory force of 'social origin' – is particularly strong when one is dealing with a position that is in the process of birth, still to be made (rather than already made, established and capable of imposing its own norms on its occupants); and, more generally, that the scope allowed to dispositions varies according to the state of the field (in particular, its autonomy), the position in the field and the degree of institutionalization of the position.

Finally, we must ask explicitly a question which is bound to be asked: what is the degree of conscious strategy, cynical calculation, in the objective strategies which observation brings to light and which ensure the correspondence between positions and dispositions? One only has to read literary testimonies, correspondence, diaries and, especially perhaps, explicit position-takings on the literary world as such (like those collected by Huret) to see that there is no simple answer to these questions and that lucidity is always partial and is, once again, a matter of position and trajectory within the field, so that it varies from one agent and one moment to another. As for awareness of the logic of the game as such, and of the *illusio* on which it is based, I had been inclined to think that it was excluded by membership of the field, which presupposes (and induces) belief in everything which depends on the existence of the field, i.e. literature, the writer, etc., because such lucidity would make the literary or artistic undertaking itself a cynical mysitification, a conscious trickery. So I thought, until I came across a text by Mallarmé which provides both the programme and the balance-sheet of a rigorous science of the literary field and the recognized fictions that are engendered within it: 'We know, captives of an absolute formula that, indeed, there is only that which is. Forthwith to dismiss the cheat, however, on a pretext, would indict our inconsequence, denying the pleasure we want to take: for that *beyond* is its agent, and the engine I might say were I not loath to perform, in public, the impious dismantling of the fiction and consequently of the literary mechanism, display the principal part or nothing. But I venerate how, by a trick, we project to a height forfended – and with thunder! – the conscious lack in us of what shines up there. What is it for? A game.'[66] This quasi-Feuerbachian theory reduces beauty, which is sometimes thought of as a Platonic Idea, endowed with an objective, transcendent existence, to no more than the projection into a metaphysical beyond of what is lacking in the here-and-now of literary life. But is that how it is to be taken? Hermeticism, in this case, perfectly fulfils its function: to utter 'in public' the true nature of the field, and of its mechanisms, is sacrilege *par excellence*, the unforgivable sin which all the censorships constituting the field seek to repress. These are things that can only be said in such a way that they are not said. If Mallarmé can, without excluding himself from the field, utter the truth about a field which excludes the *publishing* of its own truth, this is because he says it in a language which is designed to be *recognized* within the field because everything, in its very *form*, that of euphemism and *Verneinung*, affirms that he *recognizes* its censorships. Marcel Duchamp was to do exactly the same thing when he made artistic acts out of his bluffs, demystificatory mystifications which denounce fiction as mere fiction, and with it the collective belief which is the basis of this 'legitimate' imposture (as Austin would have put it). But Mallarmé's hermeticism, which bespeaks his concern not to destroy the *illusio*, has another basis too: if the Platonic illusion is the 'agent' of a pleasure which we take only because 'we *want* to take it', if the pleasure of the love of art has its source in unawareness of producing the source of what produces it, then it is understandable that one might, by another willing suspension of disbelief, choose to 'venerate' the authorless trickery which places the fragile fetish beyond the reach of critical lucidity.

# 2

# The Production of Belief: Contribution to an Economy of Symbolic Goods

Once again, I don't like this word
'entrepreneur'.

Sven Nielsen, Chairman and
Managing Director of Presses de
la Cité

In another area, I had the honour, if
not the pleasure, of losing money by
commissioning the two monumental volumes
of Carlos Baker's translation of
Hemingway.

Robert Laffont

The art business, a trade in things that have no price, belongs to the class
of practices in which the logic of the pre-capitalist economy lives on (as
it does, in another sphere, in the economy of exchanges between the
generations). These practices, functioning as practical *negations*,* can
only work by pretending not to be doing what they are doing. Defying
ordinary logic, they lend themselves to two opposed readings, both
equally false, which each undo their essential duality and duplicity by
reducing them either to the disavowal or to what is disavowed – to
disinterestedness or self-interest. The challenge which economies based
on disavowal of the 'economic' present to all forms of economism lies
precisely in the fact that they function, and can function, in practice –
and not merely in the agents' representations – only by virtue of a
constant, collective repression of narrowly 'economic' interest and of the
real nature of the practices revealed by 'economic' analysis.[1]

* *Translator's note*: The terms *negation*, *denial* and *disavowal* are used to render the French
*dénégation*, which itself is used in a sense akin to that of Freud's *Verneinung*. See J. Laplanche
and J. B. Pontalis, *The Language of Psycho-analysis* (London: Hogarth Press, 1973), entry
'Negation', pp. 261–3.

## THE DISAVOWAL OF THE 'ECONOMY'

In this economic universe, whose very functioning is defined by a 'refusal' of the 'commercial' which is in fact a collective disavowal of commercial interests and profits, the most 'anti-economic' and most visibly 'disinterested' behaviours, which in an 'economic' universe would be those most ruthlessly condemned, contain a form of economic rationality (even in the restricted sense) and in no way exclude their authors from even the 'economic' profits awaiting those who conform to the law of this universe. In other words, alongside the pursuit of 'economic' profit, which treats the cultural goods business as a business like any other, and not the most profitable, 'economically' speaking (as the best-informed, i.e. the most 'disinterested', art dealers point out) and merely adapts itself to the demand of an already converted clientele, there is also room for the *accumulation of symbolic capital*. 'Symbolic capital' is to be understood as economic or political capital that is disavowed, misrecognized and thereby recognized, hence legitimate, a 'credit' which, under certain conditions, and always in the long run, guarantees 'economic' profits. Producers and vendors of cultural goods who 'go commercial' condemn themselves, and not only from an ethical or aesthetic point of view, because they deprive themselves of the opportunities open to those who can *recognize* the specific demands of this universe and who, by concealing from themselves and others the interests at stake in their practice, obtain the means of deriving profits from disinterestedness. In short, when the only usable, effective capital is the (mis)recognized, legitimate capital called 'prestige' or 'authority', the economic capital that cultural undertakings generally require cannot secure the specific profits produced by the field – not the 'economic' profits they always imply – unless it is reconverted into symbolic capital. For the author, the critic, the art dealer, the publisher or the theatre manager, the only legitimate accumulation consists in making a name for oneself, a known, recognized name, a capital of consecration implying a power to consecrate objects (with a trademark or signature) or persons (through publication, exhibition, etc.) and therefore to give value, and to appropriate the profits from this operation.

The disavowal [*dénégation*] is neither a real negation of the 'economic' interest which always haunts the most 'disinterested' practices, nor a simple 'dissimulation' of the mercenary aspects of the practice, as even the most attentive observers have supposed. The disavowed economic enterprise of art dealers or publishers, 'cultural bankers' in whom art and business meet in practice – which predisposes them for the role of scapegoat – cannot succeed, even in 'economic' terms, unless it is guided by a practical mastery of the laws of the functioning of the field in which cultural goods are produced and circulate, i.e. by an entirely improbable, and in any case rarely achieved, combination of the realism implying minor concessions to 'economic' necessities that are disavowed but not denied and the conviction which excludes them.[2] The fact that the disavowal of the 'economy' is neither a simple ideological mask nor a complete repudiation of economic interest explains why, on the one hand, new producers whose only capital is their conviction can establish themselves in the market by appealing to the values whereby the dominant figures accumulated their symbolic capital, and why, on the other hand, only those who can come to terms with the 'economic' constraints inscribed in this bad-faith economy can reap the full 'economic' profits of their symbolic capital.

## WHO CREATES THE 'CREATOR'?

The 'charismatic' ideology which is the ultimate basis of belief in the value of a work of art and which is therefore the basis of functioning of the field of production and circulation of cultural commodities, is undoubtedly the main obstacle to a rigorous science of the production of the value of cultural goods. It is this ideology which directs attention to the *apparent producer*, the painter, writer or composer, in short, the 'author', suppressing the question of what authorizes the author, what creates the authority with which authors authorize. If it is all too obvious that the price of a picture is not determined by the sum of the production costs – the raw material and the painter's labour time – and if works of art provide a golden example for those who seek to refute Marx's labour theory of value (which anyway gives a special status to artistic production), this is perhaps because we wrongly define the unit of production or, which amounts to the same thing, the process of production.

The question can be asked in its most concrete form (which it sometimes assumes in the eyes of the agents): who is the true producer of the value of the work – the painter or the dealer, the writer or the publisher, the playwright or the theatre manager? The ideology of creation, which makes the author the first and last source of the value of his work, conceals the fact that the cultural businessman (art dealer, publisher, etc.) is at one and the same time the person who exploits the labour of the 'creator' by trading in the 'sacred' and the person who, by putting it on the market, by exhibiting, publishing or staging it, consecrates a product which he has 'discovered' and which would otherwise remain a mere natural resource; and the more consecrated he personally is, the more strongly he consecrates the work.[3] The art trader is not just the agent who gives the work a commercial value by bringing it into a market; he is not just the representative, the impresario, who 'defends the authors he loves'. He is the person who can proclaim the value of the author he defends (cf. the fiction of the catalogue or blurb) and above all 'invests his prestige' in the author's cause, acting as a 'symbolic banker' who offers as security all the symbolic capital he has accumulated (which he is liable to forfeit if he backs a 'loser').[4] This investment, of which the accompanying 'economic' investments are themselves only a guarantee, is what brings the producer into the cycle of consecration. Entering the field of literature is not so much like going into religion as getting into a select club: the publisher is one of those prestigious sponsors (together with preface-writers and critics) who effusively recommend their candidate. Even clearer is the role of the art dealer, who literally has to 'introduce' the artist and his work into ever more select company (group exhibitions, one-man shows, prestigious collections, museums) and ever more sought-after places. But the law of this universe, whereby the less visible the investment, the more productive it is symbolically, means that promotion exercises, which in the business world take the overt form of publicity, must here be euphemized. The art trader cannot serve his 'discovery' unless he applies all his conviction, which rules out 'sordidly commercial' manoeuvres, manipulation and the 'hard sell', in favour of the softer, more discreet forms of 'public relations' (which are themselves a highly euphemized form of publicity) – receptions, society gatherings, and judiciously placed confidences.[5]

## THE CIRCLE OF BELIEF

But in moving back from the 'creator' to the 'discoverer' or 'creator of the creator', we have only displaced the initial question and we still have to determine the source of the art-businessman's acknowledged power to consecrate. The charismatic ideology has a ready-made answer: the 'great' dealers, the 'great' publishers, are inspired talent-spotters who, guided by their disinterested, unreasoning passion for a work of art, have 'made' the painter or writer, or have helped him make himself, by encouraging him in difficult moments with the faith they had in him, guiding him with their advice and freeing him from material worries.[6] To avoid an endless regress in the chain of causes, perhaps it is necessary to cease thinking in the logic, which a whole tradition encourages, of the 'first beginning', which inevitably leads to faith in the 'creator'. It is not sufficient to indicate, as people often do, that the 'discoverer' never discovers anything that is not already discovered, at least by a few – painters, already known to a small number of painters or connoisseurs, authors, 'introduced' by other authors (it is well known, for example, that the manuscripts that will be published hardly ever arrive directly, but almost always through recognized go-betweens). His 'authority' is itself a credit-based value, which only exists in the relationship with the field of production as a whole, i.e. with the artists or writers who belong to his 'stable' – 'a publisher', said one of them, 'is his catalogue' – and with those who do not and would or would not like to; in the relationship with the other dealers or publishers who do or do not envy him his painters or writers and are or are not capable of taking them from him; in the relationship with the critics, who do or do not believe in his judgement, and speak of his 'products' with varying degrees of respect; in the relationship with his clients and customers, who perceive his 'trademark' with greater or lesser clarity and do or do not place their trust in it. This 'authority' is nothing other than 'credit' with a set of agents who constitute 'connections' whose value is proportionate to the credit they themselves command. It is all too obvious that critics also collaborate with the art trader in the effort of consecration which makes the reputation and, at least in the long term, the monetary value of works. 'Discovering' the 'new talents', they guide buyers' and sellers' choices by their writings or advice (they are often manuscript readers or series editors in publishing houses or accredited preface-writers for galleries) and by their verdicts, which, though offered as purely aesthetic, entail significant economic effects (juries for artistic prizes). Among the makers of the work of art, we must finally include the public, which helps to make its value by appropriating it materially (collectors) or symbolically (audiences, readers), and by objectively or subjectively identifying part of its own value with these appropriations. In short, what 'makes reputations' is not, as provincial Rastignacs naïvely think, this or that 'influential' person, this or that institution, review, magazine, academy, coterie, dealer or publisher; it is not even the whole set of what are sometimes called 'personalities of the world of arts and letters'; it is the field of production, understood as the system of objective relations between these agents or institutions and as the site of the struggles for the monopoly of the power to consecrate, in which the value of works of art and belief in that value are continuously generated.[7]

## FAITH AND BAD FAITH

The source of the efficacy of all acts of consecration is the field itself, the locus of the accumulated social energy which the agents and institutions help to reproduce through the struggles in which they try to appropriate it and into which they put what they have acquired from it in previous struggles. The value of works of art in general – the basis of the value of each particular work – and the belief which underlies it, are generated in the incessant, innumerable struggles to establish the value of this or that particular work, i.e. not only in the competition between agents (authors, actors, writers, critics, directors, publishers, dealers, etc.) whose interests (in the broadest sense) are linked to different cultural goods, 'middle-brow' theatre (*théâtre 'bourgeois'*) or 'high-brow' theatre (*théâtre 'intellectuel'*), 'established' painting or avant-garde painting, 'mainstream' literature or 'advanced' literature, but also in the conflicts between agents occupying different positions in the production of products of the same type: painters and dealers, authors and publishers, writers and critics, etc. Even if these struggles never clearly set the 'commercial' against the 'non-commercial', 'disinterestedness' against 'cynicism', they almost always involve recognition of the ultimate values of 'disinterestedness' through the denunciation of the mercenary compromises or calculating manoeuvres of the adversary, so that disavowal of the 'economy' is placed at the very heart of the field, as the principle governing its functioning and transformation.

This is why the dual reality of the ambivalent painter–dealer or writer–publisher relationship is most clearly revealed in moments of crisis, when the objective reality of each of the positions and their relationship is unveiled and the values which do the veiling are reaffirmed. No one is better placed than art dealers to know the interests of the makers of works and the strategies they use to defend their interests or to conceal their strategies. Although dealers form a protective screen between the artist and the market, they are also what link them to the market and so provoke, by their very existence, cruel unmaskings of the truth of artistic practice. To impose their own interests, they only have to take artists at their word when they profess 'disinterestedness'. One soon learns from conversations with these middle-men that, with a few illustrious exceptions, seemingly designed to recall the ideal, painters and writers are deeply self-interested, calculating, obsessed with money and ready to do anything to succeed. As for the artists, who cannot even denounce the exploitation they suffer without confessing their self-interested motives, they are the ones best placed to see the middle-men's strategies and their eye for an (economically) profitable investment which guides their actual aesthetic investments. The makers and marketers of works of art are adversaries in collusion, who each abide by the same law which demands the repression of direct manifestations of personal interest, at least in its overtly 'economic' form, and which has every appearance of transcendence although it is only the product of the cross-censorship weighing more or less equally on each of those who impose it on all the others.

A similar mechanism operates when an unknown artist, without credit or credibility, is turned into a known and recognized artist. The struggle to impose the dominant definition of art, i.e. to impose a style, embodied in a particular producer or group of producers, gives the work of art a value by putting it at stake, inside and outside the field of production. Everyone can challenge his or her adversaries' claim to distinguish art from non-art without ever calling into question this fundamental claim. Precisely because of the conviction that good and bad painting exist, competitors can exclude each other from the field of painting, thereby giving it the stakes and the motor without which it could not function. And nothing better conceals the objective collusion which is the matrix of specifically artistic value than the conflicts through which it operates.

## RITUAL SACRILEGE

This argument might be encountered by pointing to the attempts made with increasing frequency in the 1960s, especially in the world of painting, to break the circle of belief. But it is all too obvious that these ritual acts of sacrilege, profanations which only ever scandalize the believers, are bound to become sacred in their turn and provide the basis for a new belief. One thinks of Manzoni, with his tins of 'artist's shit', his magic pedestals which could turn any object placed on them into a work of art, or his signatures on living people which made them *objets d'art*; or Ben, with his many 'gestures' of provocation or derision such as exhibiting a piece of cardboard labelled 'unique copy' or a canvas bearing the words 'canvas 45 cm long'. Paradoxically, nothing more clearly reveals the logic of the functioning of the artistic field than the fate of these apparently radical attempts at subversion. Because they expose the art of artistic creation to a mockery already annexed to the artistic tradition by Duchamp, they are immediately converted into artistic 'acts', recorded as such and thus consecrated and celebrated by the makers of taste. Art cannot reveal the truth about art without snatching it away again by turning the revelation into an artistic event. And it is significant, *a contrario*, that all attempts to call into question the field of artistic production, the logic of its functioning and the functions it performs, through the highly sublimated and ambiguous means of discourse or artistic 'acts' (e.g. Maciunas or Flynt) are no less necessarily bound to be condemned even by the most heterodox guardians of artistic orthodoxy, because in refusing to play the game, to challenge in accordance with the rules, i.e. artistically, their authors call into question not a way of playing the game, but the game itself and the belief which supports it. This is the one unforgivable transgression.

## COLLECTIVE MISRECOGNITION

The quasi-magical potency of the signature is nothing other than the power, bestowed on certain individuals, to mobilize the symbolic energy produced by the functioning of the whole field, i.e. the faith in the game and its stakes that is produced by the game itself. As Marcel Mauss observed, the problem with magic is not so much to know what are the specific properties of the magician, or even of the magical operations and representations, but rather to discover the bases of the collective belief or, more precisely, the *collective misrecognition*, collectively produced and maintained, which is the source of the power the magician appropriates. If it is 'impossible to understand magic without the magic group', this is because the magician's power, of which the miracle of the signature or personal trademark is merely an outstanding example, is a *valid imposture*, a legitimate abuse of power, collectively misrecognized and so recognized. The artist who puts her name on a ready-made article and produces an object whose market price is incommensurate with its cost of production is collectively mandated to perform a magic act which would be nothing without the whole tradition leading up to her gesture, and without the universe of celebrants and believers who give it meaning and value in terms of that tradition. The source of 'creative' power, the ineffable *mana* or charisma celebrated by the tradition, need not be sought anywhere other than in the field, i.e. in the system of objective relations which constitute it, in the struggles of which it is the site and in the specific form of energy or capital which is generated there.

So it is both true and untrue to say that the commercial value of a work of art is incommensurate with its cost of production. It is true if one only takes account of the manufacture of the material object; it is not true if one is referring to the production of the work of art as a sacred, consecrated object, the product of a vast operation of *social alchemy* jointly conducted, with equal conviction and very unequal profits, by all the agents involved in the field of production, i.e. obscure artists and writers as well as 'consecrated' masters, critics and publishers as well as authors, enthusiastic clients as well as convinced vendors. These are contributions, including the most obscure, which the partial materialism of economism ignores, and which only have to be taken into account in order to see that the production of the work of art, i.e. of the artist, is no exception to the law of the conservation of social energy.[8]

## THE ESTABLISHMENT AND THE CHALLENGERS

Because the fields of cultural production are universes of belief which can only function in so far as they succeed in simultaneously producing products and the need for those products through practices which are the denial of the ordinary practices of the 'economy', the struggles which take place within them are ultimate conflicts involving the whole relation to the 'economy'. The 'zealots', whose only capital is their belief in the principles of the bad-faith economy and who preach a return to the sources, the absolute and intransigent renunciation of the early days, condemn in the same breath the merchants in the temple who bring 'commercial' practices and interests into the area of the sacred, and the pharisees who derive temporal profits from their accumulated capital of consecration by means of an exemplary submission to the demands of the field. Thus the fundamental law of the field is constantly reasserted by 'newcomers', who have most interest in the disavowal of self-interest.

The opposition between the 'commercial' and the 'non-commercial' reappears everywhere. It is the generative principle of most of the judgements which, in the theatre, cinema, painting or literature, claim to establish the frontier between what is and what is not art, i.e. in practice, between 'bourgeois' art and 'intellectual' art, between 'traditional' and 'avant-garde' art, or, in Parisian terms, between the 'right bank' and the 'left bank'.[9] While this opposition can change its substantive content and designate very different realities in different fields, it remains structurally invariant in different fields and in the same field at different moments. It is always an opposition between small-scale and large-scale ('commercial') production, i.e. between the primacy of production and the field of producers or even the sub-field of producers for producers, and the primacy of marketing, audience, sales and success measured quantitatively; between the deferred, lasting success of 'classics' and the immediate, temporary success of best-sellers; between a production based on denial of the 'economy' and of profit (sales targets, etc.) which ignores or challenges the expectations of the established audience and serves no other demand than the one it itself produces, but in the long term, and a production which secures success and the corresponding profits by adjusting to a pre-existing demand. The characteristics of the commercial enterprise and the characteristics of the cultural enterprise, understood as a more or less disavowed relation to the commercial enterprise, are inseparable. The differences in the relationship to 'economic' considerations and to the audience coincide with the differences officially recognized and identified by the taxonomies prevailing in the field. Thus the opposition between 'genuine' art and 'commercial' art corresponds to the opposition between ordinary entrepreneurs seeking immediate economic profit and cultural entrepreneurs struggling to accumulate specifically cultural capital, albeit at the cost of temporarily renouncing economic profit. As for the opposition which is made within the latter group between consecrated art and avant-garde art, or between orthodoxy and heresy, it distinguishes between, on the one hand, those who dominate the field of production and the market through the economic and symbolic capital they have been able to accumulate in earlier struggles by virtue of a particularly successful combination of the contradictory capacities specifically demanded by the law of the field, and, on the other hand, the newcomers, who have and want no other audience than their competitors – established producers whom their practice tends to discredit by imposing new products – or other newcomers with whom they vie in novelty.

Their position in the structure of simultaneously economic and symbolic power relations which defines the field of production, i.e. in the structure of the distribution of the specific capital (and of the corresponding economic capital), governs the characteristics and strategies of the agents or institutions, through the intermediary of a practical or conscious evaluation of the objective chances of profit. Those in dominant positions operate essentially defensive strategies, designed to perpetuate the status quo by maintaining themselves and the principles on which their dominance is based. The world is as it should be, since they are on top and clearly deserve to be there; excellence therefore consists in being what one is, with reserve and understatement, urbanely hinting at the immensity of one's means by the economy of one's means, refusing the assertive, attention-seeking strategies which expose the pretensions of the young pretenders. The dominant are drawn towards silence, discretion and secrecy, and their orthodox discourse, which is only ever wrung from them by the need to rectify the heresies of the newcomers, is never more than the explicit affirmation of self-evident principles which go without saying and would go better unsaid. 'Social problems' are social relations: they emerge from confrontation between two groups, two systems of antagonistic interests and theses. In the relationship which constitutes them, the choice of the moment and sites of battle is left to the initiative of the challengers, who break the silence of the *doxa* and call into question the unproblematic, taken-for-granted world of the dominant groups. The dominated producers, for their part, in order to gain a foothold in the market, have to resort to subversive strategies which will eventually bring them the disavowed profits only if they succeed in overturning the hierarchy of the field without disturbing the principles on which the field is based. Thus their revolutions are only ever partial ones, which displace the censorships and transgress the conventions but do so in the name of the same underlying principles. This is why the strategy *par excellence* is the 'return to the sources' which is the basis of all heretical subversion and all aesthetic revolutions, because it enables the insurgents to turn against the establishment the arms which they use to justify their domination, in particular asceticism, daring, ardour, rigour and disinterestedness. The strategy of beating the dominant groups at their own game by demanding that they respect the fundamental law of the field, a denial of the 'economy', can only work if it manifests exemplary sincerity in its own denial.

Because they are based on a relation to culture which is necessarily also a relation to the 'economy' and the market, institutions producing and marketing cultural goods, whether in painting, literature, theatre or cinema, tend to be organized into structurally and functionally homologous systems which also stand in a relation of structural homology with the field of the fractions of the dominant class (from which the greater part of their clientele is drawn). This homology is most evident in the case of the theatre. The opposition between 'bourgeois theatre' and 'avant-garde theatre', the equivalent of which can be found in painting and in literature, and which functions as a principle of division whereby authors, works, styles and subjects can be classified practically, is rooted in reality. It is found both in the social characteristics of the audiences of the different Paris theatres (age, occupation, place of residence, frequency of attendance, prices they are prepared to pay, etc.) and in the – perfectly congruent – characteristics of the authors performed (age, social origin, place of residence, lifestyle, etc.), the works and the theatrical businesses themselves.

'High-brow' theatre in fact contrasts with 'middle-brow' theatre (*théâtre de boulevard*) in all these respects at once. On one side, there are the big subsidized theatres (Odéon, Théâtre de l'Est parisien, Théâtre national populaire) and the few small left-bank theatres (Vieux Colombier, Montparnasse, Gaston Baty, etc.),[10] which are risky undertakings both economically and culturally, always on the verge of bankruptcy, offering unconventional shows (as regards content and/or *mise en scène*) at relatively low prices to a young, 'intellectual' audience (students, intellectuals, teachers). On the other side, there are the 'bourgeois'[11] theatres (in order of intensity of the pertinent properties: Gymnase, Théâtre de Paris, Antoine, Ambassadeurs, Ambigu, Michodière, Variétés), ordinary commercial businesses whose concern for economic profitability forces them into extremely prudent cultural strategies, which take no risks and create none for their audiences, and offer shows that have already succeeded (adaptations of British and American plays, revivals of middle-brow 'classics') or have been newly written in accordance with tried and tested formulae. Their audience tends to be

Table 1 *The overlap of audiences between theatres (the 1963–4 season)*

| | Théâtre de l'Est parisien | Théâtre national populaire | Théâtre de France (Odéon) | Athénée | Vieux Colombier | Montparnasse G. Baty | Comédie Française | Atelier | Ambigu | Michodière | Théâtre de Paris | Comédie Champs Elysées | Ambassadeurs | Moderne | Antoine | Gymnase | Variétés |
|---|---|---|---|---|---|---|---|---|---|---|---|---|---|---|---|---|---|
| Théâtre de l'Est parisien | X | 57 | 48 | | | | | | | | | | | | | | |
| Théâtre national populaire | X | X | 48 | | 35 | | | | | | | | | | | | |
| Théâtre de France (Odéon) | | 56 | X | 35 | 32 | | | | | | | | | | | | |
| Athénée | | 50 | 45 | X | 36 | | | 36 | | | | | | | | | |
| Vieux Colombier | | 49 | 47 | 36 | X | | 36 | 43 | | | | | | | | | |
| Montparnasse G. Baty | | 40 | 49 | | 41 | X | 48 | 48 | | | | | | | | | |
| Comédie Française | | | 48 | | | | X | 35 | | | | | | | | | |
| Atelier | | | 39 | | | | 38 | X | | | 47 | | | | | | |
| Ambigu | | | 48 | | | | 37 | 49 | X | | 41 | | | | | | |
| Michodière | | | 38 | | | | 49 | 47 | | X | 46 | | | | | | |
| Théâtre de Paris | | | | | | | 36 | 49 | | 38 | X | | | | | | |
| Comédie Champs Elysées | | | | | | | 38 | 55 | | 39 | 49 | X | | | | | |
| Ambassadeurs | | | | | | | | 58 | | | 46 | | X | | | | |
| Moderne | | | | | | | | 57 | | | 56 | | | X | | | |
| Antoine | | | | | | | | 43 | | | 40 | | | | X | | |
| Gymnase | | | | | | | | 40 | | | 37 | | 40 | | | X | |
| Variétés | | | | | | | | 42 | | | 46 | | 42 | | | | X |

Percentage figures are given, opposite each theatre, for the three other theatres to which their audiences have been most frequently.

Source: Société d'économie et de mathématiques appliquées, *La Situation du théâtre en France*, vol. 2, Annexe, Données statistiques, Tableau 42.

older, more 'bourgeois' (executives, the professions, businesspeople), and is prepared to pay high prices for shows of pure entertainment whose conventions and staging correspond to an aesthetic that has not changed for a century. Between the 'poor theatre' which caters to the dominant-class fractions richest in cultural capital and poorest in economic capital, and the 'rich theatre', which caters to the fractions richest in economic capital and poorest (in relative terms) in cultural capital, stand the classic theatres (Comédie Française, Atelier), which are neutral ground, since they draw their audience more or less equally from all fractions of the dominant class and share parts of their constituency with all types of theatre.[12] Their programmes too are neutral or eclectic: 'avant-garde boulevard' (as the drama critic of *La Croix* put it), represented by Anouilh, or the consecrated avant-garde.[13]

## GAMES WITH MIRRORS

This structure is no new phenomenon. When Françoise Dorin, in *Le Tournant*, one of the great boulevard successes, places an avant-garde author in typical vaudeville situations, she is simply rediscovering (and for the same reasons) the same strategies which Scribe used in *La Camaraderie*, against Delacroix, Hugo and Berlioz: in 1836, to reassure a worthy public alarmed by the outrages and excesses of the Romantics, Scribe gave them Oscar Rigaut, a poet famed for his funeral odes but exposed as a hedonist, in short, a man like others, ill-placed to call the bourgeois 'grocers'.[14]

Françoise Dorin's play, which dramatizes a middle-brow playwright's attempts to convert himself into an avant-garde playwright, can be regarded as a sort of sociological test which demonstrates how the opposition which structures the whole space of cultural production operated simultaneously in people's minds, in the form of systems of classification and categories of perception, and in objective reality, through the mechanisms which produce the complementary oppositions between playwrights and their theatres, critics and their newspapers. The play itself offers the contrasting portraits of two theatres: on the one hand, technical clarity and skill, gaiety, lightness and frivolity, 'typically French' qualities; on the other, 'pretentiousness camouflaged under ostentatious starkness', 'a confidence-trick of presentation', humourlessness, portentousness and pretentiousness, gloomy speeches and decors ('a black curtain and a scaffold certainly help . . .') In short, dramatists, plays, speeches, epigrams that are 'courageously light', joyous, lively, uncomplicated, true-to-life, as opposed to 'thinking', i.e. miserable, tedious, problematic and obscure. 'We had a bounce in our backsides. They think with theirs. There is no overcoming this opposition, because it separates 'intellectuals' and 'bourgeois' even in the interests they have most manifestly in common. All the contrasts which Françoise Dorin and the 'bourgeois' critics mobilize in their judgements on the theatre (in the form of oppositions between the 'black curtain' and the 'beautiful set', 'the wall well lit, well decorated', 'the actors well washed, well dressed'), and, indeed, in their whole world view, are summed up in the opposition between *la vie en noir* and *la vie en rose* – dark thoughts and rose-coloured spectacles – which, as we shall see, ultimately stems from two very different ways of *denying the social world*.[15]

Faced with an object so clearly organized in accordance with the canonical opposition, the critics, themselves distributed within the space of the press in accordance with the structure which underlies the object classified and the classificatory system they apply to it, reproduce, in the space of the judgements whereby they classify it and themselves, the space within which they are themselves classified (a perfect circle from which there is no escape except by objectifying it). In other words, the different judgements expressed on *Le Tournant* vary, in their form and content, according to the publication in which they appear, i.e. from the greatest distance of the critic and his readership *vis-à-vis* the 'intellectual' world to the greatest distance *vis-à-vis* the play and its 'bourgeois' audience and the smallest distance *vis-à-vis* the 'intellectual' world.[16]

### WHAT THE PAPERS SAY: THE PLAY OF HOMOLOGY

The subtle shifts in meaning and style which, from *L'Aurore* to *Le Figaro* and from *Le Figaro* to *L'Express*, lead to the neutral discourse of *Le Monde* and thence to the (eloquent) silence of *Le Nouvel Observateur* (see Table 2) can only be fully understood when one knows that they accompany a steady rise in the educational level of the readership (which, here as elsewhere, is a reliable indicator of the level of transmission or supply of the corresponding messages), and a rise in the proportion of those class fractions – public-sector executives and teachers – who not only read most in general but also differ from all other groups by a particularly high rate of readership of the papers with the highest level of transmission (*Le Monde* and *Le Nouvel Observateur*); and, conversely, a decline in the proportion of those fractions – big commercial and industrial employers – who not only read least in general but also differ from other groups by a particularly high rate of readership of the papers with the lowest level of transmission (*France-Soir*, *L'Aurore*). To put it more simply, the structured space of dis-

Table 2  Degree of penetration of newspapers and weeklies in relation to fractions of the dominant class (no. of readers at the time of this survey among 1,000 heads of families in the relevant category)

| | France-Soir | L'Aurore | La Croix | Le Figaro | L'Express | Le Monde | Le Nouvel Observateur | Total* |
|---|---|---|---|---|---|---|---|---|
| Commercial entrepreneurs | **170** | 70 | – | 102 | 190 | 77 | 44 | 463 |
| Industrialists | 111 | 75 | – | 152 | 309 | 78 | 28 | 449 |
| Private sector executives | **139** | **111** | 51 | 197 | 368 | 221 | 82 | 750 |
| Engineers | 99 | 23 | **70** | **218** | 374 | 270 | 71 | 681 |
| The professions | 87 | 37 | **54** | 167 | 371 | 163 | **131** | 585 |
| Civil servants | 121 | **100** | 22 | **234** | **375** | **385** | 103 | **943** |
| Teachers | | | | | | | | |
| Literary and scientific professions | 64 | 62 | 29 | 173 | **398** | **329** | **217** | **845** |
| For all categories | 118 | 72 | 31 | 178 | 335 | 231 | 99 | |

Bold figures indicate the two highest values in each column.
*This number, the sum of all readers in the given category, is obviously an approximation since it does not take account of double readership.
Source: Centre d'études des supports de publicité, study of press readership among top management and higher civil service, Paris, 1970.

courses reproduces, in its own terms, the structured space of the newspapers and of the readerships for whom they are produced, with, at one end of the field, big commercial and industrial employers, *France-Soir* and *L'Aurore*, and, at the other end, public-sector executives and teachers, *Le Monde* and *Le Nouvel Observateur*,[17] the central positions being occupied by private-sector executives, engineers and the professions and, as regards the press, *Le Figaro* and especially *L'Express*, which is read more or less equally by all the dominant-class fractions (except the commercial employers) and constitutes the neutral point in this universe.[18] Thus the space of judgements on the theatre is homologous with the space of the newspapers for which they are produced and which disseminate them and also with the space of the theatres and plays about which they are formulated, these homologies and all the games they allow being made possible by the homology between each of these spaces and the space of the dominant class.

Let us now run through the space of the judgements aroused by the experimental stimulus of Françoise Dorin's play, moving from 'right' to 'left' and from 'right-bank' to 'left-bank'. First, *L'Aurore*:

'Cheeky Françoise Dorin is going to be in hot water with our *snooty*, *Marxist* intelligentsia (the two go together). The author of 'Un sale égoïste' shows no respect for the solemn boredom, profound emptiness and vertiginous nullity which characterize so many so-called 'avant-garde' theatrical productions. She dares to profane with sacrilegious laughter the notorious 'incommunicability of beings' which is the alpha and omega of the contemporary stage. And this perverse *reactionary*, who flatters the lowest appetites of consumer society, far from acknowledging the error of her ways and wearing her boulevard playwright's reputation with humility, has the impudence to prefer the jollity of Sacha Guitry, or Feydeau's bedroom farces, to the darkness visible of Marguerite Duras or Arrabal. This is a crime it will be difficult to forgive. Especially since she commits it with cheerfulness and gaiety, using all the dreadful devices which make lasting successes. (Gilbert Guilleminaud, *L'Aurore*, 12 January 1973)'

Situated at the fringe of the intellectual field, at a point where he almost has to speak as an outsider ('our intelligentsia'), the *L'Aurore* critic does not mince his words (he calls a reactionary a reactionary) and does not hide his strategies. The rhetorical effect of putting words into the opponent's mouth, in conditions in which his discourse, functioning as an ironic antiphrasis, objectively says the opposite of what it means, presupposes and brings into play the very structure of the field of criticism and his relationship of immediate connivance with his public, based on homology of position.

From *L'Aurore* we move to *Le Figaro*. In perfect harmony with the author of *Le Tournant* – the harmony of orchestrated habitus – the *Figaro* critic cannot but experience absolute delight at a play which so perfectly corresponds to his categories of perception and appreciation, his view of the theatre and his view of the world:

'How grateful we should be to Mme Françoise Dorin for being a *courageously light* author, which means to say that she is *wittily* dramatic, and *smilingly serious*, irreverent without fragility, pushing the comedy into outright vaudeville, but in the subtlest way imaginable; an author who wields satire *with elegance*, an author who at all times demonstrates astounding virtuosity . . . Françoise Dorin knows *more than any of us* about the *tricks of the dramatist's art, the springs of comedy*, the *potential of a situation*, the comic or biting force of the *mot juste* . . . Yes, what skill in taking things apart, what irony in the deliberate side-stepping, what mastery in the way she lets you see her pulling the strings! *Le Tournant* gives every sort of enjoyment without an ounce of self-indulgence or vulgarity. And without ever being facile either, since it is quite clear that right now, *conformism lies with the avant-garde*, absurdity lies in gravity and imposture in tedium. Mme Françoise Dorin will *relieve a well-balanced audience* by bringing them back into *balance* with healthy laughter . . . Hurry and see for yourselves and I think you will *laugh so heartily* that you will forget to think how anguishing it can be for a writer to wonder if she is still in tune with the times in which she lives . . . In the end it is a question everyone asks themselves and only humour and *incurable optimism* can free them from it! (Jean-Jacques Gautier, *Le Figaro*, 12 January 1973)'

From *Le Figaro* one moves naturally to *L'Express*, which remains poised between endorsement and distance, thereby attaining a distinctly higher degree of euphemization:

'It's bound to be a runaway success . . . A witty and amusing play. A character. An actor who puts the part on like a glove: Jean Piat. With an *unfailing virtuosity that is only occasionally drawn out too long*, with a *sly cunning, a perfect mastery of the tricks of the trade*, Françoise Dorin has written a play on the 'turning point' in the Boulevard which is, ironically, the most traditional of Boulevard plays. *Only morose pedants will probe too far into the contrast between two conceptions of political life and the underlying private life.* The brilliant dialogue, full of *witticisms and epigrams*, is often viciously sarcastic. But Romain is not a caricature, he is much less stupid than the run-of-the-mill avant-garde writer. Philippe has the *plum role*, because he is on his own ground. What the author of 'Comme au théâtre' gently wants to suggest is that the

Boulevard is where people speak and behave 'as in real life', and this is true, but it is only a partial truth, and not just because it is a class truth. (Robert Kanters, *L'Express*, 15–21 January 1973)'

Here the approval, which is still total, already begins to be qualified by systematic use of formulations that are ambiguous even as regards the oppositions involved: 'It's likely to be a runaway success', 'a sly cunning, a perfect mastery of the tricks of the trade', 'Philippe has the plum role', all formulae which could also be taken pejoratively. And we even find, surfacing through its negation, a glimmer of the other truth ('Only morose pedants will probe too far . . .') or even of the truth *tout court*, but doubly neutralized, by ambiguity and negation ('and not just because it is a class truth').

*Le Monde* offers a perfect example of ostentatiously neutral discourse, even-handedly dismissing both sides, both the overtly political discourse of *L'Aurore* and the disdainful silence of *Le Nouvel Observateur*:

'The simple or simplistic argument is complicated by a very subtle 'two-tier' structure, as if there were two plays overlapping. One by Françoise Dorin, a conventional author, the other invented by Philippe Roussel, who tries to take 'the turning' towards modern theatre. This game performs a circular movement, like a boomerang. Françoise Dorin deliberately exposes the Boulevard clichés which Philippe attacks and, through his voice, utters a violent denunciation of the bourgeoisie. On the second tier, she contrasts this language with that of a young author whom she assails with equal vigour. Finally, the trajectory brings the weapon back on to the Boulevard stage, and the futilities of the mechanism are unmasked by the devices of the traditional theatre, which have therefore lost nothing of their value. Philippe is able to declare himself a 'courageously light' playwright, inventing 'characters who talk like everybody'; he can claim that his art is 'without frontiers' and therefore non-political. However, the demonstration is entirely distorted by the model avant-garde author chosen by Françoise Dorin. Vankovitz is an epigone of Marguerite Duras, a belated existentialist with militant leanings. He is caricatural in the extreme, as is the theatre that is denounced here ('A black curtain and a scaffold certainly help!' or the title of a play: 'Do take a little infinity in your coffee, Mr Karsov'). The audience gloats at this derisive picture of the modern theatre; the denunciation of the bourgeoisie is an amusing provocation inasmuch as it rebounds onto a detested victim and finishes him off . . . To the extent that it reflects the state of bourgeois theatre and reveals its systems of defence, *Le Tournant* can be regarded as an *important work*. Few plays let through so much anxiety about an 'external' threat and *recuperate* it with so much unconscious fury. (Louis Dandrel, *Le Monde*, 13 January 1973)'

The ambiguity which Robert Kanters was already cultivating here reaches its peaks. The argument is 'simple *or* simplistic', take your pick; the play is split in two, offering two works for the reader to choose, a 'violent' but 'recuperatory' critique of the 'bourgeoisie' and a defence of non-political art. For anyone naïve enough to ask whether the critic is 'for or against', whether he finds the play 'good or bad', there are two answers: first, an 'objective informant's' dutiful report that the avant-garde author portrayed is 'caricatural in the extreme' and that 'the audience gloats [*jubile*]' (but without our knowing where the critic stands in relation to this audience, and therefore what the significance of this gloating is); then, after a series of judgements that are kept ambiguous by many reservations, nuances and academic attenuations ('To the extent that . . .', 'can be regarded as . . .'), the assertion that *Le Tournant* is 'an important work', but, be it noted, as a document illustrating the crisis of modern civilization, as they would say at *Sciences Po*.[19]

Although the silence of *Le Nouvel Observateur* no doubt signifies something in itself, we can form an approximate idea of what its position might have been by reading its review of Felicien Marceau's play *La Preuve par quatre* or the review of *Le Tournant* by Philippe Tesson, then editor of *Combat*, published in *Le Canard enchaîné*:

'Theatre seems to me the wrong term to apply to these *society gatherings of tradesmen and businesswomen* in the course of which a famous and much loved actor recites the laboriously witty text of an equally famous author in the middle of an elaborate stage set, even a revolving one described with Folon's measured humour . . . No 'ceremony' here, no 'catharsis' or 'revelation' either, still less improvisation. Just a warmed-up dish of plain cooking [*cuisine bourgeoise*] for stomachs that have seen it all before . . . The audience, like all boulevard audiences in Paris, bursts out laughing, at the right time, in the most conformist places, wherever this spirit of easy-going rationalism comes into play. The connivance is perfect and the actors are all in on it. This play could have been written ten, twenty or thirty years ago. (M. Pierret, *Le Nouvel Observateur*, 12 February 1964, reviewing Felicien Marceau's *La Preuve par quatre*)'

'Françoise Dorin *really knows a thing or two*. She's a first-rate *recuperator* and terribly *well-bred*. Her *Le Tournant* is an excellent Boulevard comedy, which works mainly on bad faith and demagogy. The lady wants to prove that avant-garde theatre is tripe. To do so, she takes a *big bag of tricks* and need I say that as soon as she pulls one out the *audience* rolls in the aisles and shouts for more. Our author, who was just waiting for that, does it again. She gives us a young lefty playwright called Vankovitz – get it? – and puts him in various ridiculous, uncomfortable and rather shady situations, to show that this young gentleman is no more disinterested, no less bourgeois, than you and I. What common sense, Mme Dorin, what lucidity and what honesty! You at least have the courage to stand by your opinions, and very healthy, French ones they are too. (Philippe Tesson, *Le Canard enchâiné*, 17 March 1973)'

## PRESUPPOSITIONS AND MISPLACED REMARKS

Because the field is objectively polarized, critics on either side can pick out the same properties and use the same concepts to designate them ('crafty', 'tricks', 'common sense', 'healthy', etc.) but these concepts take on an ironic value ('common sense . . .') and thus function in reverse when addressed to a public which does not share the same relationship of connivance which is moreover strongly denounced ('as soon as she pulls one out, the audience rolls in the aisles'; 'the author was just waiting for that'). Nothing more clearly shows than does the theatre, which can only work on the basis of total connivance between the author and the audience (this is why the correspondence between the categories of theatres and the divisions of the dominant class is so close and so visible), that the meaning and value of words (and especially jokes) depends on the market in which they are uttered; that the same sentences can take on opposite meanings when addressed to groups with opposite presuppositions. Françoise Dorin simply exploits the structural logic of the field of the dominant class when, presenting the misadventures of an avant-garde author to a boulevard audience, she turns against avant-garde theatre the weapon it likes to use against 'bourgeois' conversation and against the 'bourgeois theatre' which reproduces its truisms and clichés (one thinks of Ionesco, describing *The Bald Prima-Donna* or *Jacques* as 'a sort of parody or caricature of boulevard theatre, a boulevard theatre decomposing and becoming insane'). Breaking the relation of ethical and aesthetic symbiosis which links 'intellectual' discourse with its audience, she turns it into a series of *'misplaced' remarks* which shock or provoke laughter because they are not uttered in the appropriate place and before the appropriate audience. They become, in the literal sense, a *parody*, a discourse which establishes with its audience the immediate complicity of laughter only because it has persuaded them to reject the presuppositions of the parodied discourse, if indeed they ever accepted those presuppositions.

## THE FOUNDATIONS OF CONNIVANCE

It would be a mistake to regard the term-for-term relationship between the critics' discourse and the properties of their readerships as a sufficient explanation. If the polemical image each camp has of its opponents leaves so much room for this type of explanation, that is because it makes it possible to disqualify aesthetic or ethical choices by reference to the fundamental law of the field, by exposing cynical calculation as their source, e.g. the pursuit of success at all costs, even through provocation and scandal (more of a right-bank argument) or self-interested servility, with the theme (favoured on the left bank) of the 'lackey of the bourgeoisie'. In fact, the *partial objectifications* of self-interested polemics (which is what almost all studies of the 'intellectuals' amount to) miss the essential point by describing as the product of a conscious calculation what is, in fact, the almost miraculous encounter of two systems of interests (which may coexist in the person of the 'bourgeois' writer) or, more precisely, of the structural and functional homology between any given writer's or artist's position in the field of production and the position of his or her audience in the field of the classes and class fractions. The so-called *écrivains de service*, whose opponents accuse them of being the servants of the bourgeoisie, are justified in protesting that strictly speaking they serve no one: they serve objectively only because, with total sincerity, in full unawareness of what they are doing, they serve their own interests, i.e. specific interests, highly sublimated and euphemized, such as the 'interest' in a particular form of theatre or philosophy which is logically associated with a certain position in a certain field and which (except in periods of crisis) has every likelihood of masking its own political implications, even in the eyes of its protagonists. Through the logic of homologies, the practices and works of the agents in a specialized, relatively autonomous field of production are necessarily *overdetermined*; the functions they fulfil in the internal struggles are inevitably accompanied by external functions, which are conferred on them in the symbolic struggles among the fractions of the dominant class and, in the long run at least, among the classes.[20] Critics serve their readerships so well only because the homology between their position in the intellectual field and their readership's position within the dominant-class field is the basis of an objective connivance (based on the same principles as that required by the theatre, especially for comedy) which means that they most sincerely, and therefore most effectively, defend the ideological interests of their clientele when defending their own interests as intellectuals against their specific adversaries, the occupants of opposing positions in the field of production.[21]

## THE POWER TO CONVINCE

'Sincerity' (which is one of the preconditions of symbolic efficacy) is only possible – and only achieved – when there is a perfect and immediate harmony between the expectations inscribed in the position occupied (in a less consecrated universe, one would say 'the job description') and the dispositions of the occupant. It is impossible to understand how dispositions come to be adjusted to positions (so that the journalist is adjusted to his newspaper and consequently to that paper's readership, and the readers are adjusted to the paper and so to the journalist) unless one is aware that the objective structures of the field of production give rise to categories of perception which structure the perception and appreciation of its products. This explains how antithetical couples – of persons (all the *maîtres à penser*) or institutions, newspapers (*Figaro/Nouvel Observateur*, or in a different practical context, *Nouvel Observateur/Humanité*), theatres (right-bank/left-bank, private/subsidized), galleries, publishers, reviews, couturiers, etc. – can function as classificatory schemes, which exist and signify only in their mutual relations, and serve as landmarks or beacons. As is seen more clearly in avant-garde painting than anywhere else, a practical mastery of these markers, a sort of sense of social direction, is indispensable in order to be able to navigate in a hierarchically structured space in which movement is always fraught with the danger of losing class, in which *places* – galleries, theatres, publishing houses – make all the difference (e.g. between 'commercial porn' and 'quality eroticism') because these sites designate an audience which, on the basis of the homology between the field of production and the field of consumption, qualifies the product consumed, helping to give it rarity or vulgarity. This practical mastery gives its possessors a 'nose' and a 'feeling', *without any need for cynical calculation*, for 'what needs to be done', where to do it, how and with whom, in view of all that has been done and is being done, all those who are doing it, and where.[22] Choosing the right place of publication, the right publisher, journal, gallery or magazine is vitally important because for each author, each form of production and product, there is a corresponding *natural site* in the field of production, and producers or products that are not in their right place are more or less bound to fail. All the homologies which guarantee a receptive audience and sympathetic critics for producers who have found their place in the structure work in the opposite way for those who have strayed from their natural site. Avant-garde publishers and the producers of best-sellers both agree that they would inevitably come to grief if they took it into their heads to publish works objectively assigned to the opposite pole in the publishing universe: Minuit best-sellers and Laffont *nouveaux romans*. Similarly, in accordance with the law that one only ever preaches to the converted, a critic can only 'influence' his readers in so far as they extend him this power because they are structurally attuned to him in their view of the social world, their tastes and their whole habitus. Jean-Jacques Gautier gives a good description of this elective affinity between the journalist, his paper and his readers: a good *Figaro* editor, who has chosen himself and been chosen through the same mechanisms, chooses a *Figaro* literary critic because 'he has the right tone for speaking to the readers of the paper', because, *without having deliberately tried,* 'he naturally speaks the language of *Le Figaro*, and is the paper's 'ideal reader'. 'If tomorrow I started speaking the language of *Les Temps Modernes*, for example, or *Saintes Chapelles des Lettres*, people would no longer read me or understand me, so they would not listen to me, because I would be assuming a certain number of ideas or arguments which our readers don't give a damn about.'[23] To each position there correspond presuppositions, a doxa, and the homology between the producers' positions and their clients' is the precondition for this complicity, which is that much more strongly required when fundamental values are involved, as they are in the theatre. The fact that the choices whereby individuals join groups or groups co-opt individuals are oriented by a practical mastery of the laws of the field explains the frequent occurrence of the miraculous agreement between objective structures and internalized structures which enables the producers of cultural goods to produce objectively necessary and overdetermined discourses in full freedom and sincerity.

The sincerity in duplicity and euphemization which gives ideological discourse its particular symbolic force derives, first, from the fact that the specific interests – relatively autonomous with respect to class interests – attached to a position in a specialized field cannot be satisfied legitimately, and therefore efficiently, except at the cost of perfect submission to the laws of the field (in this particular case, disavowal of the usual form of interest); and, second, from the fact that the homology which exists between all fields of struggle organized on the basis of an unequal distribution of a particular kind of capital means that the highly censored and euphemized discourses and practices which are thus produced by reference to 'pure', purely 'internal' ends are always predisposed to perform additional, external functions. They do so the more effectively the less aware they are of doing so, and when their adjustment to demand is not the product of conscious design but the result of a structural correspondence.

## THE LONG RUN AND THE SHORT RUN

The fundamental principle of the differences between 'commercial' businesses and 'cultural' businesses is to be found once again in the characteristics of cultural goods and of the market on which they are offered. A firm is that much closer to the 'commercial' pole (and, conversely, that much further from the 'cultural' pole), the more directly and completely the products it offers corresponds to a pre-existent demand, i.e. to pre-existent interests in pre-established forms. This gives, on the one hand, a short production cycle, based on the concern to minimize risks by adjusting in advance to the identifiable demand and provided with marketing circuits and presentational devices (eye-catching dustjackets, advertising, public relations, etc.) intended to ensure a rapid return of profits through rapid circulation of products with built-in obsolescence. On the other hand, there is a long production cycle, based on acceptance of the risk inherent in cultural investments[24] and above all on submission to the specific laws of the art trade. Having no market in the present, this entirely future-oriented production presupposes high-risk investments tending to build up stocks of products which may either relapse into the status of material objects (valued as such, by the weight of paper) or rise to the status of cultural objects endowed with an economic value incommensurate with the value of the material components which go into producing them.[25]

The uncertainty and ramdomness characterizing the production of cultural goods can be seen in the sales curves of three works published by Éditions de Minuit (Figure 3).[26] Curve A represents the sales of a prize-winning novel which, after a strong initial demand (of 6,143 copies distributed in 1959, 4,298 were sold by 1960 after deduction of unsold copies), achieves low annual sales (seventy or so a year on average). Robbe-Grillet's *La Jalousie* (curve B), published in 1957, sold only 746 copies in its first year and took four years to catch up with the initial sales of the prize-winning novel (in 1960) but, thanks to a steady annual rate of growth in sales (29 per cent a year average from 1960 to 1964, 19 per cent 1964 to 1968) had achieved a total of 29,462 in 1968. Beckett's *En attendant Godot* (curve C), published in 1952, took five years to reach 10,000 but grew at a fairly steady 20 per cent every year except 1963. From this point the curve begins to take on an exponential form and by 1968 (with an annual figure of 14,298) total sales had reached 64,897.

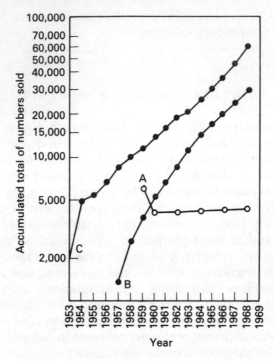

Figure 3   *Comparative growth in the sales of three books published by Éditions de Minuit*

Source: Éditions de Minuit.

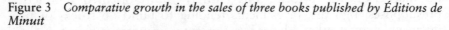

## TIME AND MONEY

Thus the various publishing houses can be characterized according to the distribution of their commitments between risky, long-term investments (*Godot*) and safe, short-term investments,[27] and, by the same token, according to the proportion of their authors who are long-term or short-term writers. The latter may include journalists extending their usual activity into 'current affairs' books, 'personalities' presenting their 'personal testimony' in essays or memoirs and professional writers who stick to the rules of a tried and tested aesthetic (award-winning literature, best-selling novels, etc.).[28]

An examination of two publishing houses that are characteristic of the two poles of the publishing field, Robert Laffont and Éditions de Minuit, will enable us to grasp the numerous aspects of the oppositions between the two sectors of the field. Robert Laffont is a large firm (700 employees) publishing a considerable number of new titles each year (about 200), overtly success-oriented (in 1976 it had seven print runs of over 100,000 copies, fourteen of over 50,000 and fifty of over 20,000). This entails a large sales department, considerable expenditure on advertising and public relations (especially directed towards booksellers), and also a systematic policy of choices guided by a sense of the safe investment (until 1975 almost half the Laffont list consisted of translations of works already successful abroad) and the hunt for best-sellers (the list of 'famous names' with which Robert Laffont refutes those who 'refuse to recognize them as serious literary publishers' includes Bernard Clavel, Max Gallo, Françoise Dorin, Georges Emmanuel Clancier and Pierre Rey). By contrast, Éditions de Minuit, a small firm employing a dozen people, publishing fewer than twenty titles a year (by no more than about forty novelists or dramatists in twenty-five years), devoting a minute proportion of its turnover to publicity (and even deriving a strategic advantage from its refusal to use the lower forms of public relations), is quite used to sales under 500 ('P's first book, which sold more than 500 copies, was only our ninth') and print runs under 3,000 (in 1975 it was stated that out of seventeen new titles published in the three years since 1971, fourteen had sold fewer than 3,000 copies and the other three had not gone beyond 5,000). The firm is always loss-making, if only its new publications are considered, but lives on its past investments, i.e. the profits regularly accruing from those of its publications which have become famous (e.g. *Godot*, which sold fewer than 200 copies in 1952 and twenty-five years later had sold more than 500,000 copies).

These two temporal structures correspond to two very different economic structures. Like all the other public companies (e.g. Hachette or Presses de la Cité), Laffont has an obligation to its shareholders (Time-Life in this case) to make profits, despite very substantial overheads, and so it must 'turn over' very rapidly what is essentially an economic capital (without taking the time required to convert it into cultural capital). Éditions de Minuit does not have to worry about profits (which are partly redistributed to the personnel) and can plough back the income from its ever-growing assets into long-term undertakings. The scale of the firm and the volume of production not only influence cultural policy through the size of the overheads and the concern with getting a return on the capital; they also directly affect the behaviour of those responsible for selecting manuscripts. The small publisher, with the aid of a few advisers who are themselves 'house' authors, is able to have personal knowledge of all the books published. In short, everything combines to discourage the manager of a big publishing house from going in for high-risk, long-term investments: the financial structure of his firm, the economic constraints which force him to seek a return on the capital, and therefore to think primarily in terms of sales, and the conditions in which he works, which make it practically impossible to have direct contact with manuscripts and authors.[29] By contrast, the avant-garde publisher is able to confront the financial risks he faces (which are, in any case, objectively smaller) by investing (in both senses) in undertakings which can, at best, bring only symbolic profits, but only on condition that he fully recognizes the specific stakes of the field of production and, like the writers or 'intellectuals' whom he publishes, pursues the sole specific profit awarded by the field, at least in the short term, i.e. 'renown' and the corresponding 'intellectual authority'.[30] The strategies which he applies in his relations with the press are perfectly adapted (without necesarily having been so conceived) to the objective demands of the most advanced fraction of the field, i.e. to the 'intellectual' ideal of negation, which demands refusal of temporal compromises and tends to establish a negative correlation between success and true artistic value. Whereas short-cycle production, like *haute couture*, is heavily dependent on a whole set of agents and institutions specializing in 'promotion' (newspaper, magazine, TV and radio critics) which must be constantly maintained and periodically mobilized (with the annual literary prizes performing a function analogous to that of fashion 'collections'),[31] long-cycle production, which derives practically no benefit from the free publicity of press articles about the prize competitions and the prizes themselves, depends entirely on the activity of a few 'talent-spotters', i.e. avant-garde authors and critics who 'make' the publishing house by giving it credit (by publishing with it, taking manuscripts there and speaking well of authors published by it) and expect it to merit their confidence by refraining from discrediting itself with excessively brilliant wordly successes ('Minuit would be devalued in the eyes of the hundred people around Saint-Germain who really count if it won the *Prix Goncourt*') and thereby discrediting those who are published by it or praise its publications ('intellectuals think less of writers who win prizes'; 'the ideal career for a young writer is a slow one').[32] It also depends on the educational system, which alone can provide those who preach in the desert with devotees and followers capable of recognizing their virtues.

The total opposition between *best-sellers*, here today and gone tomorrow, and *classics*, best-sellers over the long run, which owe their consecration, and therefore their widespread durable market, to the educational system,[33] is the basis not only of two completely different ways of organizing production and marketing, but also of two contrasting images of the activity of the writer and even the publisher: a simple businessperson or a bold 'talent-spotter' who will succeed only if he is able to sense the specific laws of a market yet to come, i.e. espouse the interests and demands of those who will make those laws, the writers he publishes.[34] There are also two opposing images of the criteria of success. For 'bourgeois' writers and their readers, success is intrinsically a guarantee of value. That is why, in this market, the successful get more successful. Publishers help to make best-sellers by printing further impressions; the best thing a critic can do for a book or play is to predict 'success' for it ('It's bound to be a runaway success' – R. Kanters, *L'Express*, 15–21 January 1973; 'I put my money on success for *Le Tournant* with my eyes closed' – Pierre Marcabru, *France-Soir*, 12 January 1973). Failure, of course, is an irrevocable condemnation; a writer without a public is a writer without talent (the same Robert Kanters refers to 'playwrights without talent and without an audience, such as Arrabal').

As for the opposing camp's vision, in which success is suspect[35] and asceticism in this world is the precondition for salvation in the next, its basis lies in the economy of cultural production itself, according to which investments are recompensed only if they are in a sense thrown away, like a gift, which can only achieve the most precious return gift, recognition (*reconnaissance*), so long as it is experienced as a one-way transaction; and, as with the gift, which it converts into pure generosity by masking the expected return-gift which the sychronization of barter reveals, it is the intervening time which provides a screen and disguises the profit awaiting the most disinterested investors.

## ORTHODOXY AND HERESY

The eschatological vision structuring the opposition between avant-garde and 'bourgeois' art, between the material ascesis which guarantees spiritual consecration and wordly success (which is marked, *inter alia*, by institutional recognition – prizes, academies, etc. – and by financial rewards), helps to disguise the true relationship between the field of cultural production and the field of power, by reproducing the opposition (which does not rule out complementarity) between the dominated and dominant fractions of the dominant class, between cultural power (associated with less economic wealth) and economic and political power (associated with less cultural wealth), in the specific logic of the intellectual field, that is, in the transfigured form of the conflict between two aesthetics. Specifically aesthetic conflicts about the legitimate vision of the world – in the last resort, about what deserves to be represented and the right way to represent it – are political conflicts (appearing in their most euphemized form) for the power to impose the dominant definition of reality, and social reality in particular. On the right, reproductive art[36] constructed in accordance with the generative schemes of 'straight', 'straightforward' representation of reality, and social reality in particular, i.e. orthodoxy (e.g., *par excellence*, 'bourgeois theatre') is likely to give those who perceive it in accordance with these schemes the reassuring experience of the immediate self-evidence of the representation, that is, of the necessity of the mode of representation and of the world represented. This orthodox art would be timeless if it were not continuously pushed into the past by the movement brought into the field of production by the dominated fractions' insistence on using the powers they are granted to change the world view and overturn the temporal and *temporary* hierarchies to which 'bourgeois' taste clings. As holders of an (always partial) delegated legitimacy in cultural matters, cultural producers – especially those who produce solely for other producers – always tend to divert their authority to their own advantage and therefore to impose their own variant of the dominant world view as the only legitimate one. But the challenging of the established artistic hierarchies and the heretical displacement of the socially accepted limit between what does and does not deserve to be preserved, admired and transmitted cannot achieve its specifically artistic effect of subversion unless it tacitly recognizes the fact and the legitimacy of such delimitation by making the shifting of that limit an artistic act and thereby claiming for the artist a monopoly in legitimate transgression of the boundary between the sacred and the profane, and therefore a monopoly in revolutions in artistic taxonomies.

The field of cultural production is the area *par excellence* of clashes between the dominant fractions of the dominant class, who fight there sometimes in person but more often through producers oriented towards defending their 'ideas' and satisfying their 'tastes', and the dominated fractions who are totally involved in this struggle.[37] This conflict brings about the integration in a single field of the various socially specialized sub-fields, particular markets which are completely separate in social and even geographical space, in which the different fractions of the dominant class can find products adjusted to their tastes, whether in the theatre, in painting, fashion or decoration.

The 'polemical' view which makes a sweeping condemnation of all economically powerful firms ignores the distinction between those which are only rich in economic capital, and treat cultural goods – books, plays or pictures – as ordinary products, i.e. as sources of immediate profit, and those which derive a sometimes very substantial economic profit from the cultural capital which they originally accumulated through strategies based on denial of the 'economy'. The differences in the scale of the businesses, measured by turnover or staff, are matched by equally decisive differences in their relation to the 'economy' which, among recently established smaller firms, separate the small 'commercial' publishers, often heading for rapid growth, such as Lattès, Laffont (as distinct from Robert Laffont), Orban, Authier or Mengès,[38] and the small avant-garde publishers, which are often short-lived (Galilée, France Adèle, Entente, Phébus), just as, at the other extreme, they separate the 'great publisher' from the 'big publisher', a great consecrated publisher like Gallimard from a big 'book merchant' like Nielsen.

Without entering into a systematic analysis of the field of the galleries, which, owing to the homology with the field of publishing, would lead to repetitions, we may simply observe that here too the differences which separate the galleries according to their seniority (and their celebrity), and therefore according to the degree of consecration and the market value of the works they own, are replicated by differences in their relation to the 'economy'. The 'sales galleries' (e.g. Beaubourg), having no 'stable' of their own, exhibit in relatively eclectic fashion painters of very different periods, schools and ages (abstracts as well as post-surrealists, a few European hyper-realists, some new realists), i.e. works whose greater 'accessibility' (owing to their more classic status or their 'decorative' potential) can find purchasers outside the circle of professional and semi-professional collectors (among the 'jet-set executives' and 'trendy industrialists', as an informant put it). This enables them to pick out and attract a fraction of the avant-garde painters who have already been 'noticed' by offering them a slightly compromising form of consecration, i.e. a market in which the prices are much higher than in the avant-garde galleries.[39] By contrast, galleries like Sonnabend, Denise René or Durand-Ruel, which mark dates in the history of painting because they have been able in their time to assemble a 'school', are characterized by a *systematic slant*.[40] Thus in the succession of painters presented by the Sonnabend gallery one can see the logic of an artistic development which leads from the 'new American painting' and pop art, with painters such as Rauschenberg, Jaspers Johns, Jim Dine, to Oldenburg, Lichtenstein, Wesselman, Rosenquist, Warhol, sometimes classified under the label minimal art, and to the most recent innovations of *art pauvre*, conceptual art and art by correspondence. Likewise, there is a clear connection between the geometric abstraction which made the name of the Denise René gallery (founded in 1945 and inaugurated with a Vasarely exhibition) and kinetic art, with artists such as Max Bill and Vasarely forming a sort of link between the visual experiments of the inter-war years (especially the Bauhaus) and the optical and technological experiments of the new generation.

## WAYS OF GROWING OLD

The opposition between the two economies, that is to say, between two relationships to the 'economy', can thus be seen as an opposition between two life-cycles of the cultural production business, two different ways in which firms, producers and products *grow old*.[41] The trajectory leading from the avant-garde to consecration and the trajectory leading from the small firm to the 'big' firm are mutually exclusive. The small commercial firm has no more chance of becoming a great consecrated firm than the big 'commercial' writer (e.g. Guy des Cars or Cécil Saint-Laurent) has of occupying a recognized position in the consecrated avant-garde. In the case of 'commercial' firms, whose sole target is the accumulation of 'economic' capital and which can only get bigger or disappear (through bankruptcy or takeover), the only pertinent distinction concerns the size of the firm, which tends to grow with time; in the case of firms characterized by a high degree of disavowal of the 'economy' and submission to the specific logic of the cultural goods economy, the chronological opposition between the newcomers and the old-established, the challengers and the veterans, the avant-garde and the 'classic', tends to merge with the 'economic' opposition between the poor and the rich (who are also the big), the 'cheap' and the 'dear', and ageing is almost inevitably accompanied by an 'economic' transformation of the relation to the 'economy', i.e. a moderating of the denial of the 'economy' which is in dialectical relation with the scale of business and the size of the firm. The only defence against 'growing old' is a refusal to 'get fat' through profits and for profit, a refusal to enter the dialectic of profit which, by increasing the size of the firm and consequently the overheads, imposes a pursuit of profit through larger markets, leading to the devaluation entailed in a 'mass appeal'.[42]

A firm which enters the phase of exploiting accumulated cultural capital runs two different economies simultaneously, one oriented towards production, authors and innovation (in the case of Gallimard, this is the series edited by Georges Lambrichs), the other towards exploiting its resources and marketing its consecrated products (with series such as the Pléiade editions and especially *Folio* or *Idées*). It is easy to imagine the contradictions which result from the incompatibility of the two economies. The organization appropriate for producing, marketing and promoting one category of products is totally unsuited for the other. Moreover, the weight of the constraints which management and marketing bring to bear on the institution and on ways of thinking tends to rule out high-risk investments – when, that is, the authors who might give rise to them are not already turned towards other publishers by the firm's prestige. (They may equally be discouraged by the fact that the 'intellectual' series tend to pass unnoticed when they appear in lists in which they are 'out of place' or even 'incongruous' e.g. as an extreme case, Laffont's *Écarts* and *Change* series.) It goes without saying that though the disappearance of the firm's founder may accelerate the process, it is not sufficient to explain a process which is inscribed in the logic of the development of cultural businesses.

The differences which separate the small avant-garde firms from the 'big firms' and 'great publishers' have their equivalents in the differences that can be found, among the products, between the 'new' product, temporarily without 'economic' value, the 'old' product, irretrievably devalued, and the 'ancient' or 'classic' product, which has a constant or constantly growing 'economic' value. One also finds similar differences among the producers, between the avant-garde, recruited mainly among the (biologically) young, without being limited to a generation, 'finished' or 'outdated' authors or artists (who may be biologically young) and the consecrated avant-garde, the 'classics'.

### THE CLASSICAL AND THE OLD-FASHIONED

It is clear that the primacy the field of cultural production accords to youth can, once again, be traced back to the disavowal of power and of the 'economy' which lies at the field's foundation. The reason why 'intellectuals' and artists always tend to align themselves with 'youth' in their manner of dress and in their whole bodily *hexis* is that, in representations as in reality, the opposition between the 'old' and the 'young' is homologous with the opposition between power and 'bourgeois' seriousness on the one hand, and indifference to power or money and the 'intellectual' refusal of the 'spirit of seriousness' on the other hand. The 'bourgeois' world view, which measures age by power or by the corresponding relation to power, endorses this opposition when it identifies the 'intellectual' with the young 'bourgeois' by virtue of their common status as dominated fractions of the dominant group, from whom money and power are temporarily withheld.[43]

But the priority accorded to 'youth' and to the associated values of change and originality cannot be understood solely in terms of the relationship between 'artists' and 'bourgeois'. It also expresses the specific law of change in the field of production, i.e. the dialectic of distinction whereby institutions, schools, artists and works which are inevitably associated with a moment in the history of art, which have 'marked a date' or which 'become dated', are condemned to fall into the past and to become *classic* or *outdated*, to drop into the 'dustbin' of history or become part of history, in the eternal present of *culture*, where schools and tendencies that were totally incompatible 'in their time' can peacefully coexist because they have been canonized, academicized and neutralized.

## BEING DIFFERENT

It is not sufficient to say that the history of the field is the history of the struggle for the monopolistic power to impose the legitimate categories of perception and appreciation. The *struggle itself* creates the history of the field; through the struggle the field is given a temporal dimension. The ageing of authors, works or schools is something quite different from the product of a mechanical slippage into the past. It is the continuous creation of the battle between those who have made their names [*fait date*] and are struggling to stay in view and those who cannot make their own names without relegating to the past the established figures, whose interest lies in freezing the movement of time, fixing the present state of the field for ever. On one side are the dominant figures, who want continuity, identity, reproduction; on the other, the newcomers, who seek discontinuity, rupture, difference, revolution. To 'make one's name' [*faire date*] means making one's *mark*, achieving recognition (in both senses) of one's *difference* from other producers, especially the most consecrated of them; at the same time, it means *creating a new position* beyond the positions presently occupied, *ahead* of them, in the *avant-garde*. To introduce difference is to produce time. Hence the importance, in this struggle for life and survival, of the *distinctive marks* which, at best, aim to identify what are often the most superficial and most visible properties of a set of works or producers. Words – the names of schools or groups, proper names – are so important only because they make things. These distinctive signs produce existence in a world in which the only way to *be* is to be *different*, to 'make one's name', either personally or as a group. The names of the schools or groups which have proliferated in recent painting (pop art, minimal art, process art, land art, body art, conceptive art, *arte povera*, Fluxus, new realism, *nouvelle figuration*, support-surface, *art pauvre*, op art, kinetic art, etc.) are pseudo-concepts, *practical* classifying tools which create resemblances and differences by naming them; they are produced in the *struggle for recognition* by the artists themselves or their accredited critics and function as *emblems* which distinguish galleries, groups and artists and therefore the products they make or sell.[44]

As the newcomers come into existence, i.e. accede to legitimate difference, or even, for a certain time, exclusive legitimacy, they necessarily push back into the past the consecrated producers with whom they are compared, 'dating' their products and the taste of those who remain attached to them. Thus the various galleries or publishing houses, like the various artists or writers, are distributed at every moment according to their artistic age, i.e. according to the age of their mode of artistic production and the degree to which this generative scheme, which is also a scheme of perception and appreciation, has been canonized and secularized. The field of the galleries reproduces *in synchrony* the history of artistic movements since the late nineteenth century. Each major gallery was an avant-garde gallery at some time or other, and it is that much more famous and that much more capable of consecrating (or, which amounts to the same thing, sells that much more dearly), the more distant its *floruit*, the more widely known and recognized its 'brand' ('geometrical abstract' or 'American pop') but also the more it is encapsulated in that 'brand' ('Durand-Ruel, the Impressionist dealer'), in a pseudo-concept which is also a destiny.

At every moment, in whichever field (the field of class struggles, the field of the dominant class, the field of cultural production), the agents and institutions involved in the game are at once contemporaries and out of phase. The field of the present is just another name for the field of struggles (as shown by the fact that an author of the past is present exactly in so far as he or she is at stake) and contemporaneity in the sense of presence in the same present, in the present and presence of others, exists, in practice, only in the struggle which synchronizes discordant times (so that, as I hope to show elsewhere, one of the major effects of great historical crises, of the events which *make history* [*font date*], is that they synchronize the times of fields defined by specific structural durations). But the struggle which *produces* contemporaneity in the form of the confrontation of different times can only take place because the agents and groups it brings together are not present in the same present. One only has to think of a particular field (painting, literature or the theatre) to see that the agents and institutions who clash, objectively at least, through competition and conflict, are separated in time and in terms of time. One group, situated at the vanguard, have no contemporaries with whom they exchange recognition (apart from other avant-garde producers), and therefore no audience, except in the future. The other group, commonly called the 'conservatives', only recognize their contemporaries in the past. The temporal movement resulting from the appearance of a group capable of 'making history' by establishing an advanced position induces a displacement of the structure of the field of the present, i.e. of the chronological hierarchy of the opposing positions in a given field (e.g. pop art, kinetic art and figurative art). Each position is moved down one rung in the chronological hierarchy which is at the same time a social hierarchy. The avant-garde is at every moment separated by an artistic generation (the gap between two modes of artistic production) from the consecrated avant-garde, which is itself separated by another artistic generation from the avant-garde that was already consecrated at the moment it entered the field. This is why, in the space of the artistic field as in social space, distances between styles or lifestyles are never better measured than in terms of time.[45]

The consecrated authors who dominate the field of production also dominate the market; they are not only the most expensive or the most profitable but also the most readable and the most acceptable because they have become part of 'general culture' through a process of familiarization which may or may not have been accompanied by specific teaching. This means that through them, the strategies directed against their domination always additionally hit the distinguished consumers of their distinctive products. To bring a new producer, a new product and a new system of tastes on to the market at a given moment is to push the whole set of producers, products and systems of tastes into the past. The process whereby the field of production becomes a temporal structure also defines the temporal status of taste. Because the different positions in the hierarchical space of the field of production (which can be equally well identified by the names of institutions, galleries, publishers and theatres or by the names of artists or schools) are at the same time tastes in a social hierarchy, every transformation of the structure of the field leads to a displacement of the structure of tastes, i.e. of the system of symbolic distinctions between groups. Oppositions homologous with those existing today between the taste of avant-garde artists, the taste of 'intellectuals', advanced 'bourgeois' taste and provincial 'bourgeois' taste, which find their means of expression on markets symbolized by the Sonnabend, Denise René and Durand-Ruel galleries, would have been able to express themselves equally effectively in 1945, when Denise René represented the avant-garde, or in 1875, when Durand-Ruel was in that position.

This model is particularly relevant nowadays, because owing to the near-perfect unification of the artistic field and its history, each artistic act which 'makes history' by introducing a new position into the field 'displaces' the whole series of previous artistic acts. Because the whole series of pertinent events is practically present in the latest, in the same way that the six digits already dialled on the telephone are contained in the seventh, an aesthetic act is irreducible to any other act in a different place in the series and the series itself tends towards uniqueness and irreversibility. As Marcel Duchamp points out, this explains why *returns* to past styles have never been more frequent than in these times of frenetic pursuit of originality: 'The characteristic of the century now coming to an end is that it is like a double-barrelled gun. Kandinsky and Kupka invented abstraction. Then abstraction died. No one was going to talk about it any more. It came back thirty-five years later with the American abstract expressionists. You could say that cubism reappeared in an impoverished form in the post-war Paris school. Dada came back in the same way. A second shot, second wind. It's a phenomenon typical of this century. You didn't find that in the eighteenth or nineteenth centuries. After the Romantics, came Courbet. And Romanticism never came back. Even the pre-Raphaelites aren't a rehash of the Romantics.'[46]

In fact, these are always *apparent* returns, since they are separated from what they rediscover by a negative reference to something which was itself the negation (of the negation of the negation, etc.) of what they rediscover (when, that is, the intention is not simply of pastiche, a parody which presupposes all the intervening history).[47] In the present stage of the artistic field, there is no room for naïveté, and every act, every gesture, every event, is, as a painter nicely put it, 'a sort of nudge or wink between accomplices'.[48] In and through the games of distinction, these winks and nudges, silent, hidden references to other artists, past or present, confirm a complicity which excludes the layperson, who is always bound to miss what is essential, namely the interrelations and interactions of which the work is only the silent trace. Never has the very structure of the field been present so practically in every act of production.

Never too has the irreducibility of the work of cultural production to the artist's own labour appeared so clearly. The primary reason is that the new definition of the artist and of artistic work brings the artist's work closer to that of the 'intellectual' and makes it more dependent than ever on 'intellectual' commentaries. Whether as critics but also the leaders of a school (e.g. Restany and the new realists), or as fellow-travellers contributing their reflexive discourse to the production of a work which is always in part its own commentary or to reflection of an art which often itself incorporates a reflection on art, intellectuals have never before so directly participated, through their work on art and the artist, in an artistic work which always consists partly of *working on oneself* as an artist. Accompanied by historians writing the chronicles of their discoveries, by philosophers who comment on their 'acts' and who interpret and over-interpret their works, artists can constantly invent the distinguishing strategies on which their artistic survival depends, only by putting into their practice the practical mastery of the objective truth of their practice, thanks to the combination of knowingness and naïveté, calculation and innocence, faith and bad faith that is required by *mandarin games*, cultivated games with the inherited culture, whose common feature is that they identify 'creation' with the introduction of *deviations* [*écarts*], which only the initiated can perceive, with respect to forms and formulae that are known to all. The emergence of this new definition of the artist and his or her craft cannot be understood independently of the transformations of the artistic field. The constitution of an unprecedented array of institutions for recording, preserving and analysing works (reproductions, catalogues, art journals, museums acquiring the most modern works, etc.), the growth in the personnel employed, full-time or part-time, in the *celebration* of works of art, the increased circulation of works and artists, with great international exhibitions and the increasing number of chains of galleries with branches in many countries – all combine to favour the establishment of an unprecedented relationship between the body of interpreters and the work of art, analogous to that found in the great esoteric traditions; to such an extent that one has to be blind not to see that discourse about a work is not a mere accompaniment, intended to assist its perception and appreciation, but a stage in the production of the work, of its meaning and value. But once again it is sufficient to quote Marcel Duchamp:

Q.    But to come back to your ready-mades, I thought that R. Mutt, the signature on *The Fountain*, was the manufacturer's name. But in the article by Rosalind Krauss, I read: 'R. Mutt, a pun on the German, Armut, or poverty'. 'Poverty' would entirely change the meaning of *The Fountain*.

M.D.   Rosalind Krauss? The redhead? It isn't that at all. You can deny it. Mutt comes from Mott Works, the name of a big firm that makes sanitary equipment. But Mott was too close, so I made it Mutt, because there was a strip cartoon in the papers in those days, Mutt and Jeff, everybody knew it. So right from the start there was a resonance. Mutt was a fat little guy, and Jeff was tall and thin . . . I wanted a different name. And I added Richard . . . Richard is a good name for a loo! You see, it's the opposite of poverty . . . But not even that, just R. – R. Mutt.

Q.    What possible interpretation is there of the *Bicycle Wheel*? Should one see it as the integration of movement into the work of art? Or as a fundamental point of departure, like the Chinese who invented the wheel?

M.D.  That machine has no intention, except to get rid of the appearance of a work of art. It was a whim, I didn't call it a work of art. I wanted to throw off the desire to create works of art. Why do works have to be static? The thing – the bicycle wheel – came before the idea. Without any intention of making a song and dance about it, not at all so as to say '*I* did that, and nobody has ever done it before me.' Besides, the originals have never been sold.

Q.  What about the geometry book left out in the weather? Can one say that it's the idea of integrating time and space? With a pun on 'geométrie dans l'espace' (solid geometry) and 'temps', the rain and sun that transforms the book?

M.D.  No, no more than the idea of integrating movement and sculpture. It was a joke. A pure joke. To denigrate the solemnity of a book of principles.

Here we see, directly exposed, the injection of meaning and value by commentary and commentary on commentary – to which the naïve but knowing exposure of the falsity of the commentary contributes in its turn. The ideology of the inexhaustible work of art, or of 'reading' as re-creation masks – through the quasi-exposure which is often seen in matters of faith – the fact that the work is indeed made not twice, but a hundred times, by all those who are interested in it, who find a material or symbolic profit in reading it, classifying it, deciphering it, commenting on it, combating it, knowing it, possessing it. Enrichment accompanies ageing when the work manages to enter the game, when it becomes a stake in the game and so incorporates some of the energy produced in the struggle of which it is the object. The struggle, which sends the work into the past, is also what ensures it a form of survival; lifting it from the state of a dead letter, a mere thing subject to the ordinary laws of ageing, the struggle at least ensures it has the sad eternity of academic debate.[49]

# 3

# The Market of Symbolic Goods

Theories and schools, like microbes
and globules, devour each other and,
through their struggle, ensure the
continuity of life.

M. Proust, *Sodom and Gomorrah*

## THE LOGIC OF THE PROCESS OF AUTONOMIZATION

Dominated by external sources of legitimacy throughout the middle ages, part of the Renaissance and, in the case of French court life, throughout the classical age, intellectual and artistic life has progressively freed itself from aristocratic and ecclesiastical tutelage as well as from its aesthetic and ethical demands. This process is correlated with the constant growth of a public of potential consumers, of increasing social diversity, which guarantee the producers of symbolic goods minimal conditions of economic independence and, also, a competing principle of legitimacy. It is also correlated with the constitution of an ever-growing, ever more diversified corps of producers and merchants of symbolic goods, who tend to reject all constraints apart from technical imperatives and credentials. Finally, it is correlated with the multiplication and diversification of agencies of consecration placed in a situation of competition for cultural legitimacy: not only academies and salons, but also institutions for diffusion, such as publishers and theatrical impresarios, whose selective operations are invested with a truly cultural legitimacy even if they are subordinated to economic and social constraints.[1]

The autonomization of intellectual and artistic production is thus correlative with the constitution of a socially distinguishable category of professional artists or intellectuals who are less inclined to recognize rules other than the specifically intellectual or artistic traditions handed down by their predecessors, which serve as a point of departure or rupture. They are also increasingly in a position to liberate their products from all external constraints, whether the moral censure and aesthetic programmes of a proselytizing church or the academic controls and directives of political power, inclined to regard art as an instrument of propaganda. This process of autonomization is comparable to those in other realms. Thus, as Engels wrote to Conrad Schmidt, the appearance of law as such, i.e. as an 'autonomous field', is correlated with a division of labour that led to the constitution of a body of professional jurists. Max Weber similarly notes, in *Wirtschaft und Gesellschaft*, that the 'rationalization' of religion owes its own 'auto-normativity' – relative independence of economic factors – to the fact that it rests on the development of a priestly corps with its own interests.

The process leading to the development of art as art is also correlated with the transformed relations between artists and non-artists and hence, with other artists. This transformation leads to the establishment of a relatively autonomous artistic field and to a fresh definition of the artist's function as well as that of his art. Artistic development towards autonomy progressed at different rates, according to the society and field of artistic life in question. It began in *quattrocento* Florence, with the affirmation of a truly artistic legitimacy, i.e. the right of artists to legislate within their own sphere – that of form and style – free from subordination to religious or political interests. It was interrupted for two centuries under the influence of absolute monarchy and – with the Counter-reformation – of the Church; both were eager to procure artists a social position and function distinct from the manual labourers, yet not integrated into the ruling class.

This movement towards artistic autonomy accelerated abruptly with the Industrial Revolution and the Romantic reaction. The development of a veritable cultural industry and, in particular, the relationship between the daily press and literature, encouraging the mass production of works produced by quasi-industrial methods – such as the serialized story (or, in other fields, melodrama and vaudeville) – coincides with the extension of the public, resulting from the expansion of primary education, which turned new classes (including women) into consumers of culture.[2] The development of the system of cultural production is accompanied by a process of differentiation generated by the diversity of the publics at which the different categories of producers aim their products. Symbolic goods are a two-faced reality, a commodity and a symbolic object. Their specifically cultural value and their commercial value remain relatively independent, although the economic sanction may come to reinforce their cultural consecration.[3]

By an apparent paradox, as the art market began to develop, writers and artists found themselves able to affirm the irreducibility of the work of art to the status of a simple article of merchandise and, at the same time, the singularity of the intellectual and artistic condition. The process of differentiation among fields of practice produces conditions favourable to the construction of 'pure' theories (of economics, politics, law, art, etc.), which reproduce the prior differentiation of the social structures in the initial abstraction by which they are constituted.[4] The emergence of the work of art as a commodity, and the appearance of a distinct category of producers of symbolic goods specifically destined for the market, to some extent prepared the ground for a pure theory of art, that is, of art as art. It did so by dissociating art-as-commodity from art-as-pure-signification, produced according to a purely symbolic intent for purely symbolic appropriation, that is, for disinterested delectation, irreducible to simple material possession.

The ending of dependence on a patron or collector and, more generally, the ending of dependence upon direct commissions, with the development of an impersonal market, tends to increase the liberty of writers and artists. They can hardly fail to notice, however, that this liberty is purely formal; it constitutes no more than the condition of their submission to the laws of the market of symbolic goods, that is, to a form of demand which necessarily lags behind the supply of the commodity (in this case, the work of art). They are reminded of this demand through sales figures and other forms of pressure, explicit or diffuse, exercised by publishers, theatre managers, art dealers. It follows that those 'inventions' of Romanticism – the representation of culture as a kind of superior reality, irreducible to the vulgar demands of economics, and the ideology of free, disinterested 'creation' founded on the spontaneity of innate inspiration – appear to be just so many reactions to the pressures of an anonymous market. It is significant that the appearance of an anonymous 'bourgeois' public, and the irruption of methods or techniques borrowed from the economic order, such as collective production or advertising for cultural products, coincides with the rejection of bourgeois aesthetics and with the methodical attempt to distinguish the artist and the intellectual from other commoners by positing the unique products of 'creative genius' against interchangeable products, utterly and completely reducible to their commodity value. Concomitantly, the absolute autonomy of the 'creator' is affirmed, as is his claim to recognize as recipient of his art none but an *alter ego* – another 'creator' – whose understanding of works of art presupposes an identical 'creative' disposition.

## THE STRUCTURE AND FUNCTIONING OF THE FIELD OF
## RESTRICTED PRODUCTION

The field of production and circulation of symbolic goods is defined as the system of objective relations among different instances, functionally defined by their role in the division of labour of production, reproduction and diffusion of symbolic goods. The field of production *per se* owes its own structure to the opposition between the *field of restricted production* as a system producing cultural goods (and the instruments for appropriating these goods) objectively destined for a public of producers of cultural goods, and the *field of large-scale cultural production*, specifically organized with a view to the production of cultural goods destined for non-producers of cultural goods, 'the public at large'. In contrast to the field of large-scale cultural production, which submits to the laws of competition for the conquest of the largest possible market, the field of restricted production tends to develop its own criteria for the evaluation of its products, thus achieving the truly cultural recognition accorded by the peer group whose members are both privileged clients and competitors.

The field of restricted production can only become a system objectively producing for producers by breaking with the public of non-producers, that is, with the non-intellectual fractions of the dominant class. This rupture is only the inverse image, in the cultural sphere, of the relations that develop between intellectuals and the dominant fractions of the dominant class in the economic and political sphere. From 1830 literary society isolated itself in an aura of indifference and rejection towards the buying and reading public, i.e. towards the 'bourgeois'. By an effect of circular causality, separation and isolation engender further separation and isolation, and cultural production develops a dynamic autonomy. Freed from the censorship and auto-censorship consequent on direct confrontation with a public foreign to the profession, and encountering within the corps of producers itself a public at once of critics and accomplices, it tends to obey its own logic, that of the continual outbidding inherent to the dialectic of cultural distinction.

The autonomy of a field of restricted production can be measured by its power to define its own criteria for the production and evaluation of its products. This implies translation of all external determinations in conformity with its own principles of functioning. Thus, the more cultural producers form a closed field of competition for cultural legitimacy, the more the internal demarcations appear irreducible to any external factors of economic, political or social differentiation.[5]

It is significant that the progress of the field of restricted production towards autonomy is marked by an increasingly distinct tendency of criticism to devote itself to the task, not of producing the instruments of appropriation – the more imperatively demanded by a work the further it separates itself from the public – but of providing a 'creative' interpretation for the benefit of the 'creators'. And so, tiny 'mutual admiration societies' grew up, closed in upon their own esotericism, as, simultaneously, signs of a new solidarity between artist and critic emerged. This new criticism, no longer feeling itself qualified to formulate peremptory verdicts, placed itself unconditionally at the service of the artist. It attempted scrupulously to decipher his or her intentions, while paradoxically excluding the public of non-producers from the entire business by attesting, through its 'inspired' readings, the intelligibility of works which were bound to remain unintelligible to those not sufficiently integrated into the producers' field.[6] Intellectuals and artists always look suspiciously – though not without a certain fascination – at dazzlingly successful works and authors, sometimes to the extent of seeing wordly failure as a guarantee of salvation in the hereafter: among other reasons for this, the interference of the 'general public' is such that it threatens the field's claims to a monopoly of cultural consecration. It follows that the gulf between the hierarchy of producers dependent on 'public success' (measured by volume of sales or fame outside the body of producers) and the hierarchy dependent upon the degree of recognition within the peer competitor group undoubtedly constitutes the best indicator of the autonomy of the field of restricted production, that is, of the disjunction between its own principles of evaluation and those that the 'general public' – and especially the non-intellectual fraction of the dominant class – applies to its productions.

No one has ever completely extracted all the implications of the fact that the writer, the artist, or even the scientist writes not only for a public, but for a public of equals who are also competitors. Few people depend as much as artists and intellectuals do for their self-image upon the image others, and particularly other writers and artists, have of them. 'There are', writes Jean-Paul Sartre, 'qualities that we acquire only through the judgements of others.'[7] This is especially so for the quality of a writer, artist or scientist, which is so difficult to define because it exists only in, and through, co-optation, understood as the circular relations of reciprocal recognition among peers.[8] Any act of cultural production implies an affirmation of its claim to cultural legitimacy:[9] when different producers confront each other, it is still in the name of their claims to orthodoxy or, in Max Weber's terms, to the legitimate and monopolized use of a certain class of symbolic goods; when they are recognized, it is their claim to orthodoxy that is being recognized. As witnessed by the fact that oppositions express themselves in terms of reciprocal excommunication, the field of restricted production can never be dominated by one orthodoxy without continuously being dominated by the general question of orthodoxy itself, that is, by the question of the criteria defining the legitimate exercise of a certain type of cultural practice. It follows that the degree of autonomy enjoyed by a field of restricted production is measurable by the degree to which it is capable of functioning as a specific market, generating a specifically cultural type of scarcity and value irreducible to the economic scarcity and value of the goods in question. To put it another way, the more the field is capable of functioning as a field of competition for cultural legitimacy, the more individual production must be oriented towards the search for culturally pertinent features endowed with value in the field's own economy. This confers properly cultural value on the producers by endowing them with marks of distinction (a speciality, a manner, a style) recognized as such within the historically available cultural taxonomies.

Consequently, it is a structural law, and not a fault in nature, that draws intellectuals and artists into the dialectic of cultural distinction – often confused with an all-out quest for any difference that might raise them out of anonymity and insignificance.[10] The same law also imposes limits within which the quest may be carried on legitimately. The brutality with which a strongly integrated intellectual or artistic community condemns any unorthodox attempt at distinction bears witness to the fact that the community can affirm the autonomy of the specifically cultural orders only if it controls the dialectic of cultural distinction, continually liable to degenerate into an anomic quest for difference at any price.

It follows from all that has just been said that the principles of differentiation regarded as most legitimate by an autonomous field are those which most completely express the specificity of a determinate type of practice. In the field of art, for example, stylistic and technical principles tend to become the privileged subject of debate among producers (or their interpreters). Apart from laying bare the desire to exclude those artists suspected of submitting to external demands, the affirmation of the primacy of form over function, of the mode of representation over the object of representation, is the most specific expression of the field's claim to produce and impose the principles of a properly cultural legitimacy regarding both the production and the reception of an art-work.[11] Affirming the primacy of the saying over the thing said, sacrificing the 'subject' to the manner in which it is treated, constraining language in order to draw attention to language, all this comes down to an affirmation of the specificity and the irreplaceability of the product and producer. Delacroix said, aptly, 'All subjects become good through the merits of their author. Oh! young artist, do you seek a subject? Everything is a subject; the subject is you yourself, your impression, your emotions before nature. You must look within yourself, and not around you.'[12] The true subject of the work of art is nothing other than the specifically artistic manner in which artists grasp the world, those infallible signs of his mastery of his art. Stylistic principles, in becoming the dominant object of position-takings and oppositions between producers, are ever more rigorously perfected and fulfilled in works of art. At the same time, they are ever more systematically affirmed in the theoretical discourse produced by and through confrontation. Because the logic of cultural distinction leads producers to develop original modes of expression – a kind of stylistic axiomatic in rupture with its antecedents – and to exhaust all the possibilities inherent in the conventional system of procedures, the different types of restricted production (painting, music, novels, theatre, poetry, etc.) are destined to fulfil themselves in their most specific aspects – those least reducible to any other form of expression.

The almost perfect circularity and reversibility of the relations of cultural production and consumption resulting from the objectively closed nature of the field of restricted production enable the development of symbolic production to take on the form of an almost reflexive history. The incessant explication and redefinition of the foundations of his work provoked by criticism or the work of others determines a decisive transformation of the relation between the producer and his work, which reacts, in turn, on the work itself.

Few works do not bear within them the imprint of the system of positions in relation to which their originality is defined; few works do not contain indications of the manner in which the author conceived the novelty of his undertaking or of what, in his own eyes, distinguished it from his contemporaries and precursors. The objectification achieved by criticism which elucidates the meaning objectively inscribed in a work, instead of subjecting it to normative judgements, tends to play a determining role in this process by stressing the efforts of artists and writers to realize their idiosyncrasy. The parallel variations in critical interpretation, in the producer's discourse, and even in the structure of the work itself, bear witness to the recognition of critical discourse by the producer – both because he feels himself to be recognized through it, and because he recognizes himself within it. The public meaning of a work in relation to which the author must define himself originates in the process of circulation and consumption dominated by the objective relations between the institutions and agents implicated in the process. The social relations which produce this public meaning are determined by the relative position these agents occupy in the structure of the field of restricted production. These relations, e.g. between author and publisher, publisher and critic, author and critic, are revealed as the ensemble of relations attendant on the 'publication' of the work, that is, its becoming a public object. In each of these relations, each of these agents engages not only his own image of other factors in the relationship (consecrated or exorcised author, avant-garde or traditional publisher, etc.) which depends on his relative position within the field, but also his image of the other factor's image of himself, i.e. of the social definition of his objective position in the field.

To appreciate the gulf separating experimental art, which originates in the field's own internal dialectic, from popular art forms, it suffices to consider the opposition between the evolutionary logic of popular language and that of literary language. As this restricted language is produced and reproduced in accordance with social relations dominated by the quest for distinction, its use obeys what one might term 'the gratuitousness principle'. Its manipulation demands the almost reflexive knowledge of schemes of expression which are transmitted by an education explicitly aimed at inculcating the allegedly appropriate categories.

'Pure' poetry appears as the conscious and methodical application of a system of explicit principles which were at work, though only in a diffuse manner, in earlier writings. Its most specific effects, for example, derive from games of suspense and surprise, from the consecrated betrayal of expectations, and from the gratifying frustration provoked by archaism, preciosity, lexicological or syntactic dissonances, the destruction of stereotyped sounds or meaning sequences, ready-made formulae, *idées reçues* and commonplaces. The recent history of music, whose evolution consists in the increasingly professionalized search for technical solutions to fundamentally technical problems, appears to be the culmination of a process of refinement which began the moment popular music became subject to the learned manipulation of professionals. But probably nowhere is this dynamic model of a field tending to closure more completely fulfilled than in the history of painting. Having banished narrative content with impressionism and recognizing only specifically pictorial principles, painting progressively repudiated all traces of naturalism and sensual hedonism. Painting was thus set on the road to an explicit employment of the most characteristically pictorial principles of painting, which was tantamount to the questioning of these principles and, hence, of painting itself.[13]

One need only compare the functional logic of the field of restricted production with the laws governing both the circulation of symbolic goods and the production of the consumers to perceive that such an autonomously developing field, making no reference to external demands, tends to nullify the conditions for its acceptance outside the field. To the extent that its products require extremely scarce instruments of appropriation, they are bound to precede their market or to have no clients at all, apart from producers themselves. Consequently they tend to fulfil socially distinctive functions, at first in conflicts between fractions of the dominant class and eventually, in relations among social classes. By an effect of circular causality, the structural gap between supply and demand contributes to the artists' determination to steep themselves in the search for 'originality' (with its concomitant ideology of the unrecognized or misunderstood 'genius'). This comes about, as Arnold Hauser has suggested,[14] by placing them in difficult economic circumstances, and, above all, by effectively ensuring the incommensurability of the specifically cultural value and economic value of a work.

### THE FIELD OF INSTANCES OF REPRODUCTION AND CONSECRATION

Works produced by the field of restricted production are 'pure', 'abstract' and 'esoteric'. They are 'pure' because they demand of the receiver a specifically aesthetic disposition in accordance with the principles of their production. They are 'abstract' because they call for a multiplicity of specific approaches, in contrast with the undifferentiated art of primitive societies, which is unified within an immediately accessible spectacle involving music, dance, theatre and song.[15] They are 'esoteric' for all the above reasons and because their complex structure continually implies tacit reference to the entire history of previous structures, and is accessible only to those who possess practical or theoretical mastery of a refined code, of successive codes, and of the code of these codes.

So, while consumption in the field of large-scale cultural production is more or less independent of the educational level of consumers (which is quite understandable, since this system tends to adjust to the level of demand), works of restricted art owe their specifically cultural rarity, and thus their function as elements of social distinction, to the rarity of the instruments with which they may be deciphered. This rarity is a function of the unequal distribution of the conditions underlying the acquisition of the specifically aesthetic disposition and of the codes indispensable to the deciphering of works belonging to the field of restricted production.[16]

It follows that a complete definition of the mode of restricted production must include not only those institutions which ensure the production of competent consumers, but also those which produce agents capable of renewing it. Consequently, one cannot fully comprehend the functioning of the field of restricted production as a site of competition for properly cultural consecration – i.e. legitimacy – and for the power to grant it unless one analyses the relationships between the various instances of consecration. These consist, on the one hand, of institutions which conserve the capital of symbolic goods, such as museums; and, on the other hand, of institutions (such as the educational system) which ensure the reproduction of agents imbued with the categories of action, expression, conception, imagination, perception, specific to the 'cultivated disposition'.[17]

Just as in the case of the system of reproduction, in particular the educational system, so the field of production and diffusion can only be fully understood if one treats it as a field of competition for the monopoly of the legitimate exercise of symbolic violence. Such a construction allows us to define the field of restricted production as the scene of competition for the power to grant cultural consecration, but also as the system specifically designed to fulfil a consecration function as well as a sytem for reproducing producers of a determinate type of cultural goods, and the consumer capable of consuming them. All internal and external relations (including relations with their own work) that agents of production, reproduction and diffusion manage to establish are mediated by the structure of relations between the instances or institutions claiming to exercise a specifically cultural authority. In a given space of time a hierarchy of relations is established between the different domains, the works and the agents having a varying amount of legitimizing authority. This hierarchy, which is in fact dynamic, expresses the structure of objective relations of symbolic force between the producers of symbolic goods who produce for either a restricted or an unrestricted public and are consequently consecrated by differentially legitimized and legitimizing institutions. Thus it also includes the objective relations between producers and different agents of legitimation, specific institutions such as academies, museums, learned societies and the educational system; by their symbolic sanctions, especially by practising a form of co-optation,[18] the principle of all manifestations of recognition, these authorities consecrate a certain type of work and a certain type of cultivated person. These agents of consecration, moreover, may be organizations which are not fully institutionalized: literary circles, critical circles, salons, and small groups surrounding a famous author or associating with a publisher, a review or a literary or artistic magazine. Finally, this hierarchy includes, of course, the objective relations between the various instances of legitimation. Both the function and the mode of functioning of the latter depend on their position in the hierarchical structure of the system they constitute; that is, they depend on the scope and kind of authority – conservative or challenging – these instances exercise or pretend to exercise over the public of cultural producers and, via their critical judgements, over the public at large.

By defending cultural orthodoxy or the sphere of legitimate culture against competing, schismatic or heretical messages, which may provoke radical demands and heterodox practices among various publics, the system of conservation and cultural consecration fulfils a function homologous to that of the Church which, according to Max Weber, should 'systematically establish and delimit the new victorious doctrine or defend the old one against prophetic attacks, determine what has and does not have sacred value, and make it part of the laity's faith'. Sainte-Beuve, together with Auger, whom he cites, quite naturally turns to religious metaphor to express the structurally determined logic of that legitimizing institution *par excellence*, the Académie Française: 'Once it comes to think of itself as an orthodox sanctuary (and it easily does so), the Académie needs some external heresy to combat. At that time, in 1817, lacking any other heresy, and the Romantics were either not yet born or had not yet reached manhood, it attacked the followers and imitators of Abbé Delille. [In 1824, Auger] opened the session with a speech amounting to a declaration of war and a formal denunciation of Romanticism: "A new literary schism", he said, "is appearing today." "Many men, brought up with a religious respect for ancient teachings, consecrated by countless masterpieces, are worried by and nervous of the projects of this emergent sect, and seem to wish to be reassured." This speech had a great effect: it brought happiness and jubilation to the adversaries. That witty swashbuckler, Henri Beyle (Stendhal), was to repeat it gaily in his pamphlets: "M. Auger said it, I'm a sectarian!" Obliged to receive M. Soumet that same year (25 November), M. Auger redoubled his anathemas against the Romantic dramatic form, "against that barbarian poetics they wish to praise", he said, and which violated, in every way, *literary orthodox*. Every sacramental word, *orthodoxy*, *sect*, *schism*, was uttered, and he could not blame himself if the Académie did not transform itself into a synod or a council.'[19]   The functions of reproduction and legitimation may, in accordance with historical traditions, be either consecrated into a single institution, as was the case in the seventeenth century with the French Académie Royale de Peinture,[20] or divided among different institutions such as the educational system, the academies, and official and semi-official institutions or diffusion (museums, theatres, operas, concert halls, etc.). To these may be added certain institutions which, though less widely recognized, are more narrowly expressive of the cultural producers, such as learned societies, literary circles, reviews or galleries; these are more inclined to reject the judgements of the canonical institutions the more intensely the cultural field asserts its autonomy.

However varied the structure of the relations among agents of preservation and consecration may be, the length of 'the process of canonization', culminating in consecration, appears to vary in proportion to the degree that their authority is widely recognized and can be durably imposed. Competition for consecration, which assumes and confers the power to consecrate, condemns those agents whose province is most limited to a state of perpetual emergency. Avant-garde critics fall into this category, haunted by the fear of compromising their prestige as discoverers by overlooking some discovery, and thus obliged to enter into mutual attestations of charisma, making them spokespersons and theoreticians, and sometimes even publicists and impresarios, for artists and their art. Academies (and the salons in the nineteenth century) or the corps of museum curators, both claiming a monopoly over the consecration of contemporary producers, are obliged to combine tradition and tempered innovation. And the educational system, claiming a monopoly over the consecration of works of the past and over the production and consecration (through diplomas) of cultural consumers, only posthumously accords that infallible mark of consecration, the elevation of works into 'classics' by their inclusion in curricula.

Among those characteristics of the educational system liable to affect the structure of its relations with other elements of the system of production and circulation of symbolic goods, the most important is surely its extremely slow rate of evolution. This structural inertia, deriving from its function of cultural conservation, is pushed to the limit by the logic which allows it to wield a monopoly over its own reproduction. Thus the educational system contributes to the maintenance of a disjunction between culture produced by the field of production (involving categories of perception related to new cultural products) and scholastic culture; the latter is 'routinized' and rationalized by – and in view of – its being inculcated. This disjunction manifests itself notably in the distinct schemes of perception and appreciation involved by the two kinds of culture. Products emanating from the field of restricted production require other schemes than those already mastered by the 'cultivated public'.

As indicated, it is impossible to understand the peculiar characteristics of restricted culture without appreciating its profound dependence on the educational system, the indispensable means of its reproduction and growth. Among the transformations which occur, the quasi-systematization and theorizing imposed on the inculcated content are rather less evident than their concomitant effects, such as 'routinization' and 'neutralization'.

The time-lag between cultural production and scholastic consecration, or, as is often said, between 'the school and living art', is not the only opposition between the field of restricted production and the system of institutions of cultural conservation and consecration. As the field of restricted production gains in autonomy, producers tend, as we have seen, to think of themselves as intellectuals or artists by divine right, as 'creators', that is as *auctors* 'claiming authority by virtue of their charisma' and attempting to impose an *auctoritas* that recognizes no other principle of legitimation than itself (or, which amounts to the same thing, the authority of their peer group, which is often reduced, even in scientific activities, to a clique or a sect). They cannot but resist, moreover, the institutional authority which the educational system, as a consecratory institution, opposes to their competing claims. They are embittered by that type of teacher, the *lector*, who comments on and explains the work of others (as Gilbert de la Porrée has already pointed out), and whose own production owes much to the professional practice of its author and to the position he or she occupies within the system of production and circulation of symbolic goods. We are thus brought to the principle underlying the ambivalent relations between producers and scholastic authority.

If the denunciation of professional routine is to some extent consubstantial with prophetic ambition, even to the point where this may amount to official proof of one's charismatic qualifications, it is none the less true that producers cannot fail to pay attention to the judgements of university institutions. They cannot ignore the fact that it is these who will have the last word, and that ultimate consecration can only be accorded them by an authority whose legitimacy is challenged by their entire practice, their entire professional ideology. There are plenty of attacks upon the university which bear witness to the fact that their authors recognize the legitimacy of its verdicts sufficiently to reproach it for not having recognized them.

The objective relation between the field of production and the educational system is both strengthened, in one sense, and undermined, in another, by the action of social mechanisms tending to ensure a sort of pre-established harmony between positions and their occupants (elimination and self-elimination, early training and orientation by the family, co-optation by class or class fraction, etc.). These mechanisms orient very diverse individuals towards the obscure security of a cultural functionary's career or towards the prestigious vicissitudes of independent artistic or intellectual enterprise. Their social origins, predominantly petit-bourgeois in the former case and bourgeois in the latter, dispose them to import very divergent ambitions into their activities, as though they were measured in advance for the available positions.[21]

Before oversimplifying the opposition between petit-bourgeois institutional servants and the bohemians of the upper bourgeoisie, two points should be made. First, whether they are free entrepreneurs or state employees, intellectuals and artists occupy a dominated position in the field of power. And second, while the rebellious audacity of the *auctor* may find its limits within the inherited ethics and politics of a bourgeois primary education, artists and especially professors coming from the petite bourgeoisie are most directly under the control of the state. The state, after all, has the power to orient intellectual production by means of subsidies, commissions, promotion, honorific posts, even decorations, all of which are for speaking or keeping silent, for compromise or abstention.

## RELATIONS BETWEEN THE FIELD OF RESTRICTED PRODUCTION AND THE FIELD OF LARGE-SCALE PRODUCTION

Without analysing the relations uniting the system of consecratory institutions with the field of producers for producers, a full definition of the relationship between the field of restricted production and the field of large-scale production would have been impossible. The field of large-scale production, whose submission to external demand is characterized by the subordinate position of cultural producers in relation to the controllers of production and diffusion media, principally obeys the imperatives of competition for conquest of the market. The structure of its socially neutralized product is the result of the economic and social conditions of its production.[22] *Middle-brow art* [*l'art moyen*], in its ideal-typical form, is aimed at a public frequently referred to as 'average' [*moyen*]. Even when it is more specifically aimed at a determinate category of non-producers, it may none the less eventually reach a socially heterogeneous public. Such is the case with the bourgeois theatre of the *belle-époque*, which is nowadays broadcast on television.

It is legitimate to define middle-brow culture as the product of the system of large-scale production, because these works are entirely defined by their public. Thus, the very ambiguity of any definition of the 'average public' or the 'average viewer' very realistically designates the field of potential action which producers of this type of art and culture *explicitly* assign themselves, and which determines their technical and aesthetic choices.

The following remarks by a French television writer, author of some twenty novels, recipient of the *Prix Interallié* and the *Grand prix du roman de l'Académie Française*, bears this out: 'My sole ambition is *to be easily read by the widest possible public*. I never attempt a "masterpiece", and *I do not write for intellectuals*; I leave that to others. For me, a good book is one that grips you within the first three pages.'[23] It follows that the most specific characteristics of middle-brow art, such as reliance on immediately accessible technical processes and aesthetic effects, or the systematic exclusion of all potentially controversial themes, or those liable to shock this or that section of the public, derive from the social conditions in which it is produced.

Middle-brow art is the product of a productive system dominated by the quest for investment profitability; this creates the need for the widest possible public. It cannot, moreover, content itself with seeking to intensify consumption within a determinate social class; it is obliged to orient itself towards a generalization of the social and cultural composition of this public. This means that the production of goods, even when they are aimed at a specific statistical category (the young, women, football fans, stamp collectors, etc.), must represent a kind of highest social denominator.[24] On the other hand, middle-brow art is most often the culmination of transactions and compromises among the various categories of agents engaged in a technically and socially differentiated field of production. These transactions occur not only between controllers of the means of production and cultural producers – who are more or less locked into the role of pure technicians – but also between different categories of producers themselves. The latter come to use their specific competencies to guarantee a wide variety of cultural interests while simultaneously reactivating the self-censorship engendered by the vast industrial and bureaucratic organizations of cultural production through invocation of the 'average spectator'.

In all fields of artistic life the same opposition between the two modes of production is to be observed, separated as much by the nature of the works produced and the political ideologies or aesthetic theories of those who disseminate them as by the social composition of the publics to which they are offered. As Bertrand Poirot-Delpech has observed, 'Apart from drama critics, hardly anyone believes – or seems to believe – that the various spectacles demanding qualification by the word "theatre" still belong to a single and identical art form. The potential publics are so distinct; ideologies, modes of functioning, styles and actors on offer are so opposed, inimical even, that professional rules and solidarity have practically disappeared.'[25]

Consigned by the laws of profitability to 'concentration' and to integration into world-wide 'show-business' production circuits, the commercial theatre in France survives today in three forms: French (or English, etc.) versions of foreign shows supervised, distributed and, to some extent, organized by those responsible for the original show; repeats of the most successful works for the traditional commercial theatre; and, finally, intelligent comedy for the enlightened bourgeoisie. The same dualism, taking the form of downright cultural schism, exists, in Western Europe at least, in the musical sphere. Here the opposition between the artificially supported market for works of restricted scope and the market for commercial work, produced and distributed by the music-hall and recording industry, is far more brutal than elsewhere.

One should beware of seeing anything more than a limiting parameter construction in the opposition between the two modes of production of symbolic goods, which can only be defined in terms of their relations with each other. Within a single universe one always finds the entire range of intermediaries between works produced with reference to the restricted market on the one hand, and works determined by an intuitive representation of the expectations of the widest possible public on the other. The range might include avant-garde works reserved for a few initiates within the peer-group, avant-garde works on the road to consecration, works of 'bourgeois art' aimed at the non-intellectual fractions of the dominant class and often already consecrated by the most official of legitimizing institutions (the academies), works of middle-brow art aimed at various 'target publics' and involving, besides brand-name culture (with, for example, works crowned by the big literary prizes), imitation culture aimed at the rising petite bourgeoisie (popularizing literary or scientific works, for example) and mass culture, that is, the ensemble of socially neutralized works.

In fact, the professional ideology of producers-for-producers and their spokespeople establishes an opposition between creative liberty and the laws of the market, between works which create their public and works created by their public. This is undoubtedly a defence against the *disenchantment* produced by the progress of the division of labour, the establishment of various fields of action – each involving the rendering explicit of its peculiar functions – and the rational organization of technical means appertaining to these functions.

It is no mere chance that middle-brow art and art for art's sake are both produced by highly professionalized intellectuals and artists, and are both characterized by the same valorization of technique. In the one case this orients production towards the search for effect (understood both as effect produced on the public and as ingenious construction) and, in the other, it orients production towards the cult of form for its own sake. The latter orientation is an unprecedented affirmation of the most characteristic aspect of professionalism and thus an affirmation of the specificity and irreducibility of producers.

> This explains why certain works of middle-brow art may present formal characteristics predisposing them to enter into legitimate culture. The fact that producers of Westerns have to work within the very strict conventions of a heavily stereotyped genre leads them to demonstrate their highly professionalized technical virtuosity by continually referring back to previous solutions – assumed to be known – in the solutions they provide to canonical problems, and they are continually bordering on pastiche or parody of previous authors, against whom they measure themselves. A genre containing ever more references to the history of that genre calls for a second-degree reading, reserved for the initiate, who can only grasp the work's nuances and subtleties by relating it back to previous works. By introducing subtle breaks and fine variations, with regard to assumed expectations, the play of internal allusions (the same one that has always been practised by lettered traditions) authorizes detached and distanced perception, quite as much as first-degree adherence, and calls for either erudite analysis or the aesthete's wink. 'Intellectual' Westerns are the logical conclusion of these pure cinematographic language games which assume, among their authors, as much the cinephile's as the cineaste's inclinations.

More profoundly, middle-brow art, which is characterized by tried and proven techniques and an oscillation between plagiarism and parody most often linked with either indifference or conservatism, displays one of the great covert truths underlying the aestheticism of art for art's sake. The fact is that its fixation on technique draws pure art into a covenant with the dominant sections of the bourgeoisie. The latter recognize the intellectual's and the artist's monopoly on the production of the work of art as an instrument of pleasure (and, secondarily, as an instrument for the symbolic legitimation of economic or political power); in return, the artist is expected to avoid serious matters, namely social and political questions. The opposition between art for art's sake and middle-brow art which, on the ideological plane, becomes transformed into an opposition between the idealism of devotion to art and the cynicism of submission to the market, should not hide the fact that the desire to oppose a specifically cultural legitimacy to the prerogatives of power and money constitutes one more way of recognizing that business is business.

What is most important is that these two fields of production, opposed as they are, coexist and that their products owe their very unequal symbolic and material values on the market to their unequal consecration which, in turn, stems from their very unequal power of distinction.[26] The various kinds of cultural competence encountered in a class society derive their social value from the power of social discrimination, and from the specifically cultural rarity conferred on them by their position in the system of cultural competencies; this system is more or less integrated according to the social formation in question, but it is always hierarchized. To be unaware that a dominant culture owes its main features and social functions – especially that of symbolically legitimizing a form of domination – to the fact that it is not perceived as such, in short, to ignore the *fact* of legitimacy is either to condemn oneself to a class-based ethnocentrism which leads the defenders of restricted culture to ignore the material foundations of the symbolic domination of one culture by another, or implicitly to commit oneself to a populism which betrays a shameful recognition of the legitimacy of the dominant culture in an effort to rehabilitate middle-brow culture. This cultural relativism is accomplished by treating distinct but *objectively* hierarchized cultures in a class society as if they were the cultures of such perfectly independent social formations as the Eskimos and the Feugians.[27]

Fundamentally heteronomous, middle-brow culture is objectively condemned to define itself in relation to legitimate culture; this is so in the field of production as well as of consumption. Original experimentation entering the field of large-scale production almost always comes up against the breakdown in communication liable to arise from the use of codes inaccessible to the 'mass public'. Moreover, middle-brow art cannot renew its techniques and themes without borrowing from high art or, more frequently still, from the 'bourgeois art' of a generation or so earlier. This includes 'adapting' the more venerable themes or subjects, or those most amenable to the traditional laws of composition in the popular arts (the Manichaean division of roles, for example). In this sense, the history of middle-brow art amounts to no more than that imposed by technical changes and the laws of competition.

However agents may dissimulate it, the objectively established hierarchical difference between the two productive systems continually imposes itself. Indeed, the practices and ideologies of consumers are largely determined by the level of the goods they produce or consume in this hierarchy. The connoisseur can immediately discern, from such reference points as the work's genre, the radio station, the name of the theatre, gallery or director, the order of legitimacy and the appropriate posture to be adopted in each case.

The opposition between legitimate and illegitimate, imposing itself in the field of symbolic goods with the same arbitrary necessity as the distinction between the sacred and the profane elsewhere, expresses the different social and cultural valuation of two modes of production: the one a field that is its own market, allied with an educational system which legitimizes it; the other a field of production organized as a function of external demand, normally seen as socially and culturally inferior.

This opposition between the two markets, between producers for producers and producers for non-producers, entirely determines the image writers and artists have of their profession and constitutes the taxonomic principle according to which they classify and hierarchize works (beginning with their own). Producers for producers have to overcome the contradiction in their relationship with their (limited) public through a transfigured representation of their social function, whereas in the case of producers for non-producers the quasi-coincidence of their authentic representation and the objective truth of the writer's profession is either a fairly inevitable effect or a prior condition of the success with their specific public. Nothing could be further, for example, from the charismatic vision of the writer's 'mission' than the image proposed by the successful writer previously cited: 'Writing is a job like any other. Talent and imagination are not enough. Above all, discipline is required. It's better to force oneself to write two pages a day than ten pages once a week. There is one essential condition for this: one has to be in shape, just as a sportsman has to be in shape to run a hundred metres or to play a football match.'

It is unlikely that all writers and artists whose works are objectively addressed to the 'mass public' have, at least at the outset of their career, quite so realistic and 'disenchanted' an image of their function. None the less, they can hardly avoid applying to themselves the objective image of their work received from the field. This image expresses the opposition between the two modes of production as objectively revealed in the social quality of their public ('intellectual' or 'bourgeois', for example). The more a certain class of writers and artists is defined as beyond the bounds of the universe of legitimate art, the more its members are inclined to defend the professional qualities of the worthy, entertaining technician, complete master of his technique and *métier*, against the uncontrolled, disconcerting experiments of 'intellectual' art.

There is no doubt, moreover, that the emergence of large collective production units in the fields of radio, television, cinema and journalism as well as in scientific research, and the concomitant decline of the intellectual artisan in favour of the salaried worker, entail a transformation of the relationship between the producers and their work. This will be reflected in his own representation of his position and function in the social structure, and, consequently, of the political and the aesthetic ideologies they profess. Intellectual labour carried out collectively, within technically and socially differentiated production units, can no longer surround itself with the charismatic aura attaching to traditional independent production. The traditional cultural producer was a master of his means of production and invested only his cultural capital, which was likely to be perceived as a gift of grace. The demystification of intellectual and artistic activity consequent on the transformation of the social conditions of production particularly affects intellectuals and artists engaged in large units of cultural production (radio, television, journalism). They constitute a proletaroid intelligentsia forced to experience the contradiction between aesthetic and political position-takings stemming from their inferior position in the field of production and the objectively conservative functions of the products of their activity.

## POSITIONS AND POSITION-TAKINGS

The relationship maintained by producers of symbolic goods with other producers, with the significations available within the cultural field at a given moment and, consequently, with their own work, depends very directly on the position they occupy within the field of production and circulation of symbolic goods. This, in turn, is related to the specifically cultural hierarchy of degrees of consecration. Such a position implies an objective definition of their practice and of the products resulting from it. Whether they like it or not, whether they know it or not, this definition imposes itself on them as a fact, determining their ideology and their practice, and its efficacy manifests itself never so clearly as in conduct aimed at transgressing it. For example, it is the ensemble of determinations inscribed in their position which inclines professional jazz or film critics to issue very divergent and incompatible judgements destined to reach only restricted cliques of producers and little sects of devotees. These critics tend to ape the learned, sententious tone and the cult of erudition characterizing academic criticism, and to seek theoretical, political or aesthetic security in the obscurity of a borrowed language.[28]

As distinct from a solidly legitimate activity, an activity on the way to legitimation continually confronts its practitioners with the question of its own legitimacy. In this way, photography – a middle-brow art situated midway between 'noble' and 'vulgar' practices – condemns its practitioners to create a substitute for the sense of cultural legitimacy which is given to the priests of all the legitimate arts. More generally, all those marginal cultural producers whose position obliges them to conquer the cultural legitimacy unquestioningly accorded to the consecrated professions expose themselves to redoubled suspicion by the efforts they can hardly avoid making to challenge its principles. The ambivalent aggression they frequently display towards consecratory institutions, especially the educational system, without being able to offer a counter-legitimacy, bears witness to their desire for recognition and, consequently, to the recognition they accord to the educational system.

All relations that a determinate category of intellectuals or artists may establish with any and all external social factors – whether economic (e.g. publishers, dealers), political or cultural (consecrating authorities such as academies) – are mediated by the structure of the field. Thus, they depend on the position occupied by the category in question within the hierarchy of cultural legitimacy.

The sociology of intellectual and artistic production thus acquires its specific object in constructing the relatively autonomous system of relations of production and circulation of symbolic goods. In doing this, it acquires the possibility of grasping the positional properties that any category of agents of cultural production or diffusion owes to its place within the structure of the field. Consequently, it acquires the capacity to explain those characteristics which products, as position-takings, owe to the *positions* of their producers within the system of social relations of production and circulation and to the corresponding positions which they occupy within the system of *objectively possible cultural positions* within a given state of the field of production and circulation.

The position-takings which constitute the cultural field do not all suggest themselves with the same probability to those occupying at a given moment a determinate position in this field. Conversely, a particular class of cultural position-takings is attached as a potentiality to each of the positions in the field of production and circulation (that is, a particular set of problems and structures of resolution, themes and procedures, aesthetic and political positions, etc.). These can only be defined differentially, that is, in relation to the other constitutive cultural positions in the cultural field under consideration. 'Were I as glorious as Paul Bourget,' Arthur Craven used to say, 'I'd present myself nightly in music-hall revues in nothing but a G-string, and I guarantee you I'd make a bundle.'[29] This attempt to turn literary glory into a profitable undertaking only appears at first sight to be self-destructive and comical because it assumes a desacralized and desacralizing relationship with literary authority. And such a stance would be inconceivable for anyone other than a marginal artist, knowing and recognizing the principles of cultural legitimacy well enough to be able to place himself outside the cultural law.[30] There is no position within the field of cultural production that does not call for a determinate type of position-taking and which does not exclude, simultaneously, an entire gamut of theoretically possible position-takings. This does not require that possible or excluded position-takings be explicitly prescribed or prohibited. But one should beware of taking as the basis of all practice the strategies half-consciously elaborated in reference to a never more than partial consciousness of structures. In this connection one might think, for example, of the knowledge of the present and future structure of the labour market that is mobilized at the moment of a change in orientation.

All relations among agents and institutions of diffusion or consecration are mediated by the field's structure. To the extent that the ever-ambiguous marks of recognition owe their specific form to the objective relations (perceived and interpreted as they are in accordance with the unconscious schemes of the habitus) they contribute to form the *subjective* representation which agents have of the *social* representation of their position within the hierarchy of consecrations. And this semi-conscious representation itself constitutes one of the mediations through which, by reference to the social representation of possible, probable or impossible position-takings, the system of relatively unconscious strategies of the occupants of a given class of positions is defined.

It would be vain to claim to assess from among the determinants of practices the impact of durable, generalized and transposable dispositions, the impact of the perception of this situation and of the intentional or semi-intentional strategies which arise in response to it. The least conscious dispositions, such as those constituting the primary class habitus, are themselves constituted through the internalization of an objectively selected system of signs, indices and sanctions, which are nothing but the materialization, within objects, words or conducts, of a particular kind of objective structure. Such dispositions remain the basis upon which all the signs and indices characterizing quite varied situations are selected and interpreted.

In order to gain some idea of the complex relations between unconscious dispositions and the experiences which they structure – or, which amounts to the same thing, between the unconscious strategies engendered by habitus and strategies consciously produced in response to a situation designed in accordance with the schemes of the habitus – it will be necessary to analyse an example.

The manuscripts a publisher receives are the product of a kind of pre-selection by the authors themselves according to their image of the publisher who occupies a specific position within the space of publishers. The authors' image of their publisher, which may have oriented the production, is itself a function of the objective relationship between the positions authors and publishers occupy in the field. The manuscripts are, moreover, coloured from the outset by a series of determinations (e.g. 'interesting, but not very commercial', or 'not very commercial, but interesting') stemming from the relationship between the author's position in the field of production (unknown young author, consecrated author, house author, etc.) and the publisher's position within the system of production and circulation ('commercial' publisher, consecrated or avant-garde). They usually bear the marks of the intermediary whereby they came to the publisher (editor of a series, reader, 'house author', etc.) and whose authority, once again, is a function of respective positions in the field. Because subjective intentions and unconscious dispositions contribute to the efficacy of the objective structures to which they are adjusted, their interlacing tends to guide agents to their 'natural niche' in the structure of the field. It will be understood, moreover, that publisher and author can only experience and interpret the pre-established harmony achieved and revealed by their meeting as a miracle of predestination: 'Are you happy to be published by Éditions de Minuit?' 'If I had followed my instincts, I would have gone there straight away . . . but I didn't dare; I thought they were too good for me . . . So I first sent my manuscript to Publisher X. What I just said about X isn't very kind! They refused my book, and so I took it to Minuit anyway.' 'How do you get on with the publisher?' 'He began by telling me a lot of things I hoped had not shown. Everything concerning time, coincidences.'[31]

The publisher's image of his 'vocation' combines the aesthetic relativism of the discoverer, conscious of having no other principle than that of defiance of all canonical principles, with the most complete faith in an absolute kind of 'flair'. This ultimate and often indefinable principle behind his choices finds itself continually strengthened and confirmed by his perception of the selective choices of authors and by the representations authors, critics, the public and other publishers have of his function within the division of intellectual labour. The critic's situation is hardly any different. The works she receives have undergone a process of pre-selection. They bear a supplementary mark, that of the publisher (and, sometimes, that of author of a preface, another author or another critic). The value of this mark is a function, once more, of the structure of objective relations between the respective positions of author, publisher and critic. It is also affected by the relationship of the critic to the predominant taxonomies in the critical world or in the field of restricted production (for example, the *nouveau roman*, 'objectal literature', etc.). 'Apart from the opening pages, which seem to be more or less voluntary pastiche of the *nouveau roman*, *L'Auberge espagnole* tells a fantastic, though perfectly clear, story, whose development obeys the logic of dreams rather than reality.'[32] So the critic, suspecting the young novelist of having entered the hall of mirrors, enters there himself by describing what he takes for a reflection of the *nouveau roman*. Schönberg describes the same type of effect: 'On the occasion of a concert given by my pupils, a critic with a particularly fine ear defined a piece for string quartet whose harmony – as can be proved – was only a very slight development of Schubert's, as a product bearing signs of my influence.' Even if such errors of identification are not rare, especially among the 'conservative' critics, they may also bring profit to the 'innovators': on account of his position, a critic may find himself predisposed in favour of all kinds of avant-garde; accordingly he may act as an initiate, communicating the deciphered revelation back to the artist from whom he received it. The artist, in return, confirms the critic in his vocation, that of privileged interpreter, by confirming the accuracy of his de-cipherment.

On account of the specific nature of his interests, and of the structural ambiguity of his position as a businessperson objectively invested with some power of cultural consecration, the publisher is more strongly inclined than the other agents of production and diffusion to take the regularities objectively governing relations between agents into account in his conscious strategies. The selective discourse in which he engages with the critic, who has been selected not merely because of his influence but also because of the affinities he may have with the work, and which may even go to the length of declared allegiance to the publisher and his entire list of publications, or to a certain category of authors, is an extremely subtle mixture, in which his own idea of the work combines with his idea of the idea the critic is likely to have, given the image he has of the house's publications

Hence, it is quite logical and highly significant that what has become the name of a literary school (the *nouveau roman*), adopted by the authors themselves, should have begun as a pejorative label, accorded by a traditionalist critic to novels published by Éditions de Minuit. Just as critics and public found themselves invited to seek the links that might unite works published under the same imprint, so authors were defined by this public definition of their works to the extent that they had to define themselves in relation to it. Moreover, confronted with the public's and the critics' image of them, they were encouraged to think of themselves as constituting more than simply a chance grouping. They became a school endowed with its own aesthetic programme, its eponymous ancestors, its accredited critics and spokespersons.

In short, the most personal judgements it is possible to make of a work, even of one's own work, are always collective judgements in the sense of position-takings referring to other position-takings through the intermediary of the objective relations between the positions of their authors within the field. Through the public meaning of the work, through the objective sanctions imposed by the symbolic market upon the producers' 'aspirations' and 'ambitions' and, in particular, through the degree of recognition and consecration it accords them, the entire structure of the field interposes itself between producers and their work. This imposes a definition of their ambitions as either legitimate or illegitimate according to whether their position objectively implies, or denies, their fulfilment.

Because the very logic of the field condemns them to risk their cultural salvation in even the least of their position-takings and to watch, uncertainly, for the ever-ambiguous signs of an ever-suspended election, intellectuals and artists may experience a failure as a sign of election, or over-rapid or too brilliant a success as a threat of damnation. They cannot ignore the value attributed to them, that is, the position they occupy within the hierarchy of cultural legitimacy, as it is continually brought home by the signs of recognition or exclusion appearing in their relations with peers or with institutions of consecration.

For each position in the hierarchy of consecration there is a cor-responding relationship – more or less ambitious or resigned – to the field of cultural practices which is, itself, hierarchized. An analysis of artistic or intellectual trajectories attests that those 'choices' most commonly imputed to 'vocation', such as choice of intellectual or artistic specialization – author rather than critic, poet rather than novelist – and, more profoundly, everything defining the manner in which one fulfils oneself in that 'chosen' speciality, depend on the actual and potential position that the field attributes to the different categories of agents, notably through the intermediary of the institutions of cultural consecration. It might be supposed that the laws governing intellectual or artistic 'vocations' are similar in principle to those governing scholastic 'choices', such as the 'choice' of faculty or discipline. Such a supposition would imply, for example, that the 'choice' of discipline be increasingly 'ambitious' (with respect to the reigning hierarchy in the university field) as one ascends towards those categories of students or teachers most highly consecrated, scholastically, and most favoured in terms of social origin. Again, it might be supposed that the greater the scholastic consecration, mediated by social origin, of a determinate category of teachers and researchers, the more abundant and ambitious would be their production.

Among the social factors determining the functional laws of any field of cultural production (literary, artistic or scientific), undoubtedly the most important is the position of each discipline or specialization and the position of the different producers in the hierarchy peculiar to each sub-field. The migrations of labour power which drive large sections of producers towards the currently most consecrated scientific discipline (or, elsewhere, artistic genre), and which are experienced as though 'inspired' by vocation or determined by some intellectual itinerary and often imputed to the effects of fashion, could be merely reconversions aimed at ensuring the best possible economic or symbolic return on a determinate kind of cultural capital. And the sensitivity necessary to sniff out these movements of the cultural value stock exchange, the audacity requisite to abandoning well-worn paths for the most opportune-seeming future, once more depend on social factors, such as the nature of the capital possessed and scholastic and social origins with their attendant objective chances and aspirations.[33] Similarly, the interest which different categories of researchers manifest in different types of practice (for example, empirical research or theory) is also a composite function. It is dependent, first, on the ambitions which their formation and their scholastic success and, thus, their position in the discipline's hierarchy allow them to form by assuring them of reasonable chances of success. Secondly, it is a function of the objectively recognized hierarchy of the very different material and symbolic profits which particular practices or objects of study are in a position to procure.[34]

If the relations which make the cultural field into a field of (intellectual, artistic or scientific) position-takings only reveal their meaning and function in the light of the relations among cultural subjects who are holding specific positions in this field, it is because intellectual or artistic position-takings are also always semi-conscious *strategies* in a game in which the conquest of cultural legitimacy and of the concomitant power of legitimate symbolic violence is at stake. To claim to be able to discover the entire truth of the cultural field within that field is to transfer the objective relations between different positions in the field of cultural production into the heaven of logical and semiological relations of opposition and homology. Moreover, it is to do away with the question of the relationship between this 'positional' field and the cultural field; in other words, it is to ignore the question of the dependence of the different systems of cultural position-takings constituting a given state of the cultural field on the specifically cultural interests of different groups competing for cultural legitimacy. It is also to deprive oneself of the possibility of determining what particular cultural position-takings owe to the social functions they fulfil in these groups' strategies.

Consequently, we can postulate that there is no cultural position-taking that cannot be submitted to a *double interpretation*: it can be related, on the one hand, to the universe of cultural position-takings constituent of the specifically cultural field; on the other hand, it can be interpreted as a consciously or unconsciously oriented strategy elaborated in relation to the field of allied or hostile positions.[35] Research starting from this hypothesis would doubtless find its surest landmarks in a methodical analysis of *privileged references*. These would be conceived, not as simple indices of information exchanges (in particular, implicit or explicit borrowings of words or ideas), but as so many landmarks circumscribing, within the common battlefield, the small network of privileged allies and adversaries proper to each category of producer.

'Citatology' nearly always ignores this question, implicitly treating references to an author as an index of recognition (of indebtedness or legitimacy). In point of fact this apparent function may nearly always be associated with such diverse functions as the manifestation of relations of allegiance or dependence, of strategies of affiliation, of annexation or of defence (this is the role, for example, of guarantee references, ostentatious references or alibi-references). We should mention here two 'citatologists' who have the merit of having posed a question systematically ignored: 'People quote another author for complex reasons – to confer meaning, authority or depth upon a statement, to demonstrate familiarity with other work in the same field and to avoid the appearance of plagiarising even ideas conceived independently. The quotation is aimed at readers of whom some, at least, are supposed to have some knowledge of the work quoted (there would be no point in quoting if this were not so) and to adhere to the norms concerning what may, and what may not, be attributed to it.'[36] When it is not immediately explicit and direct (as in the case of polemical or deforming references), the strategic function of a reference may be apprehended in its modality: humble or sovereign, impeccably academic or sloppy, explicit or implicit and, in this case, unconscious, repressed (and betraying a strong relationship of ambivalence) or knowingly dissimulated (whether through tactical prudence, through a more or less visible and naïve will to annexation – plagiarism – or through disdain). Strategic considerations may also stalk those quotations most directly oriented towards the functions commonly recognized as theirs by 'citatology'. It suffices to think of what might be termed an *a minima* reference, which consists in recognizing a precise and clearly specified debt (by the full-length quotation of a sentence or an expression) in order to hide a far more global and more diffuse debt. (We should note, in passing, the existence of *a maxima* references, whose functions may vary from grateful homage to self-valorizing annexation – when the contribution of the quoter to the thought quoted, which, in this case, must be prestigious, is fairly important and obvious.)

The construction of the system of relations between each of the categories of producers and competing, hostile, allied or neutral powers, which are to be destroyed, intimidated, cajoled, annexed or won over, presumes a decisive rupture, first, with naïve citatology, since it does not go beyond any but the most phenomenal relationships, and second – and in particular – with that supremely naïve representation of cultural production that takes only *explicit references* into account. How can we reduce Plato's presence in Aristotle's texts to explicit references alone, or that of Descartes in Leibniz's writings, of Hegel in those of Marx? We speak here more generally of those *privileged interlocutors* implicit in the writings of every producer, those revered antecedents whose thought structures he has internalized to the point where he no longer thinks except in them and through them, to the point where they have become intimate adversaries determining his thinking and imposing on him both the shape and the substance of conflict. Manifest conflicts dissimulate the *consensus* within the *dissensus* which defines the field of ideological battle in a given epoch, and which the educational system contributes to producing by inculcating an uncontested hierarchy of themes and problems worthy of discussion. Given this, implicit references allow also the construction of that intellectual space defined by a system of common references appearing so natural, so incontestable that they are never the object of conscious position-takings at all. However, it is in relation to this referential space that all the position-takings of the different categories of producers are differentially defined.

In addition to other possible functions, theories, methods and concepts in whatever realm are to be considered as strategies aimed at installing, restoring, strengthening, safeguarding or overthrowing a determinate structure of relationships of symbolic domination; that is, they constitute the means for obtaining or safeguarding the monopoly of the legitimate mode of practising a literary, artistic or scientific activity.

How, for example, could one fail to see that 'epistemological couples' (e.g. general theory and empiricism, or formalism and positivism) are nearly always covers for oppositions between different groups within the field? Such groups are led to transform interests associated with possession of a determinate type of scientific capital, and with a determinate position within the scientific field, into epistemological choices. Is it not legitimate to suppose that there is a strategic intention (which may remain perfectly unconscious) lurking behind a theory of theory such as Merton's? Does one not better understand the *raison d'être* of works by the 'high methodologists', such as Lazarsfeld, as one realizes that these scholastic codifications of the rules of scientific practice are inseparable from the project of building a kind of intellectual papacy, replete with its international corps of vicars, regularly visited or gathered together in *concilium* and charged with the exercise of rigorous and constant control over common practice?

By ignoring the systems of social relations within which symbolic systems are produced and utilized, strictly internal interpretation most frequently condemns itself to the gratuitousness of an arbitrary formalism. In point of fact, an appropriate construction of the object of analysis presupposes sociological analysis of the social functions at the basis of the structure and functioning of any symbolic system. The semiologist, who claims to reveal the structure of a literary or artistic work through so-called strictly internal analysis, exposes him or herself to a theoretical error by disregarding the social conditions underlying the production of the work and those determining its functioning.

A field of cultural production may have achieved virtually complete autonomy in relation to external forces and demands (as in the case of the pure sciences), while still remaining amenable to specifically sociological analysis. It is the job of sociology to establish the external conditions for a system of social relations of production, circulation and consumption necessary to the autonomous development of science or art; its task, moreover, is to determine those functional laws which characterize such a relatively autonomous field of social relations and which can also account for the structure of corresponding symbolic productions and its transformations. The principles of 'selection' objectively employed by the different groups of producers competing for cultural legitimacy are always defined within a system of social relations obeying a specific logic. The available symbolic position-takings are, moreover, functions of the interest-systems objectively attached to the positions producers occupy in *special power relations*, which are the social relations of symbolic production, circulation and consumption.

As the field of restricted production closes in upon itself, and affirms itself capable of organizing its production by reference to its own internal norms of perfection – excluding all external functions and social or socially marked content from the work – the dynamic of competition for specifically cultural consecration becomes the exclusive principle of the production of works. Especially since the middle of the nineteenth century, the principle of change in art has come from within art itself, as though history were internal to the system and as if the development of forms of representation and expression were merely the product of the logical development of axiomatic systems specific to the various arts. To explain this, there is no need to hypostatize the laws of this evolution. If a relatively autonomous history of art and literature (or of science) exists, it is because the 'action of works upon works', of which Brunetière spoke, explains an ever-increasing proportion of artistic or literary production. At the same time, the field as such explicates and systematizes specifically artistic principles of the production and the evaluation of the work of art. The relationship, moreover, which each category of producer enjoys with its own production is more and more exclusively determined by its relationship with the specifically artistic traditions and norms inherited from the past, and which is, again, a function of its position in the structure of the field of production.

True, cultural legitimacy appears to be the 'fundamental norm', to employ the language of Kelsen, of the field of restricted production. But this 'fundamental norm', as Jean Piaget has noted, 'is nothing other than the abstract expression of the fact that society "recognizes" the normative value of this order' in such a way that it 'corresponds to the social reality of the exercise of some power and of the "recognition" of this power or of the system of rules emanating from it'.[37] Thus, if the relative autonomy of the field of restricted production authorizes the attempt to construct a 'pure' model of the objective relations defining it and of the interactions which develop within it, one must remember that this formal construction is the product of the temporary bracketing-off of the field of restricted production (as a system of specific power relations) from the surrounding field of the power relations between classes. It would be futile to search for the ultimate foundation of this 'fundamental norm' within the field itself, since it resides in structures governed by powers other than the culturally legitimate; consequently, the functions objectively assigned to each category of producer and its products by its position in the field are always duplicated by the external functions objectively fulfilled through the accomplishment of its internal functions.

# Part II

*Flaubert and the French
Literary Field*

# 4

# Is the Structure of *Sentimental Education* an Instance of Social Self-analysis?

I have several reasons for starting this series of lectures with an analysis of Flaubert's *Sentimental Education*. First of all, it is one way for me to pay particular homage to my host Victor Brombert, who is, as everyone knows, one of the most eminent Flaubert specialists. Secondly, I believe that this fascinating and mysterious work condenses all those enigmas that literature can put to those who wish to interpret it. A true example of the absolute masterpiece, the novel contains an analysis of the social space in which the author was himself located and thus gives us the instruments we need for an analysis of him. Flaubert the sociologist gives us a sociological insight on Flaubert the man. One Flaubert gives us the means to understand the particular lucidity of the other as well as the limits within which his writing is confined. This sociological content is not readily apparent, and some may think that I, as interpreter, have inserted or imposed it through my own reading of the text. In fact, as Heidegger might have said, it is a veiled revelation. It is only a shrouded, half-hidden form which yields itself to our scrutiny or even, to some extent, to the gaze of the author himself.

My reading of the text, which will explicitly mark out a real but hitherto implicit structure, will necessarily come as an oversimplification. It may seem to transform a story, a tale, into a sociologist's model where unforeseen adventure is replaced by the protocol of some experimental construction. To sharpen this contrast, which throws light on the literary effect as well as on the scientific effect, I would like to start by reading, before coming to my model, a perfectly straightforward, traditional summary of *Sentimental Education*.

In Paris in the 1840s, student Frédéric Moreau meets and falls in love with Madame Arnoux, the wife of an art dealer who sells paintings and engravings in a shop in the Faubourg Montmartre. Frédéric harbours vague aspirations to literary, artistic or social success and tries to win acceptance at the home of Dambreuse, a high-society banker. Disappointed by his reception, he falls back into self-doubt, idleness, solitude and daydreams. He finds himself in the centre of a group of young men, Martinon, Cisy, Sénécal, Dussardier, Hussonnet, and it is while he is a guest at the Arnoux' home that his passion for Madame Arnoux takes shape. He leaves Paris for a holiday at his mother's place in Nogent, where he meets the young Louise Roque, who falls in love with him. His precarious financial situation is improved by an unexpected inheritance, and he leaves once more for Paris.

But there he is disappointed by Madame Arnoux, and he becomes interested in Rosanette, a courtesan who is Monsieur Arnoux's mistress. As commentators often remark, Frédéric is torn between diverging temptations, rebounding from one to the other. There is Rosanette and the charms of a life of luxury; there is Madame Arnoux, whom he tries in vain to seduce; and, finally, there is the wealthy Madame Dambreuse, who may well help him to fulfil his society ambitions. After protracted hesitations and many changes of mind he returns to Nogent, determined to marry Louise Roque. But he leaves once more for Paris, where Madame Arnoux agrees to a rendezvous. He waits in vain at the appointed time and place while battles rage in the streets, for it is 22 February 1848. Disappointed and angered, he seeks consolation in the arms of Rosanette.

While living through the revolution, Frédéric regularly visits Rosanette and has by her a baby son who dies very shortly thereafter. He also regularly visits the Dambreuses and becomes Madame Dambreuse's lover. After her husband's death, she even offers to marry him. But with unaccustomed energy, he first breaks off with Rosanette and then with Madame Dambreuse. He cannot see Madame Arnoux again, since she left Paris after her husband's bankruptcy. And so, bereft of their affections and once again penniless, he returns to Nogent to marry Louise Roque, only to find that she has already married his friend Deslauriers.

Fifteen years later, in March 1867, Madame Arnoux comes to visit him. They declare their love for each other, recalling the past, and part forever.

Two years later, Frédéric and Deslauriers mull over the failure of their lives. They have nothing left but memories of their youth, the most memorable of which, a visit to a brothel 'Chez la Turque', is the epitome of their failure: Frédéric, who had the money, fled from the sight of so many offered women, and Deslauriers, who had none, was obliged to follow. But they both agree: 'It was there that we had the best of our lives.'

This very sketchy and oversimplified summary, borrowed for the main from a school edition, was necessary to recall the gist of the novel, but it was above all necessary to help point out the contrast between the most generally accepted reading of the work and the one which becomes possible when one grasps the sociological model of society and the process of social ageing that Flaubert brings into play.

During this first lecture, I shall try to make this model explicit, since it seems to me to reveal the structure of *Sentimental Education* and therefore enables us to understand the novel's logic as both story and history. In the second lecture, I shall endeavour to explain Flaubert's real position in social space and how this position, structurally very similar to that of our main character, Frédéric, tended, among other things, to give the author his peculiar perception of the social world depicted in the novel, how it gave him a predisposition for perceiving and exposing with peculiar lucidity the structure of this world. I shall then attempt, in the third lecture, to bring out more systematically the model of the field of power and of the artistic field that is to be found, in a veiled form, in *Sentimental Education* and to locate my method for the analysis of literary works in the space of available models. The analysis of this novel will have thus served as a literary, and hence more easily acceptable and concrete, introduction to a sociological analysis of the literary field and of literature itself. It will also have served as an introduction to a sociological study of the relationships between the literary and sociological readings of a given text, and, hence, between sociology and literature.

The truth is that the sociologist himself cannot break out of the circle that he discovers in analysing this novel. When Flaubert describes the structure of the field of power, he gives us the key necessary for the comprehension of the novel which reveals this structure. In just the same way, the sociologist who describes this work of revelation gives the key to the understanding of his own understanding and to the understanding of the freedom that he achieves in discovering the necessity which lies at the source of his own lucidity.

Let us return to *Sentimental Education*. In this novel Flaubert presents us with a generative model. The first element of this model is a representation of the structure of the ruling class, or, as I put it, of the field of power. The social space described in this work is organized around two poles represented on the one hand by the art dealer Arnoux and on the other by the banker Dambreuse. On the one side, art and politics; on the other, politics and business. At the intersection of these two universes, at least at the beginning, before the revolution of 1848, there is only one character, Père Oudry, a regular visitor at the Dambreuses', but also invited, as neighbour, to the Arnoux'.

To reconstruct this social space, I simply noted methodically just who attends the different meetings or gatherings or dinners. The Dambreuses play host to anonymous, generically defined personalities, a former minister, a priest of a large parish, two government officials, two property owners, and well-known people from the realms of art, science and politics. The Arnoux invite more or less famous artists, always designated by their names, such as Dittmar, a painter, or Blaise, a portraitist. This is normal in a field in which one of the main stakes is to become famous or to make a name for oneself, *se faire un nom*. The receptions organized by Rosanette, the *demi-mondaine*, bring people from these two worlds together. Her world, the *demi-monde*, is an in-between, intermediate world. The two poles are totally opposed to each other: on the one hand, money and luxury, on the other, money devalued in favour of intelligence. On the one hand, serious, boring, conservative conversation; on the other, readily obscene and always paradoxical speech. While the Dambreuses serve the most expensive and most classic of dishes (venison and lobster, accompanied by the best wines, served in the finest of silver), chez Arnoux the more exotic the dish, the better.

These two poles are completely incompatible, as is fire with water. What is good at one pole is bad at the other, and vice versa. The writers and artists cultivate disinterested intelligence, the gratuitous act, deliberate poverty, all those things which characterize the artist's life; the powerful and the monied worship money and power. But throughout the whole space, all the lines of force converge on the pole of political and economic power. And from the outset, the Dambreuses are clearly indicated as the supreme pole of attraction for those with political and sentimental ambitions. It is with the Dambreuses in mind that Deslauriers says to Frédéric. 'Just think of it! A man with millions. See if you can't get into his good books and his wife's as well. Become her lover!'

*Education* may be read as an experimental novel in the true sense of the term. Flaubert first offers us a description of the field of power, within which he traces the movements of six young men, including Frédéric, who are propelled in it like so many particles in a magnetic field. And each one's trajectory – what we normally call the history of his life – is determined by the interaction between the forces of the field and his own inertia, that is, the habitus as the remanence of a trajectory which tends to orient future trajectory.

The field of power is a field of latent, potential forces which play upon any particle which may venture into it, but it is also a battlefield which

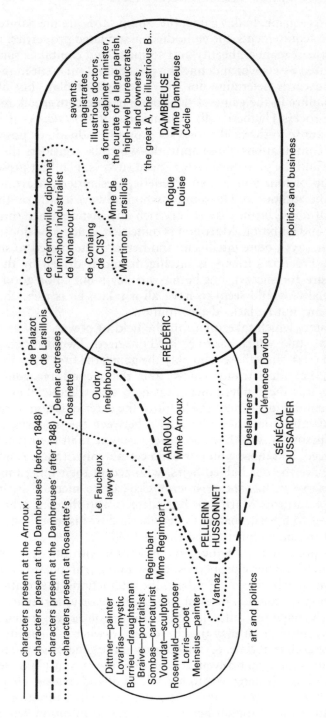

Figure 4 *The field of power according to* Sentimental Education

——— characters present at the Arnoux'

———— characters present at the Dambreuses' (before 1848)

– – – – characters present at the Dambreuses' (after 1848)

· · · · · characters present at Rosanette's

**art and politics**

Dittmer—painter
Lovarias—mystic
Burrieu—draughtsman
Braive—portraitist
Sombas—caricaturist
Vourdat—sculptor
Rosenwald—composer
Lorris—poet
Meinsius—painter

Vatnaz

PELLERIN
HUSSONNET

Regimbart
Mme Regimbart

Le Faucheux
lawyer

ARNOUX
Mme Arnoux

Deslauriers
Clémence Daviou

SÉNÉCAL
DUSSARDIER

Oudry
(neighbour)

FRÉDÉRIC

de Palazot
de Larsillois

Delmar actresses
Rosanette

de Grémonville, diplomat
Fumichon, industrialist
de Nonancourt

de Comaing
de CISY

Martinon

Mme de
Larsillois

savants,
magistrates,
illustrious doctors,
a former cabinet minister,
the curate of a large parish,
high-level bureaucrats,
land owners,
'the great A, the illustrious B...'

DAMBREUSE
Mme Dambreuse
Cécile

Rogue
Louise

**politics and business**

can be seen as a game. In this game, the trump cards are the habitus, that is to say, the acquirements, the embodied, assimilated properties, such as elegance, ease of manner, beauty and so forth, and capital as such, that is, the inherited assets which define the possibilities inherent in the field. These trump cards determine not only the style of play, but also the success or failure in the game of the young people concerned, in short, the whole process Flaubert calls *éducation sentimentale*. As if he had wished to expose to the field's forces a group of individuals possessing, in different combinations, those aptitudes which he considers the trump cards in life and the prerequisites for social success, Flaubert presents us with a group of four young men, Frédéric, Deslauriers, Martinon and Cisy, with the addition of Hussonnet, who is always a little on the edge of things. Of noble birth, Cisy is very rich and distinguished, but lacks intelligence and ambition. Martinon is quite rich, quite good-looking (or at least so he says), quite intelligent and fiercely determined to succeed. Deslauriers, Frédéric's friend, is intelligent and is driven by the same burning desire for success, but he has neither money nor good looks. Frédéric, finally, would seem to have all it takes: he is rich, charming and intelligent; but he lacks determination.

In the game, which takes place in the field of power, power itself is obviously the stake which has to be held or seized. Two distinctions can be drawn in relation to those who play the game, the first regarding their *inheritance*, i.e. their trump cards, and the second regarding their attitude towards their inheritance, that is to say, whether they possess the fundamental dimension of the habitus, the determination to succeed. There is thus an initial line to be drawn between the upstarts, Deslauriers and Hussonnet, who have no other resource than their determination to succeed, and those who possess a certain inheritance. Among the latter, there are the untroubled heirs, who accept their inheritance and seek to preserve it, like the aristocrat Cisy, or to increase it, like the swaggering bourgeois Martinon. But there is also the heir who, so to speak, refuses to inherit, that is, to be inherited by his inheritance, or to do what he should to inherit, and that is Frédéric.

With this polarized space the game is set up; with the description of the young men's intrinsic properties, the winning trump cards are dealt, and the game may begin. For Flaubert, the interactions, the relationships of competition or conflict, or even the fortunate or unfortunate coincidences which shape the different life histories concerned are merely so many opportunities to display the characters' essence as their life stories unfold in the course of time. As the creator of the generative model from which all the subsequent adventures derive, the novelist has never so obviously and totally entered into his role of divine creator. He endows himself with the *intuitus originarius*, the generative intuition which, according to Kant, distinguishes God's creative intuition from finite human intuition. In fact, as if in some Leibnizian universe, everything is given *in actu*, from the outset, to the Godlike creator–spectator. The young men's trajectories and the different forms that love, money and power give to each one's sentimental education are all determined by the forces present in the field interacting with the embodied forces of the young men's habitus. In such a universe there is no room for chance, and Victor Brombert is right to contradict Jean Bruneau[1] by saying: 'In a novel apparently submitted to the rule of chance, meetings, disappearances, opportunities missed or taken, there is in fact no room at all for chance. Henry James, for whom the novel read "like an epic without air," rightly noted that everything in it "hangs together".'[2]

In fact, in the enclosed and finite world of this novel, very similar to that of detective novels in which characters are trapped on an island or in some isolated country manor, the twenty main characters have every chance of meeting each other, and therefore of fulfilling, in the course of some necessary and eminently foreseeable adventure, all the implications of the generative formula by which they are governed. One could thus take each of the young men and demonstrate that, as essentialist philosophy would have it, his life story is nothing but the fulfilment of things already implied by his essence. For example, we learn at the end of the first comparison of the five young men's trajectories that Cisy would drop his law studies. And why should he ever finish them? After those few adolescent years in Paris, traditionally given over to the bohemian life in the company of people with heretical ways and ideas, he loses no time in getting back to the straight and narrow way which leads him to the future, already implied by his past, that is, to the country estate of his ancestors. He ends up as he should: 'sunk deep in religion and the father of eight children'.

I shall not dwell on the detailed analysis that I have carried out elsewhere concerning the opposition between Frédéric and Deslauriers.[3] This opposition is manifold: between those who inherit possessions and those who inherit only the desire for possessions, between those who have capital without necessarily having the determination to preserve or increase it and those who have the urge to succeed without having the necessary capital; the opposition, in short, between bourgeois and petit-bourgeois. As a case in point, during the visit to the brothel 'Chez la Turque', Frédéric, who ran off, had the money but lacked the audacity, while Deslauriers, who would have gone through with it, did not have the money and was obliged to follow Frédéric's lead. Everything that happens to Deslauriers is inscribed in the structural relationship between the bourgeoisie and the petite bourgeoisie.

This objective relationship takes the shape of a peculiar relationship between Deslauriers and Frédéric, where the driving force is the former's hopeless desire to become Frédéric, the desperate hope of being someone else. For Flaubert's characters, true examples of 'windowless and doorless monads' imprisoned within their own essential being, nothing can happen that is not already written into the original formula. This is true of those things which seem to come spontaneously from competition and interaction, such as the successive occasions on which Deslauriers tries to usurp Frédéric's place in the affection of Monsieur Dambreuse or Madame Arnoux, or in Deslauriers' final marriage with Louise. This urge to take another's place which leads to identifying with another, to putting oneself in another's place, to taking oneself *for* another, lies at the very heart of petit-bourgeois pretension.

We should perhaps dwell on another case, that of Hussonnet, another petit-bourgeois, whom Flaubert has some trouble in differentiating from Deslauriers. The two men are in fact at one time associated in some politico-literary undertaking, and they are always very close to each other in their behaviour and their opinions, though the one tends more towards literature and the other towards politics. Very early on, Hussonnet had embarked on a literary career. He is a typical incarnation of those bohemian souls whom Max Weber lumps together under the title of proletaroid intelligentsia, who are always predestined to material deprivation and intellectual disappointment. Year after year, Hussonnet maintains a certain status as a literary gentleman, writing rejected reviews and run-of-the-mill verse. As failures accumulate, as endlessly cherished plans for a weekly paper follow an unsuccessful daily paper down the drain, Hussonnet turns into an embittered bohemian ready to belittle all his contemporaries' efforts in art or in revolutionary action. He finally assumes a position as the recognized leading light in a group of reactionaries; completely disillusioned, particularly with intellectual things, he is ready for anything, even for writing biographies of industrial magnates, in order to gain a position of power within the intellectual field. He does in fact end up obtaining the high-ranking position from which he can dominate all the theatres and all the press, and where he can give free rein to what you Americans magnificently describe as his 'meatballism', that is, the anti-intellectual stance of dominated, underling intellectuals which found its exemplary expression as much in Zhdanovism as in National Socialist populism (such comparisons are more than simple analogies, because they are based on the homology between different structures of the ruling class).

But it is through Frédéric that one can demonstrate most fully all the implications of Flaubert's model. An heir who does not wish to be taken up by his inheritance and made what he is, i.e. a 'bourgeois', he wavers between reproduction strategies which are all quite incompatible with one another. By persistently refusing to follow the normal course of sociological and biological reproduction, for example, through a marriage with Louise, he ultimately jeopardizes those chances of reproduction that he does possess. At different stages his contradictory ambitions drive him towards each of the poles which dominate the social space in which he moves: he vacillates between an artistic or a business career and, at the same time, between the two women corresponding to these social stances, passionate love for Madame Arnoux and a more reasoned affair with Madame Dambreuse. This vacillation is the infallible sign of a being without *gravity*, lacking all the weight of character and seriousness, and hence incapable of offering the least resistance to the forces of the field.

Frédéric uses his inheritance to defer and postpone the moment when he will actually inherit; his subjective indetermination tends to prolong the state of indecision in which he exists. Lacking any impetus of his own, whether it be the bourgeois tendency to uphold an inherited dominant position or the petit-bourgeois desire to attain such a position, he breaks the golden rule of the field of power, trying to bring about the marriage of opposing extremes, the *coincidentia oppositorum*, by attempting to maintain a position of untenable equilibrium between the two worlds. In fact, Frédéric's sentimental education is nothing other than a progressive apprenticeship in the impossibility of reconciling two different worlds: art and unalloyed passion on the one hand, money and venal affection on the other. The story of his failures is nothing other than the enumeration of those unfortunate coincidences when the two worlds, which he can bring together only to the extent that he keeps them carefully apart, suddenly become entangled one with the other.

Owing to the duality of these distinct worlds, Frédéric can, as Flaubert says, lead the 'double life' which enables him to put off, for a time, any lasting or binding decision (one has only to think of all those misunderstandings which successively occur to Frédéric's advantage or disadvantage). But the risk of an *accident*, an unforeseen collision between social possibilities, each of which would normally exclude the others, is none the less inherent in the simultaneous existence of several separate and distinct series. The most typical example of this role-switching is organized by Martinon, something of a specialist in such matters. He throws Madame Dambreuse into the willing arms of Frédéric and, in the meantime, courts and marries the Dambreuses' daughter, Cécile, thus inheriting Monsieur Dambreuse's fortune, which he had formerly hoped to attain through Madame Dambreuse, who is finally disinherited by her husband at the very moment that Frédéric inherits her from him. The phenomenon of social ageing, with its correspondingly diminished range of social possibilities, is none other than the series of successive and necessary crises arising from the interplay of two incompatible universes, those of art and business.

We can check our model by observing the trajectory of Arnoux, who is, from the structural point of view, Frédéric's exact double. Arnoux, who occupies the intellectual pole of the field of power, is, like Frédéric, a double-sided character who represents money and business in the world of art. As a member of the art industry, he is really at home neither with art, nor with industry; and it is his very vagueness which, as with Frédéric, leads to his downfall. 'His intelligence could neither rise high enough to attain the realm of art, nor remain bourgeois enough to concentrate purely on the profit; so that in the end he satisfied no one and ruined himself in the process.' Like Frédéric, he endeavours to postpone the unhappy fate that awaits him as the inhabitant of two incompatible universes, but he can do so only by endlessly playing a double game with art on the one hand and money on the other. In Frédéric's case, life history, taken as a process of social ageing, is traced through a series of necessary reductions in the range of objective possibilities. As far as ambition is concerned, the oscillation of the pendulum from art (or even several arts) to money and back again tends to diminish as time goes on; but Frédéric nevertheless continues to oscillate between a position of power in the art world on the one hand and, on the other, a position in the realm of upper administration and business under the wing of Monsieur Dambreuse. Sentimentally speaking, Frédéric continues until the very end to swing widely between *amour fou* – headlong passion, the art for art's sake of love – and more mercenary affairs. On the one hand we have Madame Arnoux, and on the other, Rosanette or Madame Dambreuse, not to mention Louise, who offers Frédéric a haven in those moments when his stock is low.

To understand the losing game, the 'loser takes all' sort of game that Frédéric makes of his life, one must be aware of the correspondences that Flaubert establishes between the different forms of love and the different forms of art, as well as of the inverted relationship between the world of pure art and the world of business. The art game is, in fact, in relation to the business world, a losing game, a game of loser takes all. The real winners are the losers: those who earn money and honours (it was Flaubert who said 'honours bring dishonour'), those who achieve wordly success surely jeopardize their salvation in the world beyond. The underlying law of this paradoxical game is that it is to one's interest to be disinterested: the advantage always falls to those who seek none. The love of art is an unreasoning love, at least when considered from the point of view of the everyday world, the normal world, as portrayed in the bourgeois theatre of the day.

Flaubert gives us a model of the different forms of love which were in the process of being invented, as one can see, for example, by reading *La vie de bohème*, and he makes it clear that the historical invention of new forms of love, represented in the novel by Frédéric's relationships with

Madame Arnoux and Rosanette, is inseparable from the historical invention of new forms of love of art. A perfect homology exists between the forms of love and the forms of the love of art. The structure of the relationship between the forms of love is clearly revealed in the scene at the auction sale when Madame Dambreuse and Rosanette meet in front of the objects left by Madame Arnoux. Frédéric finds himself placed between the woman who buys love, Madame Dambreuse, and the woman who sells it, Rosanette, and between the two forms of bourgeois love, the legitimate wife and the mistress, which are complementary and hierarchized, like the *monde* and the *demi-monde*. It is there that Frédéric makes a statement of that pure love which, fixing on its object, transports it beyond all price. There is a perfect homology with the opposition between art for art's sake and bourgeois art. Just as pure love is the art for art's sake of love, so art for art's sake is the pure love of art: the term 'a work of art' is reserved exclusively for the object that has no price, which is never sold and which in any event is not created to be sold. Through his unreasoning passion for Madame Arnoux, Frédéric seeks to apply to the field of power the fundamental law of the artistic and literary fields: having chosen to play a losing game, he can do none other than lose; and he loses on all accounts, because unlike pure art, pure love is necessarily sterile, and can never be embodied through any act of creation.

It is in this equivalence between pure love and art for art's sake that we perceive the real essence of Flaubert's identification with Frédéric. By insisting on unreasoning passion and pure love, which turns upside down the laws of the conventional world of business, money, businessmen and mercenary women, Frédéric reproduces the essential features in the make-up of the modern artist, a new category invented by the creation of an autonomous artistic field: the creation of a new art of living that flouts the laws obtaining in the everyday world outside.

Flaubert is undoubtedly one of those who contributed most to the invention of the artist's life or, to be more precise, the field of art, this upside-down world whose laws are the exact contrary of those in the ordinary world and where the artist's very impotence is the mainspring of his creative potency. Writing about impotence is perhaps for Flaubert one way of grasping the truth of the very special potency which is granted to writers and their writings. This capacity for retrospective appropriation through the near-magical evocation of the past is rooted in impotence, in the powerlessness to appropriate the present and things present. We are not far from Proust, who understood Flaubert's taste for the imperfect so well.

And so we return to the phrase which, at the very end of the novel, concludes the comments of Frédéric and Deslauriers about their unsuccessful visit to the brothel: 'It was there that we had the best of our lives.' This tale of innocent impotence, this rout of naïveté and purity, stands out, in retrospect, as a peak of achievement, a fulfilment. In fact, it symbolically condenses Frédéric's whole life story, that is, the extremely gratifying awareness of being in possession of a number of possibilities among which he will not and cannot choose. If the story ends with the nostalgic account of this sort of initial scene, it is because, like the prophecies and the premonitions of tragic drama, the scene contains in coded form the entire future of the protagonists and of their relationships to one another. The immediate possession of all these possibilities, of all these possible lives, creates that uncertainty which is at the heart of the impotence, but it turns out to be a supreme form of happiness that the writer carves out for himself when he manages, through his writing, to 'live all human lives'. But, in the normal course of events, this revelation is always retrospective. 'It was there that we had the best of our lives.' Victor Brombert, who saw very clearly that this phrase holds as it were the key to *Sentimental Education*, reminds us, in the same connection, of the phrase with which Frédéric ends his account of his relationship with Madame Arnoux: 'Never mind, he says, we shall have loved each other dearly.' Because it goes against all the laws of the ordinary world and ordinary love, pure love is experienced as a future anterior, as an unrealized condition in the past. And, in the same way, art, this power to create semblances of reality which are more real than reality, is rooted in the artist's inability to face reality.

The relationship which blinds Frédéric to Madame Arnoux, this feeling to which all other earthly goals, and above all the striving after power and money, are firmly subordinated, is the precise equivalent, in a different sphere, of the feeling that the writer as defined by Flaubert entertains in relation to his art. Frédéric never quite achieves in real experience the happiness of his dreams; he is impassioned by a 'nostalgic and ineffable yearning' through the evocation of images of the mistresses of former kings; he conspires, through his clumsiness, his indecision or his fastidiousness, with those strokes of fate which come to delay or impede the fulfilment of his desires and his ambitions. One could quote twenty passages from the *Correspondence* where Flaubert himself says precisely this. For example: 'There are many things which leave me unperturbed when I see them or when others talk of them, but which arouse me, irritate me, or cut me to the quick, if I speak about them, but above all, if I write about them myself.' Or, and again I quote: 'When one is at grips with life, one perceives it badly, the suffering or the enjoyment is too keen. For me, the artist is a monstrosity, an outlaw of nature.'

This is a far cry from the usual way of stating the problem of the relationship between the writer and his hero as well as of the social and sexual potency and impotence which is, beyond all doubt, one of Flaubert's central obsessions.[4] In fact, Flaubert takes his distance from Frédéric, who is one of his own possibilities, and from his impotence, his indecisiveness and his indifference, in the very act of writing Frédéric's history. For we know that one of the aspects of Frédéric's impotence is that he cannot write. But Flaubert does not stop at affirming his own potency by objectifying impotence; he also objectifies the principle of this symbolic power of objectification. He perceives it in the incapacity or refusal to possess in naked simplicity, if you will allow me the expression, either women or money or power, and he also objectifies Frédéric's relationships with the structure of the field of power which lies behind this impotence and, although he does not say it, behind his own power to objectify this impotence in a novel.

In the character of Frédéric, Flaubert expresses the generative formula which lies at the foundation of his fictional work. This formula is a relationship of a twofold refusal, which favours a relationship of objectifying distance with the social world. This relation of double refusal is clearly evidenced in the frequent appearance in his work of those pairs of characters which serve as generative schemes: Henry and Jules in the first *Sentimental Education*, Frédéric and Deslauriers, Pellerin and Delmar in the second. The same formula explains Flaubert's taste for antithesis and symmetrical constructions, especially noticeable in *Bouvard et Péchuchet*, and his liking for parallel antithesis, for criss-crossed trajectories which lead so many of his characters from one end of the field of power to the other, with all the ensuing train of sentimental recantations and correlative political reversals. But the clearest proof of the existence of this generative formula is given in the outlines of novels published by Madame Durry and particularly in the one entitled *The Friend's Vow*. The structures that are overlaid and hidden, as the writer works and shapes his initial intuition, are now perfectly visible, and we can follow the criss-crossed trajectories of no fewer than three pairs of antithetical characters.

A good example of the double refusal leading to a stance of disillusioned social aloofness can be seen in Flaubert's use of free reported speech and quotation. Quotation, in Flaubert's hands, is eminently ambiguous and can be taken as either a token of approval or a signal of derision, and this phenomenon demonstrates quite well the way in which Flaubert may veer from hostility to identification. This ambivalence is perceptible when Flaubert, in his *Dictionnaire des idées reçues*, singles out the expression *tonner contre*, to thunder against something. One cannot help thinking that Flaubert himself falls into the trap of thundering against the bourgeois propensity for thundering against things or persons.

This aloofness from the social world, the origins of which we will analyse later, meant that Flaubert was clearly predisposed to produce the view of the social space that he puts before us in *Sentimental Education*. One could call it a sociological view of things, except that it differs from a sociological analysis by its specifically literary form. Since this form paradoxically conceals the underlying structure that it reveals – a paradox borne out by the fact that the structure is perfectly obvious as soon as it is pointed out – it has remained unnoticed so far.

The sociological reading, which abruptly unveils the structure that the literary text unveils while still veiling it, runs uncomfortably counter to the literary approach; and more often than not it gives rise to hostile reactions, since it is considered somewhat vulgar. In such a case, instead of waxing indignant and putting the reaction down to ingrained resistance to scientific analysis, the sociologist should try to understand the grounds for such behaviour: he should try to grasp the difference between literary expression and scientific expression, which comes to light when a fictional work is translated in scientific terms. For the sociologist lays bare a truth that the literary text will reveal only in veiled terms, that it will say only in such a manner as to leave it unsaid, that is, by means of negation, of *Verneinung*, as Freud uses the term. By so doing, he also uncovers the fact that the specific quality of literary expression consists precisely of this negation, this *Verneinung*, that is operative in literary form. This way of withholding things which is characteristic of the literary view of life is the thing which, above and beyond the aesthetic function it fulfils, enables an author to reveal truths that would otherwise be unbearable.

No doubt you have been wondering whether Flaubert knowingly constructed the model that I have found in his novel. In fact, literary fiction is undoubtedly, for the author and his reader, a way of making known that which one does not wish to know. It is in this light that one should consider all those fictional conventions of the novel as a game which defines what we call *realism*. The appearance of reality which satisfies the need to know is in fact achieved by that semblance of reality which allows the reader to ignore the real state of things, to refuse to see things as they really are. The sociological reading of a text breaks the spell by breaking the tacit complicity that binds author and reader together in the same relationship of negation with regard to the reality indicated in the text. Such a reading, although it reveals a truth that the text says, but in such a way as not to say it, does not reveal the text's own truth; and it would be completely erroneous if it claimed to give the entire truth contained in a text which owes its specificity precisely to the fact that it does not say what it says in a way a scientific text would say it. It is doubtless the form, the literary form in which literary objectification takes place, which enables the most deeply buried and the most safely hidden truth to emerge: indeed, the form constitutes the veil that allows author and reader to hide from themselves (as well as from others) this repressed truth (in this case, the structure of the field of power and the model of social ageing). This no doubt explains how it happens that literature so often reveals, by means of negation or *Verneinung*, truths which social sciences, with their promethean ambition, cannot quite grasp.

The charm of literature lies to a great extent in the fact that, unlike science, according to Searle, it deals with serious matters without asking to be taken completely seriously. It is the act of writing and the licence it grants for negated, disavowed confession that bestows on the author himself and his reader a negated, unavowed understanding, which is no mere half understanding but rather an understanding which is at once total and null. In his *Critique of Dialectical Reason*, Sartre says of his first readings of Marx, 'I understood everything, and I understood nothing.' Such is the understanding of life that we get through reading novels: we understand everything and we understand nothing. If through writing and reading one can, as Flaubert says, 'live all human lives', this is only because they are ways of not living those lives. And we have to learn everything again from scratch when we actually experience those situations we have lived through a hundred times in the pages of novels.

Flaubert, the novelist of novelistic illusion, reveals the essence of this illusion. In life as in novels, the romantic characters – and novelists among them – are perhaps those who take fiction seriously, not, as has been suggested, to escape reality and flee to imaginary worlds, but because, like Frédéric, they simply cannot take reality seriously, because they cannot come to grips with the present as it presents itself, the insistent and therefore terrifying present as it stands. The smooth running of all social mechanisms, whether in the literary field or in the field of power, depends on the existence of the *illusio*, the interest, the investment, in both economic and psychological senses (this investment is called *Besetzung* in German and 'cathexis' in English). But Frédéric is a man who cannot throw himself into any of the games with art or money that society produces and proposes to its members. His bovarism is a flight into unreality, motivated by his inability to take reality seriously, to take seriously the stakes in so called serious games. The novelistic illusion which, in its most radical form, as with Don Quixote and Emma Bovary, goes so far as to abolish completely the frontier between reality and fiction, seems to be powered by the fact that reality is experienced as an illusion. If such illusions or delusions thrive above all in adolescence, and if Frédéric seems a perfect example of this age, it is perhaps because the entry into adult life, that is, into one or another of the social games that society asks us to invest in, does not always seem the most obvious thing to do. Frédéric, like all difficult adolescents, serves as a formidable analyst of our deepest relationships with society. To objectify romantic, fictional illusion, and above all, the relationship with the so-called real world on which it hinges, is to be reminded that the reality against which we measure all our imaginings is merely the recognized referent for an (almost) universally recognized illusion.

Flaubert says all this without saying it, and it is quite understandable that we understand without understanding. One is reminded of Proust's comment: 'A work that is stamped with theories is like an object that is still stamped with its price.' That is to say, there is something vulgar about bringing to the surface of a literary work its underlying theories. And yet, one should go all the way and try to make explicit the theory of the literary effect, of the novel's charm that is contained within the analysis of the effect that the sociological analysis exerts upon a literary text. The novelistic vision simulates and dissimulates reality; in the very act of giving it, it withdraws it. The form of the literary creation by which writers are able to say whatever the formal conventions of the day allow them to say is itself a mask; it brings unreality to what it presents as reality. Literary charm lies in this double game: 'Quae plus latent, plus placent,' said Saint Bernard. The more a work hides, the greater the pleasure. The more the writings are able to suggest, veiling what they are unveiling, the greater is the specifically literary effect that they produce and that the objectification tends to destroy.

Literary charm lies in a relationship of veiled revelation between an historical form and an historical content or context. The 'eternal charm' that Marx himself felt obliged to confer at least to Greek art may be understood in purely historical terms. It appears when what the veiled revelation reveals is an invariant historical structure, as, in the particular case of *Sentimental Education*, the structure of the field of power that every adolescent (at least every bourgeois adolescent) must confront, in 1848 as well as in 1968.

These are my initial reflections on *Sentimental Education*. Since the novel only reveals the structure of the society which it expresses in a disguised fashion, in the next lecture we shall have to come back to the direct, frankly sociological analysis of the structure of the field of power and of the literary field in which Flaubert himself took shape and which lies behind his representation of this structure.

# 5

# Field of Power, Literary Field and Habitus

The reading of *Sentimental Education* has allowed the extraction of two bodies of information: first, Flaubert's representation of the structure of the field of power and the writer's position in that structure; and second, what I have termed Flaubert's formula, the generative scheme which, as the fundamental structure of Flaubert's habitus, is at the basis of the Flaubertian construction of the social world. In sum, on the one hand, Flaubert's sociology, meaning the sociology which he produces; on the other, the sociology of Flaubert, meaning the sociology of which he is the object. If it is true that the former furnishes us with elements for the latter, we must first of all submit it to the test. What is the structure of the social space in which the Flaubertian project was generated?

In my opinion, the approach the analyst should take in order to understand Flaubert's position, and thus uncover the principle of his work, is precisely the opposite of Sartre's approach in *The Family Idiot*. Generally speaking, Sartre seeks the genetic principle of Flaubert's work in the individual Gustave, in his infancy, in his first familial experiences. Using the method outlined in the chapter of the *Critique of Dialectical Reason* entitled 'Questions of Method', Sartre hopes to discover a mediation between social structures and the work. He finds this mediation thanks to a method of analysis which integrates psychoanalysis and sociology in a social psychology of Flaubert, and which, as evidenced by the title, accords an enormous role to Flaubert's position in his family and to the experiences associated with the relationships between Flaubert, his father and his older brother.

One may credit Sartre with having reintroduced the social dimension into intra-familial relations: the relationship to the father or the older brother is one of the probable careers which are proposed to Flaubert and thus to the *space of social possibles* available to him. Nevertheless, we do not abandon the point of view of the individual; or indeed, when we do, it is to leap, in one motion, into the 'society' taken in its entirety (vol. 2 of *The Family Idiot*). Thus we have on the one hand a macro-sociology, and on the other a social micro-psychology, without a relation between the two ever being truly established.

We find here something that happens to all who attempt a sociological analysis of literary creation; it is as much the case with Lukács or Goldmann as with Adorno in relation to Heidegger, among so many others. This is also what makes one doubt the possibility of a true sociology of literary creation. Sartre's merit is that, with his characteristically mad energy, he pushed the paradigm to its limits, setting the considerable resources of his talent and culture to the task of attempting to account totally for a creative project as a function of social variables. And I believe he failed (even if he brings interesting ideas to the psycho-sociology of Flaubert's family experience).

Thus, we must completely reverse the procedure and ask, not how a writer comes to be what he is, in a sort of genetic psycho-sociology, but rather how the position or 'post' he occupies – that of a writer of a particular type – became constituted. It is only then that we can ask if the knowledge of particular social conditions of the production of what I have termed his habitus permits us to understand that he has succeeded in occupying this position, if only by transforming it. The genetic structuralism I propose is designed to understand both the genesis of social structures – the literary field – and the genesis of the dispositions of the habitus of the agents who are involved in these structures.

This is not self-evident. For example, historians of art and literature, victims of what I call the illusion of the constancy of the nominal, retrospectively transport, in their analyses of cultural productions prior to the second half of the nineteenth century, definitions of the writer and the artist which are entirely recent historical inventions and which, having become constitutive of our cultural universe, appear to us as a given. The invention of the writer and the artist, to which Flaubert himself greatly contributed, is the end result of a collective enterprise which is inseparable from (1) the constitution of an autonomous literary field, independent of or even opposite to the economic field (e.g. bohemian vs bourgeois), and (2) the constitution of a tactical position within the field (e.g. artist vs bohemian).

What do I mean by 'field'? As I use the term, a field is a separate social universe having its own laws of functioning independent of those of politics and the economy. The existence of the writer, as fact and as value, is inseparable from the existence of the literary field as an autonomous universe endowed with specific principles of evaluation of practices and works. To understand Flaubert or Baudelaire, or any writer, major or minor, is first of all to understand what the status of writer consists of at the moment considered; that is, more precisely, the social conditions of the possibility of this social function, of this social personage. In fact, the invention of the writer, in the modern sense of the term, is inseparable from the progressive invention of a particular social game, which I term the *literary field* and which is constituted as it establishes its autonomy, that is to say, its specific laws of functioning, within the field of power.

To provide a preliminary idea of what I mean by that I will make use of the old notion of the 'Republic of Letters', of which Bayle, in his *Dictionnaire historique et critique*, had announced the fundamental law: 'Liberty is what reigns in the Republic of Letters. This Republic is an extremely free state. In it, the only empire is that of truth and reason; and under their auspices, war is naïvely waged against just about anybody. Friends must protect themselves from their friends, fathers from children, fathers-in-law from sons-in-law: it is a century of iron. In it everyone is both ruler and subject of everyone else.' Several fundamental properties of the field are enunciated in this text, in a partly normative, partly positive mode: the war of everyone against everyone, that is, universal competition, the closing of the field upon itself, which causes it to be its own market and makes each of the producers seek his customers among his competitors; the ambiguity, therefore, of this world where one may see, according to the adopted perspective, the paradise of the ideal republic, where everyone is at once sovereign and subject, or the hell of the Hobbesian battle of everyone against everyone.

But it is necessary to make the definition somewhat more precise. The literary field (one may also speak of the artistic field, the philosophical field, etc.) is an independent social universe with its own laws of functioning, its specific relations of force, its dominants and its dominated, and so forth. Put another way, to speak of 'field' is to recall that literary works are produced in a particular social universe endowed with particular institutions and obeying specific laws. And yet this observation runs counter to both the tradition of internal reading, which considers works in themselves independently from the historical conditions in which they were produced, and the tradition of external explication, which one normally associates with sociology and which relates the works directly to the economic and social conditions of the moment.

This field is neither a vague social background nor even a *milieu artistique* like a universe of personal relations between artists and writers (perspectives adopted by those who study 'influences'). It is a veritable social universe where, in accordance with its particular laws, there accumulates a particular form of capital and where relations of force of a particular type are exerted. This universe is the place of entirely specific struggles, notably concerning the question of knowing who is part of the universe, who is a real writer and who is not. The important fact, for the interpretation of works, is that this autonomous social universe functions somewhat like a prism which *refracts* every external determination: demographic, economic or political events are always retranslated according to the specific logic of the field, and it is by this intermediary that they act on the logic of the development of works.

To know Flaubert (or Baudelaire or Feydeau), to understand his work, is thus to understand, first of all, what this entirely special social universe is, with customs as organized and mysterious as those of a primitive tribe. It is to understand, in the first place, how it is defined in relation to the field of power and, in particular, in relation to the fundamental law of this universe, which is that of economy and power. Without going into detail at this point in the analysis, I will merely say that the literary field is the economic world reversed; that is, the fundamental law of this specific universe, that of disinterestedness, which establishes a negative correlation between temporal (notably financial) success and properly artistic value, is the inverse of the law of economic exchange. The artistic field is a *universe of belief.* Cultural production distinguishes itself from the production of the most common objects in that it must produce not only the object in its materiality, but also the value of this object, that is, the recognition of artistic legitimacy. This is inseparable from the production of the artist or the writer as artist or writer, in other words, as a creator of value. A reflection on the meaning of the artist's signature would thus be in order.

In the second place, this autonomous field, a kind of *coin de folie* or corner of madness within the field of power, occupies a dominated position in the field. Those who enter this completely particular social game participate in domination, but as *dominated* agents: they are neither dominant, plain and simple, nor are they dominated (as they want to believe at certain moments of their history). Rather, they occupy a dominated position in the dominant class, they are owners of a dominated form of power at the interior of the sphere of power. This structurally contradictory position is absolutely crucial for understanding the positions taken by writers and artists, notably in struggles in the social world.

Dominated among the dominant, writers and artists are placed in a precarious position which destines them to a kind of objective, therefore subjective, indetermination: the image which others, notably the dominants within the field of power, send back to them is marked by the ambivalence which is generated in all societies by beings defying common classifications. The writer – or the intellectual – is enjoined to a double status, which is a bit suspect: as possessor of a dominated weak power, he is obliged to situate himself somewhere between the two roles represented, in medieval tradition, by the *orator*, symbolic counter-weight of the *bellator*, charged with preaching and praying, with saying the true and the good, with consecrating or condemning by speech, and by the *fool*, a character freed from convention and conformities to whom is accorded transgression without consequences, inspired by the pure pleasure of breaking the rule or of shocking. Every ambiguity of the modern intellectual is inscribed in the character of the fool: he is the ugly buffoon, ridiculous, a bit vile, but he is also the alerter who warns or the adviser who brings forth the lesson; and, above all, he is the demolisher of social illusions.

Significantly, all statistical inquiries show that the social properties of agents, thus their dispositions, correspond to the social properties of the position they occupy. The literary and artistic fields attract a particularly strong proportion of individuals who possess all the properties of the dominant class *minus one*: money. They are, if I may say, *parents pauvres* or 'poor relatives' of the great bourgeois dynasties, aristocrats already ruined or in decline, members of stigmatized minorities like Jews or foreigners. One thus discovers, from the first moment, that is, at the level even of the social position of the literary and artistic field in the field of power, a property which Sartre discovered within the domestic unit and in the particular case of Flaubert: the writer is the 'poor relative', the *idiot of the bourgeois family*.

The structural ambiguity of their position in the field of power leads writers and painters, these 'penniless bourgeois' in Pissarro's words, to maintain an ambivalent relationship with the dominant class within the field of power, those whom they call 'bourgeois', as well as with the dominated, the 'people'. In a similar way, they form an ambiguous image of their own position in social space and of their social function: this explains the fact that they are subject to great fluctuation, notably in the area of politics (for example, when the centre of gravity of the field shifted towards the left in 1848, one notes a general swing towards 'social art': Baudelaire, for instance, speaks of the childish or 'puerile utopia of art for art's sake' and rises up in violent terms against pure art (see *De l'École païenne*, 1851).

The characteristics of the positions occupied by intellectuals and artists in the field of power can be specified as a function of the positions they occupy in the literary or artistic field. In other words, the position of the literary field within the field of power affects everything that occurs within the latter. In order to understand what artists and writers can say or do, one must always take into account their membership of a dominated universe and the greater or lesser distance of this universe from that of the dominant class, an overall distance that varies with different periods and societies and also, at any given time, with various positions within the literary field. One of the great principles of differentiation within the literary field, in fact, lies in the relationship towards the structural position of the field, and thus of the writer, that different positions within the literary field favour; or, if one prefers, in the different ways of realizing this fundamental relationship, that is, in the different relationships with economic or political power, and with the dominant fraction, that are associated with these different positions.

Thus the three positions around which the literary field is organized between 1830 and 1850, namely, to use the indigenous labels, 'social art', 'art for art's sake' and 'bourgeois art', must be understood first as so many particular forms of the generic relationship which unites writers, dominated-dominant, to the dominant-dominant. The partisans of social art, republican and democratic like Pierre Leroux, Louis Blanc or Proudhon, or liberal Catholics like Lamennais and many others who are now completely unknown, condemn the 'egotistical' art of the partisans of art for art's sake and demand that literature fulfil a social or political function. Their lower position within the literary field, at the intersection of the literary field with the political field, doubtless maintains a circular causal relationship with respect to their solidarity with the dominated, a relationship that certainly is based in part on hostility towards the dominant within the intellectual field.

The partisans of 'bourgeois art', who write in the main for the theatre, are closely and directly tied to the dominant class by their lifestyle and their system of values, and they receive, in addition to significant material benefits (the theatre is the most economically profitable of literary activities) all the symbols of bourgeois honour – notably the Academy. In painting, with Horace Vernet or Paul Delaroche, in literature with Paul de Kock or Scribe, the bourgeois public is presented with an attenuated, softened, watered-down version of Romanticism. The restoration of 'healthy and honest' art is the responsibility of what has been called the 'school of good sense': those like Ponsard, Émile Augier, Jules Sandeau and, later, Octave Feuillet, Murger, Cherubuliez, Alexandre Dumas fils, Maxime Ducamp. Émile Augier and Octave Feuillet, whom Jules de Goncourt called the 'family Musset', and whom Flaubert detested even more than Ponsard, subject the most frenzied Romanticism to the tastes and norms of the bourgeoisie, celebrating marriage, good management of property, the honourable placement of children in life. Thus, Émile Augier, in *L'Aventurière*, combines the sentimental reminiscences of Hugo and Musset with praise of morality and family life, a satire on courtesans and condemnation of love late in life.[1]

Thus the defenders of art for art's sake occupy a central but structurally ambiguous position in the field which destines them to feel with doubled intensity the contradictions that are inherent in the ambiguous position of the field of cultural production in the field of power. Their position in the field compels them to think of themselves, on the aesthetic as well as the political level, in opposition to the 'bourgeois artists', homologous to the 'bourgeois' in the logic of the field, and in opposition to the 'social artists' and to the 'socialist boors', in Flaubert's words, or to the 'bohemians', homologous to the 'people'. Such conflicts are felt successively or simultaneously, according to the political climate. As a result, the members of this group are led to form contradictory images of the groups they oppose as well as of themselves. Dividing up the social world according to criteria that are first of all aesthetic, a process that leads them to cast the 'bourgeois', who are closed to art, and the 'people', imprisoned by the material problems of everyday existence, into the same scorned class, they can simultaneously or successively identify with a glorified working class or with a new aristocracy of the spirit. A few examples: 'I include in the word *bourgeois*, the bourgeois in working smocks and the bourgeois in frock coats. We, and we alone, that is the cultured, are the people, or to put it better, the tradition of humanity' (letter to George Sand, May 1867). 'All must bow before the elite: the Academy of Sciences must replace the Pope.'

Brought back towards the 'bourgeois' when they feel threatened by the bohemians, they can be prompted by their disgust for the bourgeois or the bourgeois artist to proclaim their solidarity with all those whom the brutality of bourgeois interests and prejudices rejects or excludes: the bohemian, the young artist, the acrobat, the ruined noble, the 'good-hearted servant' and especially, perhaps, the prostitute, a figure who is symbolic of the artist's relationship to the market.

Their disgust for the bourgeois, a customer who is at the same time sought after and scorned, whom they reject as much as he rejects them, is fed, in the intellectual field, the first horizon of all aesthetic and political conflicts, by disgust for the bourgeois artist, that disloyal competitor who assures for himself immediate success and bourgeois honour by denying himself as a writer: 'There is something a thousand times more dangerous than the bourgeois,' says Baudelaire in his *Curiosités esthétiques*, 'and that is the bourgeois artist, who was created to come between the artist and genius, who hides each from the other.' (It is remarkable that all the partisans of art for art's sake, with the exception of Bouilhet and Banville, suffered resounding defeat in the theatre, like Flaubert and the Goncourts, or that, like Gautier and Baudelaire, they kept librettos or scripts in their portfolios.) Similarly, the scorn shown at other times by the professionals of artistic endeavour, the partisans of art for art's sake, towards the literary proletariat who are jealous of their success, inspires the image that they have of the 'populace'. The Goncourts, in their *Journal*, denounce 'the tyranny of the brasseries and of bohemian life over all real workers' and oppose Flaubert to the 'great bohemians', like Murger, in order to justify their conviction that 'one must be an honest man and an honourable bourgeois in order to be a man of talent'. Placed at the field's centre of gravity, they lean towards one pole or the other according to the state of the forces outside the field and their indirect consequences within the field, shifting towards political commitment or revolutionary sympathies in 1848 and towards indifference or conservatism under the Second Empire.

This double rejection of the two opposing poles of social space and of the literary field, rejection of the 'bourgeois' and of the 'people', at the same time a rejection of 'bourgeois art' and 'social art', is continually manifested in the purely literary domain of style. The task of writing is experienced as a permanent struggle against two opposing dangers: 'I alternate between the most extravagant grandiloquence and the most academic platitudes. This smacks alternatively of Petrus Borel and Jacques Delille' (to Ernest Feydeau, late November/early December 1857); 'I am afraid of falling into a sort of Paul de Kock or of producing Chateaubriandized Balzac' (to Louise Colet, 20 September 1851); 'What I am currently writing runs the risk of sounding like Paul de Kock if I don't impose some profoundly literary form on it' (to Louise Colet, 13 September 1852). In his efforts to distance himself from the two poles of the literary field, and by extension of the social field, Flaubert comes to refuse any mark, any distinctive sign, that could mean support, or, worse, membership. Relentlessly hunting down *commonplaces*, that is, those places in discourse in which an entire group meets and recognizes itself, and *idées reçues*, generally accepted ideas that go without saying for all members of a group and that one cannot take up without affirming one's adhesion to the group, Flaubert seeks to produce a socially utopian discourse, stripped of all social markers.

The need to distance oneself from all social universes goes hand in hand with the will to refute every kind of reference to the audience's expectations. Thus Flaubert writes to Renan about the 'Prayer on the Acropolis': 'I don't know whether there is a more beautiful page of prose in French! It's splendid and I am sure that the bourgeois won't understand a bit of it! So much the better!' The more artists affirm their autonomy and produce works which contain and impose their own norms of evaluation, the greater their chances of pushing the 'bourgeois' to the point where they are incapable of appropriating these works for themselves. As Ortega y Gasset observes: 'by its very existence new art compels the *bon bourgeois* to admit who he is: a *bon bourgeois*, a person unworthy of aesthetic feelings, deaf and blind to all pure beauty' (*The Dehumanization of Art*). The symbolic revolution through which artists free themselves from bourgeois demands and define themselves as the sole masters of their art while refusing to recognize any master other than their art – this is the very meaning of the expression 'art for art's sake' – has the effect of eliminating the market. The artist triumphs over the 'bourgeois' in the struggle to impose aesthetic criteria, but by the same token rejects him as a potential customer. As the autonomy of cultural production increases, so does the time-lag that is necessary for works to impose the norms of perceptions they bring along. This time-lag between supply and demand tends to become a structural characteristic of the restricted field of production, a very special economic world in which the producers' only customers tend to be their own competitors.

Thus the Christ-like mystique of the *artiste maudit*, sacrificed in this world and consecrated in the next, is nothing other than the retranslation of the logic of a new mode of production into ideal and ideology: in contrast to 'bourgeois artists', assured of immediate customers, the partisans of art for art's sake, compelled to produce their own market, are destined to deferred economic gratification. At the limit, pure art, like pure love, is not made to be consumed. Instant success is often seen, as with Leconte de Lisle, as 'the mark of intellectual inferiority'. We are indeed in the economic world reversed, a game in which the loser wins: the artist can triumph on the symbolic terrain only to the extent that he loses on the economic one, and vice versa. This fact can only reinforce the ambivalence of his relationship to the 'bourgeois', this unacceptable and unobtainable customer. To his friend Feydeau who is attending his dying wife, Flaubert writes: 'You have and will have some good paintings, and you will be able to do some good studies. You'll pay for them dearly. The bourgeois hardly realize that we are serving up our heart to them. The race of gladiators is not dead: every artist is one of them. He entertains the public with his death throes.' This is a case of not letting oneself become caught up in the mithridatizing effect created by our dependence on literary bombast. Gladiator or prostitute, the artist invents himself *in suffering*, in revolt, against the bourgeois, against money, by inventing a separate world where the laws of economic necessity are suspended, at least for a while, and where value is not measured by commercial success.

That being said, one cannot forget the economic conditions of that distancing of oneself from economic necessity that we call 'disinterestedness'. The 'heirs', as in *Sentimental Education*, hold a decisive advantage in a world which, as in the world of art and literature, does not provide immediate profits: the possibility that it offers for 'holding out' in the absence of a market and the freedom it assures in relation to urgent needs is one of the most important factors of the differential success of the avant-garde enterprise and of its unprofitable or, at least, very long-term investments. 'Flaubert', observed Théophile Gautier to Feydeau, 'was smarter than us. He had the wit to come into the world with money, something that is absolutely indispensable to anyone who wants to get anywhere in art.' In short, it is still (inherited) money that assures freedom from money. In painting as in literature, the most innovative enterprises are the privilege of those who have inherited both the boldness and the insurance that enable this freedom to grow . . .

Thus we come back to the individual agents and to the personal characteristics which predispose them to realize the potentialities inscribed in a certain position. I have attempted to show that the partisans of art for art's sake were predisposed by their position in the intellectual field to experience and to express in a particularly acute way the contradictions inherent in the position of writers and artists in the field of power. Similarly, I believe that Flaubert was predisposed through a whole set of properties to express in exemplary fashion the potentialities inscribed in the camp of art for art's sake. Some of these characteristics are shared by the whole group. For example, the social and educational background: Bouilhet, Flaubert and Fromentin are sons of famous provincial doctors; Théodore de Banville, Barbey d'Aurevilly and the Goncourts are from the provincial nobility. Almost every one of them studied law, and their biographers observe that, for several, the fathers 'wanted a high social position for them' (this opposes them to the partisans of 'social art' who, especially after 1850, come in large part from the middle class and even the working classes, while the 'bourgeois artists' are more often from the business bourgeoisie).

In the position within social space of what was at the time termed *les capacités* – that is, the 'liberal professions' – one can see the principle of particular affinities between writers issuing from that position and art for art's sake which occupies, as we have seen, a central position in the literary field: *les capacités* occupy an intermediary position between economic power and intellectual prestige; this position, whose occupants are relatively well endowed with both economic and cultural capital, constitutes a kind of intersection from which one can continue, with roughly equal probabilities, towards the pole of business or the pole of art. And it is truly remarkable to see how Achille-Cléophas,

Flaubert's father, invested simultaneously in the education of his children and in real estate.

The objective relation established between *les capacités* and the other fractions of the dominant class (not to mention the other classes) doubtless oriented the subconscious dispositions and the conscious representations of Flaubert's family and of Flaubert himself with respect to the various positions that could be explored. Therefore, in Flaubert's correspondence one can only be struck by the precocious appearance of the oratorical precautions, which are so characteristic of his relation to writing, and through which Flaubert, then ten years old, distances himself from commonplaces and pompous formulae: 'I shall answer your letter and, as some practical jokers say, I am setting pen to paper to write to you' (to Ernest Chevalier, 18 September 1831); 'I am setting pen to paper (as the shopkeeper says) in order to answer your letter punctually (as the shopkeeper again says)' (to Ernest Chevalier, 18 July 1835); 'As the true shopkeeper says, I am sitting down and I am setting pen to paper to write to you' (to Ernest Chevalier, 25 August 1838).

The reader of *The Family Idiot* discovers, not without surprise, the same stereotyped horror of the stereotype in a letter from Dr Achille-Cléophas to his son in which the ritualistic considerations – here not devoid of intellectual pretension – on the virtues of travel suddenly take on a typically Flaubertian tone, with vituperation against the shopkeeper: 'Take advantage of your travel and remember your friend Montaigne who reminds us that we travel mainly to bring back the mood of nations and their mores, and to "rub and sharpen our wits against other brains". See, observe, and take notes; do not travel as a shopkeeper or a salesman' (29 August 1840). This programme for a literary journey, so extensively practised by writers and, in particular, by the partisans of art for art's sake, and perhaps the form of the reference to Montaigne ('your friend'), which suggests that Gustave shared his literary tastes with his father, attests that if, as hinted by Sartre, Flaubert's literary 'vocation' may have had its origin in the 'paternal curse' and in the relationship with his elder brother – that is, in a certain division of the work of reproduction – it met very early on with the understanding and the support of Dr Flaubert who, if one can believe this letter and, among other indications, the frequency of his references to poets in his thesis, must have been not insensitive to the prestige of the literary enterprise.

But this is not all. At the risk of seeming to push the search for an explanation a bit far, it is possible, starting from Sartre's analysis, to point out the homology between the objective relationship that tied the artist as 'poor relation' to the 'bourgeois' or 'bourgeois artist' and the relationship that tied Flaubert, as the 'family idiot', to his elder brother, and through him – the clear objectification of the most probable career for their category – to his class of origin and to the objective future implied by that class. We would therefore have an extraordinary superimposition of redundant determinations. When Sartre evokes the relationship that Flaubert maintains with his family milieu, the child's and the misunderstood student's resentment, he seems to describe the relationship that the segment of artists and writers maintains with the dominant fractions: 'He is outside and inside. He never ceases to demand that this bourgeoisie, in so far as it manifests itself to him as his family milieu, *recognize* and *integrate* him.'[2] 'Excluded and compromised, victim and accomplice, he suffers from both his exclusion and his complicity.'[3] To evoke the relationship that Gustave maintained with his brother Achille, an objective realization of the objective probability of a career attached to his 'category', is to evoke the relationship of the partisans of art for art's sake with the 'bourgeois artists', 'of whom they sometimes envied the success, the resounding fame, and also the profits':[4] 'It's the older brother Achille, covered with honours, it's the stupid young heir who is satisfied with an inheritance that he does not deserve, it's the solemn physician reasoning at the bedside of a dying patient whose life he cannot save, it's the ambitious person who wants power but will be satisfied with the *Légion d'honneur* . . . This is what Henry will become at the end of the first *Education*: "the future belongs to him, and those are the people who become powerful and influential".'[5]

One could ask what has been gained by proceeding as I have, from the opposite side of the most common approach: instead of starting from Flaubert and his particular oeuvre, I went directly to the space in which he was inserted, I tried to open the biggest box, the field of power, in order to discover what the writer was about, what Flaubert was as a writer defined by a predetermined position in this space. Then, in opening the second box, I tried to reconstitute this dominated-dominant in the literary field, where I found a structure homologous to that of the field of power: on one side the 'bourgeois artists', dominated-dominants with the emphasis on the dominant, and on the other side 'social art', dominated-dominants with emphasis on the dominated; between the two, art for art's sake and Flaubert, dominated-dominants with no emphasis on either side, in a state of equilibrium, unstable between the two poles. Finally, I examined the initial position of Gustave in social space and discovered, I believe, the immobile trajectory which, starting from the position of equilibrium between the two poles of the field of power that is represented by the position of the physician, directed him to occupy this position of equilibrium in the literary field. This long aside was not superfluous, I believe, since it permitted the observation that many properties which one could be tempted to attribute to the particular characteristics of Flaubert's history, as was done by Sartre, are inscribed in the position of 'pure' writer.

What we have learned through this analysis also accounts for Flaubert's quasi-miraculous lucidity. If Flaubert was able to produce a quasi-objective representation of social space of which he was himself the product, it is because the position he never ceased to occupy in this space *from the very outset*, and the tension, even the suffering associated with the *indetermination* which defines it, promotes a *painful lucidity*, since it is rooted in powerlessness, converted into a refusal to belong to one or the other group situated at one or the other of the poles of this space. The objectifying distance, close to Frédéric's contemplative indifference, which enables Flaubert to produce a global vision of the space in which he is situated, is inseparable from the obsession of powerlessness which is associated with the occupation of neutral positions where the forces of the field are neutralized.

Flaubert's trajectory is, one might say, an *Aufhebung* of what is involved in Frédéric's position: Flaubert has passed from an indeterminate state, close to Frédéric's, in the field of power, to a homologous position in the literary field. And if Flaubert was able to project on to Frédéric his own experience of the adolescent's indetermination situated at the neutral point of the field of power, it is because he was able to situate himself, through art for art's sake, in a homologous position within the literary field, but from which he could realize the objectivization of his past position. It is indeed easy to find in young Flaubert's *Correspondence*, or even in his first works, all the traits of Frédéric's indetermination: 'I am left with all the major roads, the well-trodden paths, the clothes to sell, the employment possibilities, a thousand holes that get plugged up with imbeciles. I shall therefore be a "plug" [*bouche-trou*] in society. I'll do my duty, I'll be an honest man, and everything else, if you want, I'll be like somebody else, respectable, *just like everybody else*, a lawyer, a doctor, a sub-prefect, a notary public, an attorney, a judge, as stupid as anyone else, a man of the world or a government official, which is even more stupid. Because one has to be something, and there is no middle of the road solution. Well, I have chosen, I have made up my mind, I'll study law, which far from opening up all opportunities, directs you to *nothing*' (to Ernest Chevalier, 23 July 1839).

This description of the space of the positions objectively offered to the bourgeois adolescent of the 1840s owes its objectivistic rigour to an indifference, a lack of satisfaction and, as Claudel used to say, an 'impatience with limits', which are hardly compatible with the magical experience of the 'vocation': 'I will pass my bar examination, but I scarcely think I shall ever plead in court about a party-wall or on behalf of some poor paterfamilias cheated by a rich upstart. When people speak to me about the bar, saying "This young fellow will make a fine trial lawyer", because I'm broad in the shoulders and have a booming voice, I confess it turns my stomach. I don't feel myself made for such a completely materialistic, trivial life' (to Gourgaud-Dugazon, 22 January 1842).

So, the status of the writer devoted to pure art, situated at equal distance from the two polar positions, also appears as a means of holding on to the refusal to belong, to hold and to be held, which characterized the young Gustave. Pure art transforms Frédéric's 'inactive passion' into a wilful position, a system: 'I no longer want to be associated with a review, or to be a member of a society, a club, or an academy, no more than to be a city counsellor or an officer in the national guard' (to Louise Colet, 31 March 1853); 'No, *sacré nom de Dieu!*, no!, I shall not attempt to publish in any review. It seems to me that, under present conditions, to be *a member of anything*, to join any official organization, any association or small club [*boutique*], or even to take a title no matter what it might be, is to lose one's honour, to debase oneself, since everything is so low' (to Louise Colet, 3–4 May 1853).

Again at the risk of seeming to push the analysis too far, I should like to describe finally what appears to be the true principle of the relationship between Flaubert and Frédéric, and the true function of the work of writing through which Flaubert projected himself, and projected a self through and beyond Frédéric's character. What is at stake in this relationship is the inescapable social genesis of a sovereign position which proclaims itself free of any determination. And what if social determinations which encourage distance *vis-à-vis* all determinations did exist? What if the power that the writer appropriates for himself through writing were only the imaginary inversion of powerlessness? What if intellectual ambition were only the imaginary inversion of the failure of temporal ambitions? It is evident that Flaubert never ceased to ask himself whether the writer's scorn for the 'bourgeois' and the wordly possessions of which they are the prisoners does not owe something to the resentment of the failed 'bourgeois' who transforms his failure into elective renunciation; unless it is the 'bourgeois' who, by keeping him at a distance, enable the writer to distance himself from them.

Flaubert knew all too well that flights into the imaginary, just like revolutionary declarations, are also ways to seek refuge from powerlessness. One can return now to Frédéric who, at the apex of his trajectory, in the Dambreuses' salon, reveals, through his disdain for his failed revolutionary friends, his conviction that the artistic or revolutionary vocations are nothing but refuges from failure – the same Frédéric who never feels more intellectual than when his life goes wrong. It is when he is faced with Monsieur Dambreuse's reproach for his actions or by Madame Dambreuse's allusions to Rosanette's coach that, surrounded by bankers, he defends the positions of the intellectual in order to conclude: 'I don't give a damn about business!'

It would appear that Flaubert was not able to forget the negative determinations of his writer's 'vocation', free of all determination. The enchantment of writing enables him to abolish all determinations which are the constituent parts of social existence: 'This is why I love Art. It's because at least there, in the world of fictions, everything can happen; one is at the same time one's king and one's people, active and passive, victim and priest. No limits; humanity is a jokester with little bells that one jingles at the end of one's sentence, like a street performer at the end of his foot' (to Louise Colet, 15–16 May 1852); 'The only way to live in peace is to leap in one motion above humanity and to have nothing in common with it, except to gaze upon it.' Eternity and ubiquity are the divine attributes the pure observer appropriates for himself. 'I could see other people live, but a life different from mine: some believed, some denied, others doubted, and others finally were not at all concerned by these matters and went about their business, that is, selling in their shops, writing their books, or declaiming from their podiums.'[6]

But *Sentimental Education* is there to prove that Flaubert never forgot that the idealist representation of the 'creator' as a 'pure' subject who is inscribed in the social definition of the writer's *métier* is rooted in the sterile dilettantism of the bourgeois adolescent, temporarily freed from social determinations, and is magically realized in the ambition, that Flaubert himself professed, to 'live like a bourgeois and think like a demigod'.

# 6
# Principles for a Sociology of Cultural Works

Fields of cultural production propose to those who are involved in them a *space of possibles* that tends to orient their research, even without their knowing it, by defining the universe of problems, references, intellectual benchmarks (often constituted by the names of its leading figures), concepts in *-ism*, in short, all that one must have in the back of one's mind in order to be in the game. This is what differentiates, for example, the professionals from the amateurs or, to use a painter's idiom, the 'naïfs' (the 'Douanier' Rousseau is a 'naïf' painter, that is, a 'painter as object' who is constituted as a painter by the field). This space of possibles is what causes producers of a particular period to be both situated and dated (the problematic is the historical outcome of the specific history of the field) and relatively autonomous in relation to the direct determinations of the economic and social environment. Thus, for example, in order to understand the choices of contemporary directors [*metteurs en scène*], one cannot be satisfied with relating them to the economic conditions of the theatre, subventions, receipts, or even to the expectations of the public. Rather, one must refer to the entire history of production since the 1880s, during which time the universe of the *points under discussion* – that is, the constitutive elements of theatrical production about which any director worthy of the name would have to take a position – came into being.

This space of possibles, which transcends individual agents, functions as a kind of system of common reference which causes contemporary directors, even when they do not consciously refer to each other, to be objectively situated in relation to the others, to the extent that they are all interrelated as a function of the same system of intellectual co-ordinates and points of reference.

Literary scholars do not escape this logic, and here I would like to extract what I find to be the space of possible ways of analysing cultural works by attempting to render its theoretical presuppositions more explicit. In order to exhaust the possibilities of the method, which establishes the existence of an intelligible relation between the position-takings (the choice among the possibles) and the positions in the social field, I should present the sociological elements which are necessary in each case for the understanding of how different specialists are distributed among these approaches, why, among the different possible methods, they choose certain ones over others. But I will not do so, even though it would not be the most difficult task to undertake (I have outlined such a relational framework in my analysis of the Barthes–Picard debate in *Homo Academicus*).[1]

A well-known initial division is that which opposes internal or formal readings (Saussure was wont to speak of 'internal linguistics') and external readings, or, to use the words of Schelling and Cassirer, 'tautegorical' as opposed to 'allegorical' interpretations. The first tradition, in its most ordinary form, is that practised by *lectores*, that is, literature professors of all countries. To the degree that it is supported by all the logic of the university institution – the situation is even clearer in philosophy – it does not need to be constituted in the body of a particular doctrine and can remain as doxa. New Criticism, whose merit is having provided it with an explicit expression, has merely constituted an explicit theory from the presuppositions of the 'pure' reading of 'pure' literature based on the absolutization of the text. The historically constituted presuppositions which are inherent to 'pure' production – notably in the case of poetry – also find expression in the literary field itself, in England with the T. S. Eliot of *The Sacred Wood* and in France with the *Nouvelle revue française*, and notably Paul Valéry. From this perspective cultural works are temporal and pure forms demanding a purely internal reading that excludes all references to determinations or historical functions, which are seen as reductive.

In fact, if one insists on giving a theoretical basis to this formalist tradition which, as such, is independent of foundations, since it is rooted in the institutional doxa, one can move in two directions: on the one hand, the neo-Kantian tradition of symbolic forms or, more generally, all the traditions which seek to discover universal anthropological structures, such as Mircea Eliade's comparative mythology or Jungian or Bachelardian psychoanalysis, which academic hermeneutics easily borrow and eagerly combine; on the other hand, the structuralist tradition. In the first case, through a tautegorical reading which relates works only to themselves, critics seek to rediscover the universal forms of poetic or literary reason, ahistorical structures which are at the basis of a poetic construction of the world. This position, perhaps because it is untenable, is hardly expressed as such, although it pervades all investigations of an 'esssence' of the poetic, of the symbol, of metaphor, and so on.

The structuralist solution is intellectually and socially more powerful. Socially, it has taken over internalist doxa and bestowed a scientific aura to internal reading as a formal stripping, a dismantling of atemporal texts. Breaking with neo-Kantian universalism, structuralist hermeneutics treats cultural works (language, myths and, by extension, works of art) as structured structures without a structuring subject, which, like the Saussurean concept of *langue*, are particular historical realizations and must therefore be deciphered as such, but without any recourse to an external hermeneutics, that is, without reference to the social or economic conditions of the production of the work or the production of the producers of the work (such as the educational system). Refusing all forms of formalist universalism, structuralism, as Lévi-Strauss says clearly in opposition to Eliade and comparative mythology, seeks to extract the specific code proper to myth, that is, to a historical tradition, or, in the case of literature, to a single work, treated as a small private myth. But it in fact evades not only the question of the social conditions of the works under consideration – one forgets, for example, that the formalism that frees works from the most visible historical determinations is itself a historical invention – but also the fact that by analysing an isolated work, a sonnet by Baudelaire, for example, in the case of Jakobson and Lévi-Strauss (while it is the ensemble of Baudelaire's poems that would provide a number of keys for analysis), it also avoids the fundamental question of the delimitation of the corpus, for example, the body of poetic works of Baudelaire's contemporaries.

In fact, structuralism has 'taken' so well in the academic world, in spite of certain quarrels between the Ancients and the Moderns, such as the debate between Picard and Barthes, who harbour an underlying agreement regarding the essential details, only because it has given an *aggiornamento* to the old tradition of internal reading so dear to the *lector academicus*. However, one could profit more or perhaps better from the structuralist tradition if one posed the question of the corpus referred to above. Michel Foucault has produced what appears to me to be the only rigorous formulation (with that of the Russian formalists) of structuralism in relation to the analysis of cultural works.

Foucault's symbolic structuralism retains from Saussure what is no doubt essential, that is, the primacy of relations: '*Langue*, says Saussure, in a language that is quite close to that of the Cassirer of *Substanzbegriff und Funktionsbegriff*, is form and not substance.' Aware that a work does not exist by itself, that is, outside relationships of interdependence which unite it to other works, Michel Foucault gives the name 'field of strategic possibilities' to the 'regulated system of differences and dispersions' within which each individual work defines itself.[2] But – and in this respect he is very close to semiologists such as Trier and the use they have made of the idea of the 'semantic field' – he refuses to look outside the 'field of discourse' for the explanatory principle of each of the discourses in the field. What cultural producers have in common is a system of common references, a common framework; in short, what I have referred to as the 'space of possibles'.

But Foucault, faithful in this to the Saussurean tradition and to its absolute division between internal and external linguistics, affirms the absolute autonomy of this 'field of strategic possibilities', of this *épistème*, and he quite logically challenges as a 'doxological illusion' the claim of finding in what he calls the 'field of polemic' and 'the divergencies of interests or mental habits among individuals' (I cannot help but feel singled out . . .) the explanatory principle of what happens in the 'field of strategic possibilities'. Put another way (and here lies the boundary between orthodox structuralism and the genetic structuralism I am proposing), Michel Foucault transfers into the 'paradise of ideas', if I may put it this way, the oppositions and antagonisms which are rooted in the relations between the producers and the consumers of cultural works. Obviously, it is not a question of denying the specific determination which the space of possibles exerts, since one of the functions of the notion of the relatively autonomous field, endowed with its own history, is to account for that determination. Nevertheless, it is not possible to treat cultural order, the *épistème*, as an autonomous and transcendent system, if only because one is forbidden to account for changes which can unexpectedly take place in this separated universe, unless one attributes to it an immanent capacity suddenly to transform itself through a mysterious form of Hegel's *Selbstbewegung*. (Like so many others, Foucault succumbs to that form of essentialism or, if one prefers, fetishism, that is manifested so clearly in other domains, notably in mathematics: one should follow Wittgenstein, who recalls that mathematical truths are not eternal essences born whole from the human brain, but rather are historical productions of a certain type of historical labour undertaken in that peculiar social world called the scientific field.)

The same criticism is valid against the Russian formalists. Like Foucault, who drew from the same source, they consider only the system of works, the network of relationships among texts, or *intertextuality*. Hence, like Foucault, they are compelled to find in the system of texts itself the basis of its dynamics. Tynjanov, for example, explicitly affirms that all that is literary can be determined only by the prior conditions of the literary system (Foucault says the same thing for the sciences). From the process of banalization or debanalization, they create a kind of natural law of poetic change analogous to an effect of mechanical deterioration.

By considering the relationship between the social world and works of culture in terms of *reflection*, external analysis, in contrast, directly links these works to the social characteristics (the social origins) of their authors or of the groups for whom they were really or potentially destined and whose expectations they are intended to meet. In what seems to me the best case, the analysis that Sartre carried out with respect to Flaubert, the biographical method exhausts itself in seeking in the characteristics of the author's individual existence the explanatory principles that can only be revealed by considering the literary microcosm in which his career is realized.

Statistical analysis is not much more productive, since it often applies to *preconstructed* populations principles of classification that are themselves preconstructed. To give such an analysis the minimum of rigour, one should on the one hand study, as Francis Haskell has done for painting, the history of the process through which the *lists* of authors on which the statistician works are constructed, that is, the *process* of canonization and hierarchization that leads to the delimitation of the population of canonical writers at any given moment in time. On the other hand, one should study the genesis of the systems of classification, names of periods, schools, genres and so forth that are actually the instruments and the stakes of struggle. Without carrying out such a critical genealogy, one risks coming to a research conclusion that is but a statement of the real problem, for example, the limits of the population of writers, that is, of those who are recognized by the most consecrated writers as deserving to call themselves writers (the same thing holds for historians or sociologists). Moreover, without carrying out an analysis of the real divisions of the field, one risks destroying true examples of cohesion, by the effect of the groupings imposed through the logic of statistical analysis, thereby destroying the true statistical relationships that a statistical analysis armed with an understanding of the specific structure of the field could apprehend.

But the studies that are most typical of the external mode of analysis are those of Marxist inspiration, which with authors as different as Lukács or Goldmann, Borkenau (on the origins of mechanistic thought), Antal (on Florentine painting) and Adorno (on Heidegger) attempt to relate works to the world view or the social interests of a particular social class. It is taken for granted in this case that understanding the work means understanding the world view of the social group that is supposed to have expressed itself through the artist acting as a sort of medium. One ought to examine the presuppositions, all extremely naïve, of these imputations of spiritual inheritance, which can always be reduced to the supposition that a group can act *directly*, as final cause (function), on the production of the work (for example, is the declared artistic financier, where one exists, the true addressee of the work?). But at a deeper level, supposing that one manages to determine the social functions of the work, that is, the groups and the 'interests' that it 'serves' or expresses, would one have advanced the least bit an understanding of the structure of the work? To say that religion is 'the opium of the people' does not tell us much about the *structure* of the religious message, and, anticipating the logic of my exposition, this structure is the prerequisite for the fulfilling of its function, if it has one.

It is against this form of reduction, which I call the *short circuit* effect, that I developed the theory of the field. Exclusive attention to function (which the internalist tradition, notably structuralism, was doubtless wrong in neglecting) leads one to ignore the question of the internal logic of cultural objects, their structure as *languages*. At a deeper level, however, it leads one to forget the groups that produce these objects (priests, lawyers, intellectuals, writers, poets, artists, mathematicians, etc.), for whom they also fulfil functions. It is here that Max Weber and his theory of religious agents is of great help. While it is to his credit that he reintroduces the specialists, their particular interests, that is, the functions that their activities and products – religious doctrines, juridical corpora, etc. – fulfil for them, he does not perceive that intellectual worlds are *microcosms* that have their own structures and their own laws. It is these microcosms that I have called fields and whose general laws of operation I have attempted to describe.

In fact, if one is to profit fully from the reintroduction of the specialists, one must apply a relational or, if one prefers, a structural mode of thought to the social space of the producers: the social microcosm that I call the literary field is a space of objective relationships among positions – that of the consecrated artist and that of the *artiste maudit*, for example – and one can only understand what happens there if one locates each agent or each institution in its relationships with all the others. It is this peculiar universe, this 'Republic of Letters', with its relations of power and its struggles for the preservation or the transformation of the established order, that is the basis for the strategies of producers, for the form of art they defend, for the alliances they form, for the schools they found, in short, for their specific interests. External determinants – for example, the effect of economic crises, technical transformations or political revolutions –

which the Marxists invoke can only have an effect through resulting transformations in the structure of the field. The field exerts an effect of *refraction* (much like a prism) and it is only when one knows its specific laws of operation (its 'refraction coefficient', i.e. its *degree of autonomy*) that one can understand what is happening in the struggles between poets, between the partisans of social art and the defenders of art for art's sake, or, in a broader sense, in the relationships among genres, between the novel and the theatre, for example, when one passes from a conservative monarchy to a progressive republic.

What happens to the works in all of this? Along the way, haven't we lost what the more subtle defenders of an internal reading had contributed? The logic of operation of fields tends to make the different possibles that constitute the space of possibles at a given moment in time seem intrinsically, logically incompatible, when they are indeed incompatible, but only from a sociological perspective (such is the case, for example, of the different methods I have examined as well as of the positions of the literary and artistic fields that they propose to analyse). The logic of the struggle and the division into opposing camps which differ with respect to the possibles that are objectively offered – to the point where each one sees or wishes to see only a tiny fraction of the space – makes options that are logically compatible seem irreconcilable. Since each camp exists through opposition, it is unable to perceive the limits that are imposed on it by the very act through which it is constituted. This is very clear in the case of Foucault, who, in order to set up what I call the space of possibles, finds it necessary to exclude the social space of which that space is the expression. Very often, as here, the social antagonisms underlying theoretical oppositions and the interests connected to these antagonisms form the only obstacle to getting beyond and to synthesis.

Retaining what has been gained through the notion of intertextuality, that is, the fact that at each moment the space of works appears as a field of position-takings which can only be understood relationally, as in a system of phonemes, that is, as a system of differential discrepancies, one can form the hypothesis – a heuristic tool confirmed through analysis – of a homology between the space of creative works, the field of position-takings and the space of positions in the field of production. Thus several fundamental problems, and first of all the problem of change, find themselves at once resolved. For example, the impetus behind the process of 'banalization' and 'de-banalization' described by the Russian formalists is not inscribed in the works themselves but rather in the opposition between orthodoxy and heresy which is constitutive of all fields of cultural production and which takes on its paradigmatic form in the religious field. It is significant that Weber, speaking of religion, speaks also of 'banalization' or 'routinization' and of 'de-banalization' or 'de-routinization' with regard to the respective functions of priesthood and prophets. The process that carries works along is the product of the struggle among agents who, as a function of their position in the field, of their specific capital, have a stake in conservation, that is, routine and routinization, or in subversion, that is, a return to sources, to an original purity, to heretical criticism and so forth.

It is certain that the direction of change depends on the state of the system of possibilities (stylistic, for example) that is offered by history and that determines what is possible and impossible at a given moment within a particular field. But it is no less certain that it also depends on the interests (often totally disinterested) that orient agents – as a function of their position *vis-à-vis* the dominant pole or the dominated pole of the field – towards more open and more innovative possibilities, or towards the most secure and established possibilities, towards the newest possibilities among those which are already socially constituted, or even towards possibilities that must be created for the first time.

The science of cultural works has as its object the correspondence between two homologous structures, the structure of the works (i.e. of genres, forms and themes) and the structure of the literary field, a field of forces that is unavoidably a field of struggle. The impetus for change in cultural works – language, art, literature, science, etc. – resides in the struggles that take place in the corresponding fields of production. These struggles, whose goal is the preservation or transformation of the established power relationships in the field of production, obviously have as their effect the preservation or transformation of the structure of the field of works, which are the tools and stakes in these struggles.

The strategies of the agents and institutions that are engaged in literary struggles, that is, their position-takings (either specific, e.g. stylistic, or not, e.g. political or ethical), depend on the *position* they occupy in the structure of the field, that is, on the distribution of specific symbolic capital, institutionalized or not ('celebrity' or recognition) and, through the mediation of the dispositions constituting their habitus (which are relatively autonomous with respect to their position), on the degree to which it is in their interest to preserve or transform the structure of this distribution and thus to perpetuate or subvert the existing rules of the game. But, through the stakes of the struggle between the dominants and the challengers – the questions over which they confront each other – these strategies also depend on the state of the legitimate problematic, that is, the space of possibilities inherited from previous struggles, which tends to define the space of possible position-takings and thus orient the search for solutions and, as a result, the evolution of production.

This is why – if I may be permitted a parenthesis and a reflexive look back on what I am trying to do – it is so important, if one is to have a bit of freedom from the constraints of the field, to attempt to explore the limits of the theoretical box in which one is imprisoned. This, in my view, is the principal function of theoretical culture: to provide the means for knowing what one is doing and for freeing oneself from the naïveté associated with the lack of consciousness of one's bounds. To speak today on the literary fact is, whether one knows it or not, whether one wishes it or not, to place oneself or to be placed with respect to a space of possibilities that is the product of a long, partly repetitive, history or, more precisely, a long struggle among theories and theoreticians, writings and writers, readings and readers.

The relation that is established between the available positions and the position-takings does not entail a mechanistic determination. All agents, writers, artists or intellectuals construct their own creative project according, first of all, to their perception of the available possibilities afforded by the categories of perception and appreciation inscribed in their habitus through a certain trajectory and, secondly, to their predisposition to take advantage of or reject those possibilities in accordance with the interests associated with their position in the game. To summarize a complex theory in a few phrases: to the extent that they occupy a position in a specific space, that is, in a field of forces (irreducible to a mere aggregate of material points), which is also a field of struggle seeking to preserve or transform the field of forces, authors only exist and subsist under the structured constraints of the field (e.g. the objective relations that are established between genres). They affirm the differential deviation which constitutes their position, their point of view – understood as the perspective from a given point in the field – by assuming, actually or virtually, one of the possible aesthetic positions in the field (and thus assuming a position in relation to other positions). By being well situated – and writers or artists have no choice but to situate themselves – they distinguished themselves, even without searching for distinction. By entering the game, they tacitly accept the constraints and the possibilities inherent in that game (which are presented not in the form of rules, but rather as possible winning strategies).

The difference, the differential deviation, is the principle of the field's structure as well as of its process of change, which occurs through struggles for specific stakes, themselves produced by the struggles. No matter how great the autonomy of the field, the result of these struggles is never completely independent of external factors. Thus, the power relationships between the 'conservatives' and the 'innovators', the orthodox and the heretical, the old and the new, are greatly dependent on the state of external struggles and on the reinforcement that one or another may find from without – for example, for the heretical, in the emergence of new clienteles, whose appearance is often linked to changes in the educational system. Thus, for example, the success of the Impressionist revolution would undoubtedly have been impossible without the emergence of a public of young artists [*les rapins*] and writers who were shaped by an 'overproduction' of diplomas.

To illustrate this programme of research in a concrete fashion, it would be necessary to present an in-depth description of a given state of the literary field. At the risk of appearing simplistic or dogmatic, I will merely touch on a few of the main features of the literary field in France in the 1880s, a period when the structure of the literary field was definitively established as we know it today.

During this period, the opposition between art and money, which structures the field of power, is reproduced in the literary field in the form of the opposition between 'pure' art, symbolically dominant but economically dominated – poetry, that exemplary incarnation of 'pure' art, is not saleable – and commercial art, in its two forms, boulevard theatre, which brings in high profits and bourgeois consecration (the Academy), and industrial art: vaudeville, the popular or serialized novel [*feuilleton*], journalism, cabaret. There is thus a chiasmatic structure, homologous with the structure of the field of power, in which, as we know, the intellectuals, rich in cultural capital and (relatively) poor in economic capital, and the owners of industry and business, rich in economic capital and (relatively) poor in cultural capital, are in opposition: on the one hand, a maximal independence with regard to the demands of the market and the exaltation of values of disinterestedness; on the other, direct dependence rewarded with immediate success, with respect to bourgeois demands, in the case of theatre, petit-bourgeois or, indeed, working-class demands in the case of vaudeville or the serialized novel. This being the case, we have here all the recognized characteristics of the opposition between two sub-fields practically closed in on themselves, the sub-field of restricted production, which constitutes its own market, and the sub-field of large-scale production (see Figure 5). Intersecting vertically and overlapping with this principal opposition, one finds a secondary opposition as a function of the social quality of the works and the social quality of the corresponding audiences. At the more autonomous pole, this opposition holds between the consecrated avant-garde (for example, in the 1880s, the Parnassians and, to a lesser degree, the Symbolists) and the avant-garde that is either emerging or 'failed' (that is, ageing but not consecrated). At the more heteronomous

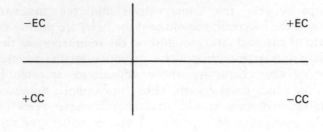

EC = economic capital; CC = cultural capital

Figure 5

pole, the opposition is less clear and appears mainly as a function of the social quality of audiences – opposing, for example, the boulevard theatre to vaudeville and all forms of 'industrial' art.

Until about 1880, the main opposition is partially superimposed on the opposition between genres, that is, between poetry and theatre, while the novel, a more 'dispersed' genre, occupied an intermediate position. The theatre, which on the whole was situated in the sub-field of large-scale production (one should recall the theatrical failures of the partisans of art for art's sake) breaks up following the appearance of a new character on the scene, the *director*, notably Antoine and Lugné-Poe who, by their very opposition, led to the rise of the whole space of possibles which would be manipulated by the subsequent history of the theatre sub-field.

Thus we have a two-dimensional space and two forms of struggle and history. On the one hand, in the horizontal dimension of the 'cross', artists in the pure and commercial sub-fields are engaged in struggles

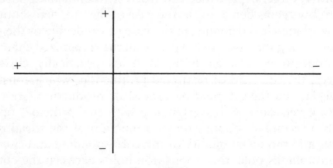

+ and − measure specific capital

Figure 6

concerning the very definition of the writer and the status of art and artist. Through this contention they engage in the struggle for the imposition of the dominant principle of domination which opposes the intellectuals of the restricted field to the 'bourgeois', who act through the intermediary of bourgeois intellectuals. On the other hand, in the vertical dimensions of the 'cross', and at the more autonomous pole, i.e. within the restricted sub-field, there are struggles between the consecrated avant-garde and the new avant-garde.

In fact, art history acknowledges and recognizes only the restricted sub-field; consequently, the representation of the field and its history are distorted. The endless changes within the field of production for producers arise from the very structure of the field, that is, from the synchronic oppositions between antagonistic positions, based on their degree of artistic consecration or, if one prefers, the position within the structure of the distribution of specific capital of recognition. This position is strongly correlated with age – the opposition between (symbolically) dominant and dominated, between orthodox and heretical, tends to take the form of a permanent revolution of the 'young' against the 'old', and the 'new' against the 'outmoded'.

Since they originate in the very structure of the field, changes within the restricted field are largely independent of the external changes which may seem to determine them because they accompany them *chronologically*. This is true even when such internal changes owe their subsequent consecration mainly to an encounter between independent series of causes (in accordance with the formula Cournot uses to define chance). It is the struggle between the dominant and the aspirants, between those who hold titles (of writers, philosophers, scholars, etc.) and their challengers, as one would say in the boxing world, that constitutes the history of the field. The social ageing of authors, schools and works results from the struggle between those who have made their mark (by producing a new position in the field) and who are fighting to persist (to become classics), and those who cannot make their own mark without pushing into the past those who have an interest in eternalizing the present state of affairs and in stopping the course of history.

In the struggles within each genre which oppose the consecrated avant-garde to the new avant-garde, the latter is compelled to question the very foundation of the genre through a return to sources and to the purity of its origins. As a consequence, the history of poetry, the novel or theatre tends to appear as a continuous process of purification through which each of these genres, at the end of a thorough reappraisal of itself, its principles and its presuppositions, finds itself reduced to the most purified quintessence. Thus, the series of poetic revolutions against fully established poetry which has marked the history of French poetry since

Romanticism tends to exclude from poetry all that makes up the 'poetic': the more standard forms, the alexandrine, the sonnet, the poem itself — in short, the poetic 'run-of-the-mill'; but also rhetorical figures, comparisons, metaphors, or even predictable feelings, lyricism, effusion, and psychology. Similarly, the history of the novel tends to exclude the 'novelistic': Flaubert, with his dream of a 'book about nothing', and the Goncourts, with their ambition of a 'novel with no adventures, without plot, and without vile entertainment', have indeed contributed to the Goncourts' project of purging the novel of 'novelistic' devices, of 'killing the novelistic'. This project, which we can trace from Joyce to Claude Simon, by way of Faulkner, has brought about the invention of a 'pure' novel, devoid of a linear story, as well as any pretence of reflecting reality, and which denounces itself as mere fiction. Finally, in similar fashion, the history of *mise en scène* increasingly tends to exclude all that is 'theatrical' and ends up with a deliberately illusionist, and therefore illusory, perspective of the comical illusion.

Paradoxically, in those fields which are the site of a *permanent revolution*, the avant-garde producers are determined by the past even in their innovations which aim to go beyond it, and which are inscribed, as in the original matrix, in the space of possibles, which is immanent in the field itself. What happens in the field is more and more dependent on the specific history of the field, and more and more independent of external history; it is therefore more and more difficult to infer or to anticipate from the knowledge of the state of the social world (economic, political situation, etc.) at any given moment.

Another consequence is that the relative autonomy of the field is more completely achieved in works owing their formal properties and their value only to the structure, thus to the history of the field, further disqualifying interpretations which, through a *short circuit*, go directly from what happens in the world to what happens in the field. Just as there is no longer any space, on the side of production, for the naïf painters, except in the role of artists as objects (one should contrast here 'Douanier Rousseau' and Marcel Duchamp), there is no longer any space for first-degree naïve perception: the work created according to the logic of a strongly autonomous field calls for a *differential* and distinctive perception, attentive to any deviations with respect to other contemporary or past works. It follows paradoxically that the adequate consumption of this art, which is the product of a permanent break with history and with tradition, tends to become completely historical: the condition for delectation is awareness and knowledge of the space of possibles from which the work emerged, its 'contribution', which can be understood only through historical comparison.

The epistemological problem posed to science by the existence of 'pure' arts (and 'formalist' theories clarifying their principles) is thus resolved: it is in history that one finds the principle of freedom with respect to history, and a social history of the autonomization process (of which I have just given an outline) can account for freedom with regard to the 'social context', which any attempt to relate directly to social conditions of the moment cancels out through the very act of explanation. The challenges issued to sociology by formalist aesthetics concerned only with form, be it in production or in reception, are overcome: the refusal that the formalist ambition opposes to any kind of historicization lies in its ignorance of its own social conditions of possibility or, more precisely, in its omission of the historical process during which the social conditions of freedom from external determinations were constituted, that is, the relatively autonomous field of production that makes pure aesthetics possible. The foundation of this independence with respect to historical conditions which stands out in the works issuing from pure attention to form resides in the historical process which has given rise to an autonomous universe.

Having thus rapidly evoked the structure of the field, the logic of its functioning and its changes (we should also have talked about relationships with the audience), we still have to describe the relationships among the individual agents, thus their habitus, and the forces of the field, which are objectified in a trajectory and a work. In contrast to ordinary biographies, the trajectory describes the series of positions successively occupied by the same writer in the successive states of the literary field, it being understood that it is only in the structure of a field that the meaning of these successive positions can be defined: journal editorships, publishing with a certain 'house', membership of particular groups or associations. It is within each state of the field, defined by a particular configuration of the structure of the possibles, that the dispositions linked to a certain social origin orient practice towards one or another of the 'possibles' offered as a function of the position which is occupied and of the more or less clearly avowed feeling of success or failure associated with it. Most often this takes place through a completely unconscious process (the habitus as a 'feel for the game' excludes and bypasses any calculation). Since I do not have the time to go into the detail of the dialectic between positions and dispositions, suffice it to say that we observe an extraordinary correspondence between the hierarchy of positions (e.g. of genres and, within genres, of styles) and the hierarchy of social origins, therefore, of associated dispositions. Just one example: within the 'popular' novel which, more often than any category of novel, is abandoned to writers issuing from dominated classes and women writers, we find yet another hierarchy: literary treatments that distance themselves most from the genre or that are semi-parodic – an excellent example of which can be found in Apollinaire's favourite novel, *Fantomas* – are the work of relatively more privileged writers. Trajectories thus appear as abruptly determined in reality as they are in *Sentimental Education*.

But I would not want to conclude without explicitly asking a question that I have not ceased to ask implicitly throughout these three lectures: What do we gain through this particular approach to the work of art? Is it worth reducing and destroying, in short breaking the spell of the work in order to account for it and to learn what it is all about?

The resolutely historicist vision which leads one to a rigorous understanding of the historical conditions of the emergence of trans-historical logic, as in art or science, has as its first effect the extrication of critical discourse from the Platonic temptation to produce essences – of the literary, or the poetic, or, in another domain, of mathematics, etc. The analytical study of essences, of which so many 'theoreticians' are guilty (notably with respect to 'literariness', the Russian formalists and Jakobson, so well versed in phenomenology and eidetic analysis, or, with regard to 'pure poetry' or 'theatricality', so many others, from Brémond and Artaud), are only re-using, without knowing it, the historical production of the slow and very gradual work of *purification* which I evoked a moment ago and which, in each of the genres – poetry, novel, theatre – accompanied the autonomization of the field of production: from purification to purification, the struggles of which the field of production is the site gradually contributed to the isolation of the specific principle of the poetic, theatrical, or novelistic effect, leaving only a kind of highly concentrated extract (such as in Ponge's poetry, for example) of the properties most apt to produce the effect of the genre under consideration – in the case of poetry, the effect of 'de-routinization', the *ostranenie* of the formalists; and this without recourse to techniques socially designated as 'poetic'. The restricted field of production, or rather the historical process which takes hold in it, is the veritable 'hair-splitter'.

But what have we gained, other than the slightly perverse pleasure of disenchantment, in reducing to history what demands to be lived as an absolute experience, immune to the contingencies of historical genesis? 'The action of works upon works', of which Brunetière spoke, can only take place through the intermediation of authors. And their strategies owe their form and content to the interests associated with the positions which they occupy in the structure of a very specific game. History can produce trans-historic universality only by instituting social universes which, by the effect of the social alchemy of their specific laws of functioning, tend to extract the sublimated essence of the universal from the often merciless clash between particular interests. This realistic vision, which transforms the production of the universal into a collective enterprise, subject to certain rules, appears to me in the end more reassuring and, if I may say so, more human than the belief in the charismatic virtues of pure interest in pure form.

# 7

# Flaubert's Point of View

The break necessary to establish a rigorous science of cultural works is something more and something other than a simple methodological reversal. It implies a true *conversion* of the ordinary way of thinking and living the intellectual enterprise. It is a matter of breaking the narcissistic relationship inscribed in the representation of intellectual work as a 'creation' and which excludes as the expression *par excellence* of 'reductionist sociology' the effort to subject the artist and the work of art to a way of thinking that is doubly objectionable since it is both genetic and generic.

It would be easy to show what the most different kinds of analysis of the work of art owe to the norms requiring that works be treated in and for themselves, with no reference to the social conditions of their production. Thus in the now-classic *Theory of Literature*, René Wellek and Austin Warren seem to advocate 'an explanation in terms of the personality and the life of the writer'. In fact, because they (no doubt along with most of their readers) accept the ideology of the 'man of genius', they are committed, in their own terms, to 'one of the oldest and best-established methods of literary study' – which seeks the explanatory principle of a work in the author taken in isolation (the uniqueness of a work being considered a characteristic of the 'creator').[1] In fact, this explanatory principle resides in the relationship between the 'space' of works in which each particular work is situated and the 'space' of authors in which each cultural enterprise is constituted. Similarly, when Sartre takes on the project of specifying the mediations through which society determined Flaubert, the individual, he attributes to those factors that can be perceived from that point of view – that is, to social class as refracted through a family structure – what are instead the effects of generic factors influencing every writer in an artistic field that is itself in a subordinate position in the field of power and also the effects specific to all writers who occupy the same position as Flaubert within the artistic field.

It is through the theory of the *projet originel* that Sartre, following his logic as far as it will go, brings out one of the basic assumptions of every form of literary analysis: that which is inscribed in the expressions of everyday life, and in particular in the many appearances of 'already', 'from then on', 'from his early years on', scattered through biographies. These ordinary expressions assume that each life is a whole, a coherent ensemble oriented in a given direction, and that it cannot be understood except as the unitary expression of a subjective and objective intention, visible in the subject's every experience, even and especially the earliest ones. Both the retrospective illusion, which establishes final events as the ends of initial experiences or behaviour, and the ideology of predestination, which credits exceptional individuals with divine foresight, tacitly assume that life is organized like a story, that it moves from an origin, understood as a point of departure and also as a first cause, or better yet, as a generative principle, and that the term of a life is also its goal. It is this philosophy that Sartre's *projet originel* makes explicit by posing the explicit consciousness of determinants implied in a social position as a principle of all existence.

Analysing the essentialist philosophy exemplified for him by Leibnizian monadology, Sartre observed in *Being and Nothingness* that this philosophical position abolished chronology by reducing it to logic. Paradoxically, Sartre's own philosophy of biography produces the same kind of effect but starting from an absolute beginning – in this case, the 'discovery' established by an act of originating consciousness.[2] Sartre is among those who, in Martin Luther's terms, 'sin bravely': we can be grateful to him for bringing out so clearly the philosophy that supports methodologies as diverse as the 'man and his work' monographs that followed the lead of Gustave Lanson, textual analyses applied to a single fragment of a given work (such as Jakobson and Lévi-Strauss's analysis of Baudelaire's 'Les Chats') or even the various enterprises of social history of art or literature which, in trying to account for a work starting from psychological or social variables for a single author, are doomed to passover the essential. A genetic sociology alone can grasp the essential, that is, the genesis and the structure of the specific social space in which the 'creative project' was formed.

THE LITERARY FIELD IN FLAUBERT'S TIME

This method centres on three elements as necessary and as necessarily tied to each other as the three levels of social reality that they grasp: first, analysis of the position occupied by the artistic or literary field within the field of power and the evolution of that position over time; second, the structure of the literary field, that is, the structure of the objective relations between the positions occupied by actors or groups competing for literary legitimacy at a given moment; and finally, genesis of the different producers' habitus.

## The Literary Field and the Field of Power

The relationships that tie the literary field to the field of power raise the question of the autonomy of the literary field with respect to those who hold political or economic power and, more specifically, the particular form of this dependence. In Flaubert's time the relationship between the producers of culture and dominant social groups was nothing like what it was in previous centuries, whether we consider direct dependence on an individual who commissions a work or loyalty to an official or unofficial patron of the arts. Henceforth we are dealing with a sort of *structural subordination* that obtained very unequally and very differently for different authors according to their position in the field. This subordination was primarily established through two intermediaries. On the one hand, the market worked either directly, through sales and so on, or indirectly, through the new jobs produced by journalism, publishing and all the forms of what Sainte-Beuve called 'industrial literature'. On the other hand, the enduring connections, founded on affinities of lifestyle and values, through the salons in particular, tied at least some kinds of writers to certain segments of high society and served to guide state subventions of the arts. This subtly hierarchical world of the salon helped structure the literary field and ensure exchange between those in power and the most conformist or the most prestigious writers.

A circular causal relationship tied the development of the market to the influx of a significant population of impecunious young men from the lower-class Parisian milieux and, especially, from the provinces, who came to Paris hoping for careers as writers or artists – careers that until then had been reserved for the aristocracy or the Parisian bourgeoisie. Despite the many new positions created by economic development, neither manufacturing nor the civil service could absorb all those with a higher education.[3] Versed in the humanities and rhetoric but devoid of the financial means or the social influence needed to make the most of these claims, the newcomers found themselves pushed back towards various literary professions and, for the artists among them, towards the artistic professions glorified by the salon. Endowed with all the prestige of romanticism, these professions had the added advantage of requiring no academic qualification.

These structural changes were undoubtedly a major determinant of the growing independence of the artistic and literary fields and the corresponding transformation of the relationship between the world of art and literature and the world of political power. However, we ought to guard against reducing this fundamentally ambiguous process to its alienating effects, as did Raymond Williams who, in analysing the English Romantics, simply forgot that this process had liberating effects as well. This new freedom, moreover, provided the very principle of the new dependence – in, for example, the possibility for what Max Weber called the 'proletaroid intelligentsia' to make a living, however precarious, from all the minor jobs tied to 'industrial literature' and journalism.

From this unprecedented gathering of so many young men hoping to live off art and separated from the rest of society by the lifestyle that they were in the process of inventing, there arose a veritable society within society. Even if, as Robert Darnton has shown, this society within a society can be traced to the eighteenth century, in the mid-nineteenth century this new social reality appeared absolutely extraordinary and without precedent. Not surprisingly, it raised all sorts of questions, even and indeed especially among its members. An ambiguous reality, 'bohemia' prompted ambivalent feelings among its most ardent advocates. In the first place, it defied classification. Close to the 'people' whose poverty it often shared, bohemia was separated from the poor by the lifestyle in which it found social definition and which, however ostentatiously opposed to bourgeois norms and conventions, situated bohemia closer to the aristocracy or to the upper bourgeoisie than to the petite bourgeoisie or the 'people'. All this is no less true for the most destitute members of bohemia, who, secure in their cultural capital and in their authority as arbiters of taste, could get at discount the outrageous sartorial splendours, the gastronomic indulgences, the affairs and liaisons – everything for which the 'bourgeois' had to pay full price.

Bohemia never ceased changing as its numbers increased, and its celebrity attracted these impoverished young men who around 1848 made up the 'second bohemia'. In contrast to the romantic dandies of 'golden bohemia' in the 1830s epitomized by Gérard de Nerval, this bohemia of Henry Murger (*Scenes of Bohemian Life*, 1848) and Champfleury, the self-proclaimed leader of the realists, constituted a veritable reserve intellectual army, directly subject to the laws of the market and often constrained to take a second job that frequently had no literary connections at all. In fact the two bohemias coexisted, but with different social weight. The true 'proletaroid intellectuals' were often so impoverished that they took themselves as their subject and ended up inventing what was called 'realism'. These 'penniless bourgeois', as Pissarro called them, bet what money they had on this enterprise, knowing they were sure to lose in the short term but ever hopeful of glory in the long term. In their divided or double habitus, these aspiring writers had already adapted to the position of being the dominated fraction of the dominant class. This contradictory position destined them to a sort of objective and therefore subjective indeterminacy, which was never more visible than in the simultaneous or successive fluctuations of their relationships with the authorities.

The relationships that these writers and artists maintained with the market no doubt contributed to their ambivalent representation of the 'general public', at once fascinating and despised, in which they mixed up the 'bourgeois' enslaved to the vulgar cares of commerce and the 'people' stultified by labour. This double ambivalence induced an ambiguous image of their own position in society and of their social function – whence their conspicuous oscillation in politics and their tendency to slide towards the pole of the field momentarily in the stronger position. Thus when the centre of gravity of the field moved to the left during the last years of the July Monarchy, and in the midst of a general slide toward 'social art' and socialist ideas, Baudelaire talked about the 'puerile utopia of art for art's sake' and protested violently against pure art. Under the Second Empire, without adhering openly to the regime and sometimes, like Flaubert, even broadcasting their disdain for the man whom Hugo dubbed 'Napoleon the Little', a good many of the most prominent writers assiduously frequented one or another of the salons held by the important members of the Imperial court.

In the absence of true legitimating institutions specifically designed for the validation of prestige (the university, for example, carried virtually no weight in the literary field), the political world and the Emperor's family exercised direct control over the literary and artistic field through sanctions on publishing (indictment, censorship and so on) and also through material or symbolic benefits (pensions, positions, honorific distinctions). Salons were not only places where like-minded writers and artists could meet those in power. They were also legitimating institutions through which those in power exerted their control over the intellectual world. The salon guests, for their part, acted as veritable lobbies to control the disbursement of various symbolic or material rewards.

An analysis that emphasizes the dependence of the literary world must simultaneously stress one of the major effects of the operation of the literary world as a field, namely, the fact that all those who claimed full membership of this world, and especially those who claimed excellence, had to demonstrate their independence *vis-à-vis* economic and political power. Indifference with respect to government authorities and the rewards they dispensed, distance from those in power and their values, tended to be asserted as the practical principle of legitimate behaviour. Most of the time these obligations did not even have to be explicit. Negative sanctions, beginning with the worst – falling into disrepute (the functional equivalent of bankruptcy) – were produced automatically by the competition that set the most prestigious authors against each other.

The effectiveness of these calls to order or injunctions, which were in some sense inscribed in the logic of the field itself, were never more obvious than in the fact that those authors apparently the most directly subject to external exigencies, in their work as in their behaviour, felt obliged to manifest a certain distance from dominant values. And we discover, to our surprise if we know them only through the sarcastic comments of Flaubert or Baudelaire, that the most typical representatives of the bourgeois theatre go beyond unequivocal praise of bourgeois life and values to satirize the very bases of bourgeois existence as well as the 'decline in morals' imputed to the court and the upper bourgeoisie. These concessions to anti-bourgeois values on the part of these model bourgeois authors confirm the patent impossibility of overlooking the fundamental law of the field since writers apparently the furthest removed from art for art's sake acknowledged that law, if only in the somewhat shamefaced or ostentatiously aggressive mode of their transgressions. Condemned for this sub-standard success, these writers have purely and simply been written out of literary history. But they were full members of the nineteenth-century art world, not only because they themselves were marked by their participation in the literary field but also because their very existence modified the functioning of that field.

The analysts who endorse these vetoes without even being aware of it, since they know only those authors from the past recognized by literary history as worthy of recognition, are destined to an intrinsically vicious-circular form of explanation and understanding. They can only register, unaware, the effects of these authors they do not know on the authors that they claim to analyse and whose refusals they take up on their own account. They thus preclude any grasp of what, in their very works, is the indirect product of these refusals. This is never clearer than in the case of a writer like Flaubert who was defined by a whole series of refusals or, more precisely, by an ensemble of double negations that opposed antagonistic doubles of styles or authors: thus his refusal of Romanticism and realism, of Lamartine no less than Champfleury.

## The Position of Art for Art's Sake within the Literary Field

A preliminary mapping of the field that was gradually fixed between 1830 and 1850 distinguishes three leading positions, namely 'social art', 'art for art's sake' and 'bourgeois art'. These categories are of course highly debatable, given the status of the intellectual field as a major battlefield over taxonomy. They nevertheless have the incontestable virtue of recalling that, in a field still in the process of institution, the internal positions must first be understood as so many specifications of the generic position of writers (or of the literary field within the political field). Or, if one prefers, as so many forms of the objective relationship to temporal power. Although writers as such belonged within the dominated fraction of the dominant class, there was considerable tension among writers, between those who tended towards the dominant pole of the literary field, those located at the dominated pole and those in between.

At the dominated pole of the literary field, the advocates of social art had their hour of glory just before and after February 1848. Republicans, Democrats or Socialists, like Proudhon and also, though less markedly, George Sand, or again liberal Catholics like Lamennais, all denounced the 'egotistical' art of art for art's sake, and demanded that literature fulfil a social or political function. These writers were structurally very close to the 'second bohemia' of Murger and company, or at least close to the 'realist' tendency that began to characterize that part of bohemia in the 1850s for which Champfleury became the theoretician. Other writers can be tied to this position, like the 'worker-poets' sponsored by George Sand. Their inferior position in the field fostered a relationship of circular causality with their solidarity with respect to the dominant social milieux. In effect, this attitude can be linked to their provincial and/or working-class background, not only directly, as they themselves wanted to believe and have everyone else believe, through the solidarity and fidelity of the group, but also indirectly, through their dominated position within the field of production to which they were assigned by their background.

At the opposite pole of the literary field, the representatives of 'bourgeois art', who wrote in the main for the theatre, were closely and directly tied to the dominant social milieux as much by their background as by their lifestyle and values. This affinity was the very principle of their success in a genre that presupposed immediate communication between author and public and assured these writers not only significant material benefits (the theatre was by far the most remunerative literary activity), but also all the tokens of success in the bourgeois world and, notably, the Academy. These writers presented their bourgeois public a bowdlerized form of Romanticism, a revival of 'healthy and honest' art which subordinated the zany aspects of Romanticism to bourgeois norms and tastes, glorified marriage, careful management of property, and establishment of children. Moralizing became more emphatic with Dumas fils, who claimed to help transform the world by a realistic depiction of the problems of the bourgeoisie (money, marriage, prostitution, and so on). Against Baudelaire's proclamation of the separation of art and morality, Dumas insisted in the preface of his play, *Le Fils naturel* (1858), that 'all literature that does not have in mind perfectibility, moralizing, the ideal, in a word, the useful, is an aborted, unhealthy literature that is born dead'.[4]

The writers located outside these two opposing positions gradually invented what was called 'art for art's sake'. Rather than a position ready for the taking, it was a position to make. Although it existed potentially within the space of the existing positions, its occupants had to invent, against the established positions and against their occupants, everything that distinguished this position from all the others. They had to invent that social personage without precedent – the modern artist, full-time professional, dedicated to his work, indifferent to the exigencies of politics as to the injunctions of morality, and recognizing no jurisdiction other than the specific norm of art. Through this they invented pure aesthetics, a point of view with universal applicability, with no other justification than that which it finds in itself. The occupants of this central yet contradictory position were destined to oppose the established positions and thereby to attempt to reconcile the irreconcilable. Against bourgeois art, they wanted ethical freedom, even transgression, and above all distance from every institution, the state, the Academy, journalism. But this desire for freedom did not mean that they accepted either the careless abandon of the bohemians who invoked this same freedom in order to legitimate transgressions devoid of properly aesthetic consequences or simple regression into what they denounced as 'vulgar'. In their concern to situate themselves above ordinary alternatives, these advocates of pure art deliberately imposed on themselves an extraordinary discipline that opposed the easy way out taken by all their adversaries. Their independence consisted in the freely chosen but total obedience to the new laws which they invented and to which they proposed to subject the Republic of Letters.

Baudelaire's own aesthetic principle resided in the double breach on which he based his position, at the price of an extraordinary strain, manifest notably in the paradoxical display of singularity in his daily life. His hatred of debased forms of Romanticism had a lot to do with his denunciation of improvisation and lyricism in favour of work and study. At the same time, Baudelaire's refusal of facile breaches of decorum lay behind his determination to be both contentious and methodical even in the mastery of freedom contained in the 'cult of the multiplied sensation'.

Flaubert was also situated in this geometric locus of contraries, along with a number of others who were all different from each other and who never formed a real group: Théophile Gautier, Leconte de Lisle, Barbey d'Aurevilly, to name the best known. I shall cite only one exemplary expression of these double refusals, which, in their general form, could be formulated as follows: 'I loathe X (writer, style, theory, school), but I loathe just as much the opposite of X.' Whence the discord among all those who rejected Romanticism, which Flaubert put so succinctly: 'Everyone thinks that I am in love with realism, whereas I execrate it. For I started on this novel [*Madame Bovary*] out of hatred of realism. But I loathe just as much false idealism, which has us hoaxed these days.'[5]

This key formula, which simply translates the contradictory properties of the position in the field, allows us to comprehend the principle behind diverse particularities in the behaviour of those who occupy this position. First of all, their political neutrality, associated with the refusal of any kind of commitment or any kind of preaching, whether glorifying bourgeois values or instructing the masses in republican or socialist principles: their horror of 'the bourgeois', in which they included, according to Flaubert, 'the bourgeois in working smocks and the bourgeois in frock coats',[6] was sustained, within the field, by the execration of the 'bourgeois artist', who secured/guaranteed his own short-term success and bourgeois honours by denying himself as a writer. But their scorn as professionals for the literary proletariat prompted by their very exacting conception of artistic work also no doubt lay at the heart of the image they had of the 'populace'.

This concern to keep distant from all social sites implied the refusal to be guided by the public's expectations. Thus Flaubert, who pushed this indifference further than anyone else, reproached Edmond de Goncourt for having addressed the public directly in the preface to his novel, *Les Frères Zemganno*, to explain the aesthetic intentions of the work: 'Why do you need to talk directly to the public? It is not worthy of our secrets' (CC, vol. 8, p. 263). The more the artist asserted himself as an artist by asserting his autonomy, the more he turned 'the bourgeois' into the 'bourgeois', the philistine. This symbolic revolution, whereby artists emancipated themselves from bourgeois standards by refusing to acknowledge any master other than their art, had the effect of making the market disappear. In the very moment that they defeated the 'bourgeois' in their struggle to master the sense and the function of artistic activity, they eliminated the bourgeois as a potential customer. And this antinomy of modern art as a pure art showed up clearly in the fact that, as the autonomy of cultural production increased, the interval of time necessary for works to impose their norms also increased.

This temporal gap between supply and demand tended to become a structural characteristic of the field of restricted production. In this anti-economic economy fixed at the pole that was economically domi-nated but symbolically dominant – with Baudelaire and the Parnassians for poetry, with Flaubert for the novel – producers could end up, at least in the short term, with only their competitors for customers. 'Bourgeois artists' were assured of an immediate clientele. The producers of commercial literature who worked on commission, like the authors of vaudeville entertainments or popular novels, could live well off their earnings and at the same time earn a secure reputation as socially concerned or even as socialist (like Eugène Sue). Quite to the contrary, the tenants of pure art were destined to deferred gratification. Some, like Leconte de Lisle, went so far as to see in immediate success 'the mark of intellectual inferiority', while the Christ-like mystique of the *artiste maudit*, sacrificed in this world and consecrated in the next, was undoubtedly the idealized or professionalized retranscription of the specific contradiction of the mode of production that the pure artist sought to establish. It was in effect an upside-down economy where the artist could win in the symbolic arena only by losing in the economic one (at least in the short term) and vice versa.

In a very paradoxical manner this paradoxical economy gave full weight to inherited economic properties and in particular to private income. In more general terms, the state of the field of production determined the probable effects of the properties of individual actors, either objectively, as with economic capital and private income, or subjectively, as in the habitus. In other words, the same dispositions engender very different, even antagonistic, positions, according to the state of the field. In short, it was still (inherited) money that assured freedom from money. A private fortune also conferred objective free-dom with respect to the authorities and those in power, which was often the condition of subjective freedom, thereby enabling 'pure' writers to avoid the compromises to which they were particularly exposed.

Thus, only after characterizing the different positions within the literary field is the analyst able to confront the individual actors and the personal properties predisposing them more or less to realize the potential inscribed in their positions. It is striking that on the whole the adherents of art for art's sake, who were objectively very close to each other by virtue of their political and aesthetic attitudes and who, though not really a group, were tied by bonds of mutual esteem and sometimes friendship, followed similar social trajectories. Flaubert was the son of a well-known provincial doctor; Baudelaire was the son of an office manager in the upper house of parliament who had ambitions of becoming a painter, and he was the step-son of a general; Barbey d'Aurevilly and the Goncourt brothers came from the provincial nobility.

To account more fully for the particular affinity that tied writers from this background of the 'liberal professions' [les capacités] as they used to say in Flaubert's time, to pure art, we can invoke the fact that the occupants of these central positions within the political field who, endowed with just about equal amounts of economic and cultural capital, wavered (like Frédéric in Sentimental Education) between the two poles of business and art and were therefore predisposed to occupy a homologous position in the literary field. Thus the dual orientation of Flaubert's father, who invested both in the education of his children and in real estate, corresponds to the indetermination of the young Flaubert, faced with various equally probable futures. Everything happened as if his position in his family and the position of this family in the political field predisposed Flaubert to experience at their strongest the force of the contradictions inscribed in the position of the writer and in the position of the pure artist, where these contradictions attained their highest degree of intensity.

### FLAUBERT'S POINT OF VIEW

So far, having grasped very partially the specificity of Flaubert, the analysis has remained generic. It has not engaged the logic specific to the work. We can almost hear Flaubert object: 'Where do you know a critic who worries about the work in itself? There are all kinds of analyses of the milieu where the work was produced and the causes that brought it about; but unknowing poetics [poétique insciente] where does it come from? its composition, its style? the author's point of view? Never!' (CC, vol. 6, p. 8). To accept the challenge, one must take Flaubert literally and reconstruct the artistic point of view from which the 'unknowing poetic' was defined which, as a view taken from a given point within an artistic space, characterized that point of view. More precisely, it is necessary to reconstruct the space of the actual and potential artistic position-takings in relationship to which Flaubert constructed his artistic project. This space, it may be supposed, is homologous with the space of positions within the field of production outlined above.

When Flaubert undertook to write *Madame Bovary* or *Sentimental Education*, he situated himself actively within the space of possibilities offered by the field. To understand these choices is to understand the differential significance that characterized them within the universe of possible choices. In choosing to write these novels, Flaubert risked the inferior status associated with a minor genre. Above all, he condemned himself to take a place within a space that was already staked out with names of authors, names of sub-genres (the historical novel, the serial, and so on) and names of movements or schools (realism). Despite Balzac's prestige, the novel was indeed perceived as an inferior genre. The Académie Française was so suspicious of the novel that it waited until 1863 to welcome a novelist as such, and when it finally did so, it chose Octave Feuillet, the author of novels full of aristocratic characters and elevated sentiments. In the manifesto of realism that was their preface to *Germinie Lacerteux* (1865), the Goncourts felt obliged to claim for 'the Novel' (a necessary capital letter) the status of a 'great, serious form'.[7] But the genre already had its history and its founding fathers. There were those claimed by Flaubert himself, like Cervantes, and also those in every educated mind, like Balzac, Musset or Lamartine. When Flaubert started to write *Madame Bovary* there was no novelist 'in view', and one found lumped together Feuillet, Murger, Barbey d'Aurevilly, Champfleury and a good many others, second-raters who are completely forgotten today but who were best-sellers at the time. In this mixed-up world Flaubert knew how to recognize his own. He reacted vehemently to everything that could be termed 'genre literature' – his own analogy with genre painting – that is, vaudeville, Dumas-type historical novels, comic opera and other works that flattered the public by tossing back its own image in the form of a hero psychologically rooted in the daily life of the petite bourgeoisie (*CP*, vol. 2, p. 358). He reacted just as fiercely to the idealistic platitudes and sentimental effusions in novels like those of the eminently successful Feuillet.

But these reactions did not put Flaubert in the realist camp, who, like him, contested the first group but who defined themselves against all the important professional writers, among whom Flaubert counted himself. His designation as leader of the realist school after *Madame Bovary*'s success, which coincided with the decline of the first realist movement, made Flaubert indignant: 'Everyone thinks that I am in love with realism, whereas I execrate it ... But I loathe just as much false idealism.' This crucial formula once again reveals the principle of the totally paradoxical, almost 'impossible' position that Flaubert was about to create for himself, thereby presenting himself as unclassifiable.

The space of positions adopted by the writer that the analyst must reconstitute does not appear as such to the writer himself. Otherwise these choices would have to be interpreted as conscious strategies of distinction. The space appears from time to time, and in a fragmentary state, in the moments of doubt concerning the reality of the difference that the writer claims, in his work, and beyond any explicit search for originality. But the threat to artistic identity is never as strong as when alterity assumes the guise of an encounter with an author who occupies an apparently nearby position in the field. This indeed happened when Flaubert's good friend Louis Bouilhet drew his attention to a novel by Champfleury then appearing as a serial and whose subject – adultery in the provinces – was very close to that of *Madame Bovary* (CP, vol. 2, pp. 562–3). There Flaubert undoubtedly found an opportunity to assert his difference and to become aware of the principle of that difference, that is, the style or, more exactly, a certain inimitable relationship in his tone between the refinement of the style and the extreme platitude of the subject, which he shared with the realists or with the Romantics or with the authors of vaudeville entertainments or, in certain cases, with all three at once.

'Write well about *mediocrity*' (CP, vol. 2, p. 429). This oxymoron condenses Flaubert's whole aesthetic programme and tells a good deal about the impossible situation in which he put himself in trying to reconcile opposites, that is, exigencies and experiences that were ordinarily associated with opposite areas of social space and of the literary field, hence socio-logically incompatible. In fact, on the lowest and most trivial forms of a genre held to be inferior Flaubert imposed the most exacting demands that had ever been advanced for the noblest genre – poetry. The very enterprise challenged the established mode of thought that set prose against poetry, lyricism against vulgarity, and it did so by banning that sacrilege represented by the mixture of genres. At the time the enterprise seemed like folly: 'To want to give to prose the rhythm of verse (but keeping it very much prose), and to want to write about ordinary life as one writes history or the epic (without denaturing the subject) is perhaps an absurdity. That's what I wonder sometimes. But perhaps it's also a grand undertaking and very original!' (CP, vol. 2, p. 287).

He was indeed putting himself in an impossible situation, and in fact, the whole time he was working on *Madame Bovary*, Flaubert never stopped talking about his suffering, even his despair. He felt like a clown performing a real *tour de force* compelled to 'desperate gymnastics'. He reproached his 'fetid' and 'foul' material for keeping him from 'bawling out' lyric themes. He waited impatiently for the time when he could once again drink his fill of stylistic beauty. But above all, he repeated over and over again that he did not, strictly speaking, know what he was doing and that it would be the product of an unnatural effort, unnatural for him in any case. The only possible assurance when confronting the unthinkable was the feeling of a *tour de force* implied by sensing the immense effort involved. 'I will have written the real, and that is rare' (CC, vol. 3, p. 268). The questioning of forms of thought by the symbolic revolution, along with the absolute originality of what that questioning engendered, had as its counterpart the absolute solitude implied by the transgression of the limits of the thinkable for a mode of thought that had become its own measure.

In fact, this mode of thinking cannot expect that minds which are structured according to those very categories it questions think the unthinkable. It is striking how the judgements of critics, applying to works the principles of division that those works have demolished, invariably undid the inconceivable combination of opposites by reducing it to one or the other of the opposite terms: thus the critic of *Madame Bovary* who deduced the vulgarity of the style from the vulgarity of the objects. Others stressed content, related *Madame Bovary* to Champfleury's novel on the same subject, and put Flaubert and Dumas fils in the same boat. Then there were those who, more attentive to tone and style, placed Flaubert in the line of formalist poets.

What made Flaubert so radically original, and what confers on his work an incomparable *value*, is his relationship, albeit negative, with the whole literary world in which he acted and whose contradictions and problems he assumed absolutely; so that the only chance of grasping and accounting for the singularity of his creative project is to proceed in exactly the reverse direction of those who sing the litany of Uniqueness. By historicizing him we can understand how he tore himself away from the strict historicity of less heroic fates. The originality of the enterprise only emerges if, instead of annexing him consciously or unconsciously to one or another prestigious position in today's literary field (like the *nouveau roman*) and to make him an inspired (if unfinished) precursor, this project is reinserted as completely as possible in the historically constituted space within which it was constructed. In other words, taking the point of view of a Flaubert who had not become Flaubert, we try to discover what he had to do and wanted to do in a world that was not yet transformed by what he in fact did, which is to say, the world to which we refer him by treating him as a 'precursor'. In effect, the familiar world keeps us from understanding, among other things, the extraordinary effort that he had to make, the exceptional resistances that he had to surmount, beginning within himself, in order to produce and impose that which, largely because of him, we now take for granted.

Flaubert is really there, in this world of relationships that should be explored one by one, in their symbolic and social dimension. At the same time, he is unquestionably beyond that world, if only because the active integration of all these partial relationships implies going beyond the given. By locating himself in the geographical locus of all perspectives, which is also the point of highest tension, Flaubert put himself so to speak in the position of pushing to their highest intensity all the questions posed by and in the field. He was able to act fully on all the resources inscribed in the space of possibilities offered by the field.

*Sentimental Education* undoubtedly offers the best example of this confrontation with all the relevant positions. The subject situates the novel at the intersection of the Romantic and realist traditions: on the one hand, Musset's *Confession of a Child of the Century* and Alfred de Vigny's *Chatterton*, but also the so-called intimate novel that anticipated the realist novel and the thesis novel; on the other hand, the second bohemia, whose Romantic intimate diary eventually turned into the realist novel, especially when, with the novels of Murger and Champfleury, it recorded the often sordid reality of these artists' existence. By taking on this subject, Flaubert confronted not only Murger and Champfleury, but also Balzac, and not only *A Great Man of the Provinces in Paris* or *A Prince of Bohemia*, but also *The Lily of the Valley*. The great ancestor is explicitly present in Deslauriers' advice to Frédéric: 'Remember Rastignac in *The Human Comedy*.' By giving the reference to Deslauriers, the petit-bourgeois *par excellence*, Flaubert authorizes us to see in Frédéric what is clear from everything else in the novel, namely, that he is the 'counterpart' of Rastignac – not a failed Rastignac, or an anti-Rastignac, but the equivalent of Rastignac in another world. In fact, Frédéric opposes Rastignac within the universe of another possible world, which really exists, at least for the critics, but also for any writer worthy of the name who masters the space of possibles well enough to foresee how what he is doing risks putting him in relationship with other creative projects which are liable to divert his intentions. Take as proof this note of Flaubert's: 'Watch out for *The Lily of the Valley*.' Nor could he avoid thinking about Eugène Fromentin's *Dominique*, and especially about Sainte-Beuve's *Volupté*. 'I wrote *Sentimental Education* for Sainte-Beuve, and he died without reading a line of it' (CC, vol. 6, p. 82).

Moreover, by assuming the impassivity of the paleontologist and the refinement of the Parnassian poet in order to write the novel of the *modern* world, and without pushing aside any of the events that passionately divided literature and politics, Flaubert broke up a whole series of obligatory associations which tied the 'realist' novel with 'literary riff-raff', or 'democracy', or 'vulgar' subjects and a 'low' style. He thereby broke the solidarities founded on the adherence to one or other of the constitutive terms of these opposites. Thus Flaubert sentenced himself to disappoint, even more than with *Madame Bovary*, those who expected literature to demonstrate something, the partisans of the moral novel as much as the defenders of the social novel.

This series of ruptures explains better than the conjuncture the cold reception that the book received. It took place at the deepest level of 'unknowing poetics'. The work on form was undoubtedly the instrument of anamnesis, which was both favoured and limited by the denegation implied by formalization. The work is not the effusions of the subject – there is a vast difference between Flaubert's objectification and the projection of Frédéric that critics have seen. Nor is the work a pure document, as some of his supposed disciples seemed to think. As Flaubert complained to George Sand, 'Goncourt is happy when he picks up in the street a word that he can stick in a book and I am content when I have written a page without assonance or repetition' (CC, vol. 7, p. 281). And if the work can reveal the deep structures of the social world and the mental worlds in which those structures were reflected, it is because the work of formalization gave the writer the opportunity to work on himself and thereby allowed him to objectify not only the positions in the field and their occupants that he opposed, but also, through the space that included him, his own position.

It is not by chance that this project was realized with *Sentimental Education*, this *Bildungsroman* in the literal sense of the term, in an unequalled effort by the writer to objectify his own intellectual experiences and the determinants that weighed on those experiences, beginning with those tied to the contradictory position of the writer in the political field. In the obsessive chiasmic structure (dual characters, crossed trajectories and so on) and in the very structure of the relationships between Frédéric and the other main characters of *Sentimental Education*, Flaubert objectified the structure of the relationship that tied him, as a writer, to the political field: or, which comes down to the same thing, to the positions in the literary field homologous to those in the political field.

There is therefore a relationship of circular causality between his social position and his exceptionally lucid consciousness of that position. If his work as a writer could take him beyond the incompatibilities established in things – in groups, schools and so on, and also in minds – as principles of vision and division, perhaps it was because, in contrast to Frédéric's passive indeterminacy, the active refusal of all the determinants associated with a given position in the intellectual field, to which he was inclined by his social trajectory and the contradictory properties that were the principle of that trajectory, predisposed him to a broader view of the space of possibles and hence to a more complete use of the freedom inherent in its constraints.

## THE INVENTION OF PURE AESTHETICS

The logic of the double refusal, and the break that the primacy given to form implied with the half-break effected by realism, provides the principle for the invention of pure aesthetics accomplished by Flaubert in an art like the novel (and in about the same degree as in painting, where Manet achieved a comparable revolution), which seemed predestined for a simple, naïve search for the illusion of reality. Realism in effect was a partial, and failed, revolution. It did not really question the tendency to mix aesthetic value and moral (or social) value which continued to guide critical judgements. If realism questioned the existence of an objective hierarchy of subjects, it was only to reverse that hierarchy out of a desire for rehabilitation or revenge, not to do away with it. For this reason realism was recognized by the social milieux that it represented rather than by the more or less 'low' or 'vulgar' way of representing them. Murger himself was perceived as a realist because he represented 'common subjects', heroes who dressed poorly, spoke disrespectfully about everything and were utterly ignorant of proper behaviour.

By breaking this privileged tie with a specific category of objects, Flaubert generalized and radicalized the partial revolution of realism. Like Manet confronted with a similar dilemma, he painted both bohemia and high society. If the pure gaze might accord special interest to objects socially designated as hateful or despicable (like Baudelaire's carrion) because of the challenge that they represented, it remained totally unaware of all the non-aesthetic differences between objects, and it could find in bourgeois worlds, by virtue of their privileged tie to bourgeois art, a particular opportunity to assert its irreducibility.

An aesthetic revolution could only occur aesthetically. It was not enough to establish as beautiful whatever official aesthetics excluded or to rehabilitate modern, 'low' or 'mediocre' subjects. It was necessary to assert through form ('write well about mediocrity') the power of art to constitute everything aesthetically, to transmute everything into literary beauty, through writing itself. 'For this reason there are neither beautiful nor ugly subjects and one could almost establish as an axiom, taking the point of view of pure Art, that there are no subjects, style by itself being an absolute manner of seeing things' (*CP*, vol. 2, p. 31). The alternative between formalism and realism to which critics tried to restrict Flaubert (and Manet as well) was patently absurd. Because he mastered the highest demands of form, he could assert almost without limitation the power of form to establish aesthetically any reality whatsoever.

The revolution of the gaze, and the rupture of the bond between ethics and aesthetics implied by that revolution, effected a total conversion of lifestyle. This revolution, which led to the aestheticization of the artistic lifestyle, could only be half accomplished by the realists of the second bohemia, enclosed within their petit-bourgeois ethos, partly because they did not accept the ethical implications of that revolution. The advocates of social art saw very clearly the ethical foundations of the new aesthetics. They denounced the ethical perversion of a literature that was 'venereal and close to an aphrodisiac'; they attacked the 'singers of ugliness and filth', who united 'moral ignominy' and 'physical decadence'; and they were especially indignant about the method and the artifice in this 'cold, reasoned, thoroughly researched depravation'.[8] This literature was deemed scandalous because of its perverse complacency, but also because of cynical indifference to infamy and to scandal itself. Thus an article on *Madame Bovary* and the 'physiological novel' reproached Flaubert's pictorial imagination for 'enclosing itself in the material world as if in a vast studio peopled with models who in his eyes all have the same value'.[9]

It is certain that the pure gaze that had to be invented (and not, as is the case today, simply put into action), at the price of breaking the ties between art and morality, required an attitude of impassivity, indifference, aloofness and even cynical extravagance. Although it never excluded a good deal of posturing (Baudelaire), this attitude presupposed very particular dispositions, associated with positions and trajectories that favoured distance with respect to the social world. This distance was the opposite of the double ambivalence, based on horror and in fascination, of the petit-bourgeois towards the 'bourgeois' and the 'people': thus, for example, Flaubert's violent anarchistic temperament, his sense of transgression and jokes, along with the distance that let him bring the most beautiful aesthetic effects out of the simple description of human misery. This aestheticism pushed to its limits tended toward a kind of neutralism, even ethical nihilism.

This freedom with respect to the moral and humanitarian conformity that constrained 'proper' people was no doubt responsible for the profound unity of the habitués of Magny's restaurant: Flaubert, Turgenev, Sainte-Beuve and Taine. Between literary anecdotes and obscene stories, they affirmed the separation of art and morality. This was also the foundation of the affinity with Baudelaire which Flaubert invoked in a letter when he was writing *Salammbô*: 'I'm getting to the dark tones. We're starting to walk around in the intestines and burn the dead. Baudelaire will be satisfied' (*CP*, vol. 3, p. 80). The aristocratic aestheticism stressed here in the provocative mode was revealed more discreetly and no doubt more authentically in a judgement of Hugo: 'why does he display such a silly morality which diminishes him so much? why the Académie? the clichés! the imitation, etc.' (*CP*, vol. 2, p. 330).

This distance from all social positions favoured by formal elaboration was inscribed by that elaboration in the literary work itself: whence the merciless elimination of all received ideas, of all clichés, and of all the other stylistic features that could mark or reveal adherence to one or another position; whence also the methodical use of free indirect discourse which leaves indeterminate, or as indeterminate as possible, the relationship of the narrator to the facts or characters in the narrative. But nothing is more revelatory of *Flaubert's point of view* than the characteristic composition of his works, and in particular of *Sentimental Education*, a novel criticized from the beginning for not being structured or for being poorly organized. Like Manet somewhat later, Flaubert abandoned the unifying perspective, taken from a fixed, central point of view, which he replaced with what could be called, following Erwin Panofsky, an 'aggregated space', if we take this to mean a space made of juxtaposed pieces without a preferred point of view. In a letter to Huysmans about his recently published novel, Flaubert wrote that 'Missing from *The Vatard Sisters*, as from *Sentimental Education*, *the falseness of a perspective!* There is no progression of effect' (*CC*, vol. 8, p. 224). Thus his declaration to Henry Céard about *Sentimental Education*: 'It's a condemned book, my good friend, because it doesn't go like that: and joining his long, elegant yet robust hands, he made a pyramid.'[10]

In itself the refusal of the pyramid construction, that is, an ascending convergence toward an idea, a conviction, a conclusion, contains a message, and no doubt the most important one: a vision, not to say a philosophy, of history in the double sense of the word. As a bourgeois who was vehemently anti-bourgeois and completely devoid of any illusions about the 'people' (though Dussardier, sincere and disinterested plebeian, is the only shining figure in *Sentimental Education*), Flaubert preserves in his absolute disenchantment an absolute conviction, which concerns the work of the writer. Against preachers of every sort, he asserted, in the only consistent way possible, without *phrases* and by the very structure of his discourse, his refusal to give the reader the deceptive satisfactions offered by the false philistine humanism of the sellers of illusion. It is here, in this narrative with no beyond, in this narrative that recounts itself, in the irreconcilable diversity of its perspectives, in the universe from which the author has deleted himself but remains, like Spinoza's god, immanent and co-extensive with his creation – it is here that we find Flaubert's point of view.

# Part III

*The Pure Gaze: Essays on Art*

# 8

# Outline of a Sociological Theory
## of Art Perception

1

Any art perception involves a conscious or unconscious deciphering operation.

1.1 An act of deciphering *unrecognized as such*, immediate and adequate 'comprehension', is possible and effective only in the special case in which the cultural code which makes the act of deciphering possible is immediately and completely mastered by the observer (in the form of cultivated ability or inclination) and merges with the cultural code which has rendered the work perceived possible.

Erwin Panofsky observes that in Rogier van der Weyden's painting *The Three Magi* we immediately perceive the representation of an apparition, that of a child in whom we recognize 'the Infant Jesus'. How do we know that this is an apparition? The halo of golden rays surrounding the child would not in itself be sufficient proof, because it is also found in representations of the nativity in which the Infant Jesus is 'real'. We come to this conclusion because the child is hovering in mid-air without visible support, and we do so although the representation would scarcely have been different had the child been sitting on a pillow (as in the case of the model which Rogier van der Weyden probably used). But one can think of hundreds of pictures in which human beings, animals or inanimate objects appear to be hovering in mid-air, contrary to the law of gravity, yet without giving the impression of being apparitions. For instance, in a miniature of the *Gospels of Otto*

*III*, in the Staatsbibliothek, Munich, a whole town is represented in the middle of an empty space, while the persons taking part in the action are standing on the ground. This actually is a real town, where the resurrection of the young people shown in the foreground took place. If, in a split second and almost automatically, we recognize the aerial figure as an apparition, whereas we see nothing miraculous about the city floating in the air, it is because 'we are reading "what we see" according to the manner in which the objects and events are expressed by forms under varying historical conditions'; more precisely, when we decipher a miniature of c.1000 AD, we unconsciously assume that the empty space serves merely as an abstract, unreal background instead of forming part of an apparently natural, three-dimensional space, in which the supernatural and the miraculous can appear as such, as in Rogier van der Weyden's painting.[1]

Since they unconsciously obey the rules which govern a particular representation of space when they decipher a picture constructed according to these rules, the educated or competent beholders of our societies can immediately apprehend as a 'supernatural vision' an element which, by reference to another system of representations in which the regions of space would be in some way 'juxtaposed' or 'aggregated' instead of being integrated into a single representation, might appear 'natural' or 'real'. 'The perspective concept', says Panofsky, 'makes it impossible for religious art to enter the realm of *magic* . . . but opens to it a completely new realm, that of the "visionary" in which the miracle becomes an experience immediately perceived by the beholder, because supernatural events burst into the apparently natural visible space which is familiar to him, and thus enable him truly to penetrate into the essence of the supernatural.'[2]

The question of the conditions that make it possible to experience the work of art (and, in a more general way, all cultural objects) as at once endowed with meaning is totally excluded from the experience itself, because the recapturing of the work's objective meaning (which may have nothing to do with the author's intention) is completely adequate and immediately effected in the case – and only in the case – where the culture that the originator puts into the work is identical with the culture or, more accurately, the *artistic competence* which the beholder brings to the deciphering of the work. In this case, everything is a matter of course and the question of the meaning, of the deciphering of the meaning and of the conditions of this deciphering does not arise.

1.2   Whenever these specific conditions are not fulfilled, misunderstanding is inevitable: the illusion of immediate comprehension leads to an illusory comprehension based on a mistaken code.[3] In the absence of the perception that the works are coded, and coded in another code, one unconsciously applies the code which is good for everyday perception, for the deciphering of familiar objects, to works in a foreign tradition. There is no perception which does not involve an unconscious code and it is essential to dismiss the myth of the 'fresh eye', considered a virtue attributed to naïveté and innocence. One of the reasons why the less educated beholders in our societies are so strongly inclined to demand a realistic representation is that, being devoid of specific categories of perception, they cannot apply any other code to works of scholarly culture than that which enables them to apprehend as meaningful objects of their everyday environment. Minimum, and apparently immediate, comprehension, accessible to the simplest observers and enabling them to recognize a house or a tree, still presupposes partial (unconscious) agreement between artist and beholder concerning categories that define the representation of the real that a historic society holds to be 'realistic' (see note 4).

1.3   The spontaneous theory of art perception is founded on the experience of familiarity and immediate comprehension – an unrecognized special case.
   1.3.1   Educated people are at home with scholarly culture. They are consequently carried towards that kind of ethnocentrism which may be called class-centrism and which consists in considering as natural (in other words, both as a matter of course and based on nature) a way of perceiving which is but one among other possible ways and which is acquired through education that may be diffuse or specific, conscious or unconscious, institutionalized or non-institutionalized. 'When, for instance, a man wears a pair of spectacles which are so close to him physically that they are "sitting on his nose", they are environmentally more remote from him than the picture on the opposite wall. Their proximity is normally so weakly perceived as to go unnoticed.' Taking Heidegger's analysis metaphorically, it can be said that the illusion of the 'fresh eye' as a 'naked eye' is an attribute of those who wear the spectacles of culture and who do not see that which enables them to see, any more than they see what they would not see if they were deprived of what enables them to see.[4]
   1.3.2   Conversely, faced with scholarly culture, the least sophisticated are in a position identical with that of ethnologists who find themselves in a foreign society and present, for instance, at a ritual to which they do not hold the key. The disorientation and cultural blindness of the less-educated beholders are an objective reminder of the objective truth that art perception is a mediate deciphering operation. Since the information presented by the works exhibited exceeds the

deciphering capabilities of the beholder, he perceives them as devoid of signification – or, to be more precise, of structuration and organization – because he cannot 'decode' them, i.e. reduce them to an intelligible form.

1.3.3   Scientific knowledge is distinguished from naïve experience (whether this is shown by disconcertment or by immediate comprehension) in that it involves an awareness of the conditions permitting adequate perception. The object of the science of the work of art is that which renders possible both this science and the immediate comprehension of the work of art, that is, culture. It therefore includes, implicitly at least, the science of the difference between scientific knowledge and naïve perception. 'The naïve "beholder" differs from the art historian in that the latter is conscious of the situation.'[5] Needless to say, there would probably be some difficulty in subsuming all the genuine art historians under the concept Panofsky defines in an excessively normative fashion.

2

Any deciphering operation requires a more or less complex code which has been more or less completely mastered.

2.1   The work of art (like any cultural object) may disclose significations at different levels according to the deciphering grid applied to it; the lower-level significations, that is to say the most superficial, remain partial and mutilated, and therefore erroneous, as long as the higher-level significations which encompass and transfigure them are lacking.

2.1.1   According to Panofsky, the most naïve beholder first of all distinguishes 'the primary or natural subject matter or meaning which we can apprehend from our practical experience', or, in other words, 'the phenomenal meaning which can be subdivided into factual and expressional'. This apprehension depends on 'demonstrative concepts' which only identify and grasp the sensible qualities of the work (this is the case when a peach is described as velvety or lace as misty) or the emotional experience that these qualities arouse in the beholder (when colours are spoken of as harsh or gay). To reach 'the secondary subject matter which presupposes a familiarity with specific themes or concepts as transmitted through literary sources' and which may be called the 'sphere of the meaning of the signified' [région du sens du signifié], we must have 'appropriately characterizing concepts' which go beyond the simple designation of sensible qualities and, grasping the stylistic characteristics of the work of art, constitute a genuine 'interpretation' of it. Within this secondary stratum, Panofsky distinguishes, on the one hand, 'the secondary or conventional meaning, the world of specific themes or concepts manifested in images, stories and allegories' (when, for instance, a group of persons seated around a table according to a certain arrangement represents the Last Supper), the deciphering of which falls to iconography; and, on the other hand, 'the intrinsic meaning or content', which the iconological interpretation can recapture only if the iconographical meanings and methods of composition are treated as 'cultural symbols', as expressions of the culture of an age, a nation or a class, and if an effort is made to bring out 'the fundamental principles which support the choice and presentation of the motifs as well as the production and interpretation of the images, stories and allegories and which give a meaning even to the formal composition and to the technical processes'.[6] The meaning grasped by the primary act of deciphering is totally different according to whether it constitutes the whole of the experience of the work of art or becomes part of a unitary experience, embodying the higher levels of meaning. Thus, it is only starting from an iconographical interpretation that the formal arrangements and technical methods and, through them, the formal and expressive qualities, assume their full meaning and that the insufficiencies of a pre-iconographic or pre-iconological interpretation are revealed at the same time. In an adequate knowledge of the work, the different levels are articulated in a hierarchical system in which the embodying form becomes embodied in its turn, and the signified in its turn becomes significant.

2.1.2 Uninitiated perception, reduced to the grasping of primary significations, is a mutilated perception. Contrasted with what might be called – to borrow a phrase from Nietzsche – 'the dogma of the immaculate perception', foundation of the Romantic representation of artistic experience, the 'comprehension' of the 'expressive' and, as one might say, 'physiognomical' qualities of the work is only an inferior and mutilated form of the aesthetic experience, because, not being supported, controlled and corrected by knowledge of the style, types and 'cultural symptoms', it uses a code which is neither adequate nor specific. It can probably be agreed that inward experience as a capacity for emotional response to the connotation (as opposed to denotation) of the work of art is one of the keys to art experience. But Raymond Ruyer very discerningly contrasts the significance, which he defines as 'epicritic', and the *expressivity*, which he describes as 'protopathic, that is to say more primitive, more blurred, of the lower level, linked with the diencephalon, whereas the signification is linked with the cerebral cortex'.

2.1.3   Through sociological observation it is possible to reveal, effectively realized, forms of perception corresponding to the different levels which theoretical analysis frames by an abstract distinction. Any cultural asset, from cookery to dodecaphonic music by way of the Western movie, can be an object for apprehension ranging from the simple, actual sensation to scholarly appreciation. The ideology of the 'fresh eye' overlooks the fact that the sensation or affection stimulated by the work of art does not have the same 'value' when it constitutes the whole of the aesthetic experience as when it forms part of an adequate experience of the work of art. One may therefore distinguish, through abstraction, two extremes and opposite forms of aesthetic pleasure, separated by all the intermediate degrees, the *enjoyment* which accompanies aesthetic perception reduced to simple *aisthesis*, and the *delight* procured by scholarly savouring, presupposing, as a necessary but insufficient condition, adequate deciphering. Like painting, perception of painting is a mental thing, at least when it conforms to the norms of perception immanent in the work of art or, in other words, when the beholder's aesthetic intention is identified with the objective intention of the work (which must not be identified with the artist's intention).

2.1.4   The most uninitiated perception is always inclined to go beyond the level of sensations and affections, that is to say *aisthesis* pure and simple: the assimilatory interpretation which tends to apply to an unknown and foreign universe the available schemes of interpretation, that is, those which enable the familiar universe to be apprehended as having meaning, becomes essential as a means of restoring the unity of an integrated perception. Those for whom the works of scholarly culture speak a foreign language are condemned to take into their perception and their appreciation of the work of art some extrinsic categories and values – those which organize their day-to-day perception and guide their practical judgement. The aesthetics of the different social classes are therefore, with certain exceptions, only one dimension of their ethics (or better, of their ethos): thus, the aesthetic preferences of the lower middle class appear as a sytematic expression of an ascetic disposition which is also expressed in other spheres of their existence.

2.2   The work of art considered as a symbolic good (and not as an economic asset, which it may also be) only exists as such for a person who has the means to appropriate it, or in other words, to decipher it.[7]

2.2.1   The degree of an agent's art competence is measured by the degree to which he or she masters the set of instruments for the appropriation of the work of art, available at a given time, that is to say, the interpretation schemes which are the prerequisite for the appropriation of art capital or, in other words, the prerequisite for the deciphering of works of art offered to a given society at a given moment.

2.2.1.1  Art competence can be provisionally defined as the preliminary knowledge of the possible divisions into complementary classes of a universe of representations. A mastery of this kind of system of classification enables each element of the universe to be placed in a class necessarily determined in relation to another class, itself constituted by all the art representations consciously or unconsciously taken into consideration which do not belong to the class in question. The *style* proper to a period and to a social group is none other than such a class defined in relation to all the works of the same universe which it excludes and which are complementary to it. The *recognition* (or, as the art historians say when using the vocabulary of logic, the *attribution*) proceeds by *successive elimination* of the possibilities to which the class is – negatively – related and to which the possibility which has become a reality in the work concerned belongs. It is immediately evident that the uncertainty concerning the different characteristics likely to be attributed to the work under consideration (authors, schools, periods, styles, subjects, etc.) can be removed by employing different codes, functioning as classification systems; it may be a case of a properly artistic code which, by permitting the deciphering of specifically stylistic characteristics, enables the work concerned to be assigned to the class formed by the whole of the works of a period, a society, a school or an author ('that's a Cézanne'), or a code from everyday life which, in the form of previous knowledge of the possible divisions into complementary classes of the universe of signifiers and of the universe of signifieds, and of the correlations between the divisions of the one and the divisions of the other, enables the particular representation, treated as a sign, to be assigned to a class of signifiers and consequently makes it possible to know, by means of the correlations with the universe of signifieds, that the corresponding signified belongs to a certain class of signifieds ('that's a forest').[8] In the first case the beholder is paying attention to the manner of treating the leaves or the clouds, that is to say to the stylistic indications, locating the possibility realized, characteristic of one class of works, by reference to the universe of stylistic possibilities; in the other case, she is treating the leaves or the clouds as indications or signals associated, according to the logic set forth above, with significations transcendent to the representation itself ('that's a poplar', 'that's a storm').

2.2.1.2  Artistic competence is therefore defined as the previous knowledge of the strictly artistic principles of division which enable a representation to be located, through the classification of the stylistic indications which it contains, among the possibilities of representation constituting the universe of art and not among the possibilities of representation constituting the universe of everyday objects or the universe of signs, which would amount to treating it as a mere monument, i.e. as a mere means of communication used to transmit a transcendent signification. The perception of the work of art in a truly aesthetic manner, that is, as a signifier which signifies nothing other than itself, does not consist of considering it 'without connecting it with anything other than itself, either emotionally or intellectually', in short of giving oneself up to the work apprehended in its irreducible singularity, but rather of noting its *distinctive stylistic features* by relating it to the ensemble of the works forming the class to which it belongs, and to these works only. On the contrary, the taste of the working classes is determined, after the manner of what Kant describes in his *Critique of Judgement* as 'barbarous taste', by the refusal or the impossibility (one should say the impossibility-refusal) of operating the distinction between 'what is liked' and 'what pleases' and, more generally, between 'disinterestedness', the only guarantee of the aesthetic quality of contemplation, and 'the interest of the senses' which defines 'the agreeable' or 'the interest of reason': it requires that every image shall fulfil a function, if only that of a sign. This 'functionalist' representation of the work of art is based on the refusal of gratuitousness, the idolatry of work or the placing of value on what is 'instructive' (as opposed to what is 'interesting') and also on the impossibility of placing each individual work in the universe of representations, in the absence of strictly stylistic principles of classification.[9] It follows that a work of art which they expect to express unambiguously a signification transcendental to the signifier is all the more disconcerting to the most uninitiated in that, like the non-figurative arts, it does away more completely with the narrative and descriptive function.

2.2.1.3   The degree of artistic competence depends not only on the degree to which the available system of classification is mastered, but also on the degree of complexity or subtlety of this system of classification, and it is therefore measurable by the ability to operate a fairly large number of successive divisions in the universe of representations and thus to determine rather fine classes. For anyone familiar only with the principle of division into Romanesque art and Gothic art, all Gothic cathedrals fall into the same class and, for that reason, remain *indistinct*, whereas greater competence makes it possible to perceive differences between the styles of the 'early', 'middle' and 'late' periods, or even to recognize, within each of these styles, the works of a school or even of an architect. Thus, the apprehension of the features which constitute the *peculiarity* of the works of one period compared with those of another period or, within this class of the works of one school or group of artists compared with another, or again, of the works of one author compared with other works of his or her school or period, or even a particular work of an author compared with his work as a whole – such apprehension is indissociable from that of *redundancies*, that is, from the grasping of typical treatments of the pictorial matter which determine a style: in short, the grasping of resemblances presupposes implicit or explicit reference to the differences, and vice versa.

2.3 The art code as a sytem of possible principles of division into complementary classes of the universe of representations offered to a particular society at a given time is in the nature of a social institution.

2.3.1 Being an historically constituted system, founded on social reality, this set of instruments of perception whereby a particular society, at a given time, appropriates artistic goods (and, more generally, cultural goods) does not depend on individual wills and consciousnesses and forces itself upon individuals, often without their knowledge, defining the distinctions they can make and those which escape them. Every period arranges artistic representations as a whole according to an institutional system of classification of its own, bringing together works which other periods separated, or distinguishing between works which other periods placed together, and individuals have difficulty in imagining differences other than those which the available system of classification allows them to imagine. 'Suppose', writes Longhi, 'that the French naturalists and impressionists, between 1860 and 1880, had not signed their works and that they had not had at their side, like heralds, critics and journalists as intelligent as Geoffroy or Duret. Imagine them forgotten, as the result of a reversal of taste and a long period of decline in erudite research, forgotten for a hundred or a hundred and fifty years. What would happen first of all, when attention was again focused on them? It is easy to foresee that, in the first phase, analysis would begin by distinguishing several entities in these mute materials, which would be more symbolic than historical. The first would bear the symbolic name of Manet, who would absorb part of Renoir's youthful production, and even, I fear, a few works of Gervex, without counting all those of Gonzalès, Morizot and the young Monet. As to Monet in later years – he also having become a symbol – he would engulf almost the whole of Sisley, a good share of Renoir, and worse still, a few dozen works of Boudin, several of Lebourand, several of Lépine. It is by no means impossible that a few of Pissarro's works and even, unflattering recompense, more than one of Guillaumin, might in such a case be attributed to Cézanne.'[10]

Still more convincing than this kind of imaginary variation, Berne Joffroy's historical study on the successive representations of the work of Caravaggio shows that the *public image* that the individuals of a specified period form of a work is, properly speaking, the product of the instruments of perception, historically constituted, and therefore historically changing, which are supplied to them by the society to which they belong: 'I know well what is said about attribution disputes: that they have nothing to do with art, that they are petty and that art is great . . . The idea that we form of an artist depends on the works attributed to him and, whether we would or not, this general idea of him colours our view of each of his works.'[11] Thus, the history of the instruments for perception of the work is the essential complement of the history of the instruments for production of the work, to the extent that every work is, so to speak, made twice, by the originator and by the beholder, or rather, by the society to which the beholder belongs.

2.3.2   The modal readability of a work of art (for a given society in a given period) varies according to the divergence between the code which the work under consideration objectively requires and the code as an historically constituted institution; the readability of a work of art for a particular individual varies according to the divergence between the more or less complex and subtle code required by the work, and the competence of the individual, as defined by the degree to which the social code, itself more or less complex and subtle, is mastered. Thus, as Boris de Schloezer observes, each period has its melodic schemes which cause the individuals to apprehend immediately the structure of the successions of sounds in conformity with these schemes: 'Nowadays we need some instruction to appreciate the Gregorian chant, and many medieval monodies seem no less baffling than a melodic phrase of Alban Berg. But when a melody enters easily into frameworks to which we are accustomed, there is no longer any need to reconstruct it, its unity is there and the phrase reaches us as a whole, so to speak, in the manner of a chord. In this case, it is capable of acting magically, again like a chord, or a gong stroke; if on the other hand it is a melody whose structure is no longer in conformity with the schemes sanctioned by tradition – the tradition of the Italian opera, that of Wagner or the popular song – the synthesis is sometimes difficult to make.'[12]

2.3.3   Since the works forming the art capital of a given society at a given time call for codes of varying complexity and subtlety, and are therefore likely to be acquired more or less easily and more or less rapidly by institutionalized or non-institutionalized training, they are characterized by different levels of emission, so that the previous proposition (2.3.2) can be reformulated in the following terms: the readability of a work of art for a particular individual depends on the *divergence between the level of emission*,[13] defined as the degree of intrinsic complexity and subtlety, of the code required for the work, and the *level of reception*, defined as the degree to which this individual masters the social code, which may be more or less adequate to the code required for the work. Individuals possess a definite and limited capacity for apprehending the 'information' suggested by the work, a capacity which depends on their knowledge of the generic code for the type of message concerned, be it the painting as a whole, or the painting of a particular period, school or author. When the message exceeds the possibilities of apprehension or, to be more precise, when the code of the work exceeds in subtlety and complexity the code of the beholders, the latter lose interest in what appears to them to be a medley without rhyme or reason, or a completely unnecessary set of sounds or colours. In other words, when placed before a message which is too rich, or 'overwhelming', as the theory of information expresses it, they feel completely 'out of their depth' (cf. 1.3.2 above).

2.3.4   It follows that to increase the readability of a work of art (or of a collection of works of art such as those exhibited in a museum) and to reduce the misunderstanding which results from the divergence, it is possible either to lower the level of emission or to raise the level of reception. The only way of lowering the level of emission of a work is to provide, together with the work, the code according to which the work is coded, in a discourse (verbal or graphic), the code of which is already mastered (partially or completely) by the receiver, or which continuously delivers the code for deciphering, in accordance with the model of perfectly rational pedagogic communication. Incidentally, it is obvious that any action tending to lower the level of emission helps in fact to raise the level of reception.

2.3.5   In each period, the rules defining the readability of contemporary art are but a special application of the general law of readability. The readability of a contemporary work varies primarily according to the relationship which the creators maintain, in a given period, in a given society, with the code of the previous period. It is thus possible to distinguish, very roughly, *classical periods*, in which a style reaches its own perfection and which the creators exploit to the point of achieving and perhaps exhausting the possibilities provided by an inherited art of inventing, and *periods of rupture*, in which a new art of inventing is invented, in which a new generative grammar of forms is engendered, out of joint with the aesthetic traditions of a time or an environment. The divergence between the social code and the code required for the works has clearly every chance of being less in classical periods than in periods of rupture, infinitely less, especially, than in the *periods of continued rupture*, such as the one we are now living through. The transformation of the instruments of art production necessarily precedes the transformation of the instruments of art perception and the transformation of the modes of perception cannot but operate slowly, because it is a matter of uprooting a type of art competence (the product of the internalization of a social code, so deeply implanted in habits and memories that it functions at a subconscious level) and of substituting another for it, by a new process of internalization, necessarily long and difficult.[14] In periods of rupture, the inertia inherent in art competences (or, if preferred, in habitus) means that the works produced by means of art production instruments of a new type are bound to be perceived, for a certain time, by means of old instruments of perception, precisely those against which they have been created. Educated people, who belong to culture at least as much as culture belongs to them, are always given to applying inherited categories to the works of their period and to ignoring, for the same reason, the irreducible novelty of works which carry with them the very categories of their own perception (as opposed to works which can be called academic, in a very broad sense, and which only put into operation a code, or, rather, a habitus which already exists). Everything opposes the devotees of culture, sworn to the worship of the consecrated works of defunct prophets, as also the priests of culture, devoted, like the teachers, to the organization of this worship, to the cultural prophets, that is to say the creators who upset the routine of ritualized fervour, while they become in their turn the object of the routine worship of new priests and new devotees. If it is true, as Franz Boas says, that 'the thought of what we call the educated classes is controlled essentially by those ideals which have been transmitted to us by past generations',[15] the fact remains that the absence of any art competence is neither a necessary nor a sufficient condition for the adequate perception of innovative works or, with stronger reason, for the production of such works. Naïveté of the artistic gaze can here be only the supreme form of sophistication. The fact of being devoid of keys is in no way favourable to the understanding of works which require only that all the old keys be rejected so as to wait for the work itself to deliver the key for its own deciphering. As we have seen, this is the very attitude that the most uninitiated, confronted by scholarly art, are least inclined to take up (cf. 2.2.1.2). The ideology according to which the most modern forms of non-figurative art are more directly accessible to the innocence of childhood or of ignorance than to the competence acquired by a training which is considered as deforming, like that of the school, is not only refuted by the facts;[16] although the most innovative forms of art only yield their message first to a few virtuosi (whose avant-garde positions are always explained partly by the position they occupy in the intellectual field and, more generally, in the social structure),[17] the fact is that they demand a capacity for breaking with all the codes, beginning obviously with the code of everyday life, and that this capacity is acquired through association with works demanding different codes and through an experience of the history of art as a succession of ruptures with established codes. In short, an ability to hold all the available codes in abeyance so as to rely entirely on the work itself, and what at first sight is the most unusual quality in it, presupposes an accomplished mastery of the code of the codes, which governs adequate application of the different social codes objectively required for the available works as a whole at a given moment.

3

Since the work of art only exists as such to the extent that it is perceived, or, in other words, deciphered, it goes without saying that the satisfactions attached to this perception – whether it be a matter of purely aesthetic enjoyment or of more indirect gratification, such as the *effect of distinction* (cf. 3.3) – are only accessible to those who are disposed to appropriate them because they *attribute a value to them*, it being understood that they can do this only if they have the means to appropriate them. Consequently, the need to appropriate goods which, like cultural goods, only exist as such for those who have received the means to appropriate them from their family environment and school, can appear only in those who can satisfy it, and it can be satisfied as soon as it appears.

3.1   It follows on the one hand that, unlike 'primary' needs, the 'cultural need' as a cultivated need increases in proportion as it is satisfied, because each new appropriation tends to strengthen the mastery of the instruments of appropriation (cf. 3.2.1) and, consequently, the satisfactions attached to a new appropriation; on the other hand, it also follows that the awareness of deprivation decreases in proportion as the deprivation increases, individuals who are most completely dispossessed of the means of appropriating works of art being the most completely dispossessed of the awareness of this dispossession.

3.2   The disposition to appropriate cultural goods is the product of general or specific education, institutionalized or not, which creates (or cultivates) art competence as a mastery of the instruments for appropriation of these goods, and which creates the 'cultural need' by giving the means to satisfy it.
3.2.1   The repeated perception of works of a certain style encourages the unconscious internalization of the rules that govern the production of these works. Like rules of grammar, these rules are not apprehended

as such, and are still less explicitly formulated and capable of being formulated: for instance, lovers of classical music may have neither awareness nor knowledge of the laws obeyed by the sound-making art to which they are accustomed, but their auditive education is such that, having heard a dominant chord, they are induced urgently to await the tonic which seems to him the 'natural' resolution of this chord, and they have difficulty in apprehending the internal coherence of music founded on other principles. The unconscious mastery of the instruments of appropriation which are the basis of familiarity with cultural works is acquired by slow familiarization, a long succession of 'little perceptions', in the sense in which Leibniz uses the expression. Connoisseurship is an 'art' which, like the art of thinking or the art of living, cannot be imparted entirely in the form of precepts or instruction, and apprenticeship to it presupposes the equivalent of prolonged contact between disciple and initiate in traditional education, i.e. repeated contact with the work (or with works of the same class). And, just as students or disciples can *unconsciously* absorb the rules of the art – including those which are not explicitly known to the initiates themselves – by giving themselves up to it, excluding analysis and the selection of elements of exemplary conduct, so art-lovers can, by abandoning themselves in some way to the work, internalize the principles and rules of its construction without there ever being brought to their consciousness and formulated as such. This constitutes the difference between the art theorist and the connoisseur, who is usually incapable of explicating the principles on which his judgements are based (cf. 1.3.3). In this field as in others (learning the grammar of one's native tongue, for instance), school education tends to encourage the conscious reflection of patterns of thought, perception or expression which have already been mastered unconsciously by formulating explicitly the principles of the creative grammar, for example, the laws of harmony and counterpoint or the rules of pictorial composition, and by providing the verbal and conceptual material essential for naming differences previously experienced in a purely intuitive way. The danger of academicism is obviously inherent in any rationalized teaching which tends to mint, within one doctrinal body, precepts, prescriptions and formulae, explicitly described and taught, more often negative than positive, which a traditional education imparts in the form of a habitus, directly apprehended *uno intuitu*, as a global style not susceptible to analytical breakdown.

3.2.2. Familiarization by repeated perceptions is the privileged mode of acquiring the means of appropriating works of art because the work of art always appears as a concrete individuality which never allows itself to be deduced from principles and rules defining a style. As is seen from the facts in the case of the musical work, the most exact and best informed discursive translations cannot take the place of the execution, as a *hic et nunc* realization of the individual form, which is irreducible to any formula; the conscious or unconscious mastery of the principles and rules of the production of this form enables its coherence and necessity to be apprehended by a symmetrical reconstruction of the creator's construction but, far from reducing the individual work to the general nature of a type, it renders possible the perception and appreciation of the originality of each actualization or, rather, of each execution, in relation to the principles and rules according to which it was produced. Although the work of art always procures the twofold feeling of the unparalleled and the inevitable, the most inventive, most improvised and the most original solutions can always be understood, *post festum*, in terms of the schemes of thought, perception and action (rules of composition, theoretical problems, etc.) which have given rise to the technical or aesthetic questions to which this work corresponds, at the same time as they guide the creator in the search for a solution irreducible to schemes and, thereby, unpredictable yet none the less in accordance, *a posteriori*, with the rules of a grammar of forms. The ultimate truth of the style of a period, a school or an author is not contained as a seed in an original inspiration, but is defined and redefined continuously as a signification in a state of flux which constructs itself in accordance with itself and in reaction against itself; it is in the continued exchange between questions which exist only for and through a mind armed with schemes of a specific type and more or less innovative solutions, obtained through the application of the same schemes, but capable of transforming the initial scheme, that this unity of style and of meaning emerges which, at least after the event, may appear to have preceded the works heralding the final outcome and which transforms, retrospectively, the different moments of the temporal series into simple preparatory outlines. If the evolution of a style (of a period, a school or an author) does not appear either as the autonomous development of an essence which is unique and always identical with itself, or as a continuous creation of unpredictable novelty, but as a progression which excludes neither leaps forward nor turnings back, it is because the creator's habitus as a system of schemes constantly guides choices which, though not deliberate, are none the less systematic and, without being arranged and organized expressly in relation to a final goal, are none the less bearers of a kind of finality which will be revealed only *post festum*. The auto-constitution of a system of works united by a set of significant relationships is accomplished in and through the association of contingency and meaning which is unceasingly made, unmade and remade according to principles which are all the more constant because they are completely unconscious, in and through the permanent transmutation which introduces the accidents of the history of techniques into the history of style while making them meaningful in and through the invention of obstacles and difficulties which are as if evoked on behalf of the very principles of their solution and of which the short-term counter-finality may conceal a higher finality.

3.2.3  Even when the educational institution makes little provision for art training proper (as is the case in France and many other countries), even when, therefore, it gives neither specific encouragement to cultural activities nor a body of concepts specifically adapted to the plastic arts, it tends on the one hand to inspire a certain *familiarity* – conferring a feeling of belonging to the cultivated class – with the world of art, in which people feel at home and among themselves as the appointed addressees of works which do not deliver their message to the first-comer; and on the other to inculcate (at least in France and in the majority of European countries, at the level of secondary education) a *cultivated disposition* as a durable and generalized attitude which implies recognition of the value of works of art and the ability to appropriate them by means of generic categories.[18] Although it deals almost exclusively with literary works, in-school learning tends to create on the one hand a transposable inclination to admire works approved by the school and a duty to admire and to love certain works or, rather, certain classes of works which gradually seem to become linked to a certain educational and social status; and, on the other hand, an equally generalized and transposable aptitude for categorizing by authors, by genres, by schools and by periods, for the handling of educational categories of literary analysis and for the mastery of the code which governs the use of the different codes (cf. 2.3.5), giving at least a tendency to acquire equivalent categories in other fields and to store away the typical knowledge which, even though extrinsic and anecdotal, makes possible at least an elementary form of apprehension, however inadequate it may be.[19] Thus, the first degree of strictly pictorial competence shows itself in the mastery of an arsenal of words making it possible to name differences and to apprehend them while naming them: these are the proper names of famous painters – da Vinci, Picasso, Van Gogh – which function as generic categories, because one can say about any painting or non-figurative object 'that suggests Picasso', or, about any work recalling nearly or distantly the manner of the Florentine painter, 'that looks like a da Vinci'; there are also broad categories, like 'the Impressionists' (a school commonly considered to include Gaugin, Cézanne and Degas), 'the Dutch School', 'the Renaissance'. It is particularly significant that the proportion of subjects who think in terms of schools very clearly grows as the level of education rises and that, more generally, generic knowledge which is required for the perception of differences and consequently for memorizing – proper names and historical, technical or aesthetic concepts – becomes increasingly specific as we go towards the more educated beholders, so that the most adequate perception differs only from the least adequate in so far as the specificity, richness and subtlety of the categories employed are concerned. By no means contradicting these arguments is the fact that the less educated visitors to museums – who tend to prefer the most famous paintings and those sanctioned by school teaching, whereas modern painters who have the least chance of being mentioned in schools are quoted only by those with the highest educational qualifications – live in large cities. To be able to form discerning or so-called 'personal' opinions is again a result of the education received: the ability to go beyond school constraints is the privilege of those who have sufficiently assimilated school education to make their own the free attitude towards scholastic culture taught by a school so deeply impregnated with the values of the ruling classes that it accepts the fashionable depreciation of school instruction. The contrast between accepted, stereotyped and, as Max Weber would say, 'routinized' culture, and genuine culture, freed from school discourse, has meaning only for an infinitely small minority of educated people for whom culture is second nature, endowed with all the appearances of talent, and the full assimilation of school culture is a prerequisite for going beyond it towards this 'free culture' – free, that is to say, from its school origins – which the bourgeois class and its school regard as the value of values (cf. 3.3).

But the best proof that the general principles for the transfer of training also hold for school training lies in the fact that the practices of one single individual and, *a fortiori*, of individuals belonging to one social category or having a specific level of education, tend to constitute a system, so that a certain type of practice in any field of culture very probably implies a corresponding type of practice in all the other fields; thus, frequent visits to museums are almost necessarily associated with an equal amount of theatre-going and, to a lesser degree, attendance at concerts. Similarly, everything seems to indicate that knowledge and preferences tend to form into constellations that are strictly linked to the level of education, so that a typical structure of preferences in painting is most likely to be linked to a structure of preferences of the same type in music or literature.[20]

3.2.4 Owing to the particular status of the work of art and the specific logic of the training which it implies, art education which is reduced to a discourse (historical, aesthetic or other) on the works is necessarily at a secondary level;[21] like the teaching of the native tongue, literary or art education (that is to say 'the humanities' of traditional education) necessarily presupposes, without ever, or hardly ever, being organized in the light of this principle, that individuals are endowed with a previously acquired competence and with a whole capital of experience unequally distributed among the various social classes (visits to museums or monuments, attending concerts, lectures, etc.).

3.2.4.1   In the absence of a methodical and systematic effort, involving the mobilization of all available means from the earliest years of school onwards, to procure for all those attending school a direct contact with the works or, at least, an approximate substitute for that experience (by showing reproductions or reading texts, organizing visits to museums or playing records, etc.), art education can be of full benefit only to those who owe the competence acquired by slow and imperceptible familiarization to their family milieu, because it does not explicitly give to all what it implicitly demands from all. While it is true that only the school can give the continuous and prolonged, methodical and uniform training capable of *mass production*, if I may use that expression, of competent individuals, provided with schemes of perception, thought and expression which are prerequisites for the appropriation of cultural goods, and endowed with that generalized and permanent inclination to appropriate them which is the mark of devotion to culture, the fact remains that the effectiveness of this formative action is directly dependent upon the degree to which those undergoing it fulfil the preliminary conditions for adequate reception: the influence of school activity is all the stronger and more lasting when it is carried on for a longer time (as is shown by the fact that the decrease of cultural activity with age is less marked when the duration of schooling was longer), when those upon whom it is exercised have greater previous competence, acquired through early and direct contact with works (which is well known to be more frequent always as one goes higher up the social scale[22]) and finally when a propitious cultural atmosphere sustains and relays its effectiveness.[23] Thus, humanities students who have received a homogeneous and homogenizing training for a number of years, and who have been constantly selected according to the degree to which they conform to school requirements, remain separated by systematic differences, both in their pursuit of cultural activities and in their cultural preferences, depending upon whether they come from a more or less cultivated milieu and for how long this has been so; their knowledge of the theatre (measured according to the average number of plays that they have seen on the stage) or of painting is greater if their father or grandfather (or, *a fortiori*, both of them) belongs to a higher occupational category; and, furthermore, if one of these variables (the category of the father or of the grandfather) has a fixed value, the other tends, by itself, to hierarchize the scores.[24] Because of the slowness of the acculturation process, subtle differences linked with the length of time that they have been in contact with culture thus continue to separate individuals who are apparently equal with regard to social success and even educational success. Cultural nobility also has its quarterings.

3.2.4.2   Only an institution like the school, the specific function of which is methodically to develop or create the dispositions which produce an educated person and which lay the foundations, quantitatively and consequently qualitatively, of a constant and intense pursuit of culture, could offset (at least partially) the initial disadvantage of those who do not receive from their family circle the encouragement to undertake cultural activities and the competence presupposed in any discourse on works, on the condition – and only on the condition – that it employs every available means to break down the endless series of cumulative processes to which any cultural education is condemned. For if the apprehension of a work of art depends, in its intensity, its modality and in its very existence, on the beholders' mastery of the generic and specific code of the work, i.e. on their competence, which they owe partly to school training, the same thing applies to the pedagogic communication which is responsible, among its other functions, for transmitting the code of works of scholarly culture (and also the code according to which it effects this transmission). Thus the intensity and modality of the communication are here again a function of culture (as a system of schemes of perception, expression and historically constituted and socially conditioned thinking) which the receiver owes to his or her family milieu and which is more or less close to scholarly culture and the linguistic and cultural models according to which the school effects the transmission of this culture. Considering that the direct experience of works of scholarly culture and the institutionally organized acquisition of culture which is a prerequisite for adequate experience of such works are subject to the same laws (cf. 2.3.2, 2.3.3 and 2.3.4), it is obvious how difficult it is to break the sequence of the cumulative effects which cause cultural capital to attract cultural capital. In fact, the school has only to give free play to the objective machinery of cultural diffusion without working systematically to give to all, in and through the pedagogical message itself, what is given to some through family inheritance – that is, the instruments which condition the adequate reception of the school message – for it to redouble and consecrate by its approval the socially conditioned inequalities of cultural competence, by treating them as natural inequalities or, in other words, as inequalities of gifts or natural talents.

3.3   Charismatic ideology is based on parenthesizing the relationship, evident as soon as it is revealed, between art competence and education, which alone is capable of creating both the disposition to recognize a value in cultural goods and the competence which gives a meaning to this disposition by making it possible to appropriate such goods. Since their art competence is the product of an imperceptible familiarization and an automatic transferring of aptitudes, members of the privileged classes are naturally inclined to regard as a gift of nature a cultural heritage which is transmitted by a process of unconscious training. But, in addition, the contradictions and ambiguities of the relationship which the most cultured among them maintain with their culture are both encouraged and permitted by the paradox which defines the 'realization' of culture as *becoming natural*. Culture is thus achieved only by negating itself as such, that is, as artificial and artificially acquired, so as to become second nature, a habitus, a possession turned into being; the virtuosi of the judgement of taste seem to reach an experience of aesthetic grace so completely freed from the constraints of culture and so little marked by the long, patient training of which it is the product that any reminder of the conditions and the social conditioning which have rendered it possible seems to be at once obvious and scandalous (cf. 1.3.1). It follows that the most experienced connoisseurs are the natural champions of charismatic ideology, which attributes to the work of art a magical power of conversion capable of awakening the potentialities latent in a few of the elect, and which contrasts authentic experience of a work of art as an 'affection' of the heart or immediate enlightenment of the intuition with the laborious proceedings and cold comments of the intelligence, ignoring the social and cultural conditions underlying such an experience, and at the same time treating as a birthright the virtuosity acquired through long familiarization or through the exercises of a methodical training; silence concerning the social prerequisites for the appropriation of culture or, to be more exact, for the acquisition of art competence in the sense of mastery of all the means for the specific appropriation of works of art is a self-seeking silence because it is what makes it possible to legitimatize a social privilege by pretending that it is a gift of nature.[25]

To remember that culture is not what one is but what one has, or rather, what one has become; to remember the social conditions which render possible aesthetic experience and the existence of those beings – art lovers or 'people of taste' – for whom it is possible; to remember that the work of art is given only to those who have received the means to acquire the means to appropriate it and who could not seek to possess it if they did not already possess it, in and through the possession of means of possession as an actual possibility of effecting the taking of possession; to remember, finally, that only a few have the real possibility of benefitting from the theoretical possibility, generously offered to all, of taking advantage of the works exhibited in museums – all this is to bring to light the hidden force of the effects of the majority of culture's social uses.

The parenthesizing of the social conditions which render possible culture and culture become nature, cultivated nature, having all the appearances of grace or a gift and yet acquired, so therefore 'deserved', is the precedent condition of charismatic ideology which makes it possible to confer on culture and in particular on 'love of art' the all-important place which they occupy in bourgeois 'sociodicy'. The bourgeoisie find naturally in culture as cultivated nature and culture that has become nature the only possible principle for the legitimation of their privilege. Being unable to invoke the right of birth (which their class, through the ages, has refused to the aristocracy) or nature which, according to 'democratic' ideology, represents universality, i.e. the ground on which all distinctions are abolished, or the aesthetic virtues which enabled the first generation of bourgeois to invoke their merit, they can resort to cultivated nature and culture become nature, to what is sometimes called 'class', through a kind of tell-tale slip, to 'education', in the sense of a product of education which seems to owe nothing to education,[26] to distinction, grace which is merit and merit which is grace, an unacquired merit which justifies unmerited acquisitions, that is to say, inheritance. To enable culture to fulfil its primary ideological function of class co-optation and legitimation of this mode of selection, it is necessary and sufficient that the link between culture and education, which is simultaneously obvious and hidden, be forgotten, disguised and denied. The unnatural idea of inborn culture, of a gift of culture, bestowed on certain people by nature, is inseparable from blindness to the functions of the institution which ensures the profitability of the cultural heritage and legitimizes its transmission while concealing that it fulfils this function. The school in fact is the institution which, through its outwardly irreproachable verdicts, transforms socially conditioned inequalities in regard to culture into inequalities of success, interpreted as inequalities of gifts which are also inequalities of merit.[27] Plato records, towards the end of *The Republic*, that the souls who are to begin another life must themselves choose their lot among 'patterns of life' of all kinds and that, when the choice has been made, they must drink of the water of the river Lethe before returning to earth. The function which Plato attributes to the water of forgetfulness falls, in our societies, on the university which, in its impartiality, though pretending to recognize students as equal in rights and duties, divided only by inequalities of gifts and of merit, in fact confers on individuals degrees judged according to their cultural heritage, and therefore according to their social status.

By symbolically shifting the essence of what sets them apart from other classes from the economic field to that of culture, or rather, by adding to strictly economic differences, namely those created by the simple possession of material goods, differences created by the possession of symbolic goods such as works of art, or by the pursuit of symbolic distinctions in the manner of using such goods (economic or symbolic), in short, by turning into a fact of nature everything which determines their 'value', or to take the word in the linguistic sense, their *distinction* – a mark of difference which, according to the Littré, sets people apart from the common herd 'by the characteristics of elegance, nobility and good form' – the privileged members of bourgeois society replace the difference between two cultures, historic products of social conditions, by the essential difference between two natures, a naturally cultivated nature and a naturally natural nature.[28] Thus, the sacralization of culture and art fulfils a vital function by contributing to the consecration of the social order: to enable educated people to believe in barbarism and persuade the barbarians within the gates of their own barbarity, all they must and need do is to manage to conceal themselves and to conceal the social conditions which render possible not only culture as a second nature in which society recognizes human excellence or 'good form' as the 'realization' in a habitus of the aesthetics of the ruling classes, but also the legitimized dominance (or, if you like, the legitimacy) of a particular definition of culture. And in order that the ideological circle may be completely closed, all they have to do is to find in an essentialist representation of the bipartition of society into barbarians and civilized people the justification of their right to conditions which produce the possession of culture and the dispossession of culture, a state of 'nature' destined to appear based on the nature of the men who are condemned to it.

If such is the function of culture and if it is love of art which really determines the choice that separates, as by an invisible and insuperable barrier, those who have from those who have not received this grace, it can be seen that museums betray, in the smallest details of their morphology and their organization, their true function, which is to strengthen the feeling of belonging in some and the feeling of exclusion in others.[29] Everything, in these civic temples in which bourgeois society deposits its most sacred possessions, that is, the relics inherited from a past which is not its own, in these holy places of art, in which the chosen few come to nurture a faith of virtuosi while conformists and bogus devotees come and perform a class ritual, old palaces or great historic homes to which the nineteenth century added imposing edifices, built often in the Greco-Roman style of civic sanctuaries, everything combines to indicate that the world of art is as contrary to the world of everyday life as the sacred is to the profane. The prohibition against touching the objects, the religious silence which is forced upon visitors, the puritan asceticism of the facilities, always scarce and uncomfortable, the almost systematic refusal of any instruction, the grandiose solemnity of the decoration and the decorum, colonnades, vast galleries, decorated ceilings, monumental staircases both outside and inside, everything seems done to remind people that the transition from the profane world to the sacred world presupposes, as Durkheim says, 'a genuine meta-morphosis', a radical spiritual change, that the bringing together of the worlds 'is always, in itself, a delicate operation which calls for precau-tion and a more or less complicated initiation', that 'it is not even possible unless the profane lose their specific characteristics, unless they themselves become sacred to some extent and to some degree'.[30] Although the work of art, owing to its sacred character, calls for particular dispositions or predispositions, it brings in return its con-secration to those who satisfy its demands, to the small elite who are self-chosen by their aptitude to respond to its appeal.

The museum gives to all, as a public legacy, the monuments of a splendid past, instruments of the sumptuous glorification of the great figures of bygone ages, but this is false generosity, because free entrance is also optional entrance, reserved for those who, endowed with the ability to appropriate the works, have the privilege of using this freedom and who find themselves consequently legitimized in their privilege, that is, in the possession of the means of appropriating cultural goods or, to borrow an expression of Max Weber, in the *monopoly* of the handling of cultural goods and of the institutional signs of cultural salvation (awarded by the school). Being the keystone of a system which can function only by concealing its true function, the charismatic representa-tion of art experience never fulfils its function of mystifying so well as when it resorts to a 'democratic' language:[31] to claim that works of art have power to awaken the grace of aesthetic enlightenment in anyone, however culturally uninitiated he or she may be, to presume in all cases to ascribe to the unfathomable accidents of grace or to the arbitrary bestowal of 'gifts' aptitudes which are always the product of unevenly distributed education, and therefore to treat inherited aptitudes as personal virtues which are both natural and meritorious. Charismatic ideology would not be so strong if it were not the only outwardly irreproachable means of justifying the right of the heirs to the inheri-tance without being inconsistent with the ideal of formal democracy, and if, in this particular case, it did not aim at establishing in nature the sole right of the bourgeoisie to appropriate art treasures to itself, to appropriate them to itself *symbolically*, that is to say, in the only legitimate manner, in a society which pretends to yield to all, 'democra-tically', the relics of an aristocratic past.[32]

# 9

# Manet and the Institutionalization of Anomie

The modern painting movement which was born in France around 1870–80 can only be understood if one analyses the situation in and against which it developed, that is, the academic institution and the conventional style which is a direct expression of it, and also if one resolutely avoids the alternatives of depreciation or rehabilitation governing most current debates.

This text represents the first stage of an analysis of the symbolic revolution brought about by Manet and, after him, by the Impressionists.[1] The contradictions introduced by the numerical increase of the population of established painters and unknown artists contributed to the overthrow of the social structures of the academic apparatus (ateliers, salons, etc.) and the mental structures associated with it. This morphological explosion favoured the emergence of an artistic and literary milieu which was highly differentiated and ready to encourage the task of ethical and aesthetic subversion that Manet was to bring about.

To understand the collective conversion of modes of thought which led to the invention of the writer and the artist through the constitution of relatively autonomous universes, where economic necessities are (partially) suspended, one has to go beyond the limits imposed by the division of specialities and abilities. The essential remains unintelligible as long as one remains enclosed within the limits of a single literary or artistic tradition. Since advances toward autonomy were brought about at different moments in both universes, in conjunction with different economic and morphological changes and with reference to different powers, such as the Academy and the market, writers were able to take advantage of the artists' achievements, and vice versa, in order to increase their independence.

The main obstacle to comprehension lies in the fact that what is to be understood is a symbolic revolution, analogous to the great religious revolutions, and also a *successful* symbolic revolution. From this revolution in the way we see the world emerged our own categories of perception and judgement, which we now commonly use to produce and comprehend representations. The illusion which causes the representation of the world born of this symbolic revolution to appear obvious – so obvious that through a surprising reversal it is the scandal caused by Manet's works which has become an object of surprise, indeed of scandal – prevents us from seeing and understanding the work of *collective conversion* that was necessary to create a new world of which our *eye* itself is the product. The social construction of an autonomous field of production, that is, a social universe able to define and impose the specific principles of perception and judgement of the natural and social world as well as of literary and artistic representations of this world, goes hand in hand with the construction of a properly aesthetic mode of perception, which places the source of artistic 'creation' in the representation and not in the thing represented. This mode never asserts itself as fully as in its capacity to give aesthetic form to the base or vulgar objects of the modern world. The social history of the genesis of this quite peculiar social world in which are produced and reproduced two mutually sustaining 'realities' – the work of art as an object of belief, and the critical discourse on the work of art – enables us to give the concepts commonly used to differentiate or designate genres, schools, styles etc., which a certain theoretical aesthetic desperately attempts to constitute into ahistorical or transhistorical essences, their only possible foundation: the historicity, which is historically necessitated without being historically necessary, of an historical structure.

## THE ACADEMIC GAZE

To account for academic art, one can adopt, as is usually done, a historical perspective and relate its major characteristics to the conditions of its genesis. Born during the French Revolution with David (who drew from the teachings of the Academy of Rome[2]) and adjusted to the taste of the new social strata of notables emerging from the Revolution and the Empire, academic art defined itself by a rejection of eighteenth-century aristocratic art, which was most often held in suspicion for 'moralistic' reasons, and by a reaction against Romanticism, that is, against the first affirmations of the autonomy of art and, above all, of the exaltation of the artist's persona and the absolutization of his point of view.

The taste for eighteenth-century painting had developed during the Revolution for historical as well as aesthetic reasons. However, it was no longer sought out at the beginning of the new century, after the restoration of classical norms during the Revolution and the Empire, except by a few eccentric collectors (among whom was Balzac's hero cousin Pons, whose gift of a fan painted by Watteau was met with indifference by some bourgeois who were not even familiar with the painter's name). As Francis Haskell demonstrates, Watteau's popularity rises again under the July Monarchy, and the supposed ancestor of Delacroix and the Romantics appears to the guardians of academic order to be a threat to David's principles and to the religious and political order. The paradoxical revival of the taste for the eighteenth-century French school of painting during the Second Republic can only be understood in relation to the nationalism of Republicans, who were anxious to restore the prestige of the French tradition. None the less it seems that these heterodox tastes were more frequent among the aristocrats than the *nouveaux riches*, such as the Pereire brothers, who had been advised in the composition of their collection by Théodore Thoré, one of the first historian-dealers (bankers, businessmen and high government officials exerted considerable power over the Salon, where their tastes were known – the paintings they had purchased were exhibited with their name on them – and recognized by the exhibitors' very orientation and by the jury's choices). But generally speaking, the classical canons are so powerful that even Dutch art, which enjoyed a great reputation, is still seen through the norms of academic perception which impede an understanding of the continuity between Ruysdael and Théodore Rousseau or Corot.[3] How is it possible not to see that nothing is more radically opposed to the inner gaze Michael Fried talks about in relation to eighteenth-century painting than the exaggerated exteriority of nineteenth-century historical paintings?[4] Furthermore, it is quite clear that the valorization of academic art is inscribed in the cultural restoration undertaken after the crises of the Revolution and the Empire, through which political regimes, seeking legitimacy, attempted to re-create a consensus around an eclectic culture of a *juste milieu*. But one can also, without negating the aforementioned argument, undertake a structural explanation of this art by relating it to the institutional conditions of its production: its aesthetic is inscribed (to the point that one can practically deduce it) in the logic of functioning of a sclerotic academic institution.

The system's whole functioning is dominated by the existence of a steady succession of *concours* or competitions with honorific awards, the most important being the annual Grand Prix competition, which rewarded the victor with a sojourn in the Villa Médicis. It is therefore not surprising once again to find all the characteristics of institutions subjected to this logic, like the preparatory classes to the *grandes écoles*[5]: the incredible docility that it assumes and reinforces in students who are maintained in an infantile dependency by the logic of competition and the frantic expectations it creates (the opening of the Salon gives rise to scenes of pathos), and the normalization brought by collective training in the ateliers, with their initiation rites, their hierarchies linked as much to seniority as to competence, and their curricula with strictly defined stages and programmes.

I was at first delighted to discover the analogy between the ateliers and preparatory classes in the writings of such a well-informed specialist as Jacques Thuillier: 'And the sort of artistic *khagne* [preparatory schools] represented by the ateliers of Léon Coigniet, Ingres or Gleyre, which were simple preparatory classes without any administrative link to the École, were perhaps more important for the future of French art than the École's own teachings and the Grand Prix laureates.'[6] But I cannot accept the role that, because of his failure to analyse his own representation of preparatory classes, Jacques Thuillier makes it play in the *process of rehabilitation* through which he seeks to annul the inversion of the scale of values brought about by Manet and Impressionism. Even if it has the merit of establishing a *raison d'être* instead of condemning without analysis, the 'comprehensive' point of view, which is suitable when it is a question of *defending* an institution, is no better than the hostile or polemical perspective when it is a question of *understanding*. The unanalysed relation to the object of analysis (I refer here to the homology of position between the analyser and the analysed, the academic master) is at the origin of an essentially anachronistic comprehension of this object, which will in all likelihood note only those institutional characteristics which are most directly opposite to the representation rejected – for example, the relatively democratic recruitment of L'École des Beaux-Arts or the interest of conventional painters in social problems – and will, on the contrary, allow all the characteristics which would permit an understanding of the works in the truth of their social genesis to escape unnoticed.

Pure products of the École, the painters emerging from this training process are neither artisans, like those of previous ages, nor artists like those who are attempting to prevail against them. They are *masters* in the true sense of the word. Differing greatly from the modern conception of the artist, these painters do not have a 'life' worth telling, or celebrating, but rather a *career*, a well-defined succession of honours, from the École des Beaux-Arts to the Institute, by way of the hierarchy of awards given at the Salon exhibitions. Like any competition, which trains the candidate through failures (preferably repeated) as much as successes, the Prix de Rome was itself a progressive conquest: one would attain the second prize, then one year later (like Alexandre-Charles Guillemot in 1808, Alexandre-Denis-Joseph Abel in 1811, etc.), two years later (like François Edouard Picot in 1813) or even three years later (like L. V. L. Pallière in 1812), the first prize. And it was the same with awards given on the occasion of the Salon: thus Meissonier received a third-class medal in 1840, the following year a second-class medal, two years later a first-class medal, the great medal in 1855, and the medal of honour in 1867.[7] One thus understands Degas's witty remark before a painting of Meissonier depicting a soldier aiming his rifle: 'Guess what he is aiming at: the Salon medal.' And one sees more clearly all that is implied by this relentless climb up the academic ladder if one realizes that even a painter as consecrated as Ingres is severely judged when he refuses to exhibit works at the Salon, after 1834, because one of his paintings had been refused.

Often coming from families belonging to artistic professions (in any case more often than the Impressionists), the academic painters have to undergo and overcome the whole long series of trials devised by the École: the ateliers preparing them for the competitions,[8] the competitions themselves, the École des Beaux-Arts, the École de Rome. The most consecrated painters among them competed all their lives for the École's laurels, which they themselves award in their turn, in their capacity as professors or jury members: throughout his life Delaroche maintained one of the most important ateliers; Gérôme kept his atelier, set up in 1865 at the École des Beaux-Arts, for more than thirty-nine years and in it he unflinchingly taught the academic tradition.[9] Trained through imitation of their master and occupied in training masters in their own image,[10] they never completely escape from the École's grasp, the necessity of which they deeply internalize through subjects which are in appearance purely technical or aesthetic but which have submission to the academic institution as an underlying principle.

The École, that is, the state, guarantees their value, by guaranteeing, like paper money, the value of the titles that they receive and confer. It also guarantees the value of their products by assuring them of a near monopoly of the only existing market, the Salon (so that the symbolic revolution, which breaks up this preferential relationship with the market, will have altogether real effects by producing a price collapse). In this sense, one can say, along with Eugenio d'Ors, that classical art, or at least academic art, is a state-sanctioned art.[11] There is a total coincidence between official success and specific consecration, between temporal and artistic hierarchies, and thus acclaim by the official instance of approbation, where the highest artistic authorities hob-nob with the representatives of political power, is the exclusive measure of value. The painter is trained through his whole apprenticeship to experience this approbation in these terms, and he perceives admission to the Salon, the prizes, election to the Academy and official commissions not so much as simple means of 'making a name for oneself', but rather as attestations of his value, genuine certificates of artistic quality. Thus Ingres, having just been elected to the Academy, 'intends to make himself worthy of his great and new artistic fortune by surpassing his old works, by transcending himself. He will look for the subject that will personalize the great principles that are indissoluble in his eyes: the True, the Beautiful, the Good. A composition which will recount, illustrate, and deify human grandeur.'[12] The artist is a high-level civil servant of Art who quite naturally exchanges its action of symbolic consecration for unprecedented temporal recognition (for the first time, living art attains parity with the most prized works of the past: 57 per cent of French paintings sold between 1838 and 1857 were signed by living artists, as opposed to 11 per cent between 1737 and 1756).[13] As Sloane observes, 'The ideas of moral grandeur which attached to the person of the king and his government were extended, in part, to apply to the art which was, so to speak, at their service. Irrespective of the quality of the results produced, a certain nobility was conferred upon any art which was related to these governmental ideas. Nationalism, love of France herself, respect for authority vested in the ruling power, and a desire to root the greatness of France deep in the past were all factors contributing to the undeniable strength of the academic system.'[14]

From the characteristics of the academic institution, which holds the monopoly of the production of painters and of the evaluation of their products, one can deduce properties of academic painting: academic art is a scholastic art which undoubtedly represents the historical quintessence of the typical productions of 'homo academicus'.[15] This is the art of the teacher, and it is his function as a teacher that grants him a statutory authority guaranteed by the institution (much like the priesthood in the religious order); it is above all an art of execution which, in so far as it implements an already established model of accomplishment based on the analysis of past masterpieces, can and must show its virtuosity only in terms of its technique and the historical culture that it can deploy. Trained in the school of copying, instructed in the respect of present and past masters, convinced that art arises from obedience to canons, and especially to the rules which define legitimate topics of painting and legitimate ways of treating them, the academic painters, when given the choice, direct their research more towards literary content than towards purely pictorial invention.

It is significant that they themselves produce copies or variations which are scarcely different from their most successful paintings (thirty-two in the case of Landelle's *Femme fellah*, which received great acclaim at the 1866 Salon),[16] and the good copies are judged almost equal to the original painting,[17] as evidenced by their place of honour in private collections, museums and provincial churches. The painters' assigned role of executant is seen through the precision of commissions entrusted to them. 'Although showered with royal favors, Horace Vernet constantly had to accept painstaking demands. Asked to paint the Fête de la Fédération, Couder was obligated to completely redo his painting in order to take Louis Philippe's remarks into account since he was a witness to the event and was concerned with the painting's historical accuracy.'[18] Jacques Lethève reproduces the extraordinarily precise instructions for a statue which was supposed to be erected in Toulon to celebrate the 'Spirit of Navigation': 'The statue holds in her right hand the helm which steers the sea shell on which the statue is set. The left arm, bending forward, holds a sextant, etc.' Along the same lines, Landelle, one of the most famous and honoured painters of the nineteenth century, who was commissioned in 1859 to depict the visit of the Empress at the Saint-Gobain factory, could not get most of his subjects to sit for him, and at the last moment he had to accept changes imposed by the Empress.[19]

The cult of technique treated as an end in itself is inscribed in the scholastic exercise seen as the solution to a scholastic problem or to an arbitrarily imposed subject which, deriving entirely from a scholastic mode of thought, only exists as a problem to be solved, often at the price of an enormous amount of work (Bouguereau was nicknamed Sisyphus). This cult is responsible for what Gombrich calls 'the error of the too well made'. The icy perfection and the indistinguishable unreality of works which are too skilful – both brilliant and insignificant by dint of impersonality[20] – characterize these virtuoso competition pieces, which seek less to say something than to show that it is well said, thus leading to a sort of 'expressionism of execution', as Joseph Levenson says in relation to Chinese painting.[21] The seal of the institution is impressed on all the works, even those which may appear to be the most felicitous (such as Flandrin's *Thésée reconnu par son père* or Boulanger's *Reconnaissance d'Ulysse par Eryclée*), in the form of concessions or feats undertaken to please a jury known for its hostility towards all originality and desirous of finding visible proof of the mastery of the techniques taught by the École.

But even when valued as a feat, technique always remains subordinated to expressive intention and to what is called the *effect*. A result of a long effort by the Academy to promote the painters' social status by transforming them into learned men and humanists, the master's very dignity is identified with the intellectual aspect of the work: 'To see nature is a formula that the slightest examination reduces almost to the proportions of nonsense. If it is only a question of opening your eyes, anybody can do it. Dogs too can see. The eye is undoubtedly the still of which the brain is the receptacle, but one must know how to use it . . . One must learn how to see.'[22] The primacy given to content and to the display of a literary culture coincides perfectly with an aesthetic of the content, and therefore of *readability*, which confers a transitive, purely referential, function on the painting, which is 'a historical subject requiring a clear exposition',[23] as Boime would have it. The work should communicate something, a meaning transcending the pure play of forms and colours which merely signify themselves, and it should do so clearly. Expressive invention turns towards the search for the most significant gestures, which are appropriate for enhancing the characters' feelings, and towards the production of the most eye-catching effects. For painters as well as for conservative critics, 'literary values are an essential element in great art, and the main function of style is to make these values clear and effective for the observer'.[24] A stylistic consequence of the primacy thus conferred on the 'subject' is that most expressive areas of the painting, where the dramatic interest is concentrated, are privileged both in the execution and in the act of reading, to the detriment of 'those gloomy areas' where, as Fénéon used to say, '[the painter] ought not to have allowed his boredom to detain him' (and which Manet will bring back into favour).

In short, this 'readerly' painting is intended to be 'read' rather than 'seen'.[25] It calls for a scholarly decoding based on a literary culture, precisely the one that was taught before the French Revolution in Jesuit schools and afterwards in the *lycées*, and which was dominated by classical languages and literatures.[26] Thus is minimized the gap which pure painting will create between the artist and the 'bourgeois', who can rely on the classics for the content and, for the technique, on successive visits to the salons (after 1816). This learned reading, which is aware of historical and literary allusions and is thus very close to academic interpretations of classical texts, looks for history in the work but without attempting to resituate the work in history, as would the perception demanded by modern art. This reading arms itself with a historical culture in order to read the work as a historically situated history, but it ignores the perception which is based on a specific knowledge of the history of styles and manners in order to situate each painting, through the play of properly pictorial comparisons and distinctions, in the specific history of painting. The eternity which academic humanism sees as its domain, devoted to the cult of timeless topics and stylistic procedures, causes the idea of rarity associated with antiquity to be absent from the academic universe, thus allowing a painting by Horace Vernet to attain a value higher than one by Titian.

History is one of the most efficient ways to put reality at a distance, to produce an effect of idealization and spiritualization, and thus para-doxically to create eternity.[27] A historicization which sanctifies and derealizes contributes, with the technical formalism which imposes gradations between colours and the continuous relief of forms, to producing the impression of cold *exteriority* that academic paintings impart. In fact, this impression is associated, on the one hand, with what Schlegel called 'pantomime', that is, the theatrical nature of the person-ages which is connected with the concern to represent the unrepresent-able, 'the soul', noble feelings and everything else that comprises that which is 'moral' and, on the other hand, with what the same Schlegel called the 'haberdashery', i.e. the clumsy and all too obvious reconstruc-tion of the dress and accessories of the period.[28] The unreal scenery of ancient civilizations can therefore authorize, through the combined virtues of exoticism and cultural consecration, a typically academic form of eroticism (such as a bordello scene by Gérôme which becomes, by virtue of stylistic neutralization and the title, a *Greek Interior*).[29] The Orient, which ignores the most aggressive forms of urban civilization, allows painters to discover the past in the present (just as it allows them to avoid the taboo of modern clothing as well as the traditional peasant world, with its costumes which are as timeless as its customs).[30] Far from being the product of a direct dependency and submission, the affinity or complicity between this orderly painting – which is hieratic, calm, serene and has modest and gentle colours, noble outlines and idealized and fixed figures – and the social and moral order it seeks to maintain or restore is born from the specific logic of the academic order, and from the relations of dependence in and through independence which link it to the political order.[31]

The concern with readability and the search for technical virtuosity combine to favour the aesthetic of the 'finished', which, as proof of integrity and discretion, also fulfils all the demands and ethical expecta-tions inscribed in the academic position. The taste for the finished never expresses itself more clearly than when confronted by works which, because they do not adhere to the major imperative of academic rigour, such as Delacroix's *La Liberté*, Courbet's *Les Baigneuses* or Manet's *Olympia,* appear physically or morally unclean, that is, dirty and immodest at the same time. These works are also easy, and thus less than honest in their intention – for integrity and cleanliness are one and the same – and, through a sort of contamination, in their subject. Thus, Delécluze, lamenting the lowering of the level of art, writes: 'The substitution of color for drawing has made the career easier to pursue.'[32] Some purely stylistic properties (the finish, cleanliness, the primacy of drawing and line) are loaded with ethical implications, notably the topos/scheme of *facility*, which leads to the perception of certain pictorial manners as being inspired by the search for rapid success at the least cost, thus tending to project the sexual connotations of all the aesthetic condemnations of the 'facile' on to the painted object itself. And it is undoubtedly because of this ethical disposition that the *antinomy of this aesthetic* is put aside or ignored. Indeed, technical virtuosity, which is, along with the exhibition of culture, the only accepted demonstration of mastery, can only be accomplished through its own negation. The finish rids the painting of all marks of work, of *manifattura* (such as the brush stroke which, according to Ingres, must not be visible, or the touch which, as Delécluze writes in *Les débats*, 'no matter how one controls or uses it, is always a sign of inferiority in the art of painting'), and even of the pictorial material (the privilege conferred on line in relation to colour, which is deemed suspicious because of its near carnal seductiveness, is well known), in sum, of all the appearances of professional specifics. The finish is responsible, at the end of this sort of self-destructive accomplishment, for transforming the painting into a literary work, like any other (*ut pictura poesis*) requiring the same deciphering as poetry.

To deepen this analysis of the fundamental principles of academic art one can recall the initial criticisms of Manet, who, in his revolutionary novelty, functions as an analyser, forcing critics to clarify the demands and presuppositions, most often tacit, of the academic vision. First, everything regarding technique: convinced that Manet is totally ignorant of the art of painting, critics take pleasure in highlighting his defects, speaking for instance of an 'almost childish ignorance of the fundamentals of drawing';[33] they perceive this style of painting, which banishes middle-range values, as being 'flat' (which led to *Balcon*'s creator to be compared to a house painter)[34] and most of all they tirelessly lament his lack of finish. 'Manet believes he is making paintings, but in reality he only brushes in sketches,' says Albert Wolff in 1869;[35] another says that Manet makes fun of the jury by sending barely outlined sketches;[36] according to a third, in 1876, Manet does not finish what he has started through sheer incompetence;[37] yet another critic, the same year, accuses him of finishing nothing.[38] In 1874 Mallarmé defends him against this never-ending stream of accusations.[39] If we cannot agree with Alfred Boime, when, while reformulating the argument already advanced by the Salon's critics, he puts forward a hypothesis (already suggested by J. C. Sloane[40]) which aims to negate the Impressionist revolution by showing that it only consisted in taking the sketches of academic painters and presenting them as finished works,[41] we can use his analysis to describe the significance of the change it brought about in the eyes of the critics.

For the academic tradition, the sketch is distinct from the painting, just as the *impression*, which is appropriate to the initial, private phase of artistic work, is distinct from the *invention*, a labour of reflection and intelligence carried out in obedience to the rules and supported by scholarly, and especially historical, research. Knowing all the moral values that were associated with the teaching of drawing, and particularly the value given to the patient and minutely detailed work leading to a 'pictorial display of laborious and diligent application'[42] ('They taught us to finish, before they taught us to compose', says Charles Blanc[43]), one understands that the members of the Academy were only able to see, in the independent artists' more direct and immediate style, the sign of an unfinished education, a subterfuge used to give themselves airs of originality while sparing themselves the long apprenticeship provided and approved by the Academy.[44] In fact, the freedom to express the direct impression in the final, public work – until then reserved to the sketch, a private, indeed intimate, moment – appears as an ethical transgression, a form of facility and carelessness, a lack of the discretion and self-effacing manner that is incumbent on the academic master. Through the process of idealization, the finish is in effect what makes the work impersonal and universal, that is, universally presentable, as in the case of the orgy of *Romains de la décadence*, an austere and heavily censored painting which is designed to arouse the ascetic delights of scholarly decoding and whose form, by dint of technical coldness, in some way cancels its substance. The rupture with academic style implies a rupture with the lifestyle that this implies and transmits. We can thus understand Couture's remark to Manet, regarding his *Buveur d'absinthe*, which was refused exhibition at the 1851 Salon: 'An absinthe drinker! Can one create such an abomination? But my poor friend, it is you who are the absinthe drinker, it is you who have lost all moral sense!'[45]

By imposing on his work a construction whose intention is not to help in the 'reading' of a meaning, Manet dooms the academic eye, used to seeing a painting as a narrative, as a dramatic representation of a 'story', to a second, undoubtedly more fundamental, disappointment.[46] Thus for Paul Mantz, the critic of the *Gazette des Beaux-Arts* (July 1869),

Manet unquestionably has something to say, but, as if wanting to leave the spectator in a state of expectation, he refuses to say it.[47] Manet, like Courbet, was often reproached for presenting 'base' subjects and especially for treating them in a cold, objective manner, without having them mean something. This criticism reveals that the painter is expected to express, if not a message then at least a feeling, preferably of a higher nature, and that aesthetic propriety comes from a sort of moral propriety, since, as Joseph Sloane has well shown, the hierarchy of subjects is based on an evaluation of their moral and spiritual importance 'for mankind in the general scheme of things' ('A hero was higher in such a scale than a banker or a street sweeper, and this was a fact which the artist was supposed to bear in mind in his painting').

Here we find the third criticism, which reveals the link between the abolition of hierarchies and the attention devoted to form: the source of all of Manet's mistakes, says Thoré in 1868, is a 'sort of pantheism which values a head no more than a slipper [and] which sometimes even attaches more importance to a bouquet of flowers than to the face of a woman' (as did Degas in *La femme et le bouquet*). All the 'defects' stressed by the critics originate in the gap between the academic eye, which is attentive to meanings, and pure painting, which is attentive to forms. Thus Thoré observed that in Zola's portrait, the head attracted little attention, lost as it was in the modulations of the colour scheme.[48] Likewise, in 1869 Odilon Redon criticized Manet for sacrificing the man and his ideas to pure technique: since he is only interested in the interplay of colours, his characters are deprived of 'moral vitality' and Zola's portrait is more a still life than the expression of a human being. The critical disarray reaches its peak in the face of paintings, such as *L'Exécution de Maximilien*, which abolish all forms of drama and erase any sort of narrative, psychological or historical relation between the objects, and especially the characters, which are thus linked only by the relations of colours and values. The unbearable lack of meaning leads either to indignant condemnation, when it is perceived as intentional, or to the arbitrary projection of a different meaning.[49] Thus Castagnary, despite the fact that he is known for his actions in favour of new works and artists, insists on seeing Whistler's *La dame blanche* as 'the bride on the morrow', 'that disturbing moment when the young woman questions herself and is astonished at no longer recognizing in herself the virginity of the night before', because he refuses to believe the painter who told him that he wanted to perform a *tour de force* by painting whites on whites; comparing the work to Greuze's *La cruche cassée*, he interprets it as an allegory.[50] Moreover, in relation to Manet's *Balcon*, the same critic wonders whether the two women depicted are sisters or whether they are mother and daughter, since he sees a contradiction in the fact that one is seated in order to look at the street, while the other is putting on her gloves as if about to take leave.[51] We thus see how the critics and writers who are most open towards the new art of painting still stubbornly persist in judging it as if they were readers attentive to the theme.

## THE MODEL: FROM *NOMOS* TO THE INSTITUTIONALIZATION OF ANOMIE

Academic art, produced by teachers who are accustomed to associating their own dignity as well as that of their activity with the affirmation of their historical and literary culture as well as with the manifestation of their technical virtuosity, is thus entirely organized around communicating a morally, that is to say, socially, edifying, and therefore hierarchical, meaning. It is subject to explicit rules and codified principles which have been drawn up *ex post*, by teachers and for the purposes of teaching, from an academically defined corpus of past works (Delaroche's famous painting, intended for the École des Beaux-Arts' Hemicycle, catalogues and magnifies these works from the past). Concerned above all with readability, academic art authorizes as its official language the legal and communicative code which is imposed as much on the conception as on the reception. Codified gestures: uplifted arms, open hands with clenched fingers to express despair, a threatening index finger to show condemnation, an open palm to express surprise or admiration, etc. Conventional symbols: blue skies, grey roads, green fields, skins with a 'flesh' tone, etc. Composition with a rigid perspective. A stereotyped definition of beauty through, for example, the ideal of regular features.

Through the Academy and its masters, the state imposes the principle of vision and legitimate division in questions of the figurative representation of the world, the artistic *nomos* which rules the production of legitimate images (through the production of producers, legitimized to produce these representations). This principle is itself a dimension of the fundamental principle of vision and legitimate division that the state, which holds the monopoly of legitimate symbolic violence, has the power to impose universally within the limits of its jurisdiction. Applied to the world of art, the monopoly of *nomination* – a creative act of designation which gives existence to what it designates in accordance with its designation – takes the form of a state monopoly of the production of producers and legitimate works or, in other words, a monopoly of the power to say who is a painter and who is not, what is a painting and what is not. In concrete terms, through the institutions charged with controlling access to the corporation, the state's monopoly

of the production of producers takes the form of a process of certification or, if one prefers, a process of consecration through which the
producers are authorized – in their own eyes as well as in those of all
legitimate consumers – as legitimate producers, known and recognized
by everyone. Thus the state, rather like a central bank, creates the
creators, guaranteeing the credit or fiduciary currency represented by
the title of duly accredited painter.

In the symbolic work that the Academy must continuously accomplish in order to impose the recognition of its own value as well as the
symbolic and economic value of the products it guarantees, and in order
to institute the belief that great painting is that of the present, the
Academy has a considerable advantage compared to other institutions
such as England's *Art Journal*. As a means of averting the threat that any
different kind of art or artistic canon could represent to its monopoly
(and consequently to the extraordinarily high prices attained by academic painters) – and especially Romantic painting which, as Francis
Haskell notes, revives a certain style from the eighteenth century,
notably that of Watteau, and professes the same indifference towards
Antiquity – the Academy, through the École des Beaux-Arts, where its
members teach, and through competitions like the Prix de Rome, which
it organizes, can control the production of legitimate producers and
exclude or excommunicate the ones who might be tempted by heretical
models. At any rate, through the jury (which it appoints) the Academy
can forbid them access to the market, since it has the power to decide
who is admitted to the Salon, which accredits the painter and assures
him a clientele. This logic of defending the profession pertains to all the
other professions (lawyers, doctors, university professors, etc.), whose
permanence in a situation of privilege depends on their capacity to
maintain control over the mechanism designed to assure their reproduction, that is, their capacity to recognize, in the double sense of
identifying and consecrating, the legitimate members of the profession.

For such professions, whose symbolic capital and, consequently,
economic capital cannot tolerate a great influx and a great dispersion,
the threat comes from numbers. Either the *de facto* or *de jure numerus
clausus* disappears, substituting open competition for a competition
limited to a chosen few (for example, state commissions go to a small
minority of painters), or the superfluous producers – that is, all those
that the mechanism controlling entrance to the profession (in this case,
the competitions) excludes from the status of producer and, consequently, from production – succeed in producing their own market and,
little by little, their own mechanism of consecration.

In fact, the Academy's monopoly rests on a whole network of
mutually reinforcing beliefs: the painters' belief in the legitimacy of the
jury and its verdicts, the state's belief in the jury's efficacy, the public's

belief in the value of the academic imprimatur (which is similar to the effect produced by the designer's label), to which the Academy contributes (notably in the matter of prices). As these interlocking beliefs gradually collapse, they drag down with them the symbolic capital that they underpin. It is not easy to establish which were the decisive triggers of this sort of bankruptcy of the central bank of symbolic capital in the art world. One may doubt, however, that the individual or collective exhibitions or the artists' and critics' never-ending criticism of the jury or changes in its composition might have struck, as J. Lethève suggests, 'irreparable blows to the public's trust'. For this institution, which, in the last analysis, gets its authority from the state, the fatal blow is doubtless the one dealt by the state: the 1863 creation of the *Salon des refusés*, which constitutes a disavowal of the admissions jury and the École des Beaux-Arts, which is 'wounded in its dignity as the guardian of the true and exclusive principles of beauty';[52] in June of the same year, the concentration of all authority to deal with the organization of artistic life in the hands of the administration (that is, the ministry of the Imperial Household and the Fine Arts); and, finally, in November 1884, the decree which deprived the Academy of the power to oversee teaching at the École des Beaux-Arts and at the Villa Médicis.

Knowing that the entire logic of the academic institution supposed the organization of competition, one understands how the ever-increasing numbers of candidates – which its very success had helped to attract to the Academy from among the products of a rapidly expanding system of secondary education – could have created conditions propitious for the success of a revolutionary challenge [*mise en question*]:[53] the proliferation of superfluous producers favours the growth, outside and then against the institution, of a negatively free artistic milieu – bohemia – which will be at one and the same time a social laboratory for the modern artists' new thinking and lifestyle, and the market where bold artistic innovation and the *art de vivre* will find the indispensable minimum of symbolic gratifications. This process, whose starting point is undoubtedly the numerical effect, culminates in the development of a critical situation within the institution which tends to favour a critical break with the institution itself and, above all, to the successful institutionalization of this break. As it ceases to operate as a hierarchical *apparatus* controlled by a professional body, the universe of the producers of art-works slowly becomes a *field* of competition for the monopoly of artistic legitimation. From now on no one can claim to be an absolute holder of the *nomos*, even if everyone has claims to the title. The constitution of a field is, in the true sense of the word, an *institutionalization of anomie*. This is a truly far-reaching revolution which, at least in the realm of the new art in the making, abolishes all references to an ultimate authority capable of acting as a court of appeal: the monotheism of the central *nomothete* gives way to a plurality of competing cults with multiple uncertain gods.[54]

In order to make this very broad model more intuitively comprehensible, and to demonstrate what severe problems the collective conversion implied by this symbolic revolution could present, it should suffice to quote a speech delivered by Count Waleski, a minister of state, on the occasion of the awards ceremony at the 1861 Salon: 'I have heard speak of artistic freedom, the right of invention and of unrecognized genius . . . Is not this exhibition, such as it is, already impressive enough? Let us write, for a moment, above the door of this Palace of Industry: "Every painter, every sculptor, every engraver, may enter here . . ." But where does the painter, the engraver, the sculptor start? If everyone has the freedom to decide as he pleases, any failed craftsman may immediately award himself a diploma, and all the errors of childhood and dotage will take place in the bright light of day . . . It is a duty for those whose mission is to keep watch over the arts and letters to fight against false gods even when they are supported by a fleeting popularity and praised by a misled public.'[55]

# 10

# The Historical Genesis of a Pure Aesthetic

Let us begin with a paradox. It has occurred to some philosophers (I have in mind Arthur Danto) to ponder the question of what enables one to distinguish between works of art and simple, ordinary things, and to suggest with unflinching sociologistic daring (which they would never accept in a sociologist) that the principle of this ontological difference must be sought in an institution. The art object, they say, is an artefact whose foundation can only be found in an *artworld*, that is, in a social universe that confers upon it the status of a candidate for aesthetic appreciation.[1] What has not yet occurred (although one of our post-modernists will surely come to it sooner or later) is for a philosopher – one perfectly 'worthy of the name' – to treat the question of what allows us to distinguish a philosophical discourse from an ordinary one. Such a question becomes particularly pertinent when, as in the case here, the philosopher, designated and recognized as such by a certain *philosophical world*, grants himself a discourse which he would deny (under the label of 'sociologism') to anyone like the sociologist, who is not a part of the philosophical institution.[2]

The radical dissymmetry which philosophy thus establishes in its relationship with the human sciences furnishes it with, among other things, unfailing means for masking what it borrows from them. In fact, it seems to me that the philosophy labelled post-modern (by one of those labelling devices until now reserved for the artworld), merely readopts in a denied form (i.e. in the sense of Freud's *Verneinung*), not only certain of the findings of the social sciences but also of historicist philosophy which is, implicitly or explicitly, inscribed in the practice of these sciences. This masked appropriation, which is legitimized by the denial of borrowing, is one of the most powerful strategies yet to be employed by philosophy against the social sciences and against the threat of relativization that these sciences have held over it. Heidegger's ontologization of historicity is, indisputably, the model for this operation.[3] It is a strategy analogous to the *double jeu* which allows Derrida to take from social science (against which he is poised) some of its most characteristic instruments of 'deconstruction'. While opposing to structuralism and its notion of 'static' structure a 'post-modernized' variant of the Bergsonian critique of the reductive effects of scientific knowledge, Derrida can give himself the air of radicalism. He does this by using, against traditional literary criticism, a critique of binary oppositions which goes back, by way of Lévi-Strauss, to the most classical analysis of 'forms of classifications' so dear to Durkheim and Mauss.[4]

But one cannot win at all the tables, and the sociology of the artistic institution which the 'deconstructor' can carry out only in the mode of *Verneinung* is never brought to its logical conclusion: its implied critique of the institution remains half-baked, although well enough done to arouse delicious shudders of a bogus revolution.[5] Moreover, by claiming a radical break with the ambition of uncovering ahistorical and ontologically founded essences, this critique is likely to discourage the search for the foundation of the aesthetic disposition and of the work of art where it is truly located, namely, in the *history* of the artistic institution.

## THE ANALYSIS OF ESSENCE AND THE ILLUSION OF THE ABSOLUTE

What is striking about the diversity of responses which philosophers have given to the question of the specificity of the work of art is not so much the fact that these divergent answers often concur in emphasizing the absence of function, the disinterestedness, the gratuitousness, etc. of the work of art,[6] but rather that they all (with the possible exception of Wittgenstein) share the ambition of capturing a transhistoric or an ahistoric essence. The pure thinker, by taking as the subject of reflection his or her own experience — the experience of a cultured person from a certain social milieu – but without focusing on the historicity of that reflection and the historicity of the object to which it is applied (and by considering it a pure experience of the work of art), unwittingly establishes this singular experience as a transhistorical norm for every aesthetic perception. Now this experience, with all the aspects of singularity that it appears to possess (and the feeling of uniqueness probably contributes greatly to its worth), is itself an institution which is the product of historical invention and whose *raison d'être* can be reassessed only through an analysis which is itself properly historical. Such an analysis is the only one capable of accounting simultaneously for the nature of the experience and for the appearance of universality which it procures for those who live it, naïvely, beginning with the philosophers who subject it to their reflections unaware of its *social conditions of possibility*.

The comprehension of this particular form of relationship with the work of art, which is an immediate comprehension, presupposes the analyst's self-understanding of himself – an understanding which can be submitted neither to simple phenomenological analysis of the lived experience (inasmuch as this experience rests on the active forgetting of the history of which it is a product), nor to the analysis of the language ordinarily used to express this experience (inasmuch as it too is the historical product of a process of dehistoricization). Instead of Durkheim's saying 'the unconscious is history', one could write 'the *a priori* is history'. Only if one were to mobilize all the resources of the social sciences would one be able to accomplish this kind of historicist actualization of the transcendental project which consists of reappropriating, through historical anamnesis, the product of the entire historical operation of which consciousness too is (at every moment) the product. In the individual case this would include reappropriating the dispositions and classificatory schemes which are a necessary part of the aesthetic experience as it is described, naïvely, by the analysis of essence.

What is forgotten in self-reflective analysis is the fact that although appearing to be a gift from nature, the eye of the twentieth-century art lover is a product of history. From the angle of phylogenesis, the pure gaze, capable of apprehending the work of art as it demands to be apprehended (i.e., in itself and for itself, as form and not as function), is inseparable from the appearance of producers of art motivated by a pure artistic intention, which is itself inseparable from the emergence of an autonomous artistic field capable of formulating and imposing its own ends against external demands. From the side of ontogenesis, the pure gaze is associated with very specific conditions of acquisition, such as the early frequenting of museums and the prolonged exposure to schooling, and to the *skholè* that it implies. All of this means that the analysis of essence which overlooks these conditions (thus universalizing the specific case) implicitly establishes as universal to all aesthetic practices the rather particular properties of an experience which is the product of privilege, that is, of exceptional conditions of acquisition.

What the ahistorical analysis of the work of art and of the aesthetic experience captures in reality is an institution which, as such, enjoys a kind of twofold existence, in things and in minds. In things, it exists in the form of an artistic field, a relatively autonomous social universe which is the product of a slow process of constitution. In minds, it exists in the form of dispositions which were invented by the same movement through which the field, to which they immediately adjusted themselves, was invented. When things and minds (or consciousness) are immediately in accord – in other words, when the eye is the product of the field to which it relates – then the field, with all the products that it offers, appears to the eye as immediately endowed with meaning and worth. This is so clearly the case that if the extraordinary question of the source of the art-work's value, normally taken for granted, were to arise at all, a special experience would be required, one which would be quite exceptional for a cultured person, even though it would be, on the contrary, quite ordinary for all those who have not had the opportunity to acquire the dispositions which are objectively required by the work of art. This is demonstrated by empirical research and is also suggested by Danto, for example.[7] Following a visit to an exhibit of Warhol's *Brillo Boxes* at the Stable Gallery, Danto discovered the arbitrary character, *ex instituto* as Leibniz would have said, of the imposition of the value created by the field through an exhibit in a place which is both consecrated and consecrating.

The experience of the work of art as being immediately endowed with meaning and value is a result of the accord between the two mutually founded aspects of the same historical institution: the cultured habitus and the artistic field. Given that the work of art exists as such (i.e. as a symbolic object endowed with meaning and value) only if it is apprehended by spectators possessing the disposition and the aesthetic competence which are tacitly required, one could say that it is the aesthete's eye which constitutes the work of art as a work of art. But one must also remember immediately that this is possible only to the extent that aesthetes themselves are the product of a long exposure to artworks.[8] This circle, which is one of belief and of the sacred, is shared by every institution which can function only if it is instituted simultaneously within the objectivity of a social game and within the dispositions which induce interest and participation in the game. Museums could bear the inscription: Entry for art lovers only. But there clearly is no need for such a sign, it all goes without saying. The game makes the *illusio*, sustaining itself through the informed player's investment in the game. The player, mindful of the game's meaning and having been created for the game because he was created by it, plays the game and by playing it assures its existence. The artistic field, by its very functioning, creates the aesthetic disposition without which it could not function. Specifically, it is through the competition among the agents with vested interests in the game that the field reproduces endlessly the interest in the game and the belief in the value of the stakes. In order to illustrate the operation of this collective endeavour and give an idea of the numerous acts of delegation of symbolic power and of voluntary or forced recognition through which this reservoir of credit (upon which the creators of fetishes draw) is engendered, it will suffice to recall the relationship among the various avant-garde critics who consecrate themselves as critics by consecrating works whose sacred value is barely perceived by cultured art lovers or even by the critic's most advanced rivals. In short, the question of the meaning and the value of the work of art, like the question of the specificity of aesthetic judgement, along with all the great problems of philosophical aesthetics, can be resolved only within a social history of the field, along with a sociology of the conditions of the establishment of the specific aesthetic disposition (or attitude) that the field calls for in each one of its states.

## THE GENESIS OF THE ARTISTIC FIELD
## AND THE INVENTION OF THE PURE GAZE

What makes the work of art a work of art and not a mundane thing or a simple utensil? What makes an artist an artist and not a craftsman or a Sunday painter? What makes a urinal or a wine rack that is exhibited in a museum a work of art? Is it the fact that they are signed by Duchamp, a recognized artist (recognized first and foremost as an artist) and not by a wine merchant or a plumber? If the answer is yes, then isn't this simply a matter of replacing the work-of-art-as-fetish with the 'fetish of the name of the master'? Who, in other words, created the 'creator' as a recognized and known producer of fetishes? And what confers its magical or, if one prefers, its ontological effectiveness upon his name, a name whose very celebrity is the measure of his claim to exist as an artist and which, like the signature of the fashion designer, increases the value of the object upon which it is affixed? That is, what constitutes the stakes in quarrels of attribution and the authority of the expert? Where is one to locate the ultimate principle of the effect of labelling, or of naming, or of theory? (Theory is a particularly apt word because we are dealing with seeing – theorein – and of making others see.) Where does this ultimate principle, which produces the sacred by introducing difference, division and separation, reside?

Such questions are quite similar in type to those raised by Mauss when, in his Theory of Magic, he pondered the principle of magic's effectiveness, and found that he had to move back from the instruments used by the sorcerer to the sorcerer himself, and from there to the belief held by his followers. He discovered, little by little, that he had to confront the entire social universe in whose midst magic evolves and is practised. Likewise, in the infinite regress in search of the primary cause and ultimate foundation of the art-work's value, one must make a similar move. And in order to explain this sort of miracle of transubstantiation (which is at the very source of the art-work's existence and which, although commonly forgotten, is brutally recalled through strokes of genius *à la* Duchamp), one must replace the ontological question with the historical question of the genesis of the universe, that is, the artistic field, within which, through a veritable continuous creation, the value of the work of art is endlessly produced and reproduced.

The philosopher's analysis of essence only records the product of the real analysis of essence which history itself performs objectively through the process of autonomization within which and through which the artistic field is gradually instituted and in which the agents (artists, critics, historians, curators, etc.) and the techniques, categories and concepts (genre, mannerisms, periods, styles, etc.) which are characteristic of this universe are invented. Certain notions which have become as banal and as obvious as the notion of artist or of 'creator', as well as the words which designate and constitute them, are the product of a slow and long historical process. Art historians themselves do not completely escape the trap of 'essentialist thought' which is inscribed in the usage – always haunted by anachronism – of historically invented, and therefore dated, words. Unable to question all that is implicitly involved in the modern notion of artist, in particular the professional ideology of the uncreated 'creator' which was developed during the nineteenth century, and unable to make a break with the apparent object, namely the artist (or elsewhere the writer, the philosopher, the scholar), in order to consider the field of production of which the artist (socially instituted as a 'creator') is the product, art historians are not able to replace the ritualistic inquiry concerning the place and the moment of the appearance of the character of the artist (as opposed to the craftsman) with the question of the economic and social conditions underlying the establishment of an artistic field founded upon a belief in the quasi-magical powers attributed to the modern artist in the most advanced states of the field.

It is not only a matter of exorcising what Benjamin called the 'fetish of the name of the master' in a simple sacrilegious and slightly childish inversion – and whether one wishes it or not, the name of the master is indeed a fetish. It is a question of describing the gradual emergence of the entire set of social conditions which make possible the character of the artist as a producer of the fetish which is the work of art. In other words, it is a matter of constituting the artistic field (which includes art analysts, beginning with art historians, even the most critical among them) as the locus where the belief in the value of art and in the artist's power of valuable creation is continually produced and reproduced. This would yield not only an inventory of the artist's indices of autonomy (such as those revealed through the analysis of contracts, the presence of a signature, or affirmations of the artist's specific competence, or the recourse in case of a dispute to the arbitration by peers, etc.), but also an inventory of the signs of the autonomy of the field itself, such as the emergence of the entire set of the specific institutions which are a necessary condition for the functioning of the economy of cultural goods. These include: places of exhibit (galleries, museums, etc.), institutions of consecration or sanction (academies, salons, etc.), instances of reproduction of producers and consumers (art schools, etc.), and specialized agents (dealers, critics, art historians, collectors, etc.), all of whom are endowed with the dispositions objectively required by the field and the specific categories of perception and appreciation, which are irreducible to those in common use and which are capable of imposing a specific measure of the value of the artist and of her products. As long as painting is measured by surface units and duration of production, by the quantity and price of the materials used (gold or ultramarine), the artist-painter is not radically different from a house painter. That is why, among all the inventions which accompany the emergence of the field of production, one of the most significant is probably the elaboration of an artistic language. This involves first establishing a way of naming painters, of speaking about them and about the nature of their work as well as of the mode of remuneration for their work, through which is established an autonomous definition of properly artistic value irreducible to the strictly economic value and also a way of speaking about painting itself, of pictorial techniques, using appropriate words (often pairs of adjectives) which enable one to speak of pictorial art, the *manifattura*, that is, the individual style of the painter whose existence it socially constitutes by naming it. By the same logic, the discourse of celebration, notably the biography, also plays a determining role. This is probably due less to what it says about painters and their work than to the fact that the biography establishes the artist as a memorable character, worthy of historical account, much like statesmen and poets. (It is known that ennobling comparisons – *ut pictura poesis* – contribute to the affirmation of the irreducibility of pictorial art, at least for a time and until they become a hindrance.) A genetic sociology should also include in its model the action of the producers themselves and their claim to the right to be the sole judges of pictorial production, to produce, themselves, the criteria of perception and appreciation for their products. Such a sociology should also take into account the effect – on themselves and the image they have of their production, and thus on their production itself – of the image of themselves and their production that comes back to them through the eyes of the agents engaged in the field – other artists, but also critics, clients, collectors. (One can assume, for example, that the interest in sketches and cartoons shown by certain collectors since the *quattrocento* has only helped to contribute to the artists' exalted view of their own worth.)

Thus, as the field is constituted as such, it becomes clear that the 'subject' of the production of the art-work – of its value but also of its meaning – is not the producer who actually creates the object in its materiality, but rather the entire set of agents engaged in the field. Among these are the producers of works classified as artistic (great or minor, famous or unknown), critics of all persuasions (who themselves are established within the field), collectors, middlemen, curators, etc., in short, all who have ties with art, who live for art and, to varying degrees, from it, and who confront each other in struggles where the imposition of not only a world view but also a vision of the artworld is at stake, and who, through these struggles, participate in the production of the value of the artist and of art.

If such is, in fact, the logic of the field, then one can understand why the concepts used to consider works of art, and particularly their classifications, are characterized (as Wittgenstein has observed) by the most extreme indeterminacy. That is the case with genres (tragedy, comedy, drama, the novel), with forms (ballad, rondeau, sonnet, sonata), with periods or styles (Gothic, baroque, classical) or with movements (Impressionist, Symbolist, Realist, Naturalist). One can also understand why confusion does not diminish when it comes to concepts used to characterize the work of art itself and the terms used to perceive and to appreciate it (such as the pairs of adjectives beautiful or ugly, refined or crude, light or heavy, etc.) which structure the expression and the experience of the work of art. Because they are inscribed in ordinary language and are generally used beyond the aesthetic sphere, these categories of judgements of taste which are common to all speakers of a shared language do allow an apparent form of communication. Yet, despite that, such terms always remain marked – even when used by professionals – by an extreme vagueness and flexibility which (again as has been noted by Wittgenstein) makes them completely resistant to essentialist definition.[9] This is probably because the use that is made of these terms and the meaning that is given to them depend upon the specific, historically and socially situated points of view of their users – points of view which are quite often perfectly irreconcilable.[10] In short, if one can always argue about taste (and everyone knows that confrontations regarding preferences play an important role in daily conversation) then it is certain that communication in these matters takes place only with a high degree of misunderstanding. That is so precisely because the commonplaces which make communication possible are the same ones that make it practically ineffective. The users of these topics each give different, at times diametrically opposed, meanings to the terms that they oppose. Thus it is possible for individuals holding opposing positions within a social space to be able to give totally opposed meanings and values to adjectives which are commonly used to describe works of art or mundane objects. The example of the adjective *soigné* comes to mind. It is most frequently excluded from 'bourgeois' taste, probably because it embodies the taste of the petit-bourgeois.[11] Situated within the historic dimension, one could go on drawing endless lists of notions which, beginning with the idea of beauty, have taken on different, even radically opposed meanings in the course of various periods or as a result of artistic revolutions. The notion of 'finish' is one example. Having condensed into one term the closely linked ethical and aesthetic ideals of academic painting, this notion was later banished from art by Manet and the Impressionists.

Thus the categories which are used in order to perceive and appreciate the work of art are doubly bound to the historical context. Linked to a situated and dated social universe, they become the subject of usages which are themselves socially marked by the social position of the users who exercise the constitutive dispositions of their habitus in the aesthetic choices these categories make possible.

The majority of notions which artists and critics use to define themselves or their adversaries are indeed weapons and stakes in the struggle, and many of the categories which art historians deploy in order to treat their subject are nothing more than skilfully masked or transfigured indigenous categories, initially conceived for the most part as insults or condemnations. (Our term 'categories' stems from the Greek *kathegoresthai*, meaning to accuse publicly.) These combative concepts gradually become technical categorems upon which – thanks to genesis amnesia – critical dissections, dissertations and academic theses confer an air of eternity. Of all the methods of entering such struggles – which must be apprehended as such from the outside in order to objectivize them – the most tempting and the most irreproachable is undoubtedly that of presenting oneself as a judge or referee. Such a method involves settling conflicts which in reality are not settled, and giving oneself the satisfaction of pronouncing verdicts – of declaring, for instance, what realism *really* is, or even, quite simply, of decreeing (through decisions as innocent in appearance as the inclusion or exclusion of so-and-so from a corpus or list of producers) who is an artist and who is not. This last decision, for all its apparent positivistic innocence, is, in fact, all the more crucial because one of the major stakes in these artistic struggles, always and everywhere, is the question of the legitimate belonging to a field (which is the question of the limits of the world of art) and also because the validity of the conclusions, notably statistical ones, which one is able to establish *à propos* a universe depends on the validity of the category *à propos* of which these conclusions were drawn.

If there is a truth, it is that truth is a stake in the struggle. And although the divergent or antagonistic classifications or judgements made by the agents engaged in the artistic field are certainly determined or directed by specific dispositions and interests linked to a given position in the field, they nevertheless are formulated in the name of a claim to universality – to absolute judgement – which is the very negation of the relativity of points of view.[12] 'Essentialist thought' is at work in every social universe and especially in the field of cultural production – the religious, scientific and legal fields, etc. – where games in which the universal is at stake are being played out. But in that case it is quite evident that 'essences' are norms. That is precisely what Austin was recalling when he analysed the implications of the adjective 'real' in expressions such as a 'real' man, 'real' courage or, as is the case here, a 'real' artist or a 'real' masterpiece. In all of these examples, the word 'real' implicitly contrasts the case under consideration to all other cases in the same category, to which other speakers assign, although unduly so (that is, in a manner not 'really' justified), this same predicate, a predicate which, like all claims to universality, is symbolically very powerful.

Science can do nothing but attempt to establish the truth of these struggles over the truth and capture the objective logic according to which the stakes, the camps, the strategies and the victories are determined. Science can attempt to bring representations and instruments of thought – all of which lay claim to universality, with unequal chances of success – back to the social conditions of their production and of their use, in other words, back to the historical structure of the field in which they are engendered and within which they operate. According to the methodological postulate (which is constantly validated by empirical analysis) of the homology between the space of the position-takings (literary or artistic forms, concepts and instruments of analysis, etc.) and the space of the positions occupied in the field, one is led to historicize these cultural products, all of which claim universality. But historicizing them means not only (as one may think) relativizing them by recalling that they have meaning solely through reference to a determined state of the field of struggle; it also means restoring to them necessity by removing them from indeterminacy (which stems from a false eternalization) in order to bring them back to the social conditions of their genesis, a truly generative definition.[13] Far from leading to a historicist relativism, the historicization of the forms of thought which we apply to the historical object, and which may be the product of that object, offers the only real chance of escaping history, if ever so small.

Just as the oppositions which structure aesthetic perception are not given *a priori*, but are historically produced and reproduced, and just as they are inseparable from the historical conditions which set them in motion, so it is with the aesthetic disposition. The aesthetic disposition which establishes as works of art objects socially designated for its use and application (simultaneously extending its activity to aesthetic competence, with its categories, concepts and taxonomies) is a product of the entire history of the field, a product which must be reproduced, by each potential consumer of the work of art, through a specific apprenticeship. It suffices either to observe the aesthetic disposition's distribution throughout history (with those critics who, until the end of the nineteenth century, have defended an art subordinated to moral values and didactic functions), or instead to observe it within society today, in order to be convinced that nothing is less natural than the disposition to adopt towards an art-work – and, more so, towards any object – the sort of pure aesthetic posture described by essentialist analysis.

The invention of the pure gaze is realized in the very movement of the field towards autonomy. In fact, without recalling here the entire argument, one could maintain that the affirmation of the autonomy of the principles of production and evaluation of the art-work is inseparable from the affirmation of the autonomy of the producer, that is, the field of production. Like pure painting, which, as Zola wrote *à propos* Manet, is meant to be beheld in itself and for itself as a painting – as a play of forms, values and colours – and not as a discourse, in other words, independently from all references to transcendent meanings, the pure gaze (a necessary correlate of pure painting) is a result of a process of purification, a true analysis of essence carried out by history, in the course of successive revolutions which, as in the religious field, always lead the new avant-garde to challenge orthodoxy – in the name of a return to the rigour of beginnings – with a purer definition of the genre. Poetry has thus been observed to purify itself of all its accessory properties: forms to be destroyed (sonnet, alexandrine), rhetorical figures to be demolished (simile, metaphor), contents and sentiments to be banished (lyricism, effusion, psychology) in order to reduce itself little by little, following a kind of historical analysis, to the most specifically poetic effects, like the break with phonosemantic parallelism.

In more general terms, the evolution of the different fields of cultural production towards a greater autonomy is accompanied by a sort of reflective and critical return by the producers upon their own production, a return which leads them to draw from it the field's own principle and specific presuppositions. This is, first, because the artists, now in a position to rebuff every external constraint or demand, are able to affirm their mastery over that which defines them and which properly belongs to them, that is, the form, the technique, in a word, the art, thus instituted as the exclusive aim of art. Flaubert in the domain of writing and Manet in painting are probably the first to have attempted to impose, at the cost of extraordinary subjective and objective difficulties, the conscious and radical affirmation of the power of the creative gaze, capable of being applied not only (through simple inversion) to base and vulgar objects, as was the aim of Champfleury's and Courbet's realism, but also to insignificant objects before which the 'creator' is able to assert his quasi-divine power of transmutation. '*Écrire bien le médiocre.*' This Flaubertian formula, which also holds for Manet, lays down the autonomy of form in relation to subject matter, simultaneously assigning its fundamental norm to cultured perception. Attribution of artistic status is, among philosophers, the most generally accepted definition of aesthetic judgement, and, as could be proven empirically, there is no cultured person today (which means, by scholastic canons, no one possessing advanced academic degrees) who does not know that any reality, a rope, a pebble, a rag peddler, can be the subject of a work of art,[14] who does not know, at the very least, that it is wise to say that such is the case, as an avant-garde painter, an expert in the art of confounding the new aesthetic doxa, made me observe. In fact, in order to awaken today's aesthete, whose artistic goodwill knows no limit, and to re-evoke in him artistic and even philosophical wonder, one must apply a shock treatment to him in the manner of Duchamp or Warhol, who, by exhibiting the ordinary object as it is, manage to prod in some way the creative power that the pure aesthetic disposition (without much consideration) confers upon the artist as defined since Manet.

The second reason for this introspective and critical return of art unto itself is the fact that, as the field closes upon itself, the practical mastery of the specific knowledge – which is inscribed in past works, recorded, codified and canonized by an entire body of professional experts in conversation and celebration, along with literary and art historians, exegetes and analysts – becomes a part of the conditions of access into the field of production. The result is that, contrary to what is taught by a naïve relativism, the time of art history is really irreversible and it presents a form of cumulativeness. Nothing is more closely linked to the specific past of the field, including subversive intention – itself linked to a state of the field – than avant-garde artists who, at the risk of appearing to be 'naïve' (in the manner of Douanier Rousseau or of

Brisset) must inevitably situate themselves in relation to all the preceding attempts at surpassing which have occurred in the history of the field and within the space of possibilities which it imposes upon the newly arrived. What happens in the field is more and more linked to the field's specific history and to it alone. It is therefore more and more difficult to deduce it from the state of the general social world at any given time (as a certain 'sociology', unaware of the specific logic of the field, claims to do). Adequate perception of works – which, like Warhol's *Brillo Boxes* or Klein's monochromatic paintings, owe their formal properties and their value only to the structure of the field and thus to its history – is a differential, diacritical perception: in other words, it is attentive to deviations from other works, both contemporary and past. The result is that, like production, the consumption of works which are a product of a long history of breaks of history, with tradition, tends to become historical through and through, and yet more and more totally dehistoricized. In fact, the history that deciphering and appreciation put into play is gradually reduced to a pure history of forms, completely eclipsing the social history of the struggles for forms which is the life and movement of the artistic field.

This also resolves the apparently insoluble problem that formalist aesthetics (which wishes to consider only form in the reception as well as the production of art) presents as a true challenge to sociological analysis. In effect, the works that stem from a pure concern for form seem destined to establish the exclusive validity of internal reading which heeds only formal properties, and to frustrate or discredit all attempts at reducing them to a social context, against which they were set up. And yet, to reverse the situation it suffices to note that the formalist ambition's objection to all types of historicization rests on the unawareness of its own social conditions of possibility. The same is true of a philosophical aesthetics which records and ratifies this ambition. What is forgotten in both cases is the historical process through which the social conditions of freedom from 'external determinations' get established; that is, the process of establishing the relatively autonomous field of production and with it the realm of pure aesthetics or pure thought whose existence it makes possible.

# Notes

EDITOR'S INTRODUCTION: PIERRE BOURDIEU
ON ART, LITERATURE AND CULTURE

1  Pierre Bourdieu was born in 1930 in Béarn. He studied philosophy at the
   École Normale Supérieure in Paris before initiating his work in anthropology and sociology. He currently holds the Chair of Sociology at the
   prestigious Collège de France and is Director of Studies at the École des
   Hautes Études en Sciences Sociales and director of the Centre de Sociologie
   Européenne.
2  Prior to the English-language publication of *Distinction: A Social Critique
   of the Judgement of Taste*, trans. Richard Nice (Cambridge, Mass.:
   Harvard University Press, 1984), originally published in French as *La
   distinction: critique social du jugement* in 1979, Bourdieu was probably
   best known in the United States and Great Britain for his ethnographic
   studies of Algerian peasant communities and his work on French education
   and its role in the reproduction of social classes. His *Outline of a Theory of
   Practice*, trans. Richard Nice (Cambridge: Cambridge University Press,
   1977), which is a much revised version of the original French edition
   *Esquisse d'une théorie de la pratique* (1972), brings together several of his
   ethnographic studies and, as the title indicates, provides the first systematic
   exposition of his theory of practice, which is re-elaborated and refined in
   *The Logic of Practice*, trans. Richard Nice (Cambridge: Polity Press;
   Stanford: Stanford University Press, 1990), originally published in French
   as *Le sens pratique* in 1980.
      On education see especially the two books by Bourdieu and Jean-Claude
   Passeron, *Reproduction in Education, Society and Culture*, trans. Richard
   Nice (London: Sage, 1979) and *The Inheritors: French Students and their*

*Relation to Culture*, trans. Richard Nice (Chicago: University of Chicago Press, 1977); also *La noblesse d'État: grandes écoles et esprit de corps* (Paris: Minuit, 1989). On the academic system in France, see *Homo Academicus*, trans. Peter Collier (Cambridge: Polity Press; Stanford: Stanford University Press, 1988).

For a complete bibliography, see Y. Delsaut, 'Bibliography of the Works of Pierre Bourdieu, 1958–1988', in Bourdieu, *In Other Words: Essays Towards a Reflexive Sociology*, trans. Matthew Adamson (Cambridge: Polity Press; Stanford: Stanford University Press, 1990), pp. 199–218.

3   For overviews of Bourdieu's work, see Rogers Brubaker, 'Rethinking Classical Theory: The Sociological Vision of Pierre Bourdieu', *Theory and Society*, 14 (1985), pp. 723–44; Paul DiMaggio, 'Review Essay: On Pierre Bourdieu', *American Journal of Sociology*, 84:6 (May 1979), pp. 1460–74; Nicholas Garnham and Raymond Williams, 'Pierre Bourdieu and the Sociology of Culture: An Introduction', in *Media, Culture and Society: A Critical Reader* (London, Beverley Hills: Sage, 1986), pp. 116–30; Axel Honneth, 'The Fragmented World of Symbolic Forms: Reflections on Bourdieu's Sociology of Culture', *Theory and Society*, 3:3 (1986), pp. 55–66; and Pekka Sulkunen, 'Society Made Visible – On the Cultural Sociology of Pierre Bourdieu', *Acta Sociologica*, 25:2 (1982), pp. 103–15.

4   In the diversity of cultural practices analysed, Bourdieu is similar to the Roland Barthes of *Mythologies*.

5   *Distinction*, pp. 6, 7. On *Distinction*, see Nicholas Garnham, 'Bourdieu's *Distinction*', *Sociological Review*, 34 (May 1986), pp. 423–33; also Bannett M. Berger, 'Review Essay: Taste and Domination', *American Journal of Sociology*, 91:6 (May 1986), pp. 1445–53.

6   Bourdieu, 'The Genesis of the Concepts of Habitus and Field', trans. Channa Newman, in *Sociocriticism*, 2, *Theories and Perspectives*, 2 (Pittsburgh, Pa., and Montpellier: International Institute for Sociocriticism, (December 1985), pp. 11–12 and esp. p. 12, n. 1.

The idea of the seminars, which included among their participants scholars such as Jean-Claude Chamboredon, Christophe Charle, Jean-Louis Fabiani, Pierre-Michel Menger and Rémy Ponton, among others, was to apply concepts developed in other areas of research, namely those of 'field' and 'habitus', to the whole of literary, artistic and intellectual production in nineteenth century France using a common card file elaborated specifically for this purpose. Studies growing out of these seminars include, among others, Christophe Charle, *La crise littéraire à l'époque du naturalisme: roman, théâtre, politique* (Paris: Presses de l'École Normale Supérieure, 1979), *Naissance des 'intellectuels', 1880–1900* (Paris: Minuit, 1990) and *Les élites de la République (1880–1900)* (Paris: Fayard, 1987); Jean-Louis Fabiani, *Les philosophes de la République* (Paris: Minuit, 1988); Rémy Ponton, 'Le champ littéraire de 1865 à 1905', doctoral dissertation École des Hautes Études en Sciences Sociales, Paris, 1977. For a 'Bourdieusian' study of the French artistic field in the late nineteenth century, see Dario Gamboni, *La plume et le pinceau: Odilon Redon et la littérature* (Paris: Minuit, 1989). Although not dealing with the same time-frame, see also Pierre-Michel Menger's *Le paradoxe du musicien: Le compositeur, le mélomane et l'État dans la société contemporaine* (Paris:

Flammarion, 1983) and Anna Boschetti, *The Intellectual Enterprise: Sartre and 'Les Temps Modernes'*, trans. Richard C. McCleary (Evanston, Ill.: Northwestern University Press, 1989).

7 See the preface to *The Logic of Practice* (pp. 1–21) for an account of Bourdieu's early intellectual influences, his ethnographic studies and his break with structuralism. The attempt to come to terms, in one way or another, with phenomenology and various forms of objectivist approaches to society, ranging from Marxism to structuralism, informed the work of a whole generation of French intellectuals, including Roland Barthes, Michel Foucault and Jacques Derrida.

8 Bourdieu's discussion of this dichotomy occurs in many different forms throughout his work. For a systematic elaboration, see *The Logic of Practice*, especially the introduction and chs. 1–2 (pp. 25–51). For a somewhat less rigorous formulation, see "Fieldwork in Philosophy . . ." ', in *In Other Words*, esp. pp. 8–14.

9 V. N. Volosinov, *Marxism and the Philosophy of Language*, trans. L. Matejka and I. R. Titunik (Cambridge, Mass.: Harvard University Press, 1986), pp. 49ff. Volosinov contrasts 'individualistc subjectivism' with 'abstract objectivism', which corresponds roughly to structural linguistics.

10 In the French intellectual field in which Bourdieu came of age, the paradigmatic figures of subjectivism and objectivism were Jean-Paul Sartre and Claude Lévi-Strauss, respectively. For Bourdieu's account of his gradual distancing from Lévi-Strauss, see the preface to *The Logic of Practice*. For this critique of Sartre's philosophy of action and his subjectivist theory of society, see *Outline of a Theory of Practice*, pp. 73–6, and 'The Imaginary Anthropology of Subjectivism', which is chapter 2 of *The Logic of Practice* (pp. 42–51).

11 *The Logic of Practice*, p. 135.

12 *Distinction*, p. 483.

13 *Outline of a Theory of Practice*, p. 73.

14 'I wanted, so to speak, to reintroduce agents that Lévi-Strauss and the structuralists, among them Althusser, tended to abolish, making them into simple epiphenomena of structure. And I mean agents, not subjects. Action is not the mere carrying out of a rule, or obedience to a rule. Social agents, in archaic societies as well as in ours, are not automata regulated like clocks, in accordance with laws they do not understand' (*In Other Words*, p. 9).

15 Ibid., p. 14.

16 Bourdieu, 'Postface', in E. Panofsky, *Architecture gothique et pensée scolastique*, trans. P. Bourdieu (Paris: Minuit, 1967; 2nd rev. edn. 1970), pp. 133–67. This volume includes translations of two essays by Panofsky, 'Abbot Suger on the Abbey Church of Saint-Denis' and 'Gothic Architecture and Scholasticism'. Bourdieu actually uses the term 'habitus' in an essay published the previous year which represents his initial attempt to outline theoretically the concept of intellectual field. See 'Intellectual Field and Creative Project', in Michael F. D. Young, ed., *Knowledge and Control* (London: Collier Macmillan, 1971), pp. 161–88. The translation first appeared in *Social Science Information*, 8:2 (1968). The original French version, 'Champ intellectuel et projet créateur' appeared in *Les temps modernes* (November 1966), pp. 865–906.

17   'The Genesis of the Concepts of Habitus and Field', pp. 12–14 at p. 14.
18   *The Logic of Practice*, p. 53; *Outline of a Theory of Practice*, p. 72.
19   *The Logic of Practice*, p. 54.
20   See Bourdieu, 'Intellectual Field and Creative Project'.
21   'The Genesis of the Concepts of Habitus and Field', pp. 16–17. See P. Bourdieu, 'Legitimation and Structured Interests in Weber's Sociology of Religion', trans. C. Turner, in Scott Lash and Sam Whimster, eds, *Max Weber: Rationality and Modernity* (London: Allen & Unwin, 1987), pp. 119–36. (Originally published in French as 'Une interprétation de la théorie de la religion selon Max Weber', *Archives européennes de sociologie*, 12:1 (1971), pp. 7–26.)
22   The essays in Bourdieu's *Language and Symbolic Power* (Cambridge: Polity, 1991) provide a rigorous analysis of various uses of linguistic capital in diverse linguistic markets.
23   *In Other Words*, pp. 22, 111.
24   The citation is from *Distinction*, p. 2. In an earlier and more abstract formulation, Bourdieu and Jean-Claude Passeron describe cultural capital as 'the cultural goods transmitted by the different family PAs [pedagogical actions], whose value qua cultural capital varies with the distance between the cultural arbitrary imposed by the dominant PA and the cultural arbitrary inculcated by the family PA within the different groups or classes' (*Reproduction in Education, Society and Culture*, p. 30).
25   *Outline of a Theory of Practice*, p. 183. Some of the 'New Historicists' have taken up much of Bourdieu's terminology, with frequent references to 'symbolic power', 'symbolic violence', 'symbolic capital', 'symbolic profit' and so forth. See, for example, H. A. Veeser's 'Introduction' to *The New Historicism* (New York, London: Routledge, 1989), pp. ix–xvi.
26   'The Genesis of the Concepts of Habitus and Field', p. 18; Brubaker, 'Rethinking Classical Theory', pp. 747–8.
27   In this sense, Bourdieu's model has clear affinities with 'depth hermeneutics', which comprises three levels of analysis: (1) social-historical analysis, which concerns the 'social and historical conditions of the production, circulation and reception of symbolic forms'; (2) discursive analysis, or the analysis of the structure and internal organization of symbolic forms; and (3) interpretation/reinterpretation, which involves the 'creative construction of possible meaning'. See J. B. Thompson, *Ideology and Modern Culture: Critical Social Theory in the Era of Mass Communication* (Cambridge: Polity; Stanford: Stanford University Press, 1990), pp. 281–91.
28   *In Other Words*, p. 147 (emphasis added).
29   Alain Viala discusses multiple components of the process of autonomization in seventeenth- and eighteenth-century France in *Naissance de l'écrivain: sociologie de la littérature à l'âge classique* (Paris: Minuit, 1985).
30   This is essentially the argument that Barbara Hernstein Smith, heavily indebted to Bourdieu, makes in *Contingencies of Value: Alternative Perspectives for Critical Theory* (Cambridge, Mass.: Harvard University Press, 1988).
31   Bourdieu refers specifically to Mircea Eliade's comparative mythology and Jungian or Bachelardian psychoanalysis, but one might think as well of

Northrop Frye's 'archetypal criticism', which has had a major impact on North American literary criticism. See N. Frye, *Anatomy of Criticism: Four Essays* (Princeton: Princeton University Press, 1957).

32 Bourdieu takes issue specifically with the Foucault of *The Archaeology of Knowledge* (1969) and other texts of the late 1960s, in which he at least temporarily sets aside the institutional analysis evident in *Madness and Civilization* (1961) and *Birth of the Clinic* (1963) and focuses on autonomous discursive systems. Clear affinities (and obvious differences) exist between Bourdieu and other aspects of Foucault's work, but will have to wait another occasion for full elaboration. See H. L. Dreyfus and P. Rabinow, *Michel Foucault: Beyond Structuralism and Hermeneutics*, 2nd edn. (Chicago: University of Chicago Press, 1983), pp. xxiv–xxv, 79–100. Also P. Bourdieu, 'Le plaisir de savoir', *Le Monde*, 27 June 1984, pp. 1, 10. For Foucault, see: *The Archaeology of Knowledge*, trans. A. M. Sheridan Smith (New York: Pantheon, 1972); *Madness and Civilization: A History of Insanity in the Age of Reason*, trans. Richard Howard (New York: Pantheon, 1965); *The Birth of the Clinic: An Archaeology of Medical Perception*, trans. A. M. Sheridan Smith (New York: Vintage Books, 1975).

33 Jakobson, cited by L. M. O'Toole and A. Shukman, 'A Contextual Glossary of Formalist Terminology', in *Russian Poetics in Translation*, 4 (1977), p. 17. Also V. Erlich, *Russian Formalism: History – Doctrine* (The Hague: Mouton, 1955), p. 172.

34 See P. Steiner, *Russian Formalism: A Metapoetics* (Ithaca: Cornell University Press, 1984), pp. 108–10.

35 *Homo Academicus*, p. xvii.

36 An example of the former is Robert Escarpit, who uses statistical regularities as explanatory factors. See Escarpit, *Sociology of Literature*, trans. Ernest Pick (Painesville, Ohio: Lake Erie College Series, vol. 4, 1965), especially part 2. The latter tendency is exemplified in art criticism by Frederick Antal, who suggests that the patrons' 'outlook on life was the ultimate factor determining the emergence of interrelations of the various styles'. See *Florentine Painting and its Social Background* (London: Kegan Paul, 1947), p. 274.

37 For Lucien Goldmann see, for example, *The Hidden God*, trans. Philip Thody (New York: The Humanities Press, 1964) and *Towards a Sociology of the Novel*, trans. Alan Sheridan (London: Tavistock, 1986).

38 See Christophe Charle, 'Situation du champ littéraire', *Littérature*, 44 (December 1981), pp. 8–20, esp. p. 10.

39 Ibid., p. 13.

40 M. M. Bakhtin, *Speech Genres and Other Late Essays*, trans. V. W. McGee, ed. Caryl Emerson and Michael Holquist (Austin: University of Texas Press, 1986), p. 2.

41 Borrowing from Bourdieu, Alain Viala speaks of the 'prismatic effects' exerted by the field: 'By prisms I mean those mediations, those realities, at once translucent and deformative that are formed by the literary codes, institutions, and fields interposed between the social referent and the text as well as between the work and its readers – those realities that determine meaning.' Among the prisms Viala outlines are (1) institutions of literary life, (2) sociopoetics, (3) theme, fashion and tradition, (4) trajectories, (5)

the psychology of the author and (6) language. See A. Viala, 'Prismatic Effects', in Philippe Desan, Priscilla Parkhurst Ferguson and Wendy Griswold, eds, *Literature and Social Practice* (Chicago: University of Chicago Press, 1989), pp. 256–66 at p. 256. Also Viala, *Naissance de l'écrivain*, esp. pp. 7–11.

42   *Homo Academicus*, pp. 115–18.
43   Edward W. Said, *The World, the Text, and the Critic* (Cambridge, Mass.: Harvard University Press, 1983; London: Faber, 1984), p. 174.
44   For a critique of Said, see Tony Bennett, *Outside Literature* (London, New York: Routledge, 1990), esp. pp. 197–205.
45   L. A. Montrose, 'The Poetics and Politics of Culture', in Veeser, *The New Historicism*, pp. 15–36 at p. 17.
46   One hears an echo of Bourdieu, furthermore, when Stephen Greenblatt writes that 'the work of art is the product of a negotiation between a creator or class of creators, equipped with a complex, communally shared repertoire of conventions, and the institutions and practices. In order to achieve the negotiation, artists need to create a currency that is valid for meaningful, mutually profitable exchange . . . normally measured in pleasure and interest' (S. Greenblatt, 'Towards a Poetics of Culture', in Veeser, *The New Historicism*, pp. 1–14, citation from p. 12).
47   For an incisive critique of New Historicism, see Vincent P. Pecora, 'The Limits of Local Knowledge', in Veeser, *The New Historicism*, pp. 243–76; also essays by E. Fox-Genovese, R. Terdiman, Frank Lentricchia and Jane Marcus in the same volume.
48   Perhaps the most compelling arguments for a rearrangement of the canon has come from feminist critics, who have quite correctly exposed the male-dominated power relations implicit in the canon. For a cogent discussion of the debate over canonicity, see John Guillory, 'Canonical and Non-canonical: A Critique of the Current Debate', *ELH*, 54:3 (Fall 1987), pp. 483–527.
49   In the 'Postscript' to *Distinction*, esp. pp. 494–5.
50   P. Bourdieu and A. Darbel, with Dominique Schnapper, *L'amour de l'art, les musées d'art et leur public* (Paris: Minuit, 1966), rev. ed. *L'amour d'art, les musées d'art européens et leur public* (1969). Published in English as *The Love of Art: European Art Museums and their Public*, trans. Caroline Beattie and Nick Merriman (Cambridge: Polity; Stanford: Stanford University Press, 1990).
51   *The Love of Art*, p. 14.
52   Ibid., pp. 62–3.
53   See, for example, P. Bourdieu, 'Cultural Reproduction and Social Reproduction', in *Knowledge, Education and Cultural Change: Papers in the Sociology of Education*, ed. Richard Brown (London: Tavistock, 1973), pp. 71–112 at p. 73.
54   Cited in *Distinction*, p. 490.
55   *Distinction*, p. 7.

## 1   THE FIELD OF CULTURAL PRODUCTION

1   Or any other kind of field; art and literature being one area among others for application of the method of object-construction designated by the concept of the field.
2   Since it is not possible to develop here all that is implied in the notion of the field, one can only refer the reader to earlier works which set out the conditions of the application in the social sciences of the relational mode of thought which has become indispensable in the natural sciences (P. Bourdieu, 'Structuralism and Theory of Sociological Knowledge', *Social Research*, 35:4 (1968), pp. 681–706) and the differences between the field as a *structure of objective relations* and the *interactions* studied by Weber's analysis of religious agents or by interactionism (P. Bourdieu, 'Une interprétation de la sociologie religieuse de Max Weber', *Archives européennes de sociologie*, 12:1 (1971), pp. 3–21).
3   M. Foucault, 'Réponse au cercle d'épistémologie', *Cahiers pour l'analyse*, 9 (1968), pp. 9–40.
4   Ibid., p. 29.
5   Ibid., p. 37.
6   See in particular S. J. Tynjanov and R. Jakobson, 'Le problème des études littéraires et linguistiques', in T. Todorov, ed., *Théorie de la littérature* (Paris: Seuil, 1965), pp. 138–9; I. Even-Zohar, 'Polysystem Theory', *Poetics Today*, 1:93 (1979), pp. 65–74; V. Erlich, *Russian Formalism* (The Hague: Mouton, 1965).
7   In this (and only this) respect, the theory of the field could be regarded as a generalized Marxism, freed from the realist mechanism implied in the theory of 'instances'.
8   H. S. Becker, 'Art Worlds and Social Types', *American Behavioral Scientist*, 19:6 (1976), pp. 703–19 at p. 703. See also H. S. Becker, 'Art as Collective Action', *American Sociological Review*, 39:6 (1974), pp. 767–76.
9   Becker, 'Art Worlds and Social Types', pp. 703–4.
10   Cf. H. Hanson, 'The Education of the Orchestra Musician', in H. Swoboda, ed., *The American Symphony Orchestra* (New York: Basic Books, 1967), especially pp. 104–5.
11   M. Weber, *Ancient Judaism* (Glencoe, Ill.: Free Press, 1952).
12   The status of 'social art' is, in this respect, thoroughly ambiguous. Although it relates artistic or literary production to external functions (which is what the advocates of art for art's sake object to about it), it shares with art for art's sake a radical rejection of the dominant principle of hierarchy and of the 'bourgeois' art which recognizes it.
13   The specific, and therefore autonomous, power which writers and artists possess *qua* writers and artists must be distinguished from the alienated, heteronomous power they wield *qua* experts or cadres – a share in domination, but with the status of dominated mandatories, granted to them by the dominant.

14   Thus, writers and artists who are 'second-rank' in terms of the specific criteria may invoke populism and social art to impose their reign on the 'leading intellectuals' who, as has happened in China and elsewhere, will protest against the disparity between the revolutionary ideal and the reality, i.e. the reign of functionaries devoted to the Party. See M. Godman, *Literary Dissent in Communist China* (Cambridge, Mass.: Harvard University Press, 1967).

15   Throughout this passage, 'writer' can be replaced by 'artist', 'philosopher' 'intellectual', etc. The intensity of the struggle, and the degree to which it takes visible, and therefore conscious, forms, no doubt vary according to the genre and according to the rarity of the specific competence each genre requires in different periods, i.e. according to the probability of 'unfair competition' or 'illegal exercise of the profession'. (This no doubt explains why the intellectual field, with the permanent threat of casual essayism, is one of the key areas in which to grasp the logic of the struggles which pervade all fields.)

16   Only just over a third of the writers in the sample studied by Rémy Ponton had had any higher education, whether or not it led to a degree. See R. Ponton, 'Le champ littéraire de 1865 à 1905' (Paris: École des Hautes Études en Sciences Sociales, 1977), p. 43. For the comparison between the literary field and other fields, see C. Charle, 'Situation du champ littéraire', *Littérature*, 44 (1981), pp. 8–20.

17   For an analysis of the play of homologies between producers, intermediaries (newspapers and critics, gallery directors, publishers, etc.) and categories of audience, see P. Bourdieu, 'The Production of Belief', ch. 2 in this volume.

18   See P. Bourdieu, *Distinction: A Social Critique of the Judgement of Taste*, trans. Richard Nice (Cambridge, Mass.: Harvard University Press, 1984), pp. 397–465.

19   This struggle can be observed as much in the literary field as in the artistic field (with the opposition between 'pure' art and 'bourgeois' art) and in each genre (with, for example, the opposition between avant-garde theatre and 'middle brow' boulevard theatre).

20   See R. W. Lee, *Ut pictura poesis: The Humanistic Theory of Painting* (New York: W. W. Norton, 1967); F. Bologna, *Dalle arte minori all' industrial design: storia di un' idealogia* (Bari: Laterza, 1972).

21   See D. Gamboni, 'Redon écrivain et épistolier', *Revue d'art* (1980), pp. 68–71, and 'Remarques sur la critique d'art, l'histoire de l'art et le champ artistique à propos d'Odilon Redon', *Revue suisse d'art et d'archéologie*, 2 (1982), pp. 57–63.

22   C. Charle, *La crise littéraire à l'époque du naturalisme* (Paris: Presses de l'École Normale Supérieure, 1979), p. 37.

23   Ibid., esp. pp. 27–54; Ponton, '*Naissance du roman psychologique*', *Actes de la recherche en sciences sociales*, 4 (1975), pp. 66–81.

24   From 1876 to 1880, Zola campaigned systematically in his regular drama reviews for the coming of a new theatre. It is remarkable that the birth of a theatrical sub-field was immediately attended by field-effects: Paul Fort's *Théâtre d'art et de l'Oeuvre* was constituted 'both on the model of the *Théâtre libre* and against it (and Naturalism was "flayed on the stage of the *Théâtre d'art*")'. See B. Dort, 'Vers un nouveau théâtre', in *Histoire littéraire de la France*, vol. 5 (Paris: Éditions Sociales, 1977), pp. 615, 619.

25 This ambiguity lies at the heart of studies in art history which claim to characterize the work – and the world view expressed in it – in terms of the group which commissions and consumes, pays and receives.

26 M. Faure, 'L'époque 1900 et la résurgence de mythe de Cythère', *Le mouvement social*, 109 (1979), pp. 15–34.

27 Ponton, 'Le champ littéraire de 1865 à 1905', pp. 223–8.

28 J.-L. Fabiani, 'La crise du champ philosophique (1880–1914): contribution à l'histoire sociale du système d'enseignement', doctoral dissertation (Paris: École des Hautes Études Sciences Sociales, 1980), p. 100.

29 Ponton, 'Le champ littéraire de 1865 à 1905', p. 206. An exemplary expression of a field-effect converted into an explicit project can be seen in this declaration of Zola's: 'Anyway, if I have time, I will do what they want!' (J. Huret, *Enquête sur l'évolution littéraire* (Vanves: Thot, 1982), p. 160; first published Paris: Charpentier, 1891). In other words: I myself will perform the suppression of Naturalism, i.e. of myself, which my adversaries vainly seek to perform.

30 Cited by Fabiani, 'La crise du champ philosophique', p. 82.

31 Zola does not fail to point out this discrepancy between positional age and 'real' age: 'In their dallying with stupidities, with such futilities, at such a grave moment in the evolution of ideas, all these young people, all between thirty and forty, remind me of nutshells bobbing on Niagara Falls! The fact is, they have nothing beneath them but a gigantic, empty pretension!' (cited by Huret, *Enquête sur l'évolution littéraire*, p. 158).

32 See P. Lidsky, *Les écrivains contre la commune* (Paris: Maspero, 1970), pp. 26–7.

33 In every field, the dominant have an interest in continuity, identity and reproduction, whereas the dominated, the newcomers, are for discontinuity, rupture and subversion.

34 Divisions between generations therefore occur in accordance with the logic specific to the struggles which characterize each field (so that oppositions formed in the literary field cannot properly be extended to the whole social field – as was often done in late nineteenth-century France, i.e. at a time when the opposition between the generations tended to be generalized to the whole literary field. See R. Wohl, *The Generation of 1914* (Cambridge, Mass.: Harvard University Press, 1979).

35 V. Shklovsky, *Sur la théorie de la prose* (Lausanne: L'Age d'Homme, 1973), p. 24.

36 On the question of returns and Duchamp's approach to it, see 'The Production of Belief' (ch. 2 in this volume).

37 The perception called for by a work produced in accordance with the logic of the field is a differential, distinctive perception, attentive to the differences, the deviations from what is normal, usual, *modal* at the moment in question, i.e. from other works, both contemporary and, especially, past ones – in short, a historical perception.

38 The limiting case is that of products with no recognized producer, raw art (of naïfs, madmen, children, etc.) which is entirely 'produced' by a sort of impresario (e.g. Dubuffet).

39 This was said in so many words by a Symbolist poet questioned by Huret: 'In all cases, I consider the worst Symbolist poet far superior to any of the writers enrolled under the banner of Naturalism' (Huret, *Enquête sur l'évolution littéraire*, p. 329). Another example, less forthright but

closer to the experience which really inflects choices: 'At fifteen, nature tells a young man whether he is cut out to be a poet or should *be content with mere prose [la simple prose]*' (ibid., p. 299, emphasis added). It is clear what the shift from poetry to the novel means for someone who has strongly internalized these hierarchies. (The division into castes separated by absolute frontiers which override real continuities and overlappings produces everywhere – e.g. in the relationships between disciplines, philosophy and the social sciences, the pure and applied sciences, etc. – the same effects, *certitudo sui* and the refusal to demean oneself, etc.)

40   The painters still had to win their autonomy with respect to the writers, without whom they would perhaps not have succeeded in freeing themselves from the constraints of the bureaucracies and academicism.

41   To those who seek to trace a direct relationship between any producers and the group from which they draw their economic support, it has to be pointed out that the logic of a relatively autonomous field means that one can use the resources provided by a group or institution to produce products deliberately or unconsciously directed against the interests or values of that group or institution.

42   It goes without saying that freedom with respect to institutions can never be truly institutionalized. This contradiction, which every attempt to institutionalize heresy comes up against (it is the antinomy of the Reformed Church), is seen clearly in the ambivalent image of institutional acts of consecration, and not only those performed by the most heteronomous institutions, such as academies (one thinks of Sartre's refusal of the Nobel Prize).

43   Although I realize that theoretical warnings count for little against the social drives which induce simplistic, apologetic or terroristic use of more-or-less scientific-seeming reference to 'father's occupation', it seems useful to condemn the inclination – in which the worst adversaries and acolytes too easily find common ground – to reduce the model that is proposed to the mechanical and mechanistic mode of thinking in which inherited capital (internalized in habitus, or objectified) determines the position occupied, which in turn directly determines position-takings.

44   *Social trajectory* or *constructed biography* is defined as the set of successive movements of an agent in a structured (hierarchized) space, itself subject to displacements and distortions, or, more precisely, in the structure of the distribution of the different kinds of capital which are at stake in the field, economic capital and the specific capital of consecration (in its different kinds). These movements, which define *social ageing*, are of two orders. They may be limited to one sector of the field and lie along the same axis of consecration, in which case ageing is marked by a positive, zero or negative accumulation of specific capital; or they may imply a change of sector and the reconversion of one kind of specific capital into another (e.g. the case of the Symbolist poets who moved into the psychological novel) or of specific capital into economic capital (in the case of shifts from poetry to the 'novel of manners' or the theatre or, still more clearly, to cabaret or serialized fiction).

45   A. Cassagne, *La Théorie de l'art pour l'art en France chez les derniers romantiques et les premiers réalistes* (Geneva: Slatkine Reprints, 1979), pp. 75ff. Originally published Paris, 1906.

46   E. de Goncourt and J. de Goncourt, *Manette Salomon* (Paris: Union générale d'éditions, 1979), p. 32.

47   The solidarity which is built up, within artistic groups, between the richest and the poorest is one of the means which enable some impecunious artists to carry on despite the absence of resources provided by the market.

48   See M. Rogers, 'The Batignolles Group: Creators of Impressionism', in M. C. Albrecht et al., eds, *The Sociology of Art and Literature* (New York: Praeger, 1970).

49   Similarity of position, especially when defined negatively, is not sufficient to found a literary or artistic group, although it tends to favour rapprochement and exchanges. This was the case, for example, with the advocates of 'art for art's sake', who were linked by relations of esteem and sympathy without actually forming a group. Gautier received Flaubert, Théodore de Banville, the Goncourt brothers and Baudelaire at his Thursday dinner parties. The rapprochement between Flaubert and Baudelaire stemmed from the near simultaneity of their early works and their trials. The Goncourts and Flaubert much appreciated each other, and the former met Bouillet at Flaubert's home. Théodore de Banville and Baudelaire were long-standing friends. Louis Ménard, a close friend of Baudelaire, Banville and Leconte de Lisle, became one of the intimates of Renan. Barbey d'Aurevilly was one of Baudelaire's most ardent advocates. Whereas they were close acquaintances, these writers were little seen in high society since their high degree of professionalization limited their social intercourse (see Cassagne, *La Théorie de l'art pour l'art*, pp. 130–4).

50   'The Decadents did not mean to *sweep away* the past. They urged necessary reforms, conducted *methodically* and *prudently*. By contrast, the Symbolists wanted to *keep nothing* of our old ways and aspired to create an entirely new mode of expression' (E. Reynaud, *La Mêlée symboliste*, vol. 1 (Paris: La Renaissance du livre, 1918), p. 118, cited by J. Jurt, 'Symbolistes et Décadentes, deux groupes littéraires parallèles', mimeo (1982), p. 12 (emphasis added).

51   Ponton, 'Le champ littéraire de 1865 à 1905', pp. 299ff; Jurt, 'Symbolistes et Décadentes', p. 12.

52   The opposition between Mallarmé and Verlaine is the paradigmatic form of an opposition which was gradually constituted and more and more strongly asserted through the nineteenth century – that between the professional writer, occupied full-time by his research and conscious of his mastery, and the amateur writer, a bourgeois dilettante who wrote as a pastime or hobby, or a frivolous, impoverished bohemian. At odds with the bourgeois world and its values, the professional writers, in the first rank of whom are the advocates of 'art for art's sake', are also set apart in countless ways from the bohemian sub-culture, its pretension, its incoherences and its very disorder, which is incompatible with methodical production. Flaubert must be cited: 'I maintain, and this should be a practical dogma for the artistic life, that one must divide one's existence into two parts: live like a bourgeois and think like a demi-god' (*Correspondence*, cited by Cassagne, *La Théorie de l'art pour l'art*, p. 307). And the Goncourt brothers: 'Literature is conceived only in silence and as it were in the sleep of the activity of the things and facts around one. Emotions are not good for the gestation of the imagination. One needs regular, calm days, a bourgeois state of one's whole being, a grocer's tranquillity, to give birth to

the grand, the tormented, the poignant, the pathetic . . . Those who spend themselves in passion, in nervous agitation, will never write a book of passion' (*Journal*, cited by Cassagne, *La Théorie de l'art pour l'art*, p. 308). This opposition between the two categories of writers is no doubt the source of specifically political antagonisms, which were particularly manifested at the time of the Commune.

53  Cited by Cassagne, *La Théorie de l'art pour l'art*, p. 218.

54  Ponton, 'Le champ littéraire de 1865 à 1905', pp. 69–70.

55  An example of this is the case of Anatole France, whose father's unusual position as a Paris bookseller enabled him to acquire a social capital and a familiarity with the world of letters which compensated for his low economic and cultural capital.

56  Ponton, 'Le champ littéraire de 1865 à 1905', p. 57.

57  P. Vernois, 'La fin de la pastorale', in *Histoire littéraire de la France* (Paris: Éditions Sociales, 1977), p. 272.

58  Cited in ibid., p. 272.

59  'As described by Champfleury (a Realist novelist, a friend of Courbet and Cladel), the Brasserie Allemande de Paris, where Realism emerged as a movement, was a Protestant village where there reigned rustic manners and a frank gaiety. The leader, Courbet, was a "journeyman", he went around shaking hands, he talked and ate a great deal, strong and stubborn as a peasant, the very opposite of the dandy of the 1830s and '40s. His behaviour in Paris was deliberately popular; he ostentatiously spoke patois, he smoked, sang and joked like a man of the people. Observers were impressed by the plebeian, domestic familiarity of his technique . . . Du Camp wrote that he painted "like a man polishing boots" ' (M. Schapiro, 'Courbet et l'imagerie populaire', in *Style, artiste et société* (Paris: Gallimard, 1982), p. 293).

60  Cladel, cited by Ponton, 'Le champ littéraire de 1865 à 1905', p. 98. To assess how much the regionalist novel, the paradigmatic expression of one of the forms of the regionalist – and, more generally, populist – enterprise, derives from being the product of a negative vocation, one would have to compare systematically all those who ended up writing populist novels after such a trajectory with those who are exceptions, such as Eugène Le Roy, a minor civil servant in the Périgord who passed through Paris, author of *Le Moulin du Frau* (1895) and *Jacquou le Croquant* (1899), etc., and especially Émile Guillaumin, a sharecropper in the Bourbonnais and author of *La Vie d'un simple* (1904).

61  Schapiro, 'Courbet et l'imagerie populaire', p. 299.

62  Ibid., p. 315ff.

63  Ponton, 'Le champ littéraire de 1865 à 1905', p. 73.

64  Dort, 'Vers un nouveau théâtre', p. 615.

65  Ibid., p. 617. In terms of the same logic, Ponton ('Le champ littéraire de 1865 à 1905', pp. 80–2) observes that among the boulevard playwrights, directly subjected to the financial sanction of bourgeois taste, writers from the working classes or petite bourgeoisie are very strongly underrepresented, whereas they are more strongly represented in vaudeville, a comic genre which gives more scope for the easy effects of farcical or salacious scenes and also for a sort of semi-critical freedom, and that the authors who write for both boulevard theatre and vaudeville have characteristics intermediate between those of specialists in each genre.

66  S. Mallarmé, 'La musique et les lettres', in *Oeuvres complètes* (Paris: Gallimard (Pléiade), 1945), p. 647. On this text and the reading put forward by Heinrich Merkl, see Jurt, 'Symbolistes et Décadentes'.

## 2  THE PRODUCTION OF BELIEF

1  From now on, the inverted commas will indicate when the 'economy' is to be understood in the narrow sense in which economism understands it.

2  The 'great' publisher, like the 'great' art dealer, combines 'economic' prudence (people often poke fun at him for his 'housekeeping' ways) with intellectual daring. He thus sets himself apart from those who condemn themselves, 'economically' at least, because they apply the same daring or the same casualness both in their commercial business and in their intellectual ventures (not to mention those who combine economic imprudence with artistic prudence: 'A mistake over the cost-prices or the print runs can lead to disaster, even if the sales are excellent. When Jean-Jacques Pauvert embarked on reprinting the Littré [multi-volume dictionary] it looked like a promising venture because of the unexpectedly large number of subscribers. But when it was about to be published, they found there had been a mistake in estimating the cost-price, and they would be losing fifteen francs on each set. Pauvert had to abandon the deal to another publisher' (B. Demory, 'Le livre à l'âge de l'industrie', *L'Expansion*, October 1970, p. 110).

It becomes clearer why Jérôme Lindon commands the admiration of both the big 'commercial' publisher and the small avant-garde publisher: 'A publisher with a very small team and low overheads can make a good living and express his own personality. This requires very strict financial discipline on his part, since he is caught between the need to maintain financial equilibrium and the temptation to expand. I have great admiration for Jérôme Lindon, the director of Les Éditions de Minuit, who has been able to maintain that difficult balance throughout his publishing life. He has been able to promote the things he liked, and nothing else, without being blown off course. Publishers like him are needed to give birth to the *nouveau roman*, and publishers like me are needed to reflect the varied facets of life and creation' (R. Laffont, *Editeur* (Paris: Laffont, 1974), pp. 291–2).

'It was during the Algerian war, and I can say that for three years I lived like an FLN militant, at the same time as I was becoming a publisher. At Éditions de Minuit, Jérôme Lindon, who has always been an example for me, was denouncing torture' (F. Maspero, 'Maspero entre tous les feux', *Nouvel Observateur*, 17 September 1973).

3  This analysis, which applies in the first instance to new works by unknown authors, is equally valid for 'underrated' or 'dated' and even 'classic' works, which can always be treated to 'rediscoveries', 'revivals' and 're-readings' (hence so many unclassifiable philosophical, literary and theatrical productions, of which the paradigm is the avant-garde staging of traditional texts).

4  It is no accident that the art trader's guarantor role is particularly visible in the field of painting, where the purchaser's (the collector's) 'economic'

investment is incomparably greater than in literature or even the theatre. Raymonde Moulin observes that a contract signed with a major gallery has a commercial value and that, in the eyes of the amateurs, the dealer is 'the guarantor of the quality of the works' (R. Moulin, *Le Marché de la peinture en France* (Paris: Minuit, 1967), p. 329).

5    It goes without saying that, depending on the position in the field of production, promotional activities range from overt use of publicity techniques (press advertisements, catalogues etc.) and economic and symbolic pressure (e.g. on the juries who award the prizes or on the critics) to the haughty and rather ostentatious refusal to make any concessions to the 'world', which can, in the long run, be the supreme form of value imposition (only available to a few).

6    The ideological representation transfigures real functions. Only the publisher or dealer, who devotes most of his time to it, can organize and rationalize the marketing of the work, which, especially in the case of painting, is a considerable undertaking, presupposing information (as to the 'worthwhile' places in which to exhibit, especially abroad) and material means. But, above all, he alone, acting as a go-between and a screen, can enable the producer to maintain a charismatic, i.e. inspired and 'disinterested', image of himself and his activity, by sparing him the tasks associated with the market, which are ridiculous, demoralizing and ineffective (symbolically at least). (The writer's or painter's craft, and the corresponding images of them, would probably be totally different if the producers had to market their products personally and if they depended directly, for their conditions of existence, on the sanctions of the market or on agencies which know and recognize no other sanctions, like 'commercial' publishing firms.)

7    In reply to those who might seek to refute these arguments by invoking a cosy picture of solidarity between 'fellow producers' or 'colleagues', one would have to point to all the forms of 'unfair competition', of which plagiarism (more or less skilfully disguised) is only the best known and the most visible, or the violence – purely symbolic, of course – of the aggressions with which producers endeavour to discredit their rivals (cf. the recent history of painting, which offers countless examples, one of the most typical, to cite only the dead, being the relationship between Yves Klein and Piero Manzoni).

8    These arguments take further and specify those which I have put forward with reference to *haute couture*, in which the economic stakes and the disavowal strategies are much more evident (see P. Bourdieu and Y. Delsaut, 'Le Couturier et sa griffe: contribution à une théorie de la magie', *Actes de la recherche en sciences sociales*, 1 (January 1975), pp. 7–36), and philosophy; in the latter case the emphasis was placed on the contribution of interpreters and commentators to the misrecognition-recognition of the work (see P. Bourdieu, 'L'ontologie politique de Martin Heidegger', *Actes de la recherche en sciences sociales*, 5–6 (November 1975), pp. 109–56). The present text does not aim to apply knowledge of the general properties of fields that have been established elsewhere to new fields. Rather, it seeks to bring the invariant laws of the functioning and transformation of fields of struggle to a higher level of explicitness and generality by comparing several fields (painting, theatre, literature and journalism) in which the

different laws do not appear with the same degree of clarity, for reasons which have to do either with the nature of the data available or with specific properties. This procedure contrasts both with theoreticist formalism, which is its own object, and with idiographic empiricism, which can never move beyond the scholastic accumulation of falsifiable propositions.

9   A couple of examples, chosen from among hundreds: 'I know a painter who has real quality as regards skill, material, etc., but for me the stuff he turns out is totally commercial; he manufactures it, like bars of soap . . . When artists become very well-known, they often tend to go in for mass production' (gallery director, interview). Avant-gardism has often nothing to offer to guarantee its convictions beyond its indifference to money and its spirit of protest: 'Money doesn't count for him; even beyond the notion of public service, he sees culture as a vehicle for social protest' (A. de Baecque, 'Faillite au théâtre', *L'Expansion* (December 1968)).

10   To remain within the limits of the information available (that provided by Pierre Guetta's excellent survey, *Le théâtre et son public*, 2 vols, roneo (Paris: Ministère des Affaires Culturelles, 1966), I have cited only the theatres mentioned in this study. Out of forty-three Parisian theatres listed in 1975 in the specialized press (excluding the subsidized theatres), twenty-nine (two-thirds) offer entertainments which clearly belong to the 'boulevard' category; eight present classical or neutral ('unmarked') works; and six present works which can be regarded as belonging to intellectual theatre.

11   Here, and throughout this text, 'bourgeois' is shorthand for 'dominant fractions of the dominant class' when used as a noun, and, when used as an adjective, for 'structurally linked to these fractions'. 'Intellectual' functions in the same way for 'dominated fractions of the dominant class'.

12   Analysis of the overlaps between the constituencies of the various theatres confirms these analyses. At one extreme is the Théâtre de l'Est parisien, which draws almost half its audience from the dominated fractions of the dominant class and shares its clientele with the other 'intellectual' theatres (Théâtre national populaire, Odéon, Vieux Colombier and Athénée; at the other extreme, the boulevard theatres (Antoine, Variétés), almost half of whose audience consists of employers, senior executives and their wives; and between the two, the Comédie Française and the Atelier, which share their audience with all the theatres.

13   A more detailed analysis would reveal a whole set of oppositions (in the different respects considered above) within avant-garde theatre and even boulevard theatre. Thus, a careful reading of the statistics on attendance suggests that a 'smart' bourgeois theatre (Théâtre de Paris, Ambassadeurs, which present works – *Comment réussir en affaires* and *Photo-finish* by Peter Ustinov – praised by *Le Figaro* (12 February 1964 and 6 January 1964) and even, in the first case, by the *Nouvel Observateur* (March 1964)), attended by an audience of cultivated bourgeois, tending to live in Paris and to be regular theatre-goers, can be contrasted with a more 'low-brow' bourgeois theatre, offering 'Parisian' entertainments (Michodière – *La preuve par quatre*, by Félicien Marceau; Antoine – *Mary, Mary*; Variétés – *Un homme comblé*, by J. Deval), which received very hostile reviews, the first from the *Nouvel Observateur* (12 February 1964) and the other two from *Le Figaro* (26 September 1963 and 28 December

1964). Their audience is more provincial, less familiar with the theatre and more petit-bourgeois, containing a higher proportion of junior executives and, in particular, craftspeople and shopkeepers. Although it is not possible to verify this statistically (as I have endeavoured to do in the case of painting and literature), everything suggests that the authors and actors of these different categories of theatres are also opposed in accordance with the same principles. Thus, the big stars in successful boulevard plays (generally also receiving a percentage of the box-office receipts) could earn up to 2,000 francs an evening in 1972, and 'known' actors 300–500 francs per performance; actors belonging to the Comédie Française, who receive less per performance than leading private-theatre actors, are paid a basic monthly rate with bonuses for each performance and, in the case of shareholding members of the company, a proportion of the annual profits, according to length of service; while the actors in the small left-bank theatres suffer precarious employment and extremely low incomes.

14 M. Descotes, *Le Public de théâtre et son histoire* (Paris: Presses Universitaires de France, 1964), p. 298. This sort of caricature would not occur so often in theatrical works themselves (e.g. the parody of the *nouveau roman* in Michel Perrin's *Haute fidelité*, 1963) and even more often in the writings of the critics, if 'bourgeois' authors were not assured of the complicity of their bourgeois' audience when they settle their scores with avant-garde authors and bring 'intellectual' comfort to the 'bourgeois' who feel threatened by 'intellectual' theatre.

15 To give an idea of the power and salience of these taxonomies, one example will suffice: statistical study of class tastes shows that 'intellectual' and 'bourgeois' preferences can be organized around the opposition between Goya and Renoir; to describe the contrasting fortunes of two concierge's daughters, one of whom 'marries into the servants' quarters' and the other becomes owner of a 'seventh floor flat with a terrace', Françoise Dorin compares the first to a Goya, the second to a Renoir. See F. Dorin, *Le Tournant* (Paris: Julliard, 1973), p. 115.

16 What is bought is not just a newspaper but also a generative principle producing opinions, attitudes, 'positions', defined by a distinctive position in a field of institutionalized position-generators. And we may postulate that readers will feel more completely and adequately expressed, the more perfect the homology between their paper's position in the field of the press and the position they occupy in the field of the classes (or class fractions), the basis of their opinion-generating principle.

17 Analysis of the overlaps in readership confirms that *France-Soir* is very close to *L'Aurore*; that *Le Figaro* and *L'Express* are more or less equidistant from all the others (*Le Figaro* inclining rather towards *France-Soir*, whereas *L'Express* inclines towards the *Nouvel Observateur*); and that *Le Monde* and the *Nouvel Observateur* constitute a final cluster.

18 Private-sector executives, engineers and the professions are characterized by a medium overall rate of readership and a distinctly higher rate of readership of *Le Monde* than businesspeople and industrialists. (The private-sector executives remain closer to the industrialists by virtue of their quantity of low-level reading – *France-Soir*, *L'Aurore* – and also their high rate of readership of financial, and business journals – *Les Echos*,

*Information, Enterprise* – whereas the members of the professions are closer to the teachers by virtue of their rate of readership of the *Nouvel Observateur*.)

19  This art of conciliation and compromise achieves the virtuosity of art for art's sake with the critic of *La Croix*, who laces his unconditional approval with such subtly articulated justifications, with understatements through double-negation, nuances, reservations and self-corrections, that the final *conciliatio oppositorum*, so naïvely jesuitical 'in form and substance', as he would say, almost seems to go without saying: '*Le Tournant*, as I have said, seems to me an admirable work, in both form and substance. This is not to say it will not put many people's teeth on edge. I happened to be sitting next to an unconditional supporter of the avant-garde and through-out the evening I was aware of his suppressed anger. However, I by no means conclude that Françoise Dorin is unfair to certain very respectable – albeit often tedious – experiments in the contemporary theatre . . . And if she concludes – her preference is delicately hinted – with the triumph of the 'Boulevard' – but a boulevard that is itself avant-garde – that is precisely because for many years a master like Anouilh has placed himself as a guide at the crossroads of these two paths' (Jean Vigneron, *La Croix*, 21 January 1973).

20  The logic of the functioning of the fields of cultural goods production as fields of struggle favouring strategies aimed at distinction means that the products of their functioning, whether *haute couture* 'creations' or novels, are predisposed to function *differentially*, as instruments of distinction, first between the class fractions and then between the classes.

21  We can believe those critics most noted for their conformity to their expectations of their readership when they insist that they never espouse their readers' opinions and often fight against them. Thus, Jean-Jacques Gautier, in *Théâtre d'aujourd'hui* (Paris: Julliard, 1972), pp. 25–6, rightly says that the effectiveness of his critiques stems not from a demagogic adjustment to the audience but from an *objective agreement*, which permits a perfect sincerity between critic and audience that is also essential in order to be believed and therefore efficacious.

22  'You're not informed like that, they're just things you feel . . . I didn't know exactly what I was doing. There are people who sent things in, I didn't know . . . Information means having a vague sense, wanting to say things and coming across the right way . . . It's lots of little things, it's feelings, not information' (painter, interview).

23  Gautier, *Théâtre d'aujourd'hui*, p. 26. Publishers are also perfectly aware that a book's success depends on where it is published. They know what is 'made for them' and what is not and observe that a certain book which was 'right for them' (e.g. Gallimard) has done badly with another publisher (e.g. Laffont). The adjustment between author and publisher and then between book and readership is thus the result of a series of choices which all involve the publisher's brand image. Authors choose their publisher in terms of this image, and he chooses them in terms of his own idea of his firm; readers are also influenced by their image of the publisher (e.g. 'Minuit is high-brow') which no doubt helps to explain the failure of 'misplaced' books. It is this mechanism which leads a publisher to say, quite correctly: 'Each publisher is the best in his category.'

24   It is said that Jean-Jacques Nathan (Fernand Nathan), who is regarded as
     being first and foremost a 'manager', defines publishing as 'a highly
     speculative trade'. The risks are indeed high and the chances of making a
     profit when publishing a young writer are minute. A novel which does not
     succeed may have a (short-term) life-span of less than three weeks; then
     there are the lost or damaged copies or those too soiled to be returned, and
     those that do come back reduced to the state of worthless paper. In the case
     of moderate short-term success, once the production costs, royalties and
     distribution costs are deducted, about 20 per cent of the retail price is left
     for the publisher who has to offset the unsold copies, finance his stocks and
     pay his overheads and taxes. But when a book extends its career beyond
     the first year and enters the back-list, it constitutes a financial 'flywheel'
     which provides the basis for forecasting and for a long-term investment
     policy. When the first edition has amortized the overheads, the book can be
     reprinted at a considerably lower cost-price and will guarantee a regular
     income (direct income and also supplementary royalties, translations,
     paperback editions, television or film adaptations), which helps to finance
     further more or less risky investments that may also eventually build up the
     back-list.

25   Because of the unequal lengths of the cycle of production it is rarely
     meaningful to compare annual statements from different publishing
     houses. The annual statement gives an increasingly incomplete picture of
     the firm's real position, as one moves away from firms with rapid turnover,
     i.e. as the proportion of long-cycle products in the firm's activity increases.
     For example, to assess the value of the stocks, one can consider the
     *production cost*, the *wholesale price*, which is unpredictable, or the *price of
     the paper*. Which of these different methods of valuation are appropriate
     depends on whether one is dealing with 'commercial' firms whose stock
     returns very rapidly to the state of printed paper or firms for which it
     constitutes a capital which constantly tends to appreciate.

26   A further case, which cannot appear on the diagram, ought to be added –
     that of simple failure, i.e. a *Godot* whose career was over by the end of
     1952 leaving a balance sheet badly in the red.

27   Among the guaranteed short-term investments, we must also include all the
     publishing strategies designed to *exploit a back-list*: new editions,
     naturally, but also paperback editions (for Gallimard, this is the *Folio*
     series).

28   Although one must never ignore the 'moiré' effect produced in every field
     by the fact that the different possible structurations (here, for example,
     according to age, size, degree of political and/or aesthetic avant-gardism)
     never coincide perfectly, the fact remains that the relative weight of
     long-term and short-term firms can probably be regarded as the dominant
     structuring principle of the field. In this respect, we find an opposition
     between the small avant-garde firms, Pauvert, Maspero and Minuit (to
     which one could add Bourgeois, if it did not occupy a culturally and
     economically ambiguous position, because of its link with Les Presses de la
     Cité), and the 'big' publishers, Laffont, Presses de la Cité and Hachette, the
     intermediate positions being occupied by firms like Flammarion (where
     experimental series coexist with specially commissioned collective works),
     Albin Michel and Calmann-Lévy, old, 'traditional' publishing houses, run

by 'heirs' whose heritage is both a strength and a brake, and above all Grasset, once a 'great' publishing house, now absorbed by the Hachette empire, and Gallimard. a former avant-garde firm that has now attained the peak of consecration and combines back-list exploitation with long-term undertakings (which are only possible on the basis of accumulated cultural capital – le Chemin, Bibliothèque des sciences humaines). The sub-field of firms mainly oriented towards long-term production and towards an 'intellectual' readership is polarized around the opposition between Maspero and Minuit (which represents the avant-garde moving towards consecration) on the one side, and Gallimard, situated in the dominant position, with Le Seuil representing the neutral point in the field (just as Gallimard, whose authors feature both in the best-seller list and in the list of intellectual best-sellers, constitutes the neutral point of the whole field). The practical mastery of this structure, which also guides, for example, the founders of a newspaper when they 'feel there is an opening' or 'aim to fill a gap' left by the existing media, is seen at work in the rigorously topographical vision of a young publisher, Delorme, founder of Galilée, who was trying to fit in 'between Minuit, Maspero and Seuil' (quoted by J. Jossin, *L'Express*, 30 August 1976).

29   It is well known in the 'trade' that the head of one of the largest French publishing houses reads hardly any of the manuscripts he publishes and that his working day is devoted to purely managerial tasks (production committee meetings, meetings with lawyers, heads of subsidiaries, etc.).

30   In fact most of his professional actions are 'intellectual acts', analogous to the signature of literary or political manifestos or petitions (with some risks, as well – consider the publication of *La Question*), which earn him the usual gratifications of 'intellectuals' (intellectual prestige, interviews, radio discussions, etc.).

31   Robert Laffont recognizes this dependence when, in order to explain the declining ratio of translations to original works, he invokes, in addition to the increased advances payable for translation rights, 'the decisive influence of the media, especially television and radio, in promoting a book': 'The author's personality and eloquence are an important factor in these media's choices and consequently in access to the public. In this respect, foreign authors, with the exception of a few international celebrities, are naturally at a disadvantage' (*Vient de paraître* – Robert Laffont's monthly publicity bulletin – January 1977).

32   Here too, cultural logic and 'economic' logic converge. As the fate of Les Éditions du Pavois shows, a literary prize can be disastrous, from a strictly 'economic' point of view, for a young publishing house suddenly faced with the enormous investments required to reprint and distribute a prize-winning book.

33   This is seen particularly clearly in the theatre, where the classics market (the 'classical matinees' at the Comédie Française) obeys quite specific rules because of its dependence on the educational system.

34   The same opposition is found in all fields. André de Baecque describes the opposition he sees as characterizing the theatrical field, between the 'businesspeople' and the 'militants': 'Theatre managers are people of all sorts. They have one thing in common; with each new show, they put an investment of money and talent at risk on an unpredictable market. But the

similarity stops there. Their motivations spring from very different ideologies. For some, the theatre is a financial speculation like any other, more picturesque perhaps, but giving rise to the same cold-blooded strategy made up of the taking of options, calculated risks, liquidity problems, exclusive rights, sometimes negotiated internationally. For others, it is the vehicle of a message, or the tool of a mission. Sometimes a militant even does good business.'

35   Without going so far as to make failure a guarantee of quality, as the 'bourgeois' writer's polemical vision would have it: 'Nowadays, if you want to succeed, you need failures. Failure inspires confidence. Success is suspect' (Dorin, *Le Tournant*, p. 46).

36   'Oh dear! All I do is reproduce what I see and hear, just arranging it and adapting it. Just my luck! What I see is always attractive, what I hear is often funny, I live in luxury and champagne bubbles' (Dorin, *Le Tournant*, p. 27). There is no need to evoke reproductive painting, nowadays incarnated by the 'impressionists' who are known to supply the publishers specializing in reproductions of works of art with all their best-sellers (apart from the *Mona Lisa*): Renoir (*Girl with Flowers*, *Le Moulin de la Galette*, Van Gogh (*L'Église d'Auvers*), Monet (*Les Coquelicots*), Degas (*Ballet Rehearsal*), Gaugin (*Peasant Women*) (information supplied by the Louvre, 1973). In the literary field, there is the vast output of biographies, memoirs, diaries and testimonies, which, from Laffont to Lattès, from Nielsen to Orban, provide 'bourgeois' readers with alternative 'real-life' experiences.

37   In literature, as elsewhere, full-time producers (and, *a fortiori*, producers for producers) are far from having a monopoly of production. Out of 100 people in *Who's Who* who have produced literary works, more than a third are non-professionals (industrialists, 14 per cent; senior civil servants, 11 per cent; doctors, 7 per cent, etc.) and the proportion of part-time producers is even greater in the areas of political writing (45 per cent) and general writing (48 per cent).

38   Among the latter, one could also distinguish between those who have come into publishing with explicitly commercial aims, such as Jean-Claude Lattès (who started as a press attaché with Laffont and originally saw his project as a Laffont series, Édition spéciale) or Olivier Orban, both of whom went straight for commissioned stories, and those who have fallen back on 'pot-boilers' after various abortive projects, such as Guy Authier or Jean-Paul Mengès.

39   By the same logic, the discoverer-publisher is always liable to see his 'discoveries' seduced by richer or more consecrated publishers, who offer their name, their reputation, their influence on prize juries, and also publicity and better royalties.

40   As opposed to the Sonnabend gallery, which brings together young (the oldest is fifty) but already relatively recognized painters, and to the Durand-Ruel gallery, whose painters are almost all dead and famous, the Denise René gallery, which stands in that particular point in the space-time of the artistic field in which the normally incompatible profits of the avant-garde and of consecration are momentarily superimposed, combines a group of already strongly consecrated painters (abstract) with an avant-garde or rear avant-garde group (kinetic art) as if it had momentarily

managed to escape the dialectic of distinction which sweeps schools away into the past.

41  The analytical opposition between the two economies implies no value judgement, although in the ordinary struggles of artistic life it is only ever expressed in the form of value judgements and although despite all the efforts to distance and objectify, it is liable to be read in polemical terms. As I have shown elsewhere, the categories of perception and appreciation (e.g. obscure/clear or easy, deep/light, original/banal, etc.) which function in the world of art are oppositions that are almost universally applicable and are based, in the last analysis, through the opposition between rarity and divulgation or vulgarization, uniqueness and multiplicity, quality and quantity, on the social opposition between the 'elite' and the 'masses', between 'elite' (or 'quality') products and 'mass' products.

42  This effect is perfectly visible in *haute couture* or perfumery, where the consecrated establishments (e.g. Caron, Chanel and especially Guerlain) are able to keep going for several generations only by means of a policy aimed at artificially perpetuating the rarity of the product (e.g. the 'exclusive concessions' which limit sales outlets to a few places which are themselves chosen for their rarity – the great couturiers' own shops, perfume shops in the smartest districts, airports). Since ageing is here synonymous with vulgarization, the oldest brands (Coty, Lancôme, Worth, Molyneux, Bourjois, etc.) have a second career, down-market.

43  We may therefore formulate the hypothesis that acquisition of the social indices of maturity, which is both the condition and the effect of accession to positions of power, and abandonment of the practices associated with adolescent irresponsibility (to which cultural and even political 'avant-gardist' practices belong) have to be more and more precocious as one moves from the artists to the teachers, from the teachers to the members of the professions, and from the professions to the employers; or to put it another way, that the members of the same biological age group, e.g. all the students in the *grandes écoles*, have different social ages, marked by different symbolic attributes and conducts, according to the objective future they are heading for. The Beaux-Arts student has to be *younger* than the *normalien*, and the *normalien* has to be younger than the *Polytechnicien* or the student at the École Nationale d'Administration. One would have to apply the same logic in analysing the relationship between the sexes within the dominant fraction of the dominant class and more specifically the effects on the division of labour (especially in culture and art) of the dominated-dominant position assigned to women in the 'bourgeoisie' which brings them relatively closer to the young 'bourgeois' and the 'intellectuals', predisposing them to the role of *mediator between the dominant and dominated fractions* (which they have always played, particularly through the 'salon').

44  Academic criticism is condemned to interminable arguments about the definition and scope of these pseudo-concepts, which are generally no more than names which identify practical groupings such as the painters assembled in an outstanding exhibition or a consecrated gallery or the authors on the list of the same publisher (and which are worth neither more nor less than convenient associations such as 'Denise René is geometric abstract', 'Alexandre Iolas is Max Ernst' or, among the painters, 'Arman is

dustbins' or 'Christo is packages'); and many concepts in literary or artistic criticism are no more than a 'learned' designation of similar practical groupings (e.g. *littérature objectale* for *nouveau roman*, itself standing for 'all the novelists published by Éditions de Minuit').

45  Tastes can be 'dated', by reference to what was avant-garde taste in different periods: 'Photography is outdated.' 'Why?' 'Because it's gone out of fashion; because it's linked to the conceptual art of two or three years ago.' 'Who would say this: "When I look at a picture, I'm not interested in what it represents"?' 'Nowadays, people who don't know much about art. It's typical of someone who has no idea about art to say that. *Twenty years ago*, I don't even know if twenty years ago the abstract painters would have said that, I don't think so. It's the sort of person who doesn't know anything and who says, "You can't fool me, what counts is whether it's pretty" ' (avant-garde painter, age thirty-five).

46  Interview published in *VH 101*, 3 (Autumn 1970), pp. 55–61.

47  That is why it would be naïve to think that the relationship between the age and the degree of accessibility of works of art disappears when the logic of distinction leads to a (second-degree) return to an old mode of expression (e.g., at present, 'neo-dadaism', 'new realism' or 'hyper-realism').

48  This game of nudges and winks, which has to be played very fast and very 'naturally', even more mercilessly excludes the 'failure', who makes the same kind of moves as everybody else, but out of phase, usually too late, who falls into all the traps, a clumsy buffoon who ends up serving as a foil for those who make him their unwilling or unwitting accomplice; unless, finally understanding the rules of the game, he turns his status into a choice and makes systematic failure his artistic speciality. (*À propos* of a painter who perfectly illustrates this trajectory, another painter said admirably: 'Once he was just a bad painter who wanted to succeed, now he's doing work on a bad painter who wants to succeed. It's excellent.')

49  The next task would be to show the contribution the economy of works of art, as a limiting case in which the mechanisms of negation and their effects are more clearly seen (and not as an exception to the laws of economy), makes to the understanding of ordinary economic practices, in which the need to veil the naked truth of the transaction is also present to varying degrees (as is shown by the use made of a whole apparatus of symbolic agents).

## 3   THE MARKET OF SYMBOLIC GOODS

1  'Historically regarded,' observes Schücking, 'the publisher begins to play a part at the stage at which the patron disappears, in the eighteenth century' (with a transition period, in which the publisher was dependent on subscriptions, which in turn largely depended on relations between authors and their patrons). There is no uncertainty about this among the poets. And indeed, publishing firms such as Dodsley in England or Cotta in Germany gradually became a source of authority. Schücking shows, similarly, that the influence of theatre managers (*Dramaturgs*) can be even greater where, as in the case of Otto Brahm, 'an individual may help to

determine the general trend of taste' of an entire epoch through his choices. See L. L. Schücking, *The Sociology of Literary Taste*, trans. E. W. Dickes (London: Routledge and Kegan Paul, 1966), pp. 50–2.

2   Thus, Watt gives a good description of the correlative transformation of the modes of literary reception and production respectively, conferring its most specific characteristics on the novel and in particular the appearance of rapid, superficial, easily forgotten reading, as well as rapid and prolix writing, linked with the extension of the public. See I. Watt, *The Rise of the Novel: Studies in Defoe, Richardson and Fielding* (Harmondsworth: Penguin, 1957).

3   The adjective 'cultural' will be used from now on as shorthand for 'intellectual, artistic and scientific' (as in cultural consecration, legitimacy, production, value, etc.).

4   At a time when the influence of linguistic structuralism is leading some sociologists towards a pure theory of sociology, it would undoubtedly be useful to enrich the *sociology of pure theory*, sketched here, and to analyse the social conditions of the appearance of theories such as those of Kelsen, de Saussure or Walras, and of the formal and immanent science of art such as that proposed by Wölfflin. In this last case, one can see clearly that the very intention of extracting the formal properties of all possible artistic expression assumed that the process of autonomization and purification of the work of art and of artistic perception had already been effected.

5   Here, as elsewhere, the laws objectively governing social relations tend to constitute themselves as norms that are explicitly professed and assumed. In this way, as the field's autonomy grows, or as one moves towards the most autonomous sectors of the field, the direct introduction of external powers increasingly attracts disapproval; as the members of autonomous sectors consider such an introduction as a dereliction, they tend to sanction it by the symbolic exclusion of the guilty. This is shown, for instance, by the discredit attaching to any mode of thought which is suspected of reintroducing the total, brutal classificatory principles of a political order into intellectual life; and it is as if the field exercised its autonomy to the maximum, in order to render unknowable the external principles of opposition (especially the political ones) or, at least intellectually, to 'overdetermine' them by subordinating them to specifically intellectual principles.

6   'As for criticism, it hides under big words the explanations it no longer knows how to furnish. Remembering Albert Wolff, Bourde, Brunetière or France, the critic, for fear of failing, like his predecessors, to recognize artists of genius, no longer judges at all' (J. Lethève, *Impressionistes et symbolistes devant la presse* (Paris: Armand Colin, 1959), p. 276).

7   Jean-Paul Sartre, *Qu'est-ce que la littérature?* (Paris: Gallimard, 1948), p. 98.

8   In this sense, the intellectual field represents the almost complete model of a social universe knowing no principles of differentiation or hierarchization other than specifically symbolic distinctions.

9   It is the same, at least objectively (in the sense that no one is supposed to be ignorant of the cultural law), with any act of consumption which finds itself objectively within the field of application of the rules governing cultural practices with claims to legitimacy.

10    Thus Proudhon, whose aesthetic writings all clearly express the petit-bourgeois representation of art and the artist, imputes the process of dissimilation generated from the intellectual field's internal logic to a cynical choice on the part of artists: 'On the one hand, artists will do anything, because everything is indifferent to them; on the other, they become infinitely specialized. Delivered up to themselves, without a guiding light, without compass, obedient to an inappropriately applied industrial law, they class themselves into genera and species, firstly according to the nature of commissions, and subsequently according to the method distinguishing them. Thus, there are church painters, historical painters, painters of battles, genre painters – that is, of anecdotes and comedy, portrait painters, landscape painters, animal painters, marine artists, painters of Venus, fantasy painters. This one cultivates the nude, another cloth. Then, each of them labours to distinguish himself by one of the competing methods of execution. One of them applies himself to drawing, the other to colour; this one cares for composition, that one for perspective, yet another for costume or local colour; this one shines through sentiment, another through the idealism or the realism of his figures; still another makes up for the nullity of his subjects by the finesse of his details. Each one labours to develop his trick, his style, his manner and, with the help of fashion, reputations are made and unmade' (P. J. Proudhon, *Contradictions économiques* (Paris: Rivière, 1939), p. 271).

11    The emergence of the theory of art which, rejecting the classical conception of artistic production as the simple execution of a pre-existent internal model, turns artistic 'creation' into a sort of apparition that was unforeseeable for the artist himself – inspiration, genius, etc. – undoubtedly assumed the completion of the transformation of the social relations of production which, freeing artistic production from the directly and explicitly formulated order, permitted the conception of artistic labour as autonomous 'creation', and no longer as mere execution.

12    E. Delacroix, *Oeuvres littéraires*, vol. 1 (Paris: Crès, 1923), p. 76.

13    It can be seen that the history leading up to what has been called a 'denovelization' of the novel obeys the same type of logic.

14    'As long as the opportunities on the art market remain favourable for the artist, the cultivation of individuality does not develop into a mania for originality – this does not happen until the age of mannerism, when new conditions on the art market create painful economic disturbances for the artist' (A. Hauser, *The Social History of Art*, vol. 2, trans. S. Godman (New York: Vintage, 1951), p. 71).

15    See J. Greenway, *Literature among the Primitives* (Hatboro: Folklore Associates, 1964), p. 37. On primitive art as a total and multiple art, produced by the group as a whole and addressed to the group as a whole, see also R. Firth, *Elements of Social Organization* (Boston: Beacon, 1963), pp. 155ff; H. Junod, *The Life of a South American Tribe* (London: Macmillan, 1927), p. 215; and B. Malinowski, *Myth in Primitive Psychology* (New York: W. W. Norton, 1926), p. 31. On the transformation of the function and significance of the dance and festivals see J. Caro Baroja, 'El ritual de la danza en el Paris Vasco', *Revista de Dialectologa y Tradiciones Populares*, 20; 1–2 (1964).

16 For an analysis of the function of the educational system in the production of consumers endowed with a propensity and aptitude to consume learned works and in the reproduction of the unequal distribution of this propensity and this aptitude, and, hence, of the *differential rarity* and the *distinctive value* of these works, see P. Bourdieu and A. Darbel, with Dominique Schnapper, *L'amour de l'art. Les musées d'art européens et leur public* (Paris: Minuit, 1969), published in English as *The Love of Art: European Art Museums and their Public*, trans. Caroline Beattie and Nick Merriman (Cambridge: Polity; Stanford: Stanford University Press, 1990).

17 The education system fulfils a culturally legitimizing function by reproducing, via the delimitation of what deserves to be conserved, transmitted and acquired, the distinction between the legitimate and the illegitimate way of dealing with legitimate works. The different sectors of the field of restricted production are very markedly distinguished by the degree to which they depend, for their reproduction, on generic institutions (such as the educational system), or on specific ones (such as the École des Beaux Arts, or the Conservatoire de Musique). Everything points to the fact that the proportion of contemporary producers having received an academic education is far smaller among painters (especially among the more avant-garde currents) than among musicians.

18 All forms of recognition – prizes, rewards and honours, election to an academy, a university, a scientific committee, invitation to a congress or to a university, publication in a scientific review or by a consecrated publishing house, in anthologies, mentions in the work of contemporaries, works on art history or the history of science, in encyclopedias and dictionaries, etc. – are just so many forms of *co-optation*, whose value depends on the very position of the co-optants in the hierarchy of consecration.

19 C. A. Sainte-Beuve, 'L'Académie Française', in *Paris-Guide, par les principaux écrivains et artistes de la France* (Paris: A. Lacroix, Verboeckhoven et Cie, 1867), pp. 96–7.

20 This academy, which accumulated the monopoly of the consecration of creators, of the transmission of consecrated works and traditions and even of production and the control of production, wielded, at the time of Le Brun, 'a sovereign and universal supremacy over the world of art. For him [Le Brun], everything stopped at these two points: prohibition from teaching elsewhere than in the Academy; prohibition from practising without being of the Academy.' Thus, 'this sovereign company . . . possessed, during a quarter of a century, the exclusive privilege of carrying out all painting and sculpture ordered by the state and alone to direct, from one end of the kingdom to the other, the teaching of drawing: in Paris, in its own schools, outside of Paris, in subordinate schools, branch academies founded by it, placed under its direction, subject to its surveillance. Never had such a unified and concentrated system been applied, anywhere, to the production of the beautiful' (L. Vitet, *L'Académie royale de Peinture et de Sculpture, Étude historique* (Paris: 1861), pp. 134, 176).

21 The same systematic opposition can be seen in very different fields of artistic and intellectual activity: between researchers and teachers, for example, or between writers and teachers in higher education and, above

all, between painters and musicians on the one hand, and teachers of drawing and music on the other.

22  Where common and semi-scholarly discourse sees a homogeneous message producing a homogenized public ('massification'), it is necessary to see an undifferentiated message produced *for* a socially undifferentiated public at the cost of a methodical self-censorship leading to the abolition of all signs and factors of differentiation. To the most amorphous messages (e.g. large-circulation daily and weekly newspapers) there corresponds the most socially amorphous public.

23  See *Télé-Sept-Jours*, 547 (October 1970), p. 45.

24  In this, the strategy of producers of middle-brow art is radically opposed to the spontaneous strategy of the institutions for the diffusion of restricted art who, as we can see in the case of museums, aim at intensifying the practice of the classes from which consumers are recruited rather than at attracting new classes.

25  B. Poirot-Delpech, *Le Monde*, 22 July 1970.

26  The educational system contributes very substantially to the unification of the market in symbolic goods, and to the generalized imposition of the legitimacy of the dominant culture, not only by legitimizing the goods consumed by the dominant class, but by devaluing those transmitted by the dominated classes (and, also, regional traditions) and by tending, in consequence, to prohibit the constitution of cultural counter-legitimacies.

27  The attempt to gain rehabilitation leads those at the forefront of the revolt against the university's conservative traditions (as well as those of the academies) to betray their recognition of academic legitimacy in the very discourse attempting to challenge it. One sociologist, for instance, argues that the leisure practices he intends to rehabilitate are genuinely cultural because they are 'disinterested', hence reintroducing an academic, and mundane, definition of the cultivated relationship to culture, and writes: 'We think that certain works said, today, to be minor, in fact reveal qualities of the first order; it seems barely acceptable to place the entire repertoire of French songs on a low level, as does Shils with American songs. The works of Brassens, Jacques Brel and Léo Ferré, all of which are highly successful, are not just songs from a variety show. All three are also, quite rightly, considered as poets.'

28  If these analyses can equally obviously be applied to certain categories of avant-garde art critics, it is because the position of the least consecrated agents of a more consecrated field may present certain analogies with the position of the most consecrated agents of a less consecrated field.

29  Cited by A. Breton, *Anthologie de l'humour noir* (Paris: J. J. Pauvert, 1966), p. 324.

30  More generally, if the occupants of a determinate position in the social structure only rarely do what the occupants of a different position think they ought to do ('if I were in his place . . .'), it is because the latter project the position-takings inscribed into their own position into a position which excludes them. The theory of relations between positions and position-takings reveals the basis of all those errors of perspective, to which all attempts at abolishing the differences associated with differences in position by means of a simple imaginary projection, or by an effort of 'comprehension' (behind which always lies the principle of 'putting oneself

in someone else's place'), or again, attempts at transforming the objective relations between agents by transforming the representations they have of these relations, are inevitably exposed.

31 *La Quinzaine littéraire*, 15 September 1966.

32 E. Lalou, *L'Express*, 26 October 1966.

33 The development of psychology in Germany at the end of the nineteenth century can be explained by the state of the university market, favouring the movement of physiology students and teachers towards other fields, and by the relatively lowly position occupied by philosophy in the academic field, which made it a dream ground for the innovative enterprises of deserters from the higher disciplines. See J. Ben-David and R. Collins, 'Social Factors in the Origins of a New Science: The Case of Psychology', *American Sociological Review*, 31:4 (August 1966), pp. 451–65.

34 Short-term movements in the cultural value stock market ought not to obscure the constants, such as the domination of the most theoretical discipline over those more practically oriented.

35 We should pay particular attention to the strategies employed in relation to groups occupying a neighbouring position in the field. The law of the search for distinction explains the apparent paradox which has it that the fiercest and most fundamental conflicts oppose each group to its immediate neighbours, for it is these who most directly threaten its identity, hence its *distinction* and even its specifically cultural existence.

36 J. S. Cloyd and A. P. Bates, 'George Homas in Footnotes: The Fate of Ideas in Scholarly Communication', *Sociological Inquiry*, 34:2 (1964), pp. 115–28 at p. 122.

37 J. Piaget, *Introduction à l'épistémologie génétique*, vol. 3 (Paris: Presses Universitaires de France, 1950), p. 239.

4   IS THE STRUCTURE OF *SENTIMENTAL EDUCATION*
AN INSTANCE OF SOCIAL SELF-ANALYSIS?

1 '*Sentimental Education* is a novel of coincidences that the characters passively observe, as if incredulous and wide-eyed before their dances of destiny' ('Le rôle du hasard dans l'*Éducation sentimentale*', *Europe*, September–November 1969), pp. 101–7.

2 V. Brombert, '*L'Éducation sentimentale*: articulations et polyvalence', in C. Gothot-Mersch, ed., *La production du sens chez Flaubert* (Paris Union générale d'éditions, series 10–18), pp. 55–69.

3 See P. Bourdieu, 'L'invention de la vie d'artiste', *Actes de la recherche en sciences sociales*, 2 (1975), pp. 67–93. An abbreviated English translation of this essay appeared as 'The Invention of the Artist's Life', trans. Erec R. Koch, *Yale French Studies*, 73 (1987), pp. 75–103.

4 Jean-Pierre Richard, for example, draws a psychological portrait of Flaubert that would suit Frédéric perfectly: Flaubert, that 'false giant . . . riddled with internal frailties', felt himself ceaselessly threatened by feelings of a lack of differentiation and by a possible fall into indistinction; incapable of heroic identification, he felt himself carried away by the

weight of failure that drags every effort, every, flight downward. J.-P. Richard, 'La création de la forme chez Flaubert', in *Littérature et sensation* (Paris: Seuil, 1954).

## 5 FIELD OF POWER, LITERARY FIELD AND HABITUS

1 See A. Cassagne, *La Théorie de l'art pour l'art en France, chez les derniers romantiques et les premiers réalistes* (Paris: 1906; Genève: Slatkine Reprints, 1979), pp. 115–18.
2 J.-P. Sartre, 'La conscience de classe chez Flaubert', *Les temps modernes*, 240 (May 1966), pp. 1921–51, and 241 (June 1966), pp. 2113–35. Citation from p. 1933.
3 Ibid., p. 1949.
4 Ibid., pp. 1943–4.
5 Cassagne, *La Théorie de l'art pour l'art*, p. 139.
6 *Novembre* (Paris: Charpentier, 1886), p. 329.

## 6 PRINCIPLES FOR A SOCIOLOGY OF CULTURAL WORKS

1 P. Bourdieu, *Homo Academicus*, trans. Peter Collier (Cambridge: Polity; Stanford: Stanford University Press, 1988), pp. 115–18.
2 I refer here to a text which is without doubt the clearest expression of the theoretical presuppositions of Foucault's work: 'Réponse au cercle d'épistémologie', *Cahiers pour l'analyse*, 9 (Summer 1968), pp. 9–40, esp. p. 40.

## 7 FLAUBERT'S POINT OF VIEW

1 R. Wellek and A. Warren, *Theory of Literature* (New York: Harcourt, Brace & World, 1956), p. 69.
2 J.-P. Sartre, 'La Conscience de classe chez Flaubert', *Les Temps modernes*, 240 (May 1966), pp. 1922–51.
3 Their number increased significantly during the first half of the nineteenth century all over Europe and again in France during the Second Empire (1852–70). See L. O'Boyle, 'The Problem of Excess of Educated Men in Western Europe, 1800–1850', *Journal of Modern History*, 42 (December 1970), pp. 471–95, and 'The Democratic Left in Germany, 1848', *Journal of Modern History*, 33 (December 1961), pp. 374–83.
4 Alexandre Dumas, preface to *Le Fils naturel* (Paris, 1894), p. 31.
5 G. Flaubert, *Correspondance*, ed. Jean Bruneau, 2 vols (Paris: Gallimard, 1980), vol. 2, pp. 643–4; further references to this work, abbreviated *CP*, are given in the text.
6 *Oeuvres complètes de Gustave Flaubert: Correspondance, nouvelle édition augmentée*, 14 vols (Paris: L. Conard, 1926–54), vol. 5, p. 300; further references to this work, abbreviated *CC*, are given in the text.

7   E. and J. de Goncourt, preface to *Germinie Lacerteux* (Naples: Edizioni scientifiche italiane, 1968), p. 2.

8   Luc Badesco, *La Génération poétique de 1860 – La Jeunesse des deux rives*, 2 vols (Paris: A.-G. Nizet, 1971), vol. 1, pp. 304–6.

9   Gustave Merlet, 'Un Réaliste imaginaire: M. Henry Murger', *Revue européenne*, 8 (1 March 1860), p. 35, cited by Bernard Weinberg, *French Realism: The Critical Reaction, 1830–1870* (New York: Oxford University Press, 1947), p. 133.

10  Cited in René Descharmes and René Dumesnil, *Autour de Flaubert*, 2 vols (Paris: Mercure de France, 1912), vol. 2, p. 48.

## 8   OUTLINE OF A SOCIOLOGICAL THEORY OF ART PERCEPTION

1   E. Panofsky, 'Iconography and Iconology: An Introduction to the Study of Renaissance Art', *Meaning in the Visual Arts* (New York: Doubleday, 1955), pp. 33–5.

2   E. Panofsky, 'Die Perspektive als symbolische Form', *Vorträge der Bibliothek Warburg: Vorträge 1924–25*, pp. 257ff.

3   Of all misunderstandings involving the code, the most pernicious is perhaps the 'humanist' misunderstanding, which, through negation, or rather, 'neutralization', in the phenomenological sense, of everything which contributes to the specificity of the cultures arbitrarily integrated into the pantheon of 'universal culture', tends to represent the Greek or the Roman as a particularly successful achievement of 'human nature' in its universality.

4   This is the same ethnocentrism which tends to take as realistic a representation of the real which owes the fact that it appears 'objective' not to its concordance with the actual reality of things (because this 'reality' is never perceptible except through socially conditioned forms of apprehension) but to its conformity with rules which define its syntax in its social usage with a social definition of the objective vision of the world; in applying the stamp of realism to certain representations of the 'real' (in photography, for instance) society merely confirms its belief in the tautological assurance that a picture of the real, in accordance with its representation of objectivity, is truly objective.

5   Panofsky, 'The History of Art as Humanistic Discipline', *Meaning in the Visual Arts*, p. 17.

6   These quotations are taken from two articles published in German: 'Über das Verhältnis der Kunstgeschichte zur Kunsttheorie', *Zeitschrift für Aesthetik und allgemeine Kunstwissenschaft*, 18 (1925), pp. 129ff; and 'Zum Problem der Beschreibung und Inhaltsdeutung von Werken der bildenden Kunst', *Logos*, 21 (1932), pp. 103. The articles were republished, with a few amendments, in 'Iconography and Iconology', pp. 26–54.

7   The laws governing the reception of works of art are a special case of the laws of cultural diffusion: whatever may be the nature of the message – religious prophecy, political speech, publicity image, technical object – reception depends on the categories of perception, thought and action of those who receive it. In a differentiated society, a close relationship is therefore established between the nature and quality of the information

transmitted and the structure of the public, its 'readability' and its effectiveness being all the greater when it meets as directly as possible the expectations, implicit or explicit, which the receivers owe chiefly to their family upbringing and social circumstances (and also, in the matter of scholarly culture at least, to their school education) and which the diffuse pressure of the reference group maintains, sustains and reinforces by constant recourse to the norm. It is on the basis of this connection between the level of transmission of the message and the structure of the public, treated as a reception level indicator, that it has been possible to construct the mathematical model of museum-going (see P. Bourdieu and A. Darbel, with D. Schnapper, *L'amour de l'art, Les musées d'art et leur public* (Paris, Minuit, 1966), pp. 99ff; published in English as *The Love of Art: European Museums and their Public*, trans. C. Beattie and N. Merriman (Cambridge: Polity; Stanford: Stanford University Press, 1990)).

8   To show that such a sequence really is the logic of the transmission of messages in everyday life, it suffices to quote the following exchange heard in a bar: 'A beer.' 'Draught or bottled?' 'Draught.' 'Mild or bitter?' 'Bitter.' 'Domestic or imported?' 'Domestic.'

9   More than through opinions expressed on works of scholarly culture, paintings and sculptures, for example, which, by their high degree of legitimacy, are capable of imposing judgements inspired by the search for conformity, it is through photographic production and judgements on photographic images that the principles of the 'popular taste' are expressed (see P. Bourdieu, *Un art moyen, Essai sur les usages sociaux de la photographie* (Paris: Minuit, 1965), pp. 113–34; published in English as *Photography: A Middle-Brow Art*, trans. S. Whiteside (Cambridge: Polity; Stanford: Stanford University Press, 1990)).

10   R. Longhi, quoted by Berne Joffroy, *Le dossier Caravage* (Paris: Minuit, 1959), pp. 100–1.

11   Joffroy, *Le dossier Caravage*, p. 9. A systematic study should be made of the relationship between the transformation of the instruments of perception and the transformation of the instruments of art production, because the evolution of the public image of past works is indissociably linked with the evolution of art. As Lionello Venturi remarks, it was by starting with Michelangelo that Vasari discovered Giotto, and by starting with Caracci and Poussin that Belloni rethought Raphael.

12   B. de Schloezer, 'Introduction à J. S. Bach', *Essai d'esthétique musicale* (Paris: Nouvelle revue française, 1947), p. 37.

13   Needless to say, the level of emission cannot be defined absolutely, because the same work may express significations of different levels according to the interpretive grid applied to it (cf. 2.1.1): just as the Western movie may be the subject of the naïve attachment of simple aesthesis (cf. 2.1.3) or of scholarly reading, coupled with a knowledge of the traditions and rules of the genre, so the same pictorial work offers significations of different levels and may, for instance, satisfy an interest in anecdotes or the informative content (especially historical) or retain attention by its formal qualities alone.

14   This holds good for any cultural training, art form, scientific theory or political theory, the former habitus being able to survive a revolution of

social codes and even of the social conditions for the production of these codes for a long time.

15 F. Boas, *Anthropology and Modern Life* (New York: Norton, 1962), p. 196.

16 A study of the characteristics of visitors to European museums shows that the museums which offer modern works of art have the highest level of emission, and therefore the most educated visitors (see Bourdieu and Darbel, *L'amour de l'art*).

17 See P. Bourdieu, 'Champ intellectuel et projet createur', *Les temps modernes* (November 1966), pp. 865–905; published in English as 'Intellectual Field and Creative Project', trans. S. France, *Social Science Information*, 8:2 (1968); also in Michael F. D. Young, ed., *Knowledge and Control* (London: Collier Macmillan, 1971), pp. 161–88.

18 School instruction always fulfils a function of legitimation, if only by giving its blessing to works which it sets up as worthy of being admired, and thus helps to define the hierarchy of cultural goods valid in a particular society at a given time. Concerning the hierarchy of cultural goods and degrees of legitimacy, see Bourdieu, *Un art moyen*, pp. 134–8.

19 L. S. Vygotsky has established experimentally the validity of the general laws governing the transfer of training in the field of educational aptitudes: 'The psychological prerequisites for instruction in different school subjects are to a large extent the same: instruction in a given subject influences the development of the higher functions far beyond the confines of that particular subject; the main psychic functions involved in studying various subjects are interdependent – their common bases are consciousness and deliberate mastery, the principal contribution of the school years' (L. S. Vygotsky, *Thought and Language*, trans. E. Hanfmann and G. Vakar (Cambridge, Mass.: MIT Press, 1962), p. 102).

20 A criticism of the ideology of the 'unevennesses' of taste and knowledge in the different art fields (music, painting, etc.) and of the widespread myth of the 'cultural breakthrough' (according to which, for instance, an individual would be able, in the absence of any pictorial culture, to produce works of art in photography), all representations which combine to strengthen the ideology of the gift, will be found in Bourdieu, *Un art moyen*, part 1.

21 This is true, in fact, of any education. Taking the native tongue, for instance, it is known that logical structures, more or less complex according to the complexity of the language used in the family circle, and acquired unconsciously, provide an unequal predisposition to the deciphering and handling of structures involved in a mathematical demonstration as well as in the comprehension of a work of art.

22 See Bourdieu and Darbel, *L'amour de l'art*, p. 90.

23 Belonging to a social group characterized by a high rate of practice helps to maintain, sustain and strengthen the cultivated disposition; but the diffuse pressures and encouragements of the reference group are more keenly felt when the disposition to receive them (linked with art competence) is greater. (On the effect of exhibitions and tourism, more strongly inserted into collective rhythms than the ordinary visit to the museums, and consequently more likely to recall the diffuse norms of practice to those who have the highest cultural ambitions, that is to say to those who belong

or who aspire to belong to the cultivated class, see Bourdieu and Darbel, *L'amour de l'art*, pp. 51 and 115–19.) Thus, for instance, if the majority of students display a kind of cultural bulimia, it is because the stimulation to practise exerted by the reference group is, in this case, particularly strong, and also – above all – because admittance to higher education marks their entrance into the cultivated world, and therefore their access to the right, and what amounts to the same thing, to the duty, to appropriate culture.

24 See P. Bourdieu and J. C. Passeron, *Les étudiants et leurs études* (Paris, The Hague: Mouton, 1964), pp. 96–7 (Cahiers du Centre de Sociologie Europeénne, no. 1).

25 It is the same autonomization of 'needs' or 'propensities' in relation to the social conditions underlying their production which leads some people to describe as 'cultural needs' the opinions or the preferences actually expressed and actually established by surveys of cultural opinion or accomplishment and, in the absence of a statement or a denunciation of the cause, to sanction the division of society into those who feel 'cultural needs' and those who are deprived of this deprivation.

26 It was understood thus by a very cultivated old man who declared during a conversation: 'Education, Sir, is inborn.'

27 See P. Bourdieu, 'L'école conservatrice', *Revue française de sociologie*, 7 (1966), pp. 325–47, and esp. pp. 346–7.

28 It is impossible to show here that the dialectics of divulgence and distinction are one of the driving forces for the change of patterns of artistic consumption, the distinguished classes being constantly driven by the divulgence of their distinctive qualities to seek elements of distinction in new forms of symbolic consumption (cf. Bourdieu, *Un art moyen*, pp. 73ff, and 'Condition de classe et position de classe', *Archives europeénnes de sociologie*, 7 (1966), pp. 201–23).

29 It is not infrequent that working-class visitors explicitly express the feeling of exclusion which, in any case, is evident in their whole behaviour. Thus, they sometimes see in the absence of any indication which might facilitate the visit – arrows showing the direction to follow, explanatory panels, etc. – the signs of a deliberate intention to exclude the uninitiated. The provision of teaching and didactic aids would not, in fact, really make up for the lack of schooling, but it would at least proclaim the right not to know, the right to be there in ignorance, the right of the ignorant to be there, a right which everything in the presentation of works and in the organization of the museum combines to challenge, as this remark overheard in the Chateau of Versailles testifies: 'This chateau was not made for the people, and it has not changed.'

30 E. Durkheim, *Les formes élémentaires de la vie religieuse*, 6th edn (Paris: Presses Universitaires de France, 1960), pp. 55–6. The holding of a Danish exhibition showing modern furniture and utensils in the old ceramic rooms of the Lille museum brought about such a 'conversion' in the visitors as can be summarized in the following contrasts, the very ones which exist between a department store and a museum: noise/silence; touch/see; quick, haphazard exploration, in no particular order/leisurely; methodical inspection, according to a fixed arrangement; freedom/ constraint; economic assessment of works which may be purchased/aesthetic appreciation of 'priceless' works. However, despite these differences, bound up with the

things exhibited, the solemnizing (and distancing) effect of the museum no less continued to be felt, contrary to expectations, for the structure of the public at the Danish exhibition was more 'aristocratic' (in respect of level of education) than the ordinary public of the museum. The mere fact that works are consecrated by being exhibited in a consecrated place is sufficient, in itself, profoundly to change their signification and, more precisely, to raise the level of their emission; were they presented in a more familiar place, a large emporium for instance, they would be more accessible (cf. Bourdieu and Darbel, *L'amour de l'art*, pp. 73–4 and 118).

31 For this reason care should be taken not to attach undue importance to the differences of pure form between the expressions 'aristocratic' and 'democratic', 'patrician' and 'paternalistic' in this ideology.

32 In the field of education, the ideology of the gift fulfils the same functions of camouflage: it enables an institution, such as literary education in France, which provides an 'awakening education', to borrow from Max Weber, assuming between the teacher and the pupil a community of values and culture which occurs only when the system is dealing with its own heirs to conceal its real function, namely, that of confirming and consequently legitimizing the right of the heirs to the cultural inheritance.

## 9  MANET AND THE INSTITUTIONALIZATION OF ANOMIE

1 This text is a chapter in a forthcoming book on Manet and the Impressionists.

2 On the genesis of David's style, see R. Rosenblum, 'La peinture sous le Consulat et l'Empire', in *De David à Delacroix, la Peinture française de 1774 à 1830* (Paris: Éditions des musées nationaux, 1974), p. 165. One could also cite Frederick Cummings, who presents David's teachings in this manner: 'He would recommend that his students use, preferentially, a *broad* composition in which full sized figures would be modelled in relief and grouped in *the same plane*; these *simplified* compositions should preserve only *the essential elements*; each object should be defined by a *color scheme of its own . . .*, its *contours* being respected in their full integrity. The search for historical *accuracy* was deemed a prime necessity' (Rosenblum, *De David à Delacroix*, p. 41, emphasis added).

3 See F. Haskell, *Rediscoveries in Art: Some Aspects of Taste, Fashion and Collections in England and France* (London: Phaidon, 1976), pp. 61–83.

4 See M. Fried, *Absorption and Theatricality: Painting and Beholder in the Age of Diderot* (Berkeley: University of California Press, 1980).

5 See P. Bourdieu, 'Épreuve scolaire et consécration sociale, les classes préparatoires aux grandes écoles', *Actes de la recherche en sciences sociales*, 39 (September 1981), pp. 3–70.

6 See J. Thuillier, 'L'artiste et l'institution: l'École des Beaux-Arts et le Prix de Rome', in Philippe Grundec, *Le Grand Prix de Peinture, les Concours du Prix de Rome de 1797 à 1863* (Paris: École Nationale Supérieure des Beaux-Arts, 1983), pp. 55–85; 'Peut-on parler d'une peinture pompier?' (Paris: Presses Universitaires de France, Essais et Conférences du Collège de France, 1984).

7  J. Lethève, *La vie quotidienne des artistes français au 19e siècle* (Paris: Hachette, 1968), p. 132.
8  Ateliers – as total institutions imposing disciplines, ordeals, and even vexations whose vulgarity or even brutality is attested by all witnesses – demand from newcomers specific dispositions and in particular a special form of docility. This undoubtedly helps explain, as has often been noted, why young artists from wealthy families would avoid the academic career, as in the cases of Géricault, Delacroix, Degas, Gustave Moreau and Manet.
9  It is remarkable that Courbet, in contrast, had tried for two months to run a studio, while at the same time refusing to give lessons, before abandoning it, and that no Impressionists became teachers. See J. Harding, *Les Peintres pompiers. La Peinture académique en France de 1830 à 1880* (Paris: Flammarion, 1980), p. 22.
10  'Each submission to the 1842 Salon . . . should be accompanied by a note bearing the artist's surname, first name, address, date and place of birth, indicating as well who is or was his master' (Lethève, *La vie quotidienne des artistes français*), p. 54.
11  The truth of this scholastic art, which is also a state art, is expressed fully in the realm of architecture: public architecture is considered the most noble and universal, and the Grand Prix programmes are always concerned with buildings with a public or national purpose – as if private buildings did not have a sufficient scale to test the candidates' abilities. The academicians are state employees who assign themselves the responsibility for the conception of public buildings. 'The members of the Académie, largely through their influence over the École des Beaux-Arts and their control of the Grand Prix competition, sought to maintain a monopoly over all national and public architecture in France in addition to carrying on private practice' (D. D. Egbert, *The Beaux-Arts Tradition in French Architecture, Illustrated by the Grand Prix de Rome* (Princeton: Princeton University Press, 1980), p. 140).
12  P. Angrand, *Monsieur Ingres et son époque* (Paris: La Bibliothèque des Arts, 1967), p. 69.
13  H. C. and C. A. White, *Canvases and Careers: Institutional Change in the French Painting World* (New York, Sydney: 1965), p. 43.
14  J. C. Sloane, *French Painting between the Past and the Present: Artists, Critics and Traditions, from 1848 to 1870* (Princeton: Princeton University Press, 1951), p. 43. Even if the academic institution is endowed with relative autonomy in relation to the government, it is perceived to be a part of official authority. Thus everyone (except Louis Peisse of the *Revue des deux mondes*) agrees to censure Ingres when, in 1841, he refuses to exhibit at the Salon: 'To refuse to exhibit alongside one's contemporaries, is to cut oneself off from national art' (A. Tabarant, *La Vie artistique au temps de Baudelaire* (Paris: Mercure de France, 1963), p. 55).
15  The search for stylistic invariants linked to the academic mode of production – which could also be applied to the writers, historians or philosophers on whom the academic institution had left its deepest marks (like the slightly ostentatious 'fine writing' of past and present authors such as Giraudoux, Alain or Lucien Febvre) – also finds perfect equivalents of Gérôme and Bouguereau in insignificant musicians with uneventful careers such as Hérold or Ambroise Thomas: of the latter, 'a pupil of Lesueur and

successor of A. Adam at the Institute, one could say he was a sage, meaning everything such a word can imply such as *very prudent*, a *voice of authority*, possessing *useful knowledge*, and guided by *moderation*. While alive, he was already a man of the past, while all around him art was being renewed with great boldness . . . the Institute formed a judgement on his submissions from Rome which one would not change, even if one wanted to apply it to his entire work: an *original but not eccentric melody*, and *expressive without exaggeration*; an *always correct* harmony, instrumentation written with *elegance* and purity' (J. Combarieu and R. Dumesnil, *Histoire de la musique*, vol. 3 (Paris: A. Colin, 1955), pp. 467–8). One could not conceive of a better definition of *academica mediocritas*. See, in the same book, the description of prize-winning cantatas written for competitions in musical composition. These were remarkable mostly for their extraordinary discretion (pp. 244–5).

16  Harding, *Les Peintres pompiers*, p. 9.
17  Lethève, *La Vie quotidienne des artistes français*, p. 184.
18  Ibid., p. 145.
19  Ibid., pp. 146–9.
20  One can find these features in the field of decoration or furniture with, for example, the objects presented in the Crystal Palace in 1851, in particular a carpet which combined the illusionism of relief, appropriate in creating depth, with stylization, instead of respecting the flatness of the surface. See N. Pevsner, *Pioneers of Modern Design, from William Morris to Walter Gropius* (Harmondsworth, Middlesex: Penguin, 1960; first published London: Faber, 1936).
21  See J. R. Levenson, *Modern China and its Confucian Past* (New York: Doubleday and Co., 1964; first published 1958).
22  Decamps, quoted by G. Cougny, 'Le dessin à l'école maternelle', no. 1, pp. 30–1.
23  A. Boime, *The Academy and French Painting in the Nineteenth Century* (London: Phaidon, 1971).
24  Sloane, *French Painting*, p. 4.
25  The metaphor of reading, which has experienced a revival in the university with semiotics, corresponds perfectly to the academic vision of the professor as *lector* (as *lecturer* and reader). It represents the absolute antithesis of the point of view of the Impressionists, and particularly that of Monet, for whom artistic perception was sensation and emotion.
26  The ateliers would recommend Pierre Chompré's classic book, *Le Dictionnaire abrégé de la fable pour l'intelligence des poètes et la connaissance des tableaux et des statues dont les sujets sont tirés de la fable*, re-edited twenty-eight times between 1727 and 1855; the painter could not work without first having brought together extensive documentation which, in the case of those such as Paul Baudry or Meissonier, rivalled the historians in precision and scrupulous regard for accuracy. See Lethève, *La Vie quotidienne des artistes français*, p. 20.
27  With regard to a painting by Robert Fleury, *Varsovie, le 8 avril 1861*, which shows the slaughter of Poles by Russians, Théophile Gautier objects: 'This is a difficult subject to deal with because of its very contemporaneity. Events need the distance of history before they can easily enter into the sphere of art' (Tabarant, *La vie artistique*, p. 380).

28    M. Baxandall, 'Jacques-Louis David et les Romantiques allemands', un-published communication, Paris, 1985.
29    On scholarly perversion of the academic eros, see Luc Boltanski's 'Pouvoir et impuissance: projet intellectuel et sexualité dans le journal d'Amiel', *Actes de la recherche en sciences sociales*, 5–6 (November 1975), pp. 80–108, esp. p. 97.
30    Orientalism thus appears as much an aesthetic solution to an aesthetic problem as the product of a specific interest in Middle Eastern countries (an interest which owes much to the literary tradition of journeys to the Orient).
31    The followers of Ingres will be the main beneficiaries of the blessing given from 1841 onwards to religious painting dedicated to the glorification of the current monarchy and Christian virtues (see Angrand, *Monsieur Ingres et son époque*, p. 201).
32    Quoted by Tabarant, *La vie artistique*, pp. 145–302.
33    G. H. Hamilton, *Manet and his Critics* (New Haven: Yale University Press, 1954), p. 72. We do not take into account here the differences in the critics' reactions, which should be related to the differences of positions held in the field of criticism (such as they are revealed through the characteristics of sites of publication – newspapers or weeklies – and of the critics themselves). Everything, and in particular the composition of groups bringing together artists and critics sharing the same convictions, leads one to think that the homology between the space of critics and the space of artists is almost perfect (cf. *French Painting*).
34    J. Lethève, *Impressionistes et Symbolistes devant la presse* (Paris: A. Colin, 1959), p. 53.
35    Hamilton, *Manet and his Critics*, p. 139.
36    Ibid., p. 191; also Lethève, *Impressionistes et Symbolistes*, p. 73.
37    Hamilton, *Manet and his Critics*, p. 196.
38    Ibid., p. 198.
39    S. Mallarmé, 'Le jury de peinture pour 1874 et M. Manet', *Oeuvres complètes* (Paris: Gallimard (La Pléiade), 1974), p. 698.
40    Sloane, *French Painters*, p. 103.
41    Boime, *The Academy and French Painting*, pp. 166ff ('The Aesthetics of the Sketch').
42    Ibid., p. 24.
43    C. Blanc, 'Les artistes de mon temps', p. 108, cited by Lethève, *La Vie quotidienne des artistes français*, p. 20.
44    Couture, whose relative freedom from the Academy often enabled him to undertake research close to that of the independent artists, particularly regarding attention to impression – especially when dealing with landscape or portraiture – was never able 'to abandon himself entirely to improvisation in definitive works, and he was always hindered by an urge to moralize' (A. Boime, *Thomas Couture and the Eclectic Vision* (New Haven: Yale University Press, 1980), p. 76). A prisoner of the aesthetic of the finished, which was imposed on him when he reached the final phase of his work, 'He identified freedom with the vivid first sketch but was bewildered when it came to projecting it on a large scale which became the public, official work' (ibid., p. 227); and the care given to realistic details, which can be seen in the picturesque portraits of his sketches which are

very similar to those of Courbet, disappears from the paintings due to his concern for the elevation and idealization through allegory which is suitable for 'great subjects'.

45 Lethève, *La Vie quotidienne des artistes français*, p. 66. Duranty started his article in the *Paris-Journal* (5 May 1870) by relating how he noticed another visitor, while they were both looking at the same painting, *La leçon de musique*, open his catalogue, see Manet's name and mutter 'What debauchery' before he walked away, shrugging his shoulders.

46 This narrative and communicative function can be put at the service of the most diverse political or moral significations. One thus understands that the winners of the 1848 competition, the purpose of which was the creation of the statue of the Republic, were academic artists who were prepared to produce meaningful works, no matter what the meaning might be. See T. J. Clark, *The Absolute Bourgeois: Artists and Politics in France, 1848–1851* (London: Thames and Hudson, 1973), p. 67.

47 Hamilton, *Manet and his Critics*, p. 135.

48 Ibid., p. 124.

49 Both reactions are observed when photographs presenting characters with no clear social links or depicting insignificant objects are shown to people with little education.

50 Castagnary, *Salons, 1857–1870* (Paris: Bibliothèque Charpentier, 1892), p. 179. Sloane, *French Painting*, pp. 186–7, n. 37.

51 Castagnary, *Salons*, p. 365.

52 Lethève, *Impressionistes et Symbolistes*, p. 29.

53 One must be careful not to forget, as often happens, that the real efficiency of morphological factors is only defined in relation to the specific constraints of a determinate social universe and that consequently, for fear of turning these factors (like technical or economic factors in other cases) into almost natural causes which are foreign to historical reality in their genesis and operation, one must proceed, in each case as is done here, to a preliminary analysis of the social space in which they intervene.

54 In a sense, the abolition of all centralized sites of certification makes the revolutionary venture more difficult. The seizure of the Hôtel Massa (headquarters of the *Société des Gens de Lettres*) in May 1968 by a group of writers immediately appeared to be ridiculous and pathetic as a misguided demonstration of a 'revolutionary' intention that was incapable of following any specific path toward realization.

55 Tabarant, *La vie artistique*, p. 285.

## 10 THE HISTORICAL GENESIS OF A PURE AESTHETIC

1 A. Danto, 'The Artworld', *Journal of Philosophy*, 61 (1964), pp. 571–84; G. Dickie, *Art and the Aesthetic* (Ithaca: Cornell University Press, 1974).

2 See P. Bourdieu, 'The Philosophical Establishment', in A. Montefiore, ed., *Philosophy in France Today* (Cambridge: Cambridge University Press, 1983), pp. 1–8.

3 See P. Bourdieu, 'L'ontologie politique de Martin Heidegger', *Actes de la recherche en sciences sociales*, 5–6 (November 1975), pp. 183–90; also

*The Political Ontology of Martin Heidegger*, trans. Peter Collier (Cambridge: Polity; Stanford: Stanford University Press, 1990).

4   One could show, following the same logic, how Nietzsche furnished Foucault with 'screening' concepts (I am thinking, for example, of the notion of genealogy functioning as a euphemistic substitute for social history). These concepts have allowed Foucault to accept, by way of denial, modes of thinking which are typical of a genetic sociology, and to generate acceptance for them. He thus renounces the plebeian methods of the social sciences, but without forfeiting them.

5   I have demonstrated elsewhere, *à propos* an analysis by Derrida of Kant's *Critique of Judgement*, how and why 'deconstruction' goes only half-way. See P. Bourdieu, 'Postscript: Towards a "Vulgar" Critique of "Pure Critiques" ', in *Distinction: A Social Critique of the Judgement of Taste*, trans. R. Nice (Cambridge, Mass.: Harvard University Press, 1984), pp. 494–8.

6   Without calling forth all the definitions which are merely variants of Kantian analysis (such as Strawson's view that the function of the work of art is to have no function; see 'Aesthetic Appraisal and Works of Art', in *Freedom and Resentment, and Other Essays* (London: Methuen, 1974), pp. 178–88), one could simply recall an ideal-typical example of the essentialist constitution of the aesthetic through an enumeration of the traits which characterize an aesthetic experience, which is nevertheless very clearly situated within social space and historical time. Such an example is Harold Osborne, for whom the aesthetic attitude is typified by the following: a concentration of attention (it separates – *frames apart* – the perceived object from its environment), the suspension of discursive and analytical activities (it disregards sociological and historical context), impartiality and detachment (it separates past and future preoccupations) and indifferences towards the existence of the object. See H. Osborne, *The Art of Appreciation* (London: Oxford University Press, 1970).

7   On the disconcertment, even confusion, which the lack of minimal mastery of the instruments of perception and of appreciation (in particular labels and references like names of genres, of schools, of periods, artists, etc.) visits upon the culturally deprived museum-goers, see P. Bourdieu and A. Darbel, *The Love of Art: European Museums and their Public*, trans. Caroline Beattie and Nick Merriman (Cambridge: Polity; Stanford: Stanford University Press, 1990); P. Bourdieu, 'Outline of a Sociological Theory of Art Perception', *International Social Science Journal*, 20 (Winter 1968), pp. 518–612 (ch. 8 in this volume). See also Danto, 'The Artworld'.

8   Sociological analysis allows one to escape the dichotomous choice between subjectivism and objectivism, and to reject the subjectivism of theories of aesthetic consciousness (*ästhetisches Bewusstsein*). Such theories reduce the aesthetic quality of a natural thing or of a human work to a simple correlate of a deliberate attitude of consciousness, an attitude which, as it confronts the thing, is actually neither theoretical nor practical but rather purely contemplative. Sociological analysis rejects these theories without falling, as does the Gadamer of *Truth and Method*, into an ontology of the work of art.

9   See R. Shusterman, 'Wittgenstein and Critical Reasoning', *Philosophy and Phenomenological Research*, 47 (1986), pp. 91–110.

10 An acute awareness of the situation in which he is positioned could lead the analyst to rather insurmountable 'aporia', especially since even the most neutral language appears inevitably – as soon as naïve reading makes it a part of the social game – as a stand within the very debate which he is only trying to objectify. Thus, for example, even if one replaced an indigenous word such as 'province', a word charged with pejorative connotations, with a more neutral concept such as 'periphery', then the opposition between the centre and the periphery which is used to analyse the effects of symbolic domination becomes a stake in the struggle within the field that is being analysed. For example, on the one hand there is the wish of the 'centrists' to describe the positions taken by those who occupy the peripheral sites as an effect of a delay, and on the other hand the resistance of the 'peripherists' against their lowered status implied in this classification, and their effort to convert a peripheral position into a central one or at least to make of it a willed gap. The example of Avignon illustrates the fact that the artist cannot produce himself as such – here as an alternative capable of effectively competing for the dominant position – unless he does so in relationship with his clients. See E. Castelnuovo and C. Ginsburg, 'Domination symbolique et géographie artistique dans l'histoire de l'art italien', *Actes de la recherche en sciences sociales*, 40 (November 1981), pp. 51–73.

11 See Bourdieu, *Distinction*, p. 194.

12 In other words, in proposing an essentialist definition of the judgement of taste or in granting the universality required by a definition which (like Kant's definition) is in accord with his own ethical-behavioural dispositions, the philosopher distances himself less than he imagines from ordinary modes of thinking and from the propensity towards making the relative absolute which typifies them.

13 Contrary to the dominant representation which claims that by relating each manifestation of taste to its social conditions of production sociological analysis reduces and relativizes the practices and representations involved, one could claim that sociological analysis does not in fact reduce and relativize these practices, but rather removes them from arbitrariness and absolutizes them by making them both necessary and unique, and thus justified in existing as they exist. One could in fact posit that two people whose habitus are different and who have not been exposed to the same conditions and stimulations (because they construct them differently) do not hear the same music and do not see the same paintings and cannot, therefore, arrive at the same judgement of value.

14 See Bourdieu, *Distinction*, pp. 34–41.

# Selected Bibliography of Works by Pierre Bourdieu

The following listing includes only those books and articles most closely related to the analysis of the cultural fields. A complete bibliography of works published by Pierre Bourdieu until 1988 can be found in *Bibliographie des travaux de Pierre Bourdieu, 1958–1988*, ed. Yvette Delsaut (Paris, Centre de Sociologie Européenne du Collège de France, 1988, mimeo). An abbreviated version appears in *In Other Words* (1990; English translation of *Choses dites*). See also the bibliography in Pierre Bourdieu and Loïc J. D. Wacquant, *An Invitation to a Reflexive Sociology* (Chicago, University of Chicago Press, 1992). For additional works by Bourdieu and his co-researchers, the reader is referred especially to the journal Bourdieu has edited since 1975, *Actes de la recherche en sciences sociales*.

## 1965

1.  *Un art moyen, essai sur les usages sociaux de la photographie*, Paris, Minuit, 1965. New rev. edn 1970 (with L. Boltanski, R. Castel and J. C. Chamboredon). English trans.: *Photography: A Middle-Brow Art* (tr. S. Whiteside), Cambridge, Polity Press; Stanford, Stanford University Press, 1990.

## 1966

1.  *L'amour de l'art, Les musées d'art et leur public*, Paris, Minuit, 1966, new augm. edn, *L'amour de l'art, Les musées d'art européens et leur public*, 1969 (with A. Darbel and D. Schnapper). English trans.: *The Love of Art: European Museums and their Public* (tr. C. Beattie and N. Merriman), Cambridge, Polity Press, 1990.

2. 'Champ intellectuel et project créateur', *Les temps modernes*, Problèmes du structuralisme, 246 (November 1966), pp. 865–906. English trans.: 'Intellectual field and creative project (S. France), *Social Science Information*, 8, no. 2 (April 1969), pp. 89–119. Also in *Knowledge and Control: New Directions for the Sociology of Education*, ed. Michael F. D. Young, London, Collier-Macmillan, 1971, pp. 161–88.

### 1967

1. 'Sociology and Philosophy in France since 1945: Death and Resurrection of a Philosophy without Subject', *Social Research*, 34, no. 1 (Spring 1967), pp. 162–212 (with J. C. Passeron).

2. Afterword to E. Panofsky, *Architecture gothique et pensée scolastique*, (tr. P. Bourdieu), Paris, Minuit, 1967, new augm. edn, 1970, pp. 133–67.

### 1969

1. 'Sociologie de la perception esthétique', in *Les sciences humaines et l'œuvre d'art*, Brussels: La connaissance S. A., 1969, pp. 161–76, 251–4.

### 1970

1. *La réproduction. Éléments pour une théorie du système d'enseignement*, Paris, Minuit, 1970 (with J. C. Passeron). English trans.: *Reproduction in Education, Society and Culture* (tr. R. Nice), London and Beverly Hills, Ca., Sage Productions, 1977.

### 1971

1. 'Champ du pouvoir, champ intellectuel et habitus de classe', *Scolies*, Cahiers de recherches d l'École normale supérieure, 1 (1971), pp. 7–26.

2. 'Une interprétation de la théorie de la religion selon Max Weber', *Archives européennes de sociologie*, 12, no. 1 (1971), pp. 3–21. English trans. (new rev. and modif. version): 'Legitimation and Structured Interests in Weber's Sociology of Religion' (tr. C. Turner), in *Max Weber, Rationality and Modernity*, ed. S. Whimster and S. Lash, London, Allen & Unwin, 1987, pp. 119–36.

3. 'Disposition esthétique et compétence artistique', *Les temps modernes*, 295 (February 1971), pp. 1345–78.

### 1972

1. *Esquisse d'une théorie de la pratique, précédé de trois études d'ethnologie kabyle*, Geneva, Droz, 1972. English trans.: pp. 162–89, 'The Three Forms of Theoretical Knowledge', *Social Science Information*, 12, no. 1 (1973), pp. 53–80; also *Outline of a Theory of Practice* (tr. R. Nice), Cambridge, Cambridge University Press, 1977.

### 1974

1. 'Les fractions de la classe dominante et les modes d'appropriation des oeuvres d'art', *Information sur les sciences sociales*, 13, no. 3 (June 1974), pp. 7–32.

### 1975

1. 'Le couturier et sa griffe. Contribution à une théorie de la magie', *Actes de la recherche en sciences sociales*, 1 (January 1975), pp. 7–36 (with Y. Delsaut).

2. 'L'invention de la vie d'artiste', *Actes de la recherche en sciences sociales*, 2 (March 1975), pp. 67–94. English trans.: 'The Invention of the Artist's Life' (tr. E. R. Koch), *Yale French Studies*, 73 (1987), pp. 75–103.

3. 'Le fétichisme de la langue', *Actes de la recherche en sciences sociales*, 4 (July 1975), pp. 2–32 (with L. Boltanski).

4. 'La critique du discours lettré', *Actes de la recherche en sciences sociales*, 5–6 (November 1975), pp. 4–8.

### 1979

1. *La distinction, Critique sociale du jugement*, Paris, Minuit, 1979, new edn augm. with an introduction, 1982. English trans.: *Distinction: A Social Critique of the Judgement of Taste* (tr. Richard Nice), Cambridge, Mass.: Harvard, 1984.

### 1980

1. *Le sens pratique*, Paris, Minuit, 1980. English trans.: *The Logic of Practice* (tr. R. Nice), Cambridge, Polity Press; Stanford, Stanford University Press, 1990.

2. *Questions de sociologie*, Paris, Minuit, 1980.

### 1981

1. 'Pour une sociologie de la perception', *Actes de la recherche en sciences sociales*, 40 (November 1981), pp. 3–9 (with Y. Delsaut).

### 1982

1. *Leçon sur la leçon*, Paris, Minuit, 1982; *Leçon inaugurale*, no. 90., Paris, Collège de France, 1982.

2. *Ce que parler veut dire, L'économie des échanges linguistiques*, Paris, Fayard, 1982. English trans. (rev. and augm.): *Language and Symbolic Power*, ed. John Thompson (tr. Gino Raymond and Matthew Adamson), Cambridge, Polity Press; Cambridge, Mass.: Harvard, 1991.

## 1983

1. 'The Philosophical Establishment' (tr. K. McLaughlin), in *Philosophy in France Today*, ed. A. Montefiore, Cambridge, Cambridge University Press, 1983, pp. 1–8.

2. 'Vous avez dit "populaire"?' *Actes de la recherche en sciences sociales*, 46 (March 1983), pp. 98–105.

## 1984

1. *Homo academicus*, Paris, Minuit, 1984. English trans.: *Homo Academicus* (tr. P. Collier), with a preface to the English Edition (pp. xi–xxvi), Cambridge, Polity Press; Stanford, Stanford University Press, 1989.

2. 'Le hit-parade des intellectuels français, ou qui sera juge de la légitimité des juges?' *Actes de la recherche en sciences sociales*, 52–53 (June 1984), pp. 5–20.

3. 'Le champ littéraire, Préables critiques et principes de méthode', *Lendemains* (Berlin and Cologne), 9, no. 36 (1984), pp. 5–20.

## 1985

1. 'The Genesis of the Concepts of Habitus and Field' (tr. C. Newman), *Sociocriticism* (Pittsburgh, Pa. and Montpellier), Theories and Perspectives II, no. 2 (December 1985), pp. 11–24.

## 1987

1. *Choses dites*, Paris, Minuit, 1987. English trans.: *In Other Words* (tr. Matthew Adamson), Cambridge, Polity Press; Stanford, Stanford University Press, 1990.

## 1991

1. 'Le champ littéraire', *Actes de la recherche en sciences sociales*, 89 (September 1991), pp. 4–46.

## 1992

1. *An Invitation to Reflexive Sociology* (with Loïc J. D. Wacquant), Chicago: University of Chicago Press, 1992.

# Index